NEVER A NATIVE

ALICE SHALVI
NEVER A NATIVE

HALBAN
LONDON

First published in Great Britain by
Halban Publishers Ltd
2018
www.halbanpublishers.com

A CIP catalogue record for this book is available
from the British Library.

ISBN 978-1-905559-98-5

Typeset by AB, Cambridgeshire
Printed in Great Britain by
CPI Group (UK) Ltd, Croydon CR0 4YY

These memoirs are dedicated with profound love and gratitude to the memory of the three men who shaped my life:

My father, Benzion Margulies, whose love for humankind I inherited;

My brother, William, who with unstinting generosity dispensed not only sound advice but also the material assistance that enabled my entire family to live well beyond our means;

My husband, Moshe Shalvi, the "rod and staff" who throughout 63 years of marriage unfailingly partnered, encouraged and supported me.

And to my children, who undoubtedly suffered as a result of my over-indulgence in public affairs, I sincerely apologise. I take comfort in seeing how different are the choices that they themselves have made.

Contents

Acknowledgements

In 1997, having retired from my academic and public activities, I was the happy recipient of a month's residency at the Rockefeller Foundation Centre in Bellagio. In its tranquil grounds, amid the natural beauty of Lake Como and the intellectual stimulus provided by my fellow residents, I succeeded in writing the first 30,000 words of my memoirs – a rich harvest.

Then I returned to the reality of Jerusalem, home, family, social and political involvement, and throughout long intervals the field of writing lay fallow. Only after a year of mourning for my husband Moshe did I find the strength of mind, soul and body to continue with my labours, urged on by the incessant queries of friends demanding to know when I would finish. They didn't crack a whip, preferring to offer lumps of sugar. Another year was devoted to editing various versions of the manuscript. The final incitement was an invitation to celebrate my 90th birthday in New York with a group of women whom Moshe had collectively dubbed "FOAs" (Friends of Alice), harking back to the years of fundraising in which I enlisted the financial and moral support of Friends of Pelech, Friends of the Israel Women's Network and so on. I could not disappoint them.

One last intensive burst of writing, comparable to that in Bellagio, and I was finished.

I cannot thank them enough.

My thanks are also due to the many friends and colleagues who provided invaluable assistance and feedback as I traversed the stony path of authorship: the late John Felstiner, who wrote the (perhaps unwarranted) glowing recommendation that won me the stay at Bellagio; my Solstice Sisters, who constituted an invaluable sounding-board for the sections I read to them at our biannual gatherings; my collaborators at the Israel women's Network, board members as well as staff, provided their recollections of our accomplishments; Aloma Halter, an experienced editor who helped me put my thoughts in order; Judy Labensohn, who served as an occasional critical reader and coach; my friend, Omi Morgenstern-Lesser, who selflessly agreed to read the entire manuscript; my beloved Rabbi, Tamar Elad-Applebaum, who restored my spirits and nourished my soul; and above all Elisheva Levy, whom the Divine Force sent to me in my hour of need, while I was sitting *shiva* for Moshe, and who has been a loyal companion and dear friend. Her intelligence, ingenuity and imperturbability are beyond compare.

Antecedents

A Portrait

THEY SIT SIDE by side on a sofa, a glimpse of its carved headboard and brocade upholstery forming a background bridge between them. Both are looking directly at the camera. He is handsome and well-groomed: a high forehead; hair, already slightly receding, neatly parted on the left; a small, carefully trimmed moustache just above the bow of his upper lip. His dress is formal and festive: a dark suit, white shirt with high, stiff collar and white bow-tie. His arms are folded across his chest; his left hand is tucked into the crook of the right, the right barely visible among the folds of his left sleeve, as if he were hugging, or restraining, himself. A whole man, self-confident, complete, with a sense of occasion.

She sits to his right, wearing a simple scoop-necked dress with elbow-length sleeves, devoid of any ornament. Her bosom is soft, uncorseted. Her thick dark hair, combed softly back from a high forehead, frames the upper part of an oval face. Her head tilts slightly to the side, like a startled bird. Her large, dark eyes, pupils – like black buttons – a focal point in the picture, are sad, beseeching, a contrast with his almost expressionless impersonal ones. Her mouth curves gently upwards, wistful, shy, perhaps attempting a smile. Although she, too, is looking directly at the camera, she leans slightly forward, her body half turned towards him. Her left arm, an echo of the curved carved back of the sofa, is concealed, from the elbow down, behind his back, as if she felt a need for physical contact, for reassurance. Her right arm lies across her body, the curled hand resting gently on her lap. His firmness and self-assurance form a sharp contrast with her hesitancy and need for contact. It is a picture not so much of a couple as of two people.

These are my parents.

Innumerable questions arise, doomed never to be answered. When was the photograph taken? It could hardly have been on their wedding day, since on that occasion, attended by numerous family members and recorded in one of the wide-lens photographs of the period, she wore white. Is this an engagement photo? I know, from an invitation that has been preserved, that a month before the wedding there was a party at my grandparents' home one Friday afternoon to mark the signing of the marriage contract. Is the simple dress she is wearing the one she brought with her from her impoverished post-war home in Galicia, her only one, which she laundered once a week?

My father's sisters didn't welcome her, although she was their cousin. They were, and forever remained, of the opinion that he could have made a far better match with one of the more elegant, wealthier, self-confident young women who had displayed an interest in him. Perhaps there was some truth in their claim that he was marrying her out of pity, having met her for the first time a year earlier, in 1919, on his way back to Germany from captivity in Russia (where he had served as a medical orderly with the Austro-Hungarian army). He was, indeed, a very compassionate man, quite capable of self-sacrifice. Were these the grounds for her insecurity, her need for reassurance?

They had, on the whole, a good marriage, despite the extreme contrast in personalities – he a dyed-in-the-wool optimist, she an eternal pessimist. They quarrelled a great deal: she contended that he was too immersed in his communal voluntary activities, too liberal in donating his hard-earned and not always plentiful income. Extremely generous by nature, he was easily moved to charitable deeds. She believed that charity begins at home, though she never turned away any of the beggars who came to our door, often inviting them in to partake of a bowl of soup and a slice of bread. Yes, they quarrelled, but he once assured me that this did not mean that they didn't love each other.

In the early summer of 1933, fully aware that Germany was no longer a safe place for Jews, he emigrated to England. For 11 months they were separated, while she, her mother, my brother and I moved to another town to live with my oldest aunt until such time as my father secured the entry permits that would enable us to join him. The anguished letters she sent him, almost daily, reveal her distress. The handwriting is uncontrolled, the lines uneven, crowded as far as possible onto one sheet, in order to save on postage. On one occasion she apologised for not having written for some days, explaining that she had lacked the money to buy stamps. She was unable to keep up contributing her share to the household expenses and felt herself disliked, unwelcome and a burden. The separation and, in particular, the uncertainty as to when, where and whether we would all be reunited were unbearable. The same need for comfort, reassurance and closeness that had already found expression in the photograph taken a decade and a half earlier filled her once again.

When my father died, too young and too soon, she was desolate. She had nursed him devotedly, tended to his every physical need during his last years of illness. She mourned him until the day she, too, died.

Perl Margulies, My Mother

Perl Margulies was born in Huyzhatyn, Galicia (in today's Ukraine), on 25 January 1893, the daughter of Ze'ev and Margola (née Margulies). She was the fourth child, with two sisters and two brothers. She attended a German-speaking school, receiving a grounding in Hebrew and Jewish practice at home. In 1920 she moved to Mannheim, where she married her cousin, Benzion (Benno) Margulies (born in 1890 in Skalat, also in Ukraine). Their oldest son, Ze'ev, was born in 1921, before the couple moved to Essen, where two daughters, Edit (1922-9) and Alice (1926), were born.

In 1933, when Benzion emigrated to England, Perl wound up the family business, and moved with her mother and children to Mannheim, where she remained until May 1934 before receiving entry visas to join her husband in London. Early in 1949, Benno suffered a stroke that left him partly paralysed until his death of a second stroke in February 1955. Perl died in Jerusalem on 21 November 1962, while on a visit to her daughter. She is buried in the Sanhedria cemetery, to which Benno's body was also transferred.

These are the facts, the bare bones to which flesh and blood must be added if we wish to know and perhaps understand this woman, my mother.

Whence does one derive that flesh, that blood, the details that constitute a life, a being, a personality? From oft-repeated family stories, frequently told by unreliable, biased narrators; stories that differ, *Rashomon*-like, according to the speaker's point of view; an occasional revelatory remark; family lore and mythology, tales passed down from generation to generation, with inevitable omissions, distortions and accretions; overheard conversations; documents; old letters and photographs; one's own relationship with the object of scrutiny. No two people experience an event in identical fashion or have exactly the same impression of a person's appearance or character. All is subjective, open to interpretation.

My portrait of my mother is based on personal observation, shared experiences, stories repeatedly told by my maternal grandmother as she sat at my bedside before I went to sleep, events reported by my father, my brother, other relations. My mother herself spoke comparatively little about the details of her life until the autumn of 1960, when I spent six weeks in London in our family home, speaking to each other for the first time as two adult women, married (in her case already widowed) and mothers of children.

I was conducting research for my PhD, spending my days at the British Library (then in the British Museum), returning home each evening to find dinner – always my favourite dishes – waiting for me. After dinner, we would sit together and talk. I would brush her hair, which she liked, and slowly I gained a greater knowledge and a deeper understanding of a life dominated by memories of deprivation and disaster.

My mother's parents, Welwel (Ze'ev) and Margola, were both members of Hasidic families, a tradition so devoutly carried on by her father that he transferred his home from Skalat, where his parents and siblings remained until their move to Germany prior to the First World War, in order to study at the court of the saintly Rebbe of Huyzhatyn. Here he spent all his days and frequently even his nights, while his wife ran a small grocery store that provided the family income. Perl was the fourth of their five children, preceded by Sarah, Lazel and Rebekka, and followed by Avraham, an ardent communist for whom his mother regularly baked two additional Shabbat *chalot* (plaited bread loaves) to be given to needy neighbours of his choice. While Perl received her Hebrew and Jewish practice at home, where Yiddish was spoken, she attended a German-language school where she became particularly fond of poetry. For many years, she enjoyed reciting poems by Heine, Goethe and Schiller. Years later, when I had to learn poetry by heart, she used to hold the texts, while I recited works by the English Romantics – Coleridge, Wordsworth, Keats and Shelley – and she loved them too.

She assisted her mother in the shop, where customers included a number of colourful characters whose activities inside and outside the shop provided material for many lively anecdotes. My mother's stories, unlike those of my grandmother, tended to focus on the less salubrious townsfolk, who for her were a source of disgust rather than humour. The monotonous life in the *shtetl* was relieved by trips to the nearby city of Tarnapol, to purchase hats and dress patterns in an attempt to be fashionable. There was a young man to whom she was attracted.

4

And there were occasional blissful moments. One of them was sitting on a balcony with a friend who taught her the words of the *Merry Widow* waltz.

Then came the war. Located on the border with Russia, Huyzhatyn changed hands several times. Each time, the population was transported and then returned, by sled, in storms, snow and ice. On one of these journeys, Sarah contracted typhus and died in 1916. The following year, Avraham left to join the Revolution in Russia. Welwel died. Rebekka married and also moved to Russia. Lazel moved to Lemberg (Lvov) in search of employment. Perl was left to care for her widowed mother. They were poor, anxious. Their future was uncertain. Then, in 1919, her cousin Benzion arrived to find out what had become of his uncle and his family. At this point the facts are fairly clear but the motives become blurred.

Fact: in summer 1920, Benno sent for my mother and on 20 August they were married. Conjectures regarding motives: was it love at first sight? My mother was not a classical beauty but she had beautiful, expressive eyes, a sweet, shy smile and an aura of vulnerability that must (might?) have moved my father. I have always wanted to believe that they married for love but have no proof of any kind to support that belief. My aunts, on the other hand, had very strong opinions on what they considered an inappropriate match. They maintained – and continued to maintain, even after my mother's death – that he felt intense pity for her and in his customary generosity decided he must help her in the only way he could. They behaved coldly to her. They contrasted her with the numerous women – more beautiful, wealthier, better connected – who were pursuing my father. They didn't hesitate to show their dislike. My mother told me she had arrived in Mannheim with only one dress. When it had to be laundered, she had no option but to stay in bed until it dried. In consequence, my aunts accused her of laziness, of behaving like a "lady", which she was not, of not contributing her share to the running of the household. She became a Cinderella and was relieved when, in 1921, after the arrival of their firstborn, Ze'ev, she and my father moved to Essen. They sent for my grandmother, who had been present at neither the wedding nor the *Pidyon Ha-ben* (Redemption of the Firstborn) 11 months later but now remained with her daughter till she died in 1938.

It was the Depression. My parents set out to buy their furniture with a suitcase full of banknotes which, by the time they reached their destination, barely sufficed to purchase what they had hoped to buy. They were, and remained, middle class but ours was a cultured home: a gramophone, records of Gigli, Jan Kipura, famous cantors; opera, cinema, theatre. In 1932, a performance of *The Merchant of Venice* aroused so much anti-Semitic venom in the audience that my parents fled in fear. There were outings to the *Stadtwald* (municipal woods). They read books, newspapers and periodicals. Unlike my uncles and aunts, they never played cards. My father was active in the *Ostjüdische Gemeinde* (East European Jewish Community), the religious Zionist organisation and his synagogue. My mother worked with him in their wholesale business of linens and cutlery. My grandmother kept house. We had a *Kindermädchen* (nanny).

In the middle of it all came tragedy again. Black-eyed Edit died of pleurisy in 1929, just before Purim, the festival on which Jews are commanded to rejoice. It is our carnival. But from then on, my mother could never bring herself to celebrate. Each year, as she lit the memorial candle for my sister, she would say, in Yiddish, "*ein finstere Purim!*" ("a black Purim!"). In June 1933, after our house had been searched by the Gestapo, my father left for London. She had difficulty eliciting payment from debtors and was harassed by creditors. Meanwhile, *Ostjuden* were leaving, with threats of expulsion hanging like thunderclouds. When would the lightning strike? In September, we moved to Mannheim. Once again she was the subject of opprobrium, as the expected few weeks stretched into months. Finally the longed-for visas arrived. We reached London on Sunday 12 May 1934.

This was life in a new and very different country, in a new language, with different foods and customs. It took a while to adjust, also now to being a full-time homemaker. She'd asked my father to find a one-floor flat. He found a three-storey house, with two rooms we used only when there were visitors and insufficient bedrooms. There was a great deal of housework, with a mother-in-law who never lifted a finger but went to the cinema and for walks, while Perl and her mother toiled for a household that now numbered five adults (my youngest uncle lived with us) and two children.

Matters improved when my paternal grandmother went to Palestine in 1935 and we moved to a modern house. I went with her to buy our first gas stove and refrigerator. We had an electric water-heater. Life was easier. We even took a holiday by the sea but could afford only a single room. So my father went alone, and the following week my mother and I shared a bed. I lay watching her at the wash basin, soaping her face, her neck, lifting her heavy breasts to sponge the body underneath. In January 1938, my grandmother, who had lived with Perl since her marriage, died of a stroke.

"She had too short a better life," my mother said.

When the Second World War broke out and I was evacuated with my school, my parents and brother moved to a country house in Waddesdon, in

Buckinghamshire, with my uncle and his very Anglo-Jewish wife. Once again my mother was a "guest", with no say in what was on the menu or *entrée* to the kitchen. There was a cook for that. She had to go into the nearby town surreptitiously to buy my brother the cream cakes he liked. She became ill, vomiting whenever she ate. This was dismissed as psychosomatic: Perl and her problems again! But it was, in fact, gallstones, which were successfully treated by our family doctor. My parents moved back to London and I too returned but when the Blitz began they moved back to Waddesdon in Buckinghamshire, now to a less luxurious house of their own.

Throughout her life, my mother practised two cardinal virtues of Judaism: charity and hospitality. No one asking for help was ever turned away. Even in the harshest of times there were a small coin, a slice of bread, a bowl of soup. People who needed a meal were welcome. There was hardly a Friday night or Shabbat lunch without a needy guest, sometimes a stranger from out of town whom my father had met at synagogue. One Passover during the war my father was asked to find hospitality for Jewish soldiers stationed in the neighbourhood. On the Seder night, the eve of Passover, we ourselves ended up hosting over 30 of them, for whom no other hospitality had been found.

In 1946, returning from the third commemoration of the Ghetto Uprising in Warsaw, my father phoned from Paris to say he was bringing three Yiddish notables (two writers and a singer) for the Seder. By way of compensation he also brought a huge carp – a fish much-loved by east European Jews but barely available in England. My mother took everything in her stride. Hating to see food wasted and always trying to diet, she rarely served herself but ate the leftovers of others. Then she would wail, "Why am I so fat? I never eat anything!" Feeding, life-giving, characterised her. She sent endless parcels – to my brother and me when we were at university (a weekly portion of Shabbat chicken, her tasty *rogalkes*, yeast pastries, chocolate wafers and other delicacies). When I left for Israel in 1949, she cried, asking my father "Why are we letting her do this?" He replied, "We raised her for it" ("*Wir haben Sie dazu erzogen*"). I left. Parcels continued to arrive, with items unavailable in Israel due to austerity and rationing.

After the war our family was wealthier. We had a car, chauffeur and daily help. My parents occupied the best seats at concerts and operas. My mother reluctantly bought some fashionable clothes. My father bought her a fur coat and diamond jewellery (which she seldom wore).

"What are you saving it for?" he asked.

7

Then, *"Was tut Gott?"* ("What does God do?"), my mother asked back in Yiddish.

In February 1955, my father had a second stroke while he was in the bathroom, preparing himself for the day. My mother heard him fall and rushed upstairs but it was too late. For years she would each week rehearse the sequence of events: "It was Tuesday, at such and such o'clock…". He was buried on the day of my oldest son's third birthday. My mother went into lasting mourning. She deprived herself of every pleasure. On my visits to London my brother would purchase three tickets for theatre or opera but even as we reached the front door she would stop and turn back. "I can't", she'd say and would not be persuaded. She was alone and lonely. My brother travelled a great deal. I came with my sons in the summer of 1956 to begin my doctoral research but she had difficulty coping with two lively young boys, so we went to Cambridge, visiting her at weekends – and receiving food parcels.

Early in 1962, quite by chance, my mother discovered that her sister Rebekka was alive and living at the same address she had lived at before the war. Letters my parents wrote to the USSR had remained unanswered out of fear of the authorities. My uncle Avraham had been executed for corresponding with someone in fascist Germany. My mother and brother travelled to the USSR and ultimately met my aunt, her widowed daughter, daughter-in-law and granddaughter in Kharkov. Avraham had been posthumously "rehabilitated". My mother visited his widow, dying of leukemia in a hospital. It was a profoundly emotional experience that affected her health. Half a year later, when she had a heart attack in Jerusalem, I told my wise German-born doctor about this reunion. His response was:

"The heart cannot bear such extremes of joy and sadness. It is like a glass that is moved from the heat to a cold surface. It breaks."

What word could sum up my mother? She "cared", in every sense of the word. She cared about, she cared for, she was involved with her family, her children – perhaps sometimes too involved. We were the centre of her life, her reason for being. Nothing was too good for us. No prospective spouses were sufficiently eligible. She had an uncanny psychic connection with me. She knew I was pregnant with my fourth child before I did. When I had a rare eye infection, she urged me, in a letter penned the previous week, to take care of my eyes, since they were essential to my livelihood.

In October 1962 she came on what proved to be her final visit to us. I watched her cross the tarmac from the plane, a little old lady weighed down with hand-luggage that contained smoked salmon and chopped liver, and my heart went out to her. She thought I was having too many children and was annoyed to find me pregnant once again. *"Wann wirst Du aus den Windeln kriechen?"* ("When will you crawl out of your nappies?") But the following month, as she lay on her deathbed and I stood opposite her, she prophesied, in Yiddish, referring to my pregnancy:

"You are carrying your father". (The son to whom I gave birth three months later indeed bore his name, Benzion.) She begged us not to send her to hospital. The doctor said it was the only hope for saving her life but I suspect she did not really want her life to be saved, though she worried over who would take care of my brother's laundry. I shall never forget the beseeching look in her eyes as the ambulance men carried her out of our house. We should have heeded her request. Instead, she lay in a hospital bed, tubes attached to wrists and nose, suffering, still worrying. Her last words to me were "You have no bread in the house". I was not with her when she died in the night. I cannot forgive myself for having gone home, exhausted, and failing to respond to the phone call in which my brother suggested to my husband that I join him again at the hospital. I did not give her a final farewell kiss. I was not privileged to close her eyes. My brother was.

Benzion Margulies, My Father

Clusters of nouns and adjectives spring to mind when I think of my father, son of Mordechai and Feige (née Kesten). Ardour, fervour, gusto; optimist, idealist; tolerant, generous in spirit and deed (sometimes to a fault); compassionate and charitable; wise and understanding… He did nothing by halves, yet he was not an extremist. A good Jew.

Perhaps because I was never as close to his mother as to my maternal grandmother and he told me little of his early life, I'm largely ignorant about my father's family background and his early years. Skalat, where he was born, draws a blank, unlike the vivid (though perhaps erroneous) impression I have of Huyszatyn, where my mother was born. The family was well-to-do and lived in bourgeois comfort. Mordechai's occupation, as cited in official documents, was "banker", though my brother suspected that this was a euphemism for the less dignified "money-lender". My father was largely an autodidact, widely read in classical Jewish texts and general literature, and always keeping abreast of social and political theories and practices. I assume he received a traditional Jewish education. He was certainly knowledgeable in all areas of Jewish studies. While the language spoken in the home was Yiddish, he was also fluent in Polish and German. At some point, he studied commerce in Vienna.

Beginning in 1910, the family moved one by one to Mannheim. When the First World War broke out, all but the youngest of the five brothers were conscripted to serve in the Austro-Hungarian army. A medical orderly on the Eastern Front, my father was taken into captivity by the Russians in 1917. From the one incident he unfailingly recounted at our family Seder, I learnt that he had determinedly ensured the observance of a Passover Seder by collecting eggs and other essential ingredients from the Jewish residents of the region. At the *shiva* (the seven day period of mourning after a funeral) for my father, my Uncle Aaron provided information that my father had omitted. When he went to the officer in charge to request permission to hold the Seder, he unfortunately failed fully to button up his jacket. For this lapse, his punishment was several hours of *"Abhengen"*: being suspended by the wrists from a high bar. Only when he had completed serving this sentence was he free to continue preparing the Seder for which he had, fortunately, previously received permission.

Released at the end of the war, he travelled back to his home via Huyszatyn, where he hoped to learn what had befallen the family of his Uncle Welwel, the oldest of Mordechai's brothers. There he first met his cousin Perl, whom in 1920 he invited to join him in Mannheim, where they married on 20 August. Their first child, a son, was born in June 1921. Soon after the *Pidyon Ha-ben* (Redemption of the Firstborn) a month later, my parents moved to Essen. For some years my father worked as a self-employed travelling salesman, including the vending of linens, silver cutlery and reproductions of famous works of art about which he spoke with some humour, reserving his most caustic comments for the portrait of the *"Büsende Magdalena"* that depicted a penitent Mary Magdalene, bare-breasted, hair dishevelled, eyes cast to heaven. "Very popular!" he'd say. "Who doesn't want legitimate pornography in his living room?" He had a reasonably flourishing business by the time I was four.

Throughout his years in Essen, my father was an active and prominent Zionist. This might be why the Gestapo searched our home in 1933: a warning that worse might follow. My father left for London, where his youngest brother, Alexander, had two years earlier established Elco, a wholesale firm dealing in clocks, watches and jewellery. They remained in partnership until my father's death. An ardent Yiddishist and also a fervent student of Hebrew, he employed private tutors for himself and his children. Struggling with S.Y. Agron's enigmatic *T'mol Shilshom*

10

he asked plaintively, in Yiddish, "What does he want with that dog?" He was not alone in finding that question hard to answer. It continues to plague readers to this day.

In 1942, together with my uncle, my brother and Oscar Phillips, he founded the aptly named Ararat Publishing Company. Under the editorship of historian-philosopher Shimon Rawidowicz, then teaching at Leeds University, Ararat kept Hebrew writing alive in Europe through a series of *belles lettres* entitled "Mezuda" (Fortress) and numerous monographs. He supported the writers who came to England as impoverished refugees. Outstanding among these was Itzik Manger, whom – as Benzion used to say – he "kept in cigarettes and whiskey". To augment his own support, he enlisted that of several fellow Yiddishists in the UK and abroad. Knowing what a spendthrift Manger was, he prudently retained the donations, doling them out in weekly portions. My mother refused to have Manger in the house because he dropped cigarette ash all over the carpet. She had a poor opinion of him as an ingrate, "not a *Mensch*". She was not mistaken. Although he dedicated one of his poems to my father and uncle, and inscribed the copy of *Wolken übern Dach* (Clouds Over the Roof) that Ararat published in 1948 with the words "To the modern Maecenas, Benzion Margulies", when he learnt of my father's death all he wrote in a letter to a friend was: "It's a pity that Benzion Margulies died. He was of some help to me in London."

My father was among those who founded a weekly, the *Polish-Jewish Observer*, the back page of which was devoted to Yiddish writing. The contributors, Manger among them, spent most of their time in the basement coffee shop of Ohel, a clubhouse on Gower Street my father and uncle helped establish in the early years of the war. At the end of the war he was instrumental in initiating the publication of *Unser Weg* (Our Way), a Yiddish paper for Displaced Persons (DPs) published by the Mizrachi Federation of Great Britain. Earlier, he had helped launch the weekly *Jewish Observer*. He was wise, understanding and tolerant. In 1945, when Sonny, my fiancé, went to see him after our childishly impetuous engagement, he did not chide him for his rashness or disrespect, as my mother would have. Instead, he told him that if we required a *hechsher,* a kosher certificate, to kiss, he would gladly provide it. Religiously observant, he never imposed Orthodoxy on others. He did, however, stress the need to know what one was rejecting. "Be an *apikoros* [non-believer]," he would say, "but don't be an *am ha'aretz* [ignoramus]." When I asked him if I could study Kabbalah, he gently suggested I should begin with the Pentateuch, move on to the Prophets, study Mishna or Talmud and then, he concluded, "you can go on to Kabbalah".

11

He was gregarious. On our first post-war trip to Europe, he disappeared from our carriage while we were in a train in Switzerland, travelling along a one-rail track. My mother worried. Where could he possibly be? Ten minutes passed. A quarter of an hour. Still no sign of him. Her fertile imagination, fuelled, as always, by her innate pessimism, conjured up a variety of mishaps. Perhaps he was locked in the toilet; even worse – he'd fallen off one of the narrow platforms that linked the carriages. Then he returned, excited. He'd gone to speak to the engine-driver, from whom he'd elicited interesting data not only about the Swiss railways in general and our present one in particular but also about the landscape through which we were travelling, the sites we should visit, even the marital status of his interlocutor.

He was compassionate. On our first visit to Paris, friends took us to the Moulin Rouge, considered a "must" for tourists. As the near-naked young women paraded before us, my father sighed: "*Nebech* [poor things]! What a way to have to earn a living!" He was also inordinately generous. Once, my cousin Yaakov, on a visit from Israel, was in his office when an elderly man entered reciting a long tale of woe and asking for money. My father gave him several pounds, a large sum at that time. When the man left, Yaakov reprimanded my father:

"You could see he was lying. He's a fake, a swindler."

"I know," my father responded, "but if he demeans himself by asking for *tzedaka* [charity], why should I put him to shame?" He was by nature a philanthropist in the most literal sense of the word – a lover of human beings.

He also had a great sense of humour. In 1954, five years after his first stroke, my parents came to visit us in Jerusalem. One afternoon, when I arrived at their hotel, my father was waiting impatiently to report an exciting event: he had been able to take a shower by himself – impossible in their London home, which had only a hand-shower. Look, he said, how the bathroom is arranged. I followed him to be shown how he had operated the taps. Place this shower on the hook above (there it still was), turn on the taps to adjust the heat of the water, then turn the middle tap from one side to the other, from bath tap to shower. But as he began to demonstrate he forgot that he'd never turned the middle tap back and so, as he leaned over the tub and began to turn on the water, it came sprinkling down, startling us, wetting his bald head and his shoulders in their grey sweater. Quickly, he straightened up. We looked at each other, and, as one, burst into laughter.

The laughter attracted my mother, who came into the bathroom to investigate. She saw my father's wet head and noted the dampness of the sweater. A cry of alarm: he'd catch pneumonia! (It was May in Jerusalem: the temperature was 27°C at least.) She threw a towel over him, rushed to remove the sweater, hurried him back to the bedroom and dependency. Within seconds our laughter was extinguished and my father's new-found independence was forgotten. The shadows of sickness, bereavement, deportation, typhus, loss – my mother's memories and experiences – extinguished my father's joy and mine.

He *was* a Zionist. When he alighted from the plane that brought him on his first visit to Eretz Israel, he knelt down to kiss the earth. For him, this was both the Holy Land and the homeland. On 29 November 1947 I went to the cinema with my brother and a friend. As we approached our house on return, we saw my father standing at the front door, impatient, eager to share with us the momentous news: the UN had approved the establishment of a Jewish state in Palestine. He had no one except my mother with whom to share his joy. A bottle of brandy was ready. Now, he had fellow celebrants with whom to drink a toast of jubilation.

He loved Jerusalem. Sitting in the hotel room, he pointed to the Mountains of Moab opposite us. "Those are the hills to which David raised his eyes!" he said. Everywhere in Israel had a biblical association. He longed to spend the final years of his life in Israel. In one of the last letters he sent me, he asked whether we could make space in the house we were planning to build, for him and my mother to live independently but also in close proximity to us. The very last letter he wrote, to my oldest son Joel on his third birthday, ended with the words "*L'hitraot, l'hitraot, yakiri*" ("au revoir, au revoir my dearest"). But he did not live to see us again. He died on the day of the birthday. A man for all seasons, a man of infinite curiosity, nothing human was alien to him. How I loved him and do, to this day.

My youngest son, Benzion, didn't like his name, which was, in any case, in customary Israeli fashion, soon abbreviated into Benzi. He found it burdensome, demanding, too strongly implying that he should be like my father in character and behaviour. Indeed, although he resembled my father in the generosity of his heart, he was unlike him in almost every other respect. While my father had on many occasions acted impulsively, his essential gravitas served as a counterbalance. Such Aristotelian moderation was alien to Benzi. From early childhood he displayed a dare-devil intrepidness that frequently made Moshe and myself hold our breaths for fear that some disabling accident – or worse – might befall him; that, given his self-confident foolhardiness, he would overreach human capacity.

Intrepid to the point of recklessness, wild and undisciplined, he was at the same time profoundly compassionate. He couldn't abide injustice or cruelty. Assigned to the Military Investigation Police, he excelled at detecting infringements of army regulations, yet without fail (and to no avail) he begged the police who arrested the culprit not to treat him violently. "We've already caught him," he would say, aware that the defector was invariably motivated by the need to provide for his family. Choosing to make private investigation his profession, he found the majority of his clients to be women seeking evidence of their spouses' infidelity.

"How can they do it?" he bewailed. "The wives are so nice, so loveable."

He soon turned to a very different field of employment. As an excellent chef, he provided his clients not only with satiety but pleasure. Later, as the owner of a highly rated falafel stand, he gladly fed impoverished Arab workmen. "They can't afford it," he explained, when we chided him for failing to provide adequately for his family.

Aged four, he became addicted to cigarettes. A workman who was painting our home acceded to his request "just to take a puff", unreasonably assuming that the child would find distasteful what an adult enjoyed. He was wrong. Whenever possible, Benzi would steal cigarettes from colleagues who visited me, skilfully whisking away entire packs, leaving the victims bewildered. "I could have sworn I had my cigarettes with me," they would say and I was too embarrassed to admit the truth.

By the age of eight, he was a competent driver. On one occasion he took my brother's car-keys and drove around the block. His misdeed was discovered because my brother returned immediately after his departure to complain that his car was not where he had parked it. Finding that spot occupied when he arrived back at home, Benzi had been compelled to seek an alternative. Moshe would thereafter from time to time take him to the square at the Givat Shaul cemetery in the late evening, when there are seldom funerals, and permit him to drive round and round until his cravings were satisfied. Eventually, he found his true calling as a taxi-driver. Courteous, tactful, helpful, with classical music softly playing by way of calming background, he developed a devoted clientèle, specialising in transporting frequent travellers to and from Ben-Gurion Airport.

While he never smoked when driving, he remained addicted to cigarettes. None of the cures that others found effective – acupuncture, hypnosis, "patches" – proved permanently effective. I begged him to have a check-up. He remained obstinate. "I'm alright," he would assure me. But he wasn't. In the early hours of Thursday 29 September 2016, Benzi died at the airport of a heart-attack, leaving a wife and four children.

Not a synagogue goer, he was gratified when the older of his sons became more Orthodox in practice, an active member of the little synagogue in the village where they lived and a frequent reader of Torah.

"He stood at the doorway," the rabbi said, when he came to see us on the morning of Benzi's death. "He didn't much care for entering a synagogue. But he stood there, face shining with pride as Ido read." He took even greater pride in the football talent of his youngest child. Unfailingly, he drove him to and from thrice-weekly practice and weekend games. Did he ever consider how his addiction to tobacco would impact on these lives? The innumerable friends, many of them from childhood, who came to comfort the mourners were evidence of his ability to inspire love and maintain close relationships during a too-short lifetime.

Grandmothers I: Margola, My *Oma*

Like everybody else, I had two grandmothers. Unlike most others, however, I lived in the same household as one or both of them until I was 12.

My mother's mother, Margola, was the more sombre of the two. In her passport photograph, she is austere, lugubrious, sad-eyed and unsmiling. Lips folded in wan resignation, a prematurely wrinkled face dominated by a long nose, a very plain wig and over it, in added modesty, a black kerchief, a dark high-necked dress: all indicate the poverty, hardship, losses and suffering she had endured in the Galician *shtetl* where she gave birth to her five children. While my brother alleges that she never smiled, she brought me much joy. She was my *Oma*, whereas my brother had a closer relationship with my father's mother. My *Oma* played a favourite game with me. While she sat by the stove in the kitchen, I would run around the table nearby, at every turn evading the outstretched arms with which she was supposedly trying to catch me. When, breathless, I allowed myself to be caught, we would hug and kiss in mutual delight.

For most of the years of my childhood we slept in the same room, so that I became acquainted with her most intimate habits. Her possessions were few and she kept most of them in a large, flat carton under her bed, denying herself a share in the scant cupboard space. There she kept a better-quality wig exclusively for Shabbat and Yom Tov (high holiday), another kerchief to put over that wig. Less austere, it had lavender-coloured flowers on a black background. Alongside these articles lay a *siddur*, (the daily and Shabbat prayerbook) its cover frayed with use, and a *teitsch-chumash* (the Hebrew Pentateuch with Yiddish translation) with a shiny maroon leather binding and a gold relief engraved with the Hebrew words of its title: *Torah, Nevi'im, Ketuvim*. Every morning, as I lazed in bed, half-asleep, half-awake, savouring the last few minutes in the warmth of my feather eiderdown, I would watch as she dressed, carefully combed her wispy silver hair, donned the wig, tied the kerchief over it, knotted it under her chin, then stood by the window, lips moving silently, rapt in her devotions. She regaled me with stories of her life in Huyzhatyn, where she had kept a grocery store, while her husband spent most of his time studying at the court of the Huyzhatyner Rebbe. Singling out various customers who were distinguished either due to some vagary or because they committed a singular act, she created a folk narrative, a saga composed solely for my benefit.

Since I demanded these stories over and over again, I soon became familiar with the deserter who hid in the cellar when the recruitment officers made their rounds and whose wife periodically called out to him, *"Woynen, Leib, woynen!"* ("Stay there, Leib, stay there!"), warning him not to emerge until the danger was past; with Yossel der Royter, the hapless red-headed thief who rashly picked a tin of food from the bottom of the pile, toppling the entire pyramid down in accusation; Reizel, the snot from whose constantly dripping nose fell on the counter, revolting my mother, who assisted in the shop and who, in consequence, ran away whenever this distasteful customer entered; and Die Chemershtike, a learned woman who always had eyes downcast, reading as she walked and hence repeatedly stumbling, to the malicious delight of the little boys who swarmed around her.

I never tired of hearing these stories. Eventually, some of their key phrases became catchwords in our conversational exchanges, a secret code my brother could not comprehend.

Other stories aroused no amusement: the Cossacks who swept through the village with whirling swords, the girls who hid in the outdoor latrines to avoid them; the First World War's repeated deportations to and fro between their village on the border of Austria and Russia, and the land on the other side – each time the territory changed hands, its inhabitants were driven out by the conquerors.

She told me anecdotes about her children. The oldest daughter, Rebecca, had married and, after the war, moved to Russia, where the younger son, Avraham, was already living. He was shot during the purges of the 1930s. She never learnt of his fate, nor of that of an older son, Lazel, who was murdered by the Nazis on the streets of Lvov. After my parents brought her to live with them in Germany in 1921, she only once again saw Lazel, who came on a short visit. She never again saw the others. About herself, her childhood and youth, she said nothing, so that there is a forever unfillable void in my portrait of her.

The best part of the day came once I was in my bed. Then my grandmother would take out the *teitsch-chumash* and, opening it at random at one of the numerous etchings, would "read" me the story. Fascinated, I would avidly listen to her vivid narratives, relating to the characters as though they, too, had been part of the *shtetl* experience, people my grandmother had known intimately. To this day, my "vision" of the crossing of the Red Sea is that of a stern, long-bearded Moshe Rabbenu, standing high on a promontory, his staff outstretched over the parted waves, in which the Egyptians and all their forces are being swallowed up – chariots overturned, armed men disappearing in the waves, helpless horses, their mouths open in screams, vainly struggling to keep their heads above water. Nonetheless, even as a young child I was aware that the characters of The Book, unlike those of my grandmother's strictly oral narratives, had an aura of holiness about them that derived precisely from their being enshrined in a real book, in pictures as well as text, not merely in my grandmother's memory. Yet the stern long-bearded Moshe Rabbenu was as real to me as Yossel der Royter.

Finally, when the story came to an end, my grandmother, sitting on the bed by my side, would recite the *Shema* (the prayer said before going to sleep), carefully intoning each word for me to repeat until, by the age of three, I was able to say the prayer by myself, as she listened to check that I'd got all the words right. The clear, though never explicitly stated, implication was that if one recited these words before falling asleep, no harm would befall one during the night. So, having offered up the prayer, I would close my eyes and, firmly clasping my grandmother's hand for further reassurance, settle down to sleep. A favourite ruse of mine was to pretend to be asleep, wait till my grandmother began slowly, carefully, to withdraw her hand, then snatch it back. I was afraid of the dark and needed the reassurance of her presence but I couldn't bring myself to confess what I assume she in any case realised, that I was scared of being alone, even if I had said the *Shema*. And so I kept her at my side with this "practical joke", in which she colluded.

Although we were not by any means wealthy, my uncle bought a car – at the time a rare feature among middle-class families. On fine Sundays, we would go for an outing, to the seaside or to a place in the country where we could picnic. Unfortunately, the car could hold only five passengers, so I ended up on the lap of whichever of my parents was sitting next to the driver. My *Oma* never went on any of these trips, even though my father and brother repeatedly offered to stay at home in her stead. Did she not want to go or did she not want to deprive anybody else of the pleasure; or was it a combination of the two – a minor sacrifice made in order not to spoil another person's enjoyment?

She made few demands, lived frugally and shrank from contact with anyone outside the family circle. She died early in 1938, just after I had been able to make her happy by telling her I'd won a scholarship to a prestigious girls' high-school. Typically, she had been sitting in her usual narrow place in the kitchen, between the stove and the refrigerator, when she had a stroke, so that some time elapsed before anyone noticed that she had been stricken, one side of her body paralysed, unable to speak and hence unable to call for help. For a short while she was confined to bed in our common bedroom, while I was exiled elsewhere. Our room was filled with a sour smell, whether emanating from her body or from the medicine I couldn't tell. Although she couldn't speak to me, her eyes were full of love.

She died on a Sunday morning, as if not to disturb the workday routine. I was in the entrance hall of our house when I saw my father come down the stairs sombre-faced and heard him say gently to my mother in the kitchen: "*Die Mamme ist gestorben*". In retrospect, I don't think she had any true happiness in her life, apart perhaps from being able to make me happy.

Grandmothers II: *Oma* Feige

A significant change in our household once we arrived in England derived from the fact that my paternal grandmother, Feige, had followed Alex, her youngest, favourite, most devoted and still unmarried son to England even before my father's arrival. For the first time, I was living together with both my grandmothers and with a jovial, sybaritic uncle. Though both had been born in Galicia, had similar backgrounds in terms of upbringing and education, and had even married two brothers, the two women could not have been more different from each other, nor could my relationships with them.

Because my brother spent some summer holidays at her home in Mannheim, where he had been born and where most of my father's siblings still lived, he had developed a strong bond with what I now perceived as "his" *Oma*. In sharp contrast to the physique and bearing of "my" *Oma*, Feige, who was short and plump, loved to dress well. Her numerous frocks, most of them silk, fell to the ground, out of fashion, and yet utterly appropriate and elegant. Her wigs, of which she had several, were equally elegant, never hidden by a kerchief. When she went out, she wore little round hats perched saucily on top of the wig. Though markedly less devout than her sister-in-law, she went to synagogue every Shabbat, to show off her clothes or perhaps simply to be in company, unconfined.

She was not one to sit around in the house. That is not to say that she took part in running the household. She probably thought two people in the kitchen were enough. As for the cleaning, that was performed twice weekly by a charwoman. For her part, she took walks, visited her friends and at least once a week went to the cinema. Although she was so spunky, ready to try anything new, she never learnt English and yet, when she got lost one Shabbat, she managed to find her way home with the help of strangers, while my father and uncle were desperately trying to get the police search for her.

When my mother, grandmother, brother and I also came to England we all lived together in a narrow three-storey house in Hampstead, with two rooms on every floor except the top, which had a tiny additional room that became the bedroom of my *Oma*. My uncle, my brother and "his" grandmother now shared a bedroom, while I slept with my parents. It was almost as if we were two separate parties. Indeed, my mother always maintained that her mother-in-law spurned my other grandmother, relating to her, if at all, rather as a servant than as an equal. Certainly I don't recall them ever sitting down to talk to each other or even being in the same room save in the presence of the entire family. One had the kitchen and her own little room in which to spend time. The other had the living-room, which opened on to a garden with lawn and flowerbeds.

My brother would be invited to accompany my grandmother to afternoon film-screenings, at which he served as interpreter until she fell asleep, leaving him to enjoy the double features until she woke up. Since he was always with an adult, he was able to see A-rated films, to which nobody under the age of 16 was admitted unaccompanied. I envied him but found a certain comfort from secretly searching out the weekly editions of *Picturegoer* he hid away. From the text, summaries, reviews and particularly photographs I derived a vicarious pleasure. I was able to reconstruct the contents of the films, just as I had done in Essen in earlier years, basing myself on the skills developed outside the cinema. Now, however, I had far more details to go by.

Poor *Oma* Feige was rudely expelled from her paradise when my uncle finally became engaged at the advanced age of 35. Stella Levy, his English-born, semi-assimilated wife-to-be, who came from a well-to-do family of industrialists, had no common language, either literally or metaphorically, with her mother-in-law.

She soon made it clear that she had no intention of sharing either her new home or her new husband with a rival for his affection. So, even before the wedding, Feige was bundled off to Palestine, where several of her children were already living. My uncle and his wife moved into a grand four-bedroom house in a more elegant suburb and, as my mother used to say, "my" *Oma*, her mother and she herself enjoyed an all-too-brief respite, especially once we too moved to a larger house in a new suburb, where everybody could have a room of their own, even though my grandmother and I chose to continue to share one.

My father and uncle never saw their mother again. She died in the home of one of her daughters in a suburb of Tel Aviv, surrounded by children and grandchildren who cared for her when she was already half-blind and bedridden. The last photo I have is of her lying in bed, a white kerchief over her head, eyes staring unseeingly at the camera, shrunken, toothless, the lower lip tucked beneath the upper – a very far cry from the dapper little lady who took my brother to the pictures.

Outsider

Childhood

I AM SITTING on the top step of the narrow flight of stairs that leads from the open front door of our apartment house to the first floor, where my parents have their wholesale linen and cutlery business. I am alone. Slowly, the door below the stairs, which leads to the cellar, opens. As I sit gripped with terror, an enormous black shoe gradually creeps out. It is a woman's shoe, a court shoe, with a Louis heel and a tongue-shaped protrusion rising at the instep, such a shoe as was fashionable in the late 1920s and 1930s. Menacingly, it slides out of the darkness while I sit, petrified, hardly daring to breathe, waiting for this animated object to strike at me, as it clearly intends to do. At the height of the terror, I awake, my body tense with fear, my arm and leg muscles rigid with the effort of remaining still.

Turning in my bed one night, I see, over by the far wall, a hunchback with a large hat that comes down over his forehead to the bridge of a threatening beak of a nose, like a bird of prey waiting to pounce on its victim. He has come to kill me but if I lie motionless he will not know I am there. Yet how long can I remain utterly motionless? At some point, the bright moonlight will inevitably penetrate to the corner of the room where my bed is and I shall be revealed. Seemingly hours go by before I realise that the hunchback is the shadow cast by clothes hung on the back of the bedroom door.

My grandmother, my brother and I are asleep in the large bedroom we share. There is a loud, rhythmic knocking at the front door downstairs. My parents are out. Our maid, Maria, comes into the room, as frightened as we are. None of us is prepared to open the door. Who could want to be admitted in the middle of the night? We huddle together, waiting, fearing that the door will ultimately give under the persistent hammering. My parents return and reassure us. There is no one at the door. A new neighbour has chosen this untimely hour to put up shelves in an adjoining room.

These three occasions of intense fear and helplessness remain vivid in my memory, marring recollections of what was on the whole a carefree, uneventful childhood. They might account for my lifelong fear of the dark and of remaining alone in the house at night. I was a solitary child, five and a half years younger than my brother. From a very early age he resented my presence. A story frequently related in our family told how on one occasion, when I was peacefully asleep in my pram, he had placed a large saucepan over my head. Perhaps he would have preferred a brother.

My paternal grandfather had died a little over a month after my brother was born, living just long enough to attend the *Pidyon Ha-ben*, customarily celebrated with a festive meal. Following the family tradition of commemorating forefathers, my parents named my brother after my maternal grandfather. Two years later, my mother gave birth to a daughter who, like one of my aunts and several of my cousins, was named after my paternal great-grandmother, Sarah Ettel. When my mother again became pregnant, in 1926, my parents hoped they would be able to name the child after my father's father, Mordechai. "And then you came along!" as my brother later told me, in an accusatory tone. So the honour of my grandfather's name fell to our cousin, the youngest son of my father's older brother, who in turn some 40 years later named his son after his own father.

My pretty, gentle, black-eyed sister Edit died of pleurisy when I was two. How different my life might have been had she lived, a companion and confidante for me, or perhaps a rival in my parents' attention and affection. I compensated for that lack by developing a fruitful imagination. I created an alter ego, who, like me, enjoyed the things I enjoyed and kept me constant company, engaging in contemplative or amusing dialogue, according to my mood or the circumstances in which we found ourselves. I played on the staircase of our house; the entrance housed the workshop of Herr Pick, a frame-maker who seemed to enjoy conversation with me, particularly when I told him the plots of films screened in the cinema on the opposite side of the street.

I knew the plots not because I went to the cinema but because each time there was a new, rich display of stills I crossed the road and, adroitly linking the film's title and the apparent contents of the scenes illustrated, concocted what I assumed was the storyline. I never knew whether Herr Pick really believed I knew what the films were about. He might simply have been amused by what my childish imagination had fabricated but he always listened intently and interrupted me with appropriate expressions of amazement, horror or amusement comparable to those the film itself might have elicited had he seen it. Encouraged by an appreciate audience, I composed ever-more fanciful stories, until one day Herr Pick remonstrated with my parents for permitting me to attend films intended for adults only. My mother tried to elicit the truth from me. How had I managed to slip into the cinema to see forbidden films? Had Maria taken me with her? The most strident denials failed to persuade her that I had not seen a single one: the apparent accuracy of my forays into semiotics was overwhelming evidence against me and I was sternly bidden on no account to repeat my escapades.

If I were now to see a film it would be in the company of my parents only. With them I saw Charlie Chaplin and Jackie Coogan in *The Kid*. What particularly impressed me about that first visit to a cinema was that, when I turned round to kneel on my seat to survey the surroundings during the interval, I saw, to my amazement, one of my uncles sitting a few rows behind us. This extraordinary real-life coincidence impressed me far more than the film itself. How fascinating that other people also went to the cinema, even when they had no need to accompany their children.

Early on I taught myself to read the few children's books we had. Once, I gathered some children of my own age, sat them down in a semi-circle facing me and read aloud to them from a large-format story book, missing its first page, called *Die Puppenmutter*, "The Doll Mother". I had to make up the book's opening but given my experience in reconstructing film scenarios that was a simple matter. When the mother of one of the absorbed listeners came to fetch her, she assumed I was merely pretending to read. A peek over my shoulder revealed, to her astonishment, that this particular four-year-old could indeed read. I don't recall anybody teaching me to do so.

Once a week I accompanied my mother to the market to buy fish and poultry. The chickens were carefully selected for their plumpness, pulled out of their coops by the vendor and carried by their legs to the nearest ritual slaughterer, where their throats were slit according to the rules of *Kashrut* (dietary laws), and then, if money sufficed, taken to be professionally plucked. When money ran out, the plucking was done at home by my grandmother. A flurry of feathers filled the kitchen. In the interests of economy, every possible part of the chicken was utilised. The fat was rendered down, mixed with finely minced onions, to create delicious *Schmaltz*, the crackling vied for by my brother and me. The liver was then fried in that same fat and chopped to serve as an *entrée* for Shabbat lunch, with hardboiled eggs mashed in to eke out the quantity so that it could serve the entire family. The neck was stuffed with a savoury mixture of flour, chicken fat and onion, and together with the throat-bone, feet, gizzard, comb and wings turned into a *fricassée*. The carcass was used first for soup (to which home-made noodles were added for the forthcoming Friday-night meal) and then, lightly browned, served as the main course. Often there were embryo eggs inside the chicken, which made a delicious addition to the soup.

Essen was and still is not beautiful. Dominated by the coalmines and steelworks of the Krupp family, it had also been built by them. Its overall grey was relieved by a well-kept park and the *Stadtwald*, both planted for the workers' welfare and recreation by the wealthy landowner, who built an imposing villa for himself on a hillock outside the city. There had once been a wall surrounding the city and some of its remains stood behind the last house in which we lived, possibly accounting for the name of the street, Schützenbahn ("sluice passage"). I was unaware of this history, as also of the fact that there was a brothel at the back of our house, occupied by what my mother, in a letter to my father, referred to as the *"Damen"*. There were other remains of Essen's medieval past, including an abbey built in 845CE. It stood, as did the Lichtburg cinema, on the main street leading to the *Marktplatz*, yet I never noticed it and none of our family entered it. However, I don't recall my parents crossing to the other side of the road and certainly not spitting at it, as some Orthodox Jews do to this day when they pass a church.

In the summer we occasionally took the train out of grimy, smoky Essen to the *Stadtwald*, where we picnicked on rolls, fruit and sweet cold tea my mother brought in dark green bottles with hinged corks. One of the delights of these outings was rolling down the hillsides, competing with my cousins as to who could roll fastest. Since I was the plumpest in the family, I never won these races. Indeed, my excessive weight caused me much embarrassment. I do not know by how much I was overweight but it was apparently enough to cause my mother to consult our family doctor when I was about six. I was ordered to cut bread and potatoes out of my diet but this was as nothing compared to the chagrin I felt one morning when I came down, still in my nightdress, to sit, as I often did, under the counter in the warehouse where my parents served the travelling salesmen who came to fill their suitcases with the linens and silver they then peddled to retailers.

There were two brothers among these salesmen. One, David Stern, dark, gentle and good-looking, was the object of my first love. He would always greet me as if I were a grown-up and chat with me whenever he came. His brother, Willy, was a joker, caustic and worldly. As I sat quietly, thinking myself unobserved, I suddenly heard him remark (using the nickname by which I was known until adulthood), "Though we don't know what will become of Mausi when she grows up, of one thing we can be sure: she'll always have a broad behind". The peals of laughter this comment aroused brought home to me for the first time in my life the extent to which physical appearance can be a source of humiliation. Forgetting that my presence was supposed to be a secret, I burst into tears and fled from the room back to the comforting arms of my grandmother.

Why, in fact, was I referred to as "Mausi"? I had, after all, been named Hinde, the Yiddish name being Germanised as Hilde. However, since it was deemed desirable to distinguish me from the numerous cousins who bore the same name (all of us in memory of our paternal great-grandmother), my parents further Germanised mine into Hildegard. Yet how could a little Jewish girl go around in an Aryan world bearing that pretentious name? They therefore sought an alternative, using as a source the *Stammbuch*, a compendium of birth certificates every family owned. Systematically starting their search at the beginning of the alphabet, they came upon Alice, the name which was bestowed on me as more acceptable than Hildegard.

My brother's name also underwent mutations. The Hebrew Ze'ev (wolf) was Germanised to Wilhelm. In England it became William. In both countries family and friends called him Willy.

I don't recall ever being called by my given name until I went to school. Instead, the nickname I believe originated with my nursemaid Maria came into general use: "Mausi" or the diminutive "Mausilein". How inured I was to being addressed and referred to by this name is borne out by an incident that occurred when I was 11, on holiday with my mother the seaside. Early one evening I went for a walk on the beach with a fellow guest at our hotel, a girl of my own age, to watch the fishermen bring in their catch. Suddenly I heard a call of "Mausi!" and, turning, saw my mother and my companion's mother on the promenade above, beckoning us to join them. Obediently, I climbed the stairs, whereupon my mother began to scold me, rebuking me for not having responded at once when she called me.

"But I came as soon as you called," I remonstrated. Apparently not. She had been calling me by my "official" name and I had simply not taken it in. Only when, in exasperation, she reverted to my nickname did I hear her call. My close relations continued to refer to me by my nickname, so much so that when I was in my 50s and telephoned one of my cousins, identifying myself as Alice, I had to repeat the name several times, until it occurred to me that I might be more readily identifiable as "Mausi".

"Ah," he said, "*Mausi!* Why didn't you say so?!"

I began my education at the Jewish primary-school in Essen. My teacher was Frau Redner. This was an occasion I had really looked forward to, more because of the accoutrements that in Germany accompanied the *Ersten Schulgang* (first day at school) than because of what I expected to happen once I entered the classroom. I inherited from my brother a slightly worn but still handsome leather satchel, in which I carried a wooden-framed slate, an oblong pencil-box for the slate pencils and a small round box in which a damp sponge must be ever ready to erase errors. While this was slung on my back, I bore on my chest a metal-lined lunchbox for the fresh, richly buttered rolls I was given to consume during the morning break. In the satchel was also a reader entitled *Tritt Auf!* that combined short rhymes, one-page stories, tongue-twisters and pictures. Having already acquired the skills of reading and writing I soon knew it by heart.

To mark the auspicious occasion children received a *Tütte*, a cone-shaped, gaudily decorated container, an outsize version of the paper cones in which grocers wrapped sugar and tea. These cones friends and relations filled with goodies: sweets, cakes, paper cut-outs to be used as bookmarks, chocolate balls in silver paper. On the first day of school, to mark the transition to a new regime and perhaps sweeten the experience of freedom curtailed, one carried the cones to school, to compare the contents with those of fellow pupils and, presumably, gloat over the superior quality of your own booty. To my bitter disappointment, I received no *Tütte*. This might have been because my parents were unaware of the immutability of German traditions, or because they simply could not afford what must have seemed an unnecessary expense. I recall my almost inconsolable grief at being deprived of what I had so keenly anticipated.

Learning of this, distant cousins made me some cut-outs of coloured tissue paper, ensuring that I, too, would have at least something to show to my classmates. That was, however, not my only disappointment with school. I soon discovered that, far from reading exciting books and writing your own compositions, the first weeks of the school year were spent in endlessly delineating the various strokes, slanting, upright or curly, that constitute Gothic script. Although I already wrote this script fluently, I too was subjected to this demeaning exercise. The kindness and warmth of my teacher did nothing to relieve my

26

boredom, and I passed the first few weeks in a haze of unmitigated disbelief and resentment.

One cold February night in 1933 sharp shouts and cries broke the silence and awoke the entire household. My parents came into our bedroom to reassure us that there was no need for concern but I sensed that they themselves were far from calm. The next morning, joining my father, who was looking out of the window into our back yard, I saw red spots on the snow.

"They got the Bolsheviks," my father told my mother. I had no idea who "they" were, nor what was meant by Bolsheviks. I don't think I even realised that the red spots, blooming like flowers in the snow, were blood. My parents had said nothing to deter me when, some weeks earlier, I had stood in the front doorway next to Herr Pick to watch Brownshirts march along our street singing the *Horst Wessel Lied* as they formed part of a motorcade surrounding Hermann Göring. I joined in the cheering, because that seemed the right thing to do. Herr Pick remained silent.

Then my brother returned from school with his shirt torn, and weals on his face and shoulders from the lashes he had been given by a group of Nazi youths. While members of the Jewish youth movements had been forbidden to wear the shoulder straps that were an indispensable part of their uniforms, these oafs used their straps to beat up Jewish boys. Shortly afterwards, I found the contents of the kitchen cupboard in which I kept my few toys and books scattered on the floor. The Gestapo had visited. It was the signal for my father to return to England. Among the earliest anti-Semitic edicts published by the Nazis was one that no longer exempted Jews from the "East" from being expelled. A month later, a further edict forbade their entry into Germany. We were now in danger of deportation.

After my father had gone my mother was left with the formidable tasks of trying to collect outstanding debts from customers, paying the creditors, dissolving the firm and packing up our household goods, all so far as possible without unduly arousing the suspicions of the authorities. She informed my father that the police had come to ask when we were leaving and that there was some evidence of ongoing surveillance. Our neighbours had moved out, we were alone in the house and she was frightened. We would have to leave Essen for a place where she was unknown. The most obvious refuge was Mannheim, where most of my father's family lived. There, we would await the British entry visas that would enable us to join him. She expected our stay in Mannheim to be a matter of weeks. In the event, we were there for eight months.

Homeless for a short while prior to our departure from Essen, we went to live with my father's oldest brother Welwel. He ran a small restaurant at home, his grossly overweight wife serving as cook. Grease seemed to be everywhere: rolling down my aunt's face as she laboured in the kitchen, on the pots, the frying pans, the plates themselves and the tablecloths. Having seen its preparation, I often found it hard to swallow the food. *Tante* Malcze's poppy seed-filled yeast cakes were, however, too delicious to resist.

My uncle was a gentle, loving, good-humoured man who in his few spare hours engaged in ornate calligraphy and pen-and-ink drawing. His ambition had been to become an artist or a scribe but these were not considered appropriate professions in a middle-class Jewish household. He remained frustrated, fitfully employed in a variety of enterprises, in none of which he found either prosperity or personal fulfilment. In features, he resembled my father. Like him, he sported a van Dyck beard and, to my surprise and delight, I discovered one day as I sat on his lap that he too, like my father, had gold teeth that gleamed when he laughed.

Uncle Welwel had three children, the oldest of whom, Jakob, was a member of the left-wing Zionist movement, *Ha-Shomer Ha-Zair* ("The Young Guard"), determined, despite his parents' opposition, to emigrate to Palestine. He was extremely fond of us, particularly of my mother, who sympathised with his Zionism. When we went to say goodbye to him early in the morning, as he still lay in bed, he turned his face to the wall to hide his tears. Fourteen years later, when we met after the war, he told me he had been certain that we would never see each other again.

"Did you think we had no flowers in Mannheim?" This caustic comment on the bouquet I had tenderly carried all the way from Essen, coming from my oldest cousin Salli as he met us at the station, proved indicative of what came to be a far from auspicious stay. My brother and I were regular targets of Salli's sarcasm. When Wilhelm took a second piece of cake at the Friday-night Shabbat meal, Salli would sneer: "Why don't you take yet another piece?" Once, when the object of one such comment, I burst into tears and went in search of my mother. I found her alone in the kitchen, crying. All we could do was embrace.

We lived at the home of Etti, my father's oldest sister, whose husband had recently been killed in a motor accident, leaving Salli, at the age of 23, the family's sole income-earner. Both his brothers were away on *hachshara*, the pioneering training-communities that prepared young people for agricultural and artisan work in Palestine, while the youngest sibling, a 17-year-old daughter, Hilde, remained at home, nursing an ambition to become a dancer. Unlike industrial Essen, Mannheim was an elegant, well-planned city with a castle, a castle-park and two rivers, one of which could be crossed either by walking over the bridge or by taking the ferry. Visible in the distance along the Rhine was the fabled university town of Heidelberg.

My brother already knew both Mannheim and the many relations who lived there because he'd spent several summer holidays with them. For me all was new and exciting. An imposing green-tiled, freestanding ceramic stove such as I had never before seen heated the living-room. With few exceptions, the streets, planned on a grid system, bore block numbers rather than names, each house and apartment being designated by an additional number. We lived at A2, 4, another aunt at H7, 17, yet another aunt across the River Neckar. In Essen there had been no "real" aunts, only two by marriage. Here there were three and, in addition, there were new-found cousins, several of them more or less my age, who owned innumerable, hitherto unfamiliar toys – not only dolls but a scooter, roller-skates and doll carriages that still (unlike the battered green one I had abandoned in Essen) possessed hoods that could be raised and lowered.

All four of us – my mother, grandmother, Willy and I – crowded into one bedroom. However, my aunt's flat proved spacious enough to accommodate another family. Shortly after our arrival, one of the rooms was made over to my youngest aunt, Lotte, a 34-year-old full of *joie de vivre*, incongruously married to a hypochondriac scholar cousin, Leo, considerably older than herself, to whom (according to her sisters) she had been attracted chiefly by the enticing prospect that she would henceforth be able to lay claim to the designation of "*Frau Doktor Rabbinerin*". Their only son, Gerd, a precocious three-year-old nicknamed Bubi, soon became a favourite playmate of my brother's, arousing considerable jealousy as I found myself excluded from their games.

Throughout the eight months we spent in Mannheim neither Willy nor I attended school. One reason was that my mother never knew when our entry permits to England would arrive. In the meantime, my brother studied a little by himself, assisted in Latin by the erudite Uncle Leo, but he was less diligent than before, spending much time in football and Zionist youth activities. Exceptionally mature for his age, he wrote for the Habonim movement's magazine and attended lectures by eminent Zionist thinkers, including Martin Buber and Ernst Simon when they passed through town. The decision to keep me at home stemmed from my well-known habit of chatting with all and sundry. Since we were not officially resident in Mannheim and my mother was all the while under threat of expulsion, the fear was that I would unwittingly reveal the truth. I therefore spent much of the day drawing or, as my mother put it in a letter to my father, "scribbling". She encouraged me to write in Gothic script, in which I occasionally added a few words to her letters to my father, seldom containing anything more original than the customary "Many regards and kisses".

The sudden influx of numerous relations who far outstayed their welcome (such as it was) must have placed an immense strain on both the hosts and their unwilling "guests". Along with Salli's meanness to me and Willy, my mother suffered the barbs of my aunt's comments on my father's failure to send an allowance adequate to covering the expense of our maintenance. I first became aware of how much pain this caused her only on the Passover eve of our stay. The entire family gathered at *Tante* Etti's, numerous adults at the upper end of the table and all the even more numerous youngsters seated together at the other. As the man of the house, Salli presided at the head of the table, while I sat immediately opposite him, at the very far end. Presumably because I was the one on whom his gaze involuntarily rested, I was also the one directly reproached when, perhaps bored by the lengthy recital of the *Haggadah*, some of us caused an interference by chatting and laughing. Whatever the reason, it was I to whom he addressed a loud chiding comment, which sent me, crying, in search of my mother. I found her, like myself in tears having been rebuked by one of the aunts for not doing her fair share of the innumerable tasks involved in preparing for this most demanding of festivals. For me, the evening ended happily. My cousin Alex, a handsome young man of 22, whose good nature contrasted sharply with his older brother's misanthropy, gathered all of us little ones and taught us how to dance a *horah*, the circle dance that was the pioneer Zionists' favourite pastime, accompanied by Hebrew songs, the words of which all related to the joy of their imminent *aliyah*, going home to "the Land", the Promised Land of Palestine, their ultimate destination.

For my mother there was ongoing misery. She had to pay for board and lodging, and was reproached whenever she failed to do so promptly or adequately. She wrote detailing the items for which she required money: £2 or £3 would suffice to cover a new corset or new pair of shoes and a few toys so that we (particularly I) wouldn't have to rely on the dubious generosity of my cousins. When they went to the theatre or on outings I was not invited to accompany them. They were often downright nasty. In one of her letters my mother cites me as tearfully asking why nobody liked me. She asked my father to send a photo of himself, since I had forgotten what he looked like. Fortunately, there was a treasure-trove of children's books in the apartment: the Grimm Brothers, Hans Christian Anderson and other classics. Some were so frightening that they brought bad dreams – that were soothed away by the proximity of my ample-bosomed mother, with whom I shared a bed.

Despite the fact that she now lived surrounded by more relations than ever before, my mother felt profoundly lonely. She didn't know when, if ever, she would see Benno again: when she would once more kiss him on the mouth rather than on paper. She had little in common with his sisters. A woman who enjoyed reading and music, she poured scorn on the gossip and bickering that characterised family interactions. She felt happiest when everybody was occupied elsewhere, while she remained alone in the apartment, free to read, reflect and write letters to my father. It was at such times that the letters became longer and more informative, less concerned with money or lack of it.

Trapped in the increasingly menacing threat of expulsion, she constantly consulted him as to the best way out of the horror: should she go to France, like some of their friends and even his brother Mendel, or to Belgium, like others? She sent letters and document after document to the British consul in Frankfurt, travelling there in the hope of persuading him to expedite the visas. On one occasion, when she had taken Willy with her for moral support, he wrote to describe the futility of the journey: my mother was too upset to do so herself. In the hope of ensuring at least his safety, she tried, with the help of my cousin Alex, to register him for *aliyah* to Palestine, only to learn that he was two years too young to be included in the programme.

She began to question Benno's love for her. Perhaps he would have preferred one of the more eligible young women his sisters were constantly referring to. Occasionally, memories of past happiness brightened the present. Alone in the apartment, she heard through the open window the waltz from *The Merry Widow* coming from a neighbour's radio and recalled the happy time 15 years earlier when, sitting with a friend on a balcony in Tarnopol, she'd been taught the words.

In May 1934 the longed-for tidings came in the form of a registered letter, hand-delivered. Choked by emotion, Perl could write no more than a brief three lines to apprise Benno of the fact, reporting that Willy, overcome by joy, had flung himself into her arms, weeping "like a baby".

At last, 11 months after my father's departure, we set off for England and safety.

*

We left Mannheim by rail for Ostend on a Saturday evening: 12 May 1934. Wedged into the corner by the window, I sensed my mother's apprehension. Presumably she feared that something might still happen to prevent our departure, which had been made possible only because the British authorities finally succumbed to my uncle's threat that, if his brother were unable to reunite with his family, he would close down the business he had founded in 1931 and throw eight employees out of work. Coming at a time of widespread unemployment and economic depression, the threat proved effective, particularly since we four new immigrants could hardly be perceived as competing with anyone in the British labour force.

There were moments of tension through the long night journey. A brown-uniformed SA man came to check our passports, which, because of my parents' place of birth, had been issued by the Polish government. We were part of the despised community of *Ostjuden* who a few years later were deported *en masse* to Zbaszyn, only to find themselves equally rejected by the anti-Semitic Polish regime. Would he find fault with our passports, our *laissez-passer* papers? He scrutinised us suspiciously, checking whether the photographs corresponded with our real-life features, and, finally, to our relief, handed the passports back to my mother without comment.

Then came an unanticipated dilemma. A jovial fat man opposite took a suitcase from under the banquette and drew out a large sausage, a loaf of bread and a knife. Spearing a slice of the *Wurst* on the point of the knife, he politely offered it to my grandmother, to whom the very thought of so much as touching non-kosher food was anathema. Shrinking back, she shook her head in refusal of the offer. Would this be interpreted as an unforgiveable slight? Would it reveal our Jewishness? Each of us was then offered the tempting morsel, only to reject it as firmly as my grandmother had done. Now, of course, it was impossible to unpack the sandwiches my mother had prepared, since our only valid reason for refusal of the sausage was that we weren't hungry. We couldn't risk offending this burly man with his knife: who could tell whether he might not turn the weapon against us? Fears and fantasies kept us hungry throughout the long train-ride, on which even the respite of sleep was interrupted at each of the numerous stops for further examination of passports and visas.

At 8.30 the next morning we reached Ostend and there on the platform to meet us was my father. But was it him? The familiar van Dyck beard had been shaved off: without it, the set of his mouth looked different. The doubt lasted a few seconds. My mother's sobs as she embraced him, his arms around me, hugging me tight – the kisses to which my usually undemonstrative brother, always so shy of physical contact, readily submitted – all convinced me that we were indeed together again. Crossing the Channel, I chatted away, showing off a new coat I had received for the journey, trying to tell him as much as possible about our life in Mannheim, waiting impatiently while he talked to my mother for the moment when he would resume listening to me.

After the boat, the train to London and then, finally, arrival at the house in West Hampstead to which my father, uncle and paternal grandmother had moved some time earlier from the nearby boarding-house at which they had stayed on first coming to England. My mother had explicitly requested a flat with all its rooms on one floor: one that had a large kitchen, and a separate room where my brother and I could spend time away from the adults and their talk; not, she stipulated, two storeys. We ended up with three. My father had chosen something infinitely less convenient in terms of housekeeping. Oblivious to practicalities, I was delighted. A whole house to ourselves! Three storeys, including a bathroom, which we had lacked in Essen, and a living-room with French windows that opened straight onto a garden – a garden of our own, with a pear tree, a fig tree, a bed of my favourite sweet-scented lilies of the valley and some deep purple, almost black iris. Later I was to discover that the pear tree leant over the fence in such a way that all the fruit was quite legitimately picked by our neighbours, so that we never tasted it, while the English climate frigidly precluded the ripening of the figs. But that never detracted from the delight of having an open, yet private space in which I could play my games of imagination.

The first evening, my father took my brother and me for a walk through the quiet streets around our house, so different from the main road on which we had lived in Essen. Some of the houses had signs reading "To Let". When I asked my father, who had already acquired a fair amount of English, what the words meant, he told me they meant "to permit, allow". This reply left me more puzzled than before. What was it one was so openly permitted to do in this remarkable Newfoundland? I was filled with excited anticipation – of roast chickens flying into my mouth, long hours of leisure in pleasant woods, innumerable books to read, unlimited free time that my father would be able to spend with us…

Although reality proved disappointingly commonplace, we soon encountered a variety of delicious unfamiliar foods: smoked haddock, fried kippers with egg, toast, tea with milk. The most impressive of these delicacies was the British birthday-cake – a foundation of rich fruit cake containing more sultanas, raisins, currants and almonds than flour, covered with a thick layer of marzipan, which was in turn smothered in an even thicker layer of almond icing, customarily embellished with flowers of angelica and often bearing an inscription appropriate to the occasion, be it a birthday, anniversary or wedding. This magnificent concoction appeared on our table for the first – and also last – time, four days after our arrival in England, on the Shabbat of my brother's bar-mitzvah. I assumed that this, like the hanging baskets of summer flowers that adorned the synagogue, was an accustomed English mode of celebration of which my brother's rite of passage was the principal cause. I was soon disabused regarding the flowers, since they remained in place for *Shavuot*, the feast of first fruits, a few days later.

Only many years later did my brother reveal to me his own ambivalence regarding what was to me a magical event. Naturally, he was happy to have our father at his side but he had hoped to be together with the entire family who, had we remained in Germany, would all have been present. In addition, although he had diligently and with his customary thoroughness prepared to recite the entire Torah portion as well as the subsequent section from the Prophets, the local rabbi, unaware of his abilities, severely curtailed his reading, so that he was unable to demonstrate his skills. And finally, standing on the *bimah* facing the rabbi, he could not understand a single word of the speech addressed to him. No wonder that, unlike mine, his recollections were bittersweet.

Willy went almost immediately to the Jewish Secondary School, an hour's journey away on the far side of London. For me, no Jewish education was available and for some time I stayed at home, playing by myself, looking longingly at the few books in the glass-fronted bookcase in the living-room, trying to decipher the meaning of the words on their spines. One in particular fascinated me, because it bore my own name and had extraordinary illustrations. With *Alice in Wonderland* on my lap I tried to piece together a narrative, as I used to do with the cinema stills, but the fantastic figures proved more difficult to integrate into a convincing story than the glamorous women and handsome men of the UFA films. Fortunately, before long my English became adequate enough to enable me to comprehend what has remained one of my very favourite books.

We lived at 10 Priory Road. Next door, at Number 12, was a family with three children – two boys and a girl who seemed to be my own age. They spent a great deal of time playing in their garden, which had a large wooden seesaw at one end. I would hear their chatter and laughter on the other side of the fence, and from time to time would go up to the rarely used dining-room on the first floor of our house to stand behind the long damask curtain watching them, supposing myself invisible from below.

One day, the girl (whose name I later learnt was Ethel) looked up, caught sight of me, and beckoned me to come and join them, adding *"Ich spreche Deutsch"*. Though the accent was strange, I was delighted at the thought of finally being able to play with someone my own age and ran next door eagerly. This misleading phrase proved the single German expression that the children's mother, Mrs Grasse, wisely anticipating such an encounter, had imparted to them. However, we quickly learnt to understand each other and I was soon spending every afternoon at our neighbours' home, joining them regularly for what was another English innovation: high tea, with bread and butter, sticky buns, scones and, very occasionally, toasted crumpets.

Mrs Grasse was a Scotswoman who had converted to Judaism in order to marry her physician husband, an Orthodox Jew who had come from Poland to Glasgow to study medicine. She presided over the tea-table, dispensing tea from a large, cosy-covered pot and playing educational games such as "20 Questions". Unlike my own mother, Mrs Grasse was a careless housekeeper. As we played with clockwork trains and tin soldiers on the carpet in the living-room, I would notice the fluff accumulated under the sofa and armchairs, and think how my mother would tut-tut in disapproval were she to see it. One day, as I was crawling on the carpet, a large darning needle pierced my knee. It penetrated so deeply that Dr Grasse had to be summoned to pull it out with forceps. Afterwards, I heard him scolding his wife for her carelessness, an occurrence so rare that Ethel has, like me, never forgotten it.

Michael, two or three years older than Ethel and me, only occasionally deigned to play with us. Like Ethel, he had absorbed some of their mother's guttural Scots, which I found fascinating and occasionally imitated. I was intrigued at seeing him set out for synagogue on Saturday mornings wearing an incongruous tartan kilt. Dr Grasse would give his children Hebrew lessons once a week but they were reluctant learners and I, hanging over the back of the sofa on which they were seated, would often impatiently provide the correct answers, keen to play more. In consequence, I heard myself praised and being held up as a shining example by the doctor, something that helped to compensate for my awareness that I still had a great deal of idiomatic English to learn.

As I was about to return home one afternoon, Ethel informed me that the entire family would be away the next day because they were going to the seaside "for tonight". A day passed before I went back to knock at the kitchen entrance but there was no reply. The same happened the next day and the next, for two weeks. Each day I would knock and each day I would return home disappointed.

Finally, after two weeks, not only was Ethel back but she had brought me a new kind of sweet, sticks of "rock", each a different colour, each with its own flavour, but each one with the same name of a seaside resort imprinted on the white inner surface, so that no matter how far one sucked or bit, the name remained legible to the end. However, I was not to be so easily mollified. In a reproachful tone, I accused Ethel of having misled me by not revealing the length of her proposed absence.

"But I told you," she remonstrated. "I said we were going away for a fortnight."

There were three cinemas in our vicinity. My parents enjoyed films but since they went to evening performances while I was permitted to attend only the afternoon matinées, we seldom went together. Rather, it was Ethel who was my most constant companion. Together we enthused over Fred Astaire and Ginger Rogers, who became the joint protagonists of our favourite game, played only on the secluded strip of paving that lay between the French windows of our living-room and the lawn. We were too shy and self-conscious to engage in make-believe in the presence of adults or siblings. In private, we played out the hackneyed archetypal plot, which never varied from one film to another, of the handsome witty man pursuing the disdainful lady, wooing her in dance and song until she finally succumbs to his charms. We didn't strictly distinguish between the male and female roles. Although we were both imaginative dancers, we never presumed to compare our efforts with the awe-inspiring grace and incomparable skill of our beloved Astaire, whom Rudolf Nureyev much later referred to as the greatest of all dancers.

When my uncle Alex married in 1935, his wife presented me with two of her cast-off evening dresses. One of black silk, the other of pink satin, both had gauze skirts. Ethel and I donned the frocks, twirling ecstatically. We thought ourselves unobserved but were disabused when one of our next-door neighbours came to see my parents in order to suggest that we become more competent by attending the tap-dancing classes she and her sister gave on Saturday mornings. My parents were initially opposed to this desecration of the Shabbat but when it became clear that the classes were within walking distance and that one did not need to pay for them on the day of attendance, they succumbed.

I acquired a pair of tap-dancing shoes but none of the other accoutrements I discovered were sartorially *de rigueur*: wide-legged sailor trousers, a bolero top, coloured bows in one's hair. My initial shame at this lack became more acute when I realised that my plumpness was a distinct disadvantage in tap-dancing in concert with fellow pupils. I was painfully embarrassed when my turn came to perform the solos under the eyes not only of my encouraging teacher but also of my disdainful fellow pupils, who did not hesitate to express their contempt. After several weeks of misery, I abandoned the forlorn attempt to emulate my American movie idols.

First day at Kingsgate Road Primary School was one of shame and distress. My father had taken me to see the headmaster, Mr Elton, who decided I should go straight into Class 10, the third one up from the bottom, where I would be with my coevals. I was the first immigrant pupil the school had ever admitted and the staff were uniformly ignorant of ways in which they might help absorb what was referred to as "our little refugee girl". All I needed to know, my father conveyed to me, was to put up my hand and say "Please, teacher". And so I was led into a class full of children, all sitting at rows of desks that sloped upwards, like an auditorium, facing a wall with a large blackboard. I was put in the front row, presumably so that the teacher would be able to help me.

Soon after I was seated, a sum of arithmetic appeared on the board and the teacher turned to the class, clearly expecting someone to provide an answer to the mathematical problem she had posed. I raised my hand. With a kindly expression, the teacher, Miss Armstrong, turned to me. "Please, teacher", I said confidently, assuming this to be a kind of magical, all-powerful portmanteau phrase that could mean anything one could want or intend it to mean. She waited, expectantly. "Please, teacher", I repeated, more firmly. Why was she still gazing at me with a puzzled expression? And why was the class beginning to giggle? I tried once more, "Please, teacher". But by this time she had realised she would elicit nothing more from me and I, too, had become aware that something had gone terribly wrong. My beloved father had betrayed me. He had failed to provide me with the right words. Barely able to hold back my tears, I sat through the morning in a miasma of suffering.

Hearing my account of this disaster, my parents realised the difficulty of my situation and the helplessness of a teacher untrained in dealing with non-speakers of English. They arranged for me to have private lessons with the daughter of the owner of the boarding-house in which my father had lived. In a matter of weeks I could read *Alice in Wonderland*, and before the end of my first school year my rich vocabulary and skill in spelling brought me to the top of the class in English. The school was a 10-minute walk from our house but took much longer to reach on the frequent mornings of thick yellow fog when one could see barely a yard ahead. On these occasions, traversing the busy Abbey Road was a frightening experience, even once the flashing orange Belisha beacons were installed to mark pedestrian crossings. Yet nobody ever accompanied me. The school was a large and grimy Victorian building, with separate entrances for girls and boys, littered and foul-smelling lavatories out in the yard and no toilet paper. On the oversized blackboard Miss Armstrong daily greeted us with a passage from Scripture: the 10 Commandments, each numbered; the 23rd Psalm, still my favourite; the Beatitudes. Some of these we learnt by heart. The psalm we sang in a tender two-part melody entitled "Brother James's Air". Composed in the 19th century, it nevertheless sounded medieval.

All the school furniture appeared, like the building itself, to date back to the 19th century. Numerous initials had been carved into desktops, each one of which had an inkwell that was replenished daily by the class monitor. In winter, as the days grew short, the school caretaker would come around carrying a long taper to light the gas-lamps that hung from the ceiling. There was no heating of any kind, for the British are – or were – a stoical people, hardened to the vagaries of their climate. While "serious" studies, of the "three Rs", history and geography, as well as (in the top classes) science, took up the morning hours, most of what we now refer to as "enrichment" enlivened the afternoons. When weather permitted, we played in the yard: netball for the girls, soccer for the boys. I constantly felt I was letting my fellow teamsters down because I couldn't run fast enough. My talents lay elsewhere. At the end of term, the class considered most talented presented a theatrical performance. Due to my histrionic gifts I invariably had a leading role. Parents were invited to the end-of-year presentation but mine never attended, unaware that their absence caused me disappointment and resentment. I couldn't understand their lack of interest, their failure to appreciate that they should share not only in the undoubted pleasure of witnessing what we'd accomplished but also of hearing the applause my performances elicited.

The illogic of English orthography continued to perplex me from time to time. When Ethel and I began to collect a new series of cigarette cards, we sought clarification of the incomprehensible meaning of its title: "Radio sell-a-bright-eyes". Only when we showed him the cards did her father helpfully elucidate that the word was actually "celebrities": *sa-le-bra-tès*. Pronunciation again. We had prayers in the hall every morning, the entire pupil body in attendance. Hymns were sung, presumed to be so familiar that hymnals were deemed unnecessary (or perhaps too expensive). I came home puzzled to ask first my parents, themselves still far from fluent in English, and then my tutor: "What is a mickamile?" Called on to provide the context, I replied that the previous words were "Gentle Jesus". It was some time before my tutor realised that the attributes applied to the son of God referred to his being meek and mild.

The vagaries of English pronunciation were also the occasion for a frightening example of the British tradition of corporal punishment. In the absence of our teacher, an older pupil had been sent in to keep us occupied by engaging us in reading aloud. We all had the same text before us and went around the room, each reading a number of sentences before handing the task on to our neighbour. One word had us so stymied that the same sentence went from pupil to pupil until there was an uncontrollable uproar. Hearing the noise, Mr Elton came in, carrying his cane and the punishment book in which every instance of corporal punishment had to be recorded, though for what purpose I never knew. Without enquiring into the causes of the commotion or bothering to ask who were the culprits, he arbitrarily picked on the little boy who'd been the last one to attempt the task, bade him stretch out his hands and administered six sharp cuts of the cane to each one.

The scapegoat slumped into his seat, each hand cradled in the opposite armpit, trying hard not to cry but succeeding only in reducing his tears to a mild sniffle. Mr Elton left the room, where a terrified silence now reigned. Fortunately, the lesson was over. The tyrannical, smirking pupil was released from her task and a professional, more experienced teacher was sent in to replace her. The episode remains traumatically to haunt me. I cannot bear to see physical violence in any form. I close my eyes and cover my ears, even when my grandchildren, like their parents before them, reassure me that "It's only a film, silly!"

On 24 May, we went to Grange Park, conveniently located next to the school, to dance around a maypole, to celebrate Empire Day and vaunt the glories of the vast areas coloured red on the maps inside the cover of our multiplication tables. We bellowed "Rule Britannia, Britannia rule the waves. Britons never, never, never shall be slaves!" This was supplemented with "Land of Hope and Glory", irreverently travestied by the pupils as Land of Soap and Water.

Despite the implied mockery of imperialism, pride in the achievements of British colonialism infused our studies, especially of history. Devoted exclusively to the conquests of Africa and Asia, the lessons simplistically portrayed these heroic achievements as victories of the civilised, enlightened and morally upright white Englishman over demonic, dark-skinned, ruthlessly vicious, treacherous villains. Clive of India and the Black Hole of Calcutta were anachronistically linked. Rhodes of Africa was lauded to the extent that we were treated *en masse* to a screening of the film by that name at the nearby Grange Cinema. The native populations were uniformly referred to in derogatory terms: niggers, Hottentots, savages. Civilising them was the "white man's burden". We read Kipling and memorised "If", which prescribed the model of British manhood. To behave fairly and honestly was to "play cricket", a uniquely British game, exported to the colonies – but unknown in Europe – the rules of which were unwarrantedly presumed to be universally comprehensible. The more sordid, less glorious, aspects of imperial growth – the slave trade, the greed for gold, forced conversions to Christianity, the contempt for native culture and tribal practices – were never mentioned. Indeed, I doubt whether our teachers, themselves captivated by the glories of the empire, were aware of the dark side of colonialism.

In 1936, Mr Elton announced a London County Council decision to hold a competition for the best essays on the British Empire. We could write on whatever country we chose. Since I knew very little about any of them, I decided to write about the only place with which I was now familiar: London. I had come to love the city, or at least the parts with which I had become acquainted, not only the Edwardian-dowager façades of West Hampstead but the various parks we visited at weekends, each with its distinct character: Regent's Park's lake, rose garden and bandstand, where military brass bands performed; the expanses and ancient trees of Hyde Park; the Serpentine; Hampstead Heath with its pond on which children sailed their toy boats.

My parents had taken me with them to hear child prodigy Yehudi Menuhin play at the Royal Albert Hall. Unaware that even children required a ticket, they had failed to purchase one at the box office but they were able to persuade the usher to let me in and we climbed what seemed to be endless staircases to reach the very top of the gallery, from where I gazed down to see the tiny figure on the stage and marvel not so much at his virtuosity as at the vast auditorium, the thousands of people who crowded it, the excitement and anticipation that preceded his performance and the volume of applause that burst forth at its close. We had also been to see a performance at the Open Air Theatre in Regent's Park, where a summer shower dampened actors and audience but not my enthusiasm. In addition, since I read the daily papers and was an observant child, good at deduction and inference, I had picked up a great deal of second-hand knowledge of what London had to offer.

Our most exciting venture into the West End took place in the course of the Silver Jubilee celebrations in 1935. I was besotted with the royal family, the

40

nobility of George V in his naval uniform garnished with the blue sash of the Order of the Garter and the statuesque beauty of Queen Mary. I studied with some envy the photos of the little princesses, Elizabeth and Margaret Rose, and demanded that the next time I was made a new coat and hat they would be similar to those they wore. Aware that there were many more of their subjects who, like myself, wished to see them in the flesh, the royal couple took several carriage rides around the streets of the West End that lay beyond the Palace-to-St Paul's route. So it was that one Sunday my father, Willy and I stood on Baker Street, enthusiastically cheering the incarnation of an institution for which my father showed little regard. When King George died the following winter, I burst into tears on hearing the news on the radio as I was dressing to go to school. My mother tied a black ribbon round my arm and I was lauded by my teacher, because I alone, "the little refugee", had cared sufficiently to express my grief.

My infatuation with my environment, England as a whole and its even then already outmoded class system, inspired a gushing paean of praise for the country and its capital. My essay on London won a prize, a book called *Zambezi Days*, which I found too boring to read but which has remained on my shelves. The inscription, in Mr Elton's florid handwriting, specifically cited my impressive loyalty to King and Country. While this filled me with pride, I suspect it caused my parents considerable amusement. I doubt whether they had ever expected a child of theirs to become so ardent a monarchist.

My love of books and skill in composition made me a favourite of several teachers. I was frequently asked to read aloud to the class, especially in lessons when the pupils were engaged in tasks that required the teacher's individual attention. I delightedly became acquainted with *Little Women* during a year of sewing lessons. When a few chapters remained unread at the end of the year, Miss Williams presented me with the book. I was deeply disappointed to find the final page missing. On other occasions, I was encouraged to entertain the class with stories of my own composition. The admiration and applause with which these met fuelled my ambition of becoming an author.

My closest relationship was with Miss Amy Burnham, in whose class I spent my last two years at Kingsgate Road Primary School. Tall, angular and well-spoken, Miss Burnham was also well-read and evidently determined to instil in her pupils a knowledge of literature comparable to her own. To this end, she regularly devoted a class every few weeks to giving us a literature quiz. This was in fact a simple test, in which we were asked to name the author of a particular book or to identify the book in which a certain character appeared. Since I had read many though not all of the works, I always did well. But even if one hadn't actually read a specific book, it was easy to memorise the correct answer to any of the frequently repeated questions. Thus, although I never completed *Coral Island* and indeed found it hard going when I did begin it, I could cite the names of both its author and its hero. Ethel disliked Miss Burnham as much as I loved her and the feeling was mutual. Our teacher must have been aware of Ethel's dislike, rebelliousness and contempt. Although there was never a cause for sanctions or punishment of any kind, she didn't spare her criticism. Ethel herself eventually became a very successful, innovative teacher in working-class neighbourhoods. To this day our differing opinions of Miss Burnham are a source of rare argument between us.

Alex was my favourite uncle. A handsome *bon vivant*, he seemed always to be in a jovial mood. When he went on holiday, he never failed to bring back presents for Willy and me. There were several lady friends who were obviously as taken with him as I was. They sometimes accompanied us on an outing, crowding the car uncomfortably. They were without exception pretty and good company but he showed no sign of marrying until, one day in 1935, he brought home a far from beautiful woman whose main attractions seemed to lie in her being both English-born and possessed of a temptingly ample dowry. Stella Levy wore coloured nail-polish, a lot of very red lipstick and her eyebrows were mere pencilled lines, totally hairless. Her black hair was pulled back into a bun and she was, quite simply, plain.

The best linen tablecloth, the finest china and the precious silver cutlery were brought out for the occasion and we ate in the seldom-used first-floor dining-room, which held all the dark, heavy, wooden furniture my parents had brought from Germany. My mother's cooking, as always, was superb and we all did our best to make a good impression. In my case this involved acting out in full the entire dramatised version of the Grimm Brothers' *The Fisherman and his Wife*, for which I was currently rehearsing the part of the titular fisherman's wife, who ends up with a large sausage stuck to her nose. My histrionic skills were considerable and I knew all the parts by heart, so I was able to present a preview of the play in toto. My uncle's guest was certainly amused, though whether by the play or the way I leapt around to face "myself" each time I switched parts I can't tell.

We must have made a good impression, because a few months later, in December, we travelled to Liverpool for the first wedding of my life. This occasion, however, also provided my first experience of adult perfidy. When I learnt of the impending celebration, I asked shyly whether I could be a bridesmaid and carry the train of the wedding-dress. I had learnt that such a function existed in England, and I longed to wear a floor-length dress and have a wreath in my hair, like the little girls in the newspaper photographs of society and royal weddings. The Duke of Kent had shortly before married the graceful Princess Marina of Greece and I was charmed by the images of elegance that appeared in the press. However, Stella responded that there were to be no bridesmaids at her wedding and I had no option but to accept the sacrifice of serving as a potentially impressive ornament for the wedding.

In Liverpool, we were taken to the Levy home, a large, double-fronted residence far more imposing than our semi-detached Edwardian home in London. Having changed into our festive garments, we went to see my aunt-to-be, who was being dressed in her bedroom. To my consternation, at her side stood a slender, very pretty little girl of my own age, wearing a floor-length dress and a wreath in her hair. She was introduced as Beryl, my future Aunt Stella's niece. Feeling the blood rush to my cheeks and the tears to my eyes, I angrily blurted out, "But you said you weren't having any bridesmaids!" There was an embarrassed silence. Nobody knew how to respond to my accusation. The reason for Stella's deception was all too clear – to me, my mother, my father's sisters, who had come from Germany to attend the wedding: Beryl was slim and pretty, I was fat and plain. She would grace the wedding cortège and increase the number of compliments received, while I would have aroused nothing but disdainful ridicule.

Hurt and envious, I sobbed throughout the ceremony in the impressively capacious synagogue. I thought that I, despised and rejected, had good reason to cry but why were my aunts sobbing as well? Why did my *Tante* Lotte, who had been Alex's constant companion while they were both unmarried, and had attended operas and dances with him, keep muttering, between sobs, "My foolish brother!" There seemed all too little joy on the part of my family, though everybody cheered up once we arrived at the elegant Adelphi Hotel, where cocktails preceded a lavish dinner and a prominently displayed seating-plan indicated that Beryl and I were to be neighbours at the very bottom of the table, as far as possible from the bride and groom. This impending proximity brought us together almost immediately and we toured the room begging for the maraschino cherries from people's cocktails, which we consumed with relish. If I was envious of her pretty appearance, she was rapidly awestruck by my superior general knowledge, the books I had read, the fact that I already spoke a foreign language and, above all, by my being a Londoner, while she had never been out of Liverpool. I soon forgave Beryl but I never fully forgave Stella for her insensitivity and selfish, if unwitting, cruelty.

With my uncle and one grandmother departed from our family circle, my parents decided that they too would move to a more modern and convenient residence, one in which a gas-stove would be installed, and where the bathroom and lavatory would be on the same floor as the bedrooms, rather than, as in Priory Road, entailing a descent to the floor below. Unable to afford as expensive a neighbour-hood or as large a house as the one my uncle and aunt had purchased in the "posh" suburb of Brondesbury, they found a neat, four-bedroom, semi-detached one slightly further from the city centre, in new and less elegant Neasden. On the day on which they were to make their final decision, I took the bus there with them and was overwhelmed with delight at the realisation that I would no longer have to share a bedroom. The house was new and we were its first owners. No flowers, shrubs or trees had yet been planted in either the front or back garden; there was virgin territory for us to develop. The entire prospect was utterly pleasing.

My father was still not wholly satisfied. First he had to ascertain whether we would have an adequate number of Jewish neighbours, a factor likely to indicate the prospect of a synagogue within walking distance. And so he set off to inspect first the houses on our side of the road and then those on the other. When he returned he reported that of the 40 houses he had found only two that had no *mezuzah* outside their front door. Thus there would be no shortage of Jewish neighbours; as for a synagogue, further reconnaissance led to the satisfying discovery of an albeit small one in the very next street. And so, with no further reservations or obstacles, in the early summer of 1937 we moved into 4 Sonia Gardens, London NW10. Now Willy, too, had a room of his own, while one of the best rooms, like my parents' with a large bow-window facing the street but with the addition of a window seat such as I had long dreamt of, was designated as mine.

However, I was still terrified of the dark. Whenever I had to go upstairs by myself I would insist not only on putting on all the lights on both floors but also on maintaining a dialogue with whoever of the family members remained below. My fertile imagination led me to conjure up a variety of terrors that might be awaiting me: burglars, murderers, kidnappers, ghosts and demons. It was best to keep my family informed of my whereabouts so that they could rapidly come to my rescue if need be. Fearing solitude, I returned to sleeping with my

44

grandmother, who still kept the cardboard box that held her possessions under her bed, even though she now had a built-in cupboard in her room. And still she told me Bible stories and said the *Shema* with me each night and held my hand till I fell asleep.

My parents were able once again, as in Germany, to afford household help. A charwoman came twice a week to do the laundry, scrub the scullery, and polish the kitchen linoleum and parquet floors, under the eagle-eyed supervision of my mother, who would follow her around, running her finger over every conceivable surface, whether visible or concealed, to make sure that all was free of dust. Since my mother now took over all the cooking and baking, my grandmother was at last able to enjoy a more leisurely existence. She still never left the house but she could sit and read in quiet, and pray three times a day, as she had always done, though now with no sense of haste or guilt at not contributing to the family's physical wellbeing.

Moving house led to changing schools. After the summer holidays I transferred to Wykeham, the local primary-school for children in the Neasden area. The difference between it and Kingsgate Road was even greater than the difference between our two homes. Wykeham was a modern, light, two-storey building that surrounded a central grass playing-field. Electricity replaced the gas-lamps. The lavatories were clean though still devoid of toilet paper. Instead of raked classrooms, we all sat on the same level. Mr Venn, our all-purpose teacher for everything except PT, was a handsome young man with wavy brown hair and athletic build, who appeared fully aware of his good looks, dressed well and carried himself proudly.

Yet despite the modernity of the building, teaching methods remained very much what they had been at Kingsgate Road and there was all too little intellectual stimulation. Here, too, infringe-ment of rules incurred the threat of corporal punishment. I vividly recall the occasion when Mr Venn, his patience and ingenuity exhausted, came into the room carrying the dreaded cane and punishment book. Excellent deterrents, they instantly restored order – to my great relief, since I feared witnessing a second miscarriage of justice. My indignation knew no bounds when I learnt of one that I didn't witness but of which I was informed by a classmate. There were two orphan girls who, it seems (I never knew for certain), lived in a home not far from mine, where the inmates were expected to help with household tasks, including clearing up after lunch. On one occasion this resulted in one them, Audrey, returning late to school for the afternoon classes. For that she was caned, by the headmistress herself. The cruelty, the lack of understanding and sympathy, appalled me.

45

Entering the class as a new pupil, without the prestige of scholastic excellence acquired at Kingsgate Road, I felt a desperate need to make a favourable impression. I had little difficulty in doing this vis-à-vis Mr Venn, who soon discerned my incomparable fund of general knowledge. One day, having used the term "*joie de vivre*", he asked the class whether anyone knew its meaning. I did, because I had seen it in the advertisements for Heinz 57 Varieties, where it appeared in various languages, each time accompanied by the English translation. A simple enough deduction that no other pupil had made. Once again I became a teacher's favourite but that didn't carry much weight with my classmates, for whom intellectual achievement was less desirous a goal than my family had encouraged me to consider it.

Needing to find another way of making an impression, fantasies once again came to my aid. I developed for myself a new persona: I was the daughter of an incredibly wealthy family, owners of a large house with servants, who took regular holidays abroad in winter and summer. This fantasy properly awed the other children, who all lived in the lower-middle-class district immediately surrounding the school, while I lived in the newer and more distant part of the suburb, to which they seldom went. But it got me into tight corners, from which I extracted myself with difficulty. When Mr Venn pinned up an illustrated poster which portrayed numerous species of dogs, one among them – a superb, sleek, white Russian Borzoi – drew gasps of admiration from the pupils.

"Oh," I said airily, "We have two of those at home." Immediately, interest was aroused and I found myself bombarded by a series of questions regarding the origin of the hounds, the care they demanded, the food they liked. Since the rest of the class was as ignorant as I was as to the correct answers to most of the queries, I was able to invent what I thought appropriate. Some months later I made the mistake of inviting one of my fellow-pupils home with me.

"Where are the Borzois?" she asked, as soon as we got in.

"They're out walking with the maid," I replied, relieved at the fact that we were out of earshot of my mother, who would have expressed some surprise at our having a servant, let alone dogs. On another occasion, I gave the same girl a graphic description of our winter holiday: the excitement of skiing in the Swiss Alps, the wooden châlets in which we stayed, the scintillating sleigh-rides through the snow, the cosmopolitan group of fellow-guests (with whom I was able to converse in German). Her response was everything I could have desired.

"I wish I could have a holiday like that," she sighed, her eyes bright with envy. Tempted to improve my standing in her opinion even further, I went too far.

"Would you like to come with us?" I asked. "I'm sure my parents wouldn't mind." To my horror, she rushed up to me the next morning and, in great excitement, told me she had asked her mother if she could go.

"She doesn't mind a bit," she said. "But she has to talk to your mum first." Fortunately, telephones in 1937 were rare, so I was able to inform her the following day that, to my deepest regret, my parents had decided not to go away that year. I had had a narrow escape. By next winter I would be at another school, out of touch with my current classmates, most of whom chose to go to a co-ed secondary-school. My own choice was the Brondesbury and Kilburn High School for Girls, which to me was as close as I would ever get to a British public school.

I had acquired an intimate, though possibly quite inaccurate knowledge of the culture of such institutions from my favourite weekly, *The Schoolgirl*, from which I gathered the details of uniforms, remittances, midnight feasts in the dormitory and an assortment of high jinks that enlivened the existence of Babs, obese Bessie Bunter and their schoolmates. The author of the stories was Hilda Richards. On one occasion I noticed, paging through a comparable weekly intended for boys, that the name of one of the major characters, a grossly overweight creature who was the hapless butt of practical jokes, was Billy Bunter. In this instance, the author's name was Frank Richards. Intrigued, I sent a letter to the editor of *The Schoolgirl*, asking whether Hilda and Frank were related. Though it occurred to me that they might be one and the same, I did not dare give explicit expression to this suspicion, since it implied deception on the part of the author(s) or editors. I never received a reply.

In addition to weekly perusal of *The Schoolgirl* I remained a voracious reader of books. While still at Kingsgate Road, I had gone to the nearby library after school almost every day. Borrowers were allowed two books at a time, one fiction and one non-fiction. I doted on series and read the entire *oeuvre* of Louisa M. Alcott, all the Dr Doolittle books in sequence, *What Katy Did* and *What Katy Did Next*, *Mary Poppins* and other works by P. L. Travers, E. Nesbit's hilarious accounts of Edwardian family life and many classics of children's literature. I would start reading on my way home, sometimes protracting what should have been no more than a 20-minute walk to one that lasted close to an hour. Reading took up most of my evening and even when I was in bed I would continue until my mother came to insist I go to sleep.

In Neasden, the library was next door to the school: I could easily continue to enjoy my favourite pastime, which in turn further nourished my fantasy world. When Aunt Stella inquired what I would like for my 11th birthday, I asked for

David Copperfield and received a shiny, leather-bound, cased volume, with a satin bookmark and a few illustrations. This at once filled me with a desire to own additional works in the same uniform edition. Aunt Stella continued to give me Dickens novels for several years and meanwhile I succeeded in wheedling my parents into buying others between birthdays. I could never resist buying books and whenever I had any pocket-money that was what I spent it on. No purchases ever excited me as much or evoked a similar visceral thrill – neither clothes, nor jewellery, nor cosmetics, until, much later, I began to collect works of art.

My passion for books early on led me to want to write them. At Kingsgate Road I was an acknowledged storyteller, frequently asked by teachers to entertain the class while other pupils learnt to sew or to paint. Because of my clear enunciation and, where appropriate, dramatic intonation I would read books aloud, with the result that I never learnt to sew. At other times I was asked to tell a story of my own devising and I readily did so, encouraged by the evident enjoyment of pupils and teachers. Most of these stories were about goblins, fairies and fantastic creatures comparable to those that later featured in the works of Tolkien. Almost all had a clear, though sometimes subtle moral content, which pleased my teachers, though in all probability it went unnoticed by my fellow pupils.

I decided to set down my creations in writing. To make them look more professional, I travelled an hour by bus from home to Holborn, where the family business was located, in Hatton Gardens, a street dedicated to trade in gold, jewellery, clocks and watches. There I was given free use of one of the typewriters, spending hours leisurely copying out my works. I also made the acquaintance of the girls in the basement packing department – pert, cheeky, cheerful young Cockneys, who took delight in embarrassing my brother by singing George Formby's mildly risqué songs in his presence and watching him blush as he hurried through his tasks, to escape as quickly as possible to the upper, more decorous, regions of the office.

Literature continued to be an essential, indispensable element in my life but my authorial ambitions were eventually jettisoned in favour of another occupation. The change was the result of a chance encounter. Neasden Library furnished the setting for a critical epiphany. While the day began with fine weather, clouds gathered before I left school. By the time I had chosen my new library books, rain was pelting down so heavily that walking home was out of the question. I would be drenched and the books ruined. So I stood in the doorway and waited for the rain to abate, starting to read one of the books. Suddenly, I became aware that I was no longer alone. Someone had taken shelter in the doorway but it was not a fellow library-user. It was an old man, poorly dressed, ill-shod, unshaven. His clothes were already sodden and he hugged himself in an attempt to ward off the cold. His appearance and the acrid smell that emanated from him nauseated me, yet I was simultaneously filled with an overwhelming desire to help him, ease his discomfort, improve his lot. Had I had any money I would have given it to him but children of my age did not carry money. In fact, unlike my friends the Grasses, who were granted a weekly penny, I never received pocket-money but would ask my parents for the required, usually modest sum if I wanted to make a particular purchase.

I could think of nothing to do. I was too shy even to talk to him. In any case, what was there to say? I could not venture expressions of pity; idle conversation – about the rain, for instance – seemed inappropriate. Had I known it then, Lear's "Poor naked wretches" would have sprung to mind but I'd not yet become acquainted with Shakespeare's tragedies. What did suddenly overwhelm me was a determination to eliminate such suffering and ensure that there would be no more poverty, hunger or beggars, like the disabled ex-servicemen who sang on Kilburn High Road, cap in hand, hoping for pennies from passersby. Then and there, I decided I would become a philanthropist. I was convinced it was a profession.

Adolescence

Together with its parent institute, the Maria Grey Teachers College, which was located across the road, Brondesbury and Kilburn High School for Girls was established in the last quarter of the 19th century, at a time when many women were fighting not only for electoral franchise but also for the right to education at levels equal to those available to boys and men.

In that spirit, the "houses" into which pupils were divided for purposes primarily of sports competitions (rather than as residences, as was the custom at boarding-schools) were named after notable women pioneers – Clough, Garrett Anderson, Fry and Nightingale. Apart from (Florence) Nightingale, the pioneer of modern nursing, the names meant nothing to me (nor, as I discovered, to my fellow pupils) and nobody saw fit to enlighten us. Only many years later, when I went to Cambridge, did I learn that Anne Jemima Clough had served as the first Principal of Newnham College. When, even later, I became interested in the

Bloomsbury Circle, I discovered that Marjorie Fry, the sister of Roger, had been a pioneering prison reformer and at one time Principal of Summerville College. Elizabeth Garrett Anderson was among the first women to qualify as a doctor. Maria Grey created the National Union for Improving the Education of Women of all Classes, which had furthered the establishment of girls' schools like my own.

Although I had successfully passed the scholarship exam in 1937, my father was deemed too wealthy to be exempted from paying the school fees – a substantial sum of £5 per term. Nor was this the sole expense involved in transition to a select secondary-school. I had to be outfitted with the full mandatory school uniform, which comprised clumsy, long-legged blue woollen knickers that had a pocket in one leg for a handkerchief, a navy-blue belted gymslip with a broad black ribbon belt, a square-necked white blouse, long black stockings, brown shoes (why *brown* with *black* stockings?), a felt or velour hat shaped like a pudding-basin, round which was bound a hatband in the school colours of red-white-red that bore the heraldic emblem of a shield, with "BKHS" inscribed on it in gold.

In summer, there was mercifully more choice. We were allowed Viyella gingham or cotton dresses in a variety of peppermint stripes, either narrow or broad, yellow, blue, green or red on a white ground. Even the style in which these were sewn was left to our own devising. Panama hats replaced the felt or velour but were in no way more flattering. Now we all undoubtedly looked far more individual and distinctive, and I was impressed by the ingenious creativity with which the more fashion-conscious girls, particularly those whose figures were already budding into womanhood, made their uniforms appear positively chic.

A new world of knowledge opened up before me: French, English literature, chemistry, biology – and mathematics with the wondrous Mrs Gee. Mrs Gee was an exception among our teachers, since all the others were "spinsters" or, to use an even more negative term, "old maids". She must have been a widow, since divorce was still considered reprehensible. She was tall, had a sebaceous shock of thick white hair that stood stiffly away from her head and wore dramatic, brightly coloured woollen shawls and little knitted capes. She was also the school's Spanish teacher. Profoundly concerned with the Civil War, her prime activity in this sphere was helping to bring Basque orphans to England and placing them in foster homes. Whenever we wanted to avoid a maths lesson, as we too frequently did, we had only to ask her a question about the war as soon as she entered the classroom and off she would go – reporting, analysing, decrying the evils of dictatorship, preaching the imperatives of democracy. From her I first imbibed the importance of political awareness and the passion of active involvement in asserting and preserving the values in which one believes and ensuring their triumph over opposing forces. Later, when I became a school principal, I would invoke Mrs Gee as the outstanding example of my contention that every teacher, no matter what subject she teaches, is also essentially an educator, one who can (and should) have a lasting moral impact on her pupils.

With several hours of homework to prepare every afternoon, leisurely reading time was severely curtailed; I could no longer exchange books at a public library. However, the classroom had its own amply stocked bookcase and from it I became acquainted not only with Arthur Ransome but also with the Bulldog Drummond thrillers. At the same time, my brother was developing his own library, from which I borrowed Hemingway's *A Farewell to Arms* and, a little later, *Gone with the Wind*. It was from these books that I derived my earliest, extremely limited and distorted sex education. Neither my mother nor any other adult had ever spoken to me about female physiology or menstruation. Conjugal relations and childbirth, presumed to lie in a distant future, were considered appropriate topics only at a later age, as preparation for marriage. Extra-marital relations were never spoken of, even during the months when the Prince of Wales's affair with the twice-divorced Mrs Simpson finally became headline news. It was a time during which the American Hays censorship still forbade explicit sex on the screen, so that only the upper, fully clothed halves of the protagonist lovers' bodies were visible. My norms regarding romantic relations were informed by Fred and Ginger who, as I realised only many years later, never exchanged so much as a kiss, though their dancing clearly exuded eroticism.

Hemingway and Margaret Mitchell now acquainted me with graphic scenes of childbirth: labour is a torture and the end result is death, whether of the infant, the mother or both. Hemingway's hero, confronted with his stillborn child, compares it to a skinned rabbit. Horrified, unable to bring myself to consult my mother regarding my discoveries, I spoke in hushed tones with some of my friends, whom I soon discovered to be as ignorant as myself. We still couldn't fathom what exactly occurred between a man and a woman to bring about these disastrous results. We assumed that, since the belly expands during pregnancy, it was from there that the infant emerged. In our current era of sex-infused media, open display of colourful condoms in pharmacies and vending-machines dispensing them in public places, nudity and copiously presented on stage and screen, it is hard to convey the extent of our ignorance. When I awoke one morning soon after my 13th birthday to find my pyjama trousers stained with blood, it took me some time to realise that this was the "period" of which my more mature friends had spoken and at which my mother had vaguely hinted in one of our confidential talks some months earlier. For over a year, the onset of my periods was accompanied by excruciating cramps, thus confirming my perception of womanhood as profoundly painful.

Menstruation, like other uniquely female phenomena, including breasts, was not spoken of in public and even between women was referred to as though it were a disgusting but unavoidable disease. Since tampons had not yet been invented, we used sanitary towels made of cotton wool held together by thin red netting, which had to be secured by a belt worn around the waist or hips. Disposable napkins became available only after the war and meanwhile, like so many other essential items, what existed, though not rationed, was hard to find. I vividly recall going from shop to shop in search of them on my way home from school while I was evacuated to Northampton, finally finding myself in a haberdashery where there was only a young male assistant. When I told him what I was looking for, he fled, red-faced, to the back of the shop to fetch his mother.

At Brondesbury and Kilburn, I developed close friendships with several classmates, most of them Jewish. Since Jews constituted one-third of the total of 600 pupils, we held our own prayers in the gym, before trooping into the main assembly hall to join the rest of the school for announcements. And so the year passed happily. I felt a surge of new knowledge and comprehension. I wrote excellent compositions. I made friends with whom I learnt to play the new game of Monopoly. I went to birthday parties. I discovered I could paint competent watercolours, one of which was inspired by our teacher's reading aloud Tennyson's "The Lady of Shalott". There were, however, some clouds even on this blissful horizon. Already during my first term at Brondesbury and Kilburn, parents had been invited to an assembly at which they were informed of the contingency plans for the school's evacuation should a war break out. The Munich Agreement allayed our fears, and in the summer of 1939 my mother and I went, for the second year in succession, for a holiday at the seaside resort of Boscombe – the poor man's Bournemouth. Small, family-run boarding-houses replaced the grand hotels of the neighbouring, more elegant town, which one could easily reach by walking through shaded combes where pine trees scented the sea air.

I shared a single room and bed with my mother at a shabby Jewish establishment run by Mr and Mrs Pantel. Every morning we would make our way down to the beach, where I swam, read or lazed in the sand with a girl of my own age, who grandly informed me that next year her family would be holidaying in

Perl and Benzion Margulies, early August 1920.

The wedding, August 20, 1920. My mother in the centre with my father at one side and his parents on the other. Surrounding them are my father's siblings, the spouses of those already married and the children of some.

"My" Oma, Margola.   Rebekka, my mother's older sister.

Reunion in Poltava, Ukraine, May 1962. My mother on the left with her cousin Sonia and her sister Rebekka, whom she had not seen since 1920.

My uncle Avraham: an ardent communist
executed by Stalin in 1937.

Avraham and his wife Anna, vacationing at
the Black Sea in happier days.

Benzion, son of Rebekka.

The Rebbe of Huyzhatyn.

Oma Feige and Opa Mordechai still in Skalat, with Tante Etti (standing left) and her husband Georg; my uncles Josef and Welwel, my Aunt Lotte, the youngest, in front of her mother and, seated below, Uncle Max, Aunt Pepi and Uncle Alex.

Opa Mordechai with (l – r) Georg, Etti holding Alex her second son and next to him her oldest, Salli. Standing are Georg's brother Chaim, Uncle Josef and (seated) my father. Mannheim 1912.

My father as medical orderly in the Austro-Hungarian Army during World War 1.

Oma Feige in Israel, with Tante Malcze (right), and the latter's daughter-in-law Eva and her daughter Raya.

With Edit, 1927.

Willy and Edit with our nursemaid
Maria, 1924.

With my mother, circa 1930.

Edit starts school.

With Willy 1931.

Christmas 1936 at Kingsgate Road School. I am third from left seated on the floor. At extreme left is my friend Ethel Grasse.

BKHS – Summer and Winter uniforms.

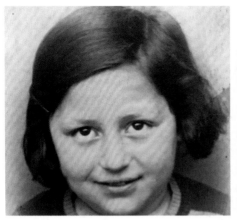

In 1937.

With my mother in the field of the Waddesdon house, 1942.

With Willy in Waddesdon, 1941.

20, High Street, Waddesdon.

My father in 1946.

France. Although our bed was narrow, I delighted in sharing it with my mother: in some way this compensated me for the loss of my grandmother. She was as fastidious in her personal hygiene as in her household cleanliness, and I lovingly watched her every evening and morning as she carefully soaped her face, her neck and her armpits before lifting each breast in succession to wash the skin underneath. She smelled sweet. Sometimes now, when I breathe in the smell of my own skin after I have bathed, I catch the same scent of warmth and softness and am happy at the thought of resembling her in this, as I do in my facial features.

Occasionally it rained even on the south coast, renowned for a warm, sunny climate – an exceptional and highly valued uncharacteristic phenomenon in England. Then I would resort to the bookshelf in the hotel lounge, where I made my first acquaintance with the green-backed Penguin editions of Agatha Christie. I was enthralled by Hercule Poirot and the plot of *The Mysterious Affair at Styles*. With frequent reference to the map of the country house helpfully provided at the beginning of the book, I tried to anticipate the story's outcome, to keep a step ahead of the perceptive Belgian detective and his denser British foil of a policeman. I loved it all. "Who Cares Who Killed Roger Ackroyd?" Edmund Wilson dismissively entitled his essay on Christie and her ilk. I did and eagerly went through all the works that previous guests of the Pantels had discarded. Detective stories have remained my favourite form of light fiction when I'm too tired to think about what I'm reading. I was delighted eventually to discover that this was a genre in which a number of women excelled. I soon came to appreciate Dorothy Sayers and Ngaio Marsh, both of whom wrote more satisfyingly sophisticated books than those of Christie.

My Boscombe playmate didn't holiday in France the year after our second meeting. In September 1939 our lives were changed forever by the outbreak of war. At the beginning of term, the contingency plans for school evacuation were rehearsed once again, though everyone hoped and prayed that there would be a repetition of the previous year's last-minute reprieve. On the morning of Sunday 3 September, my parents, my brother and I were in our dining-room, anxiously taping window-panes to prevent their being shattered by bombs. The radio was already on in the next room and soon we heard Neville Chamberlain sombrely declare that Britain was at war. Seconds later, almost simultaneously with the end of the announcement, the air-raid sirens wailed. Panic-stricken, we raced to fetch the gas-masks that had been issued to us and set off, running to the park in which our district's air-raid shelter was located.

Halfway down the street, my mother remembered she had not taken her passport. Why she should have felt it necessary to have this with her I shall never know, though I now surmise that her panic derived from the numerous crossings of borders from one country to another that she had experienced in an earlier war. Fortunately, the all-clear sounded before she had even reached home but this first incident made us aware that the public shelter was too distant from our house to constitute refuge. Henceforth, whenever the sirens sounded, we rapidly repaired to the narrow coat cupboard under the stairs, into which we all squeezed, donning our gas-masks and fighting not to let the nausea aroused by their foul smell of rubber overwhelm us. I shook uncontrollably with fear every time we took shelter in this way. I think it might have been my all too perceptible terror combining with the fact that all London schools had been closed that convinced my parents that I had, after all, better join Brondesbury and Kilburn in Northampton – place of its wartime relocation – than stay and risk being killed or maimed together with them.

So my father and I took the train to this industrial city in the East Midlands, famous for shoe- manufacturing. Through some preliminary enquiries, he had located the town's sole Jewish family, whom he hoped to persuade to offer me accommodation. The proposed refuge was the home of an elderly tailor and his wife, a childless couple who led us to the one place where they could accommodate me – a closet, the door of which, like the one offered to Mr Lockwood on his first visit to Wuthering Heights, opened on to a narrow bed. The opposite side – fortunately or unfortunately – lacked a window through which Cathy's ghost might have attempted to penetrate. I was too polite to give verbal expression to my revulsion at the thought of occupying this space but the appalled look on my face couldn't have escaped the owners any more than it did my father, who at first explained away our rejection of their offer by saying he still wanted to reflect on whether at all to send me away from home. I returned to London with very mixed feelings, on the one hand wanting to stay with my parents, on the other deeply fearing death by aerial bombardment such as had obliterated Warsaw. Before long, my father informed me that my school had helped him find a more congenial alternative to the tailor and his wife. Again we went off to Northampton, taking with us a case of clothing that unmistakably indicated that this time I wouldn't be so readily returned home.

The house to which we went from the station was a well-kept, semi-detached three-bedroom abode not unlike our Neasden home, though considerably smaller. Located in a quiet street, it had a carefully tended garden in which, at that season, yellow and brown chrysanthemums were in full bloom. The two women who greeted us appeared to me to be elderly but were probably, at least in the case of the younger one, only in their 40s or early 50s. The younger, dark-haired one, who had sallow skin, was introduced as Miss Watts. The older, white-haired and rosy-cheeked, with a more motherly air, was Miss Mundin. Immediately, I was reassured: these were clearly more appropriate hosts than the tailor and his wife would have been, and the bedroom to which I was shown, though smaller than my own at home, had not only a bed but a chest of drawers with a large mirror on it, as well as a comfortable chair. Having expressed delighted approval of these quarters, we were led down to a cosy living-room to become better acquainted.

As we sat drinking tea, a raucous voice abruptly interrupted our conversation. "Auntie Clara's Ray of Sunshine, Auntie Lily's Sunny Jim." Startled, I sought the source of these appellations. Other than us, there was nobody in the room. An amused explanation quickly followed. Directing our gaze to a corner of the room, our hosts pointed to a large gilded cage, in which perched a blue-and-grey-feathered budgerigar. Head cocked to one side, he was scrutinising us as closely as we were examining him. Miss Mundin was as astonished as we were.

"Joey doesn't normally talk when there are strangers in the room," she commented. His making such an exception was interpreted as a favourable omen of acceptance, an indication of approval, and I was wholeheartedly welcomed into the household. Despite the war, these ladies led a placid life. Joey was like a child on whom they lavished love and tender care. They took pride in his accomplishments and bought him gifts – small toys for his cage and, once, a tiny celluloid bird, which he battered mercilessly around the cage, as though fearing it might be a rival in their affection. I soon learnt that he had a wider vocabulary than that which he had so surprisingly uttered when he first set eyes on me. He also had a sense of humour, the prime object of his teasing being Scamp, a large tabby tomcat. Every morning, as the cloth covering his cage was removed, Joey would call out, "Good morning, Scamp! Pretty Pussy, Pretty Pussy! Miaou! Miaou!" In the course of my stay, he added a mild curse: "Scuttle old Hitler!" Released from his cage every evening, he fluttered around the room, flying precariously close to Scamp, who clearly longed to pounce on him, before settling on the head of one of his owners or balancing on the end of the long needles with which they knitted blankets for the troops.

Miss Mundin and Miss Watts were devout Methodists, and they understood and appreciated my father's request that I not be compelled to infringe Jewish dietary laws more than was strictly necessary in those times, when stringent rationing precluded readily and regularly finding adequate sources of protein.

Whenever they themselves partook of pork, bacon or ham, there would be an alternative for me, even though this was sometimes beef, which was perceived as less of an anathema than any pig-derived product. Furthermore, Miss Mundin and Miss Watts were concerned for my spiritual well-being and careful of my religious observance. They encouraged me to attend regularly the Shabbat morning services that, now that there was a sizeable Jewish community composed of evacuees from London, were held each week in a church hall not far from where we lived. To assure doubly, they also invited me to join them in attendance at chapel twice every Sunday. Curious to discover a new form of worship and reluctant to stay at home alone, even in the company of Joey and Scamp, I went along a first time and found myself greatly enjoying the hymn-singing, though the long sermon and the minister's rambling, improvised prayers were not wholly to my taste. Nor did they always meet with the critical approval of Miss Mundin and Miss Watts, who would earnestly discuss their contents on the way home and over lunch.

My school was permitted the use of the buildings that housed the Northampton High School for Girls but only in the afternoon hours. In the mornings we did our homework or amused ourselves in one of the local church halls, often without any staff supervision. We organised play readings, each of us laboriously copying our part from the sole available printed volume of an entire play. Once I starred as Eliza in Shaw's *Pygmalion*, hugely enjoying the opportunity not only to switch from broad Cockney to something "posh" but also to utter the forbidden swearword: "bloody". Miss Evans, one of the English teachers, directed a full-scale adaptation of *Pride and Prejudice*, creating two parallel casts in order to maximise the number of pupils who could be fruitfully occupied in this way. In one of the casts I played Lady Lucas, a small part, but one which allowed me fair scope for acting the role of a rural snob. The performance was written up in the local press, providing the thrill of seeing my name in print for the first time.

Theatre became an important part of my cultural life. Miss Mundin and Miss Watts were subscribers to the excellent Northampton Repertory Company, which, in the praiseworthy manner of provincial theatres, presented a different play each week. I thus became acquainted with many English classics, as well as with Chekhov, Molière and Ibsen. A performance of *The Mikado* introduced me to Gilbert and Sullivan, whose quintessentially English texts were unknown, and might well have been unintelligible, to my European family. As a treat, the whole school was taken by bus to Stratford-upon-Avon, where we were allowed to wander about unsupervised to sightsee before attending a matinée of *Hamlet*.

Since I had never read the play and nobody took the trouble of preparing us, I was ignorant of its plot. As a result, the appearance of the Ghost in the opening scene was as much of a shock to me as to the characters on stage and as it must have been to Shakespeare's original audience. It was the first, though not the last, occasion in my life when my entire scalp tingled. It was a sensation I experienced again the first time I saw Ibsen's *Ghosts*, when Oswald begs his mother, then memorably played by Beatrix Lehman, to "Give [him] the sun".

Because we studied only in the afternoon and our school day customarily ended after dark, we were formed into "convoys" according to the area in which we were billeted to walk home together through the unlit streets. The Vale was among the streets furthest from the school. As a result, only three of us were left to complete the journey alone. One of my companions was Muriel Barnett, who had become a close friend of mine during the previous school year and who, with her younger sister, Ruth, lived with the family directly across the road from Miss Mundin and Miss Watts. Whether because her hosts received only the mandatory official allowance of seven shillings and sixpence per child, whereas my father, sensibly having made his own private arrangement, was paying twice that sum, or because they were simply less kind people than I had had the good fortune to find, Muriel and Ruth were often miserable, never more so than when they were served distinctly non-kosher meat, with a take-it-or-leave-it gesture that gave them a choice only between eating it or remaining hungry. On one occasion, having learnt only after she had partaken of it, that what she had just consumed was rabbit, Muriel, to her own dismay, threw up her entire lunch.

As the school year passed, we listened anxiously to every news bulletin, growing more and more concerned and depressed as country after country fell to the Germans: Holland, Belgium, France, Norway, Denmark… My parents and Willy had left London to join my uncle and aunt in Waddesdon. Perhaps because she once again felt herself a not entirely welcome guest in someone else's household, my mother was profoundly unhappy and soon became ill, suffering from severe abdominal pains and vomiting. Without my being informed, she was hospitalised in London and diagnosed as suffering from gallstones. The doctors decided not to operate but rather to put her on a severe diet. As a result, when I went to London for the Easter vacation, I was greeted by a small, slim figure, very different from the overweight, cushiony one I had known all my life, but astonishingly attractive, her always brilliant, expressive, black eyes even more beautiful now in her much thinner face: "*Meine kleine Mamma*", I called her.

At the end of the school year, emboldened by the apparent calm and reluctant to have me continue to live away from them in a non-Jewish home, however hospitable, my parents decided to bring me back to London. My father installed an Anderson shelter in our back garden – a domed structure of corrugated iron, half-buried in the ground and covered with a mound of earth – and I was duly transferred to Willesden County School, which temporarily served a vast catchment area that comprised the school district around it.

I knew none of the teachers and only those few Brondesbury and Kilburn girls who had, like me, returned from Northampton. Nor in the few weeks I spent at the school did I come to know anyone better. The Blitz began almost simultaneously with the school year. Although we dutifully continued going to school, taking refuge in strange doorways every time an alarm sounded, most of our time once arrived there was spent in the air-raid shelters, where all I accomplished was a great deal of knitting. When the night raids first began, we would get out of bed at every alarm and hasten to our shelter, where we were joined by our neighbours at Number 6. The shelter was intended to accommodate 16 people but that was on the assumption that everybody would be seated and only for a brief period. Once it became clear that we were to be subjected to frequent alerts and that we would be unable to function normally for lack of sleep, our neighbours purchased a shelter of their own, while ours was equipped to serve as permanent night-quarters. My parents each occupied one of the benches that ran down either side while I was short enough to fit on the bench that ran across the far end. Willy was to sleep on the floor, where a mattress had been laid down for his comfort, but he preferred to remain in the house, bedding down under the kitchen table.

While the East End of London, the dock areas and the City suffered severe attacks, the north-west districts where we lived remained relatively undamaged. However, one night the sounds of explosion came perilously near and suddenly the ground heaved below us as if hit by an earthquake. At once came an urgent banging on the shelter door. It was my brother, badly shaken, wanting to be admitted. A bomb had fallen close by, on the other side of the main road that ran through our neighbourhood. A few days later, before we settled down outside, my brother, who had gone upstairs to the toilet, called us to join him in my bedroom at the front of the house. In the distance we could see the night sky glowing bright red. The City was burning.

Fearful for our lives, my parents once again moved to Waddesdon. This time they purchased, for £1,000, a house of their own in the centre of the village and I went with them. With a population of a mere 1,000, Waddesdon is one of a constellation of villages that surround Aylesbury. Not only was there a weekly cattle and market-gardening market in the town square on Saturdays but the local branch of Boots had a lending library from which one could order even the latest publications. There were two cinemas, both of which changed their programmes on Thursdays, thus offering a weekly total of eight films. There was also – most importantly, as far as I was concerned – a grammar-school where I would be able to continue my war-interrupted education.

Aylesbury was a short bus-ride from Waddesdon. Rural buses ran frequently, as they no longer do. However, my father's attempt to register me at the school at first met with a negative response. Like the Northampton School for Girls, Aylesbury Grammar School had been compelled to host an entire London establishment, the Ealing Boys' School, and although not all the Ealing pupils had chosen to be evacuated the premises were grossly overcrowded. Since at the time there was a general assumption that the war would soon be over and the Londoners able to return whence they'd come, there was no great readiness to come to their aid. Londoners were considered outsiders; "foreigners" was the local term applied to them.

The tightly knit rural communities, unlike the residents of large towns such as Northampton, disliked and resented the intrusion on their placid lives. The poorer families perceived us as in some way depriving them of space and income, while the snobbish "county" families, whose children went to private schools with smart uniforms, wanted nothing to do with the middle-class city parvenus. Somehow, we fell into a strange hybrid, all grouped together as "evacuees", although families like my own had little in common with the bombed-out East Enders who were accommodated in the totally inadequate space of Waddesdon's village-hall, where camp-beds were set up for them and the few toilets soon became smelly and squalid, thus contributing to a further deterioration in the evacuees' reputation.

After a few weeks spent restlessly in our little house on the High Street, I decided to write to the headmaster, describing my frustration at not being allowed to continue my studies and begging him to admit me to the school as soon as possible. Whether my letter moved him or whether he or the local education authorities now realised that, given the continued bombardment of London, our stay in Buckinghamshire was likely to be longer than initially anticipated I don't know. Almost at once I was invited for an interview and admitted into the school.

For the first time since leaving Wykeham in the summer of 1938, I found myself at an entirely co-educational establishment. The difference was that I was now an adolescent, very conscious of what I considered my plain face and heavy body, scared of how boys would react to me, profoundly aware that academic distinction could never compete with the pert sexual attractiveness of some of my classmates. I recall the amused look the school secretary, herself an "old girl" of Aylesbury Grammar School, gave me, when I anxiously inquired, while I was waiting to be escorted to my classroom, whether I would have to be studying together with boys. She was able to allay my fears by assuring me that my particular class was comprised entirely of girls, since, in the interest of economy of space and staff, all the female evacuees had been herded together, irrespective of age, while the boys were, with only a very few exceptions, assigned to the Ealing school.

I thus found myself in a motley class comprised not only of 14-year-olds like me but also of others, two or even three years older, some of whom were already anxious to take the school-leaving certificate exams that would give future employers an indication of their talents and achievements. Very few intended to stay on for the final two years in the sixth form that prepared pupils for the Higher School Certificate, a qualification required for entrance to university. I eventually benefited from the school's haphazard response to this anomalous situation. At the beginning of the 1941-2 school year, we were informed that the syllabus would be the one required for the exams, that a mock would be held at Easter and that anyone passing it would be permitted to take the exam at the end of the year, whether or not she had had the customary amount of prior high-school education. I passed the "mock-matric" with flying colours in everything except maths, in which I received a dismal mark of 6% in algebra, 12 in geometry and less than the required 40 in arithmetic. Never instructed in the basics of either algebra or geometry, I had been totally perplexed during the lessons, at a loss to understand anything being said or written on the board by the (far from competent) teacher. I was reluctant to reveal my ignorance, while he was so bent on getting through the material that he never bothered to invest the effort required in doing more than mark my exercise books with red crosses and contemptuous exclamation marks that indicated the grossness of my errors.

Warned that I would not be allowed to sit for the exams at the end of the year if I did not improve in maths, I enlisted the help of my brilliant brother, who patiently explained what Mr Rowse was too lazy or impatient to explain. To my surprise, I found myself loving a subject I'd always loathed. I thoroughly enjoyed the intellectual exercise of solving simultaneous equations, applying the theorems I had memorised and seeing the problems unravel into logical solutions "QED".

At Easter, my marks were sufficiently good to justify my being allowed to take the exam at the end of the year. Astonishingly, I came second in the school, with a distinction in algebra, a credit in arithmetic and a respectable pass in geometry. I attained my Lower School Certificate and progressed to the elect sixth form, with only two years to go before I could continue to university, a year earlier than I would have, had I stayed at Brondesbury and Kilburn.

Built in the late 1890s, Waddesdon Manor bears clear architectural evidence of the French origin of the Rothschild who erected it. It resembles a château rather than an English country house. Now it was the home of James and Dorothy de Rothschild. Around its grounds lay the village. The house was partly occupied by convalescing soldiers, while many rooms were temporarily shuttered. The parterres of flowers in the front courtyard were off limits to outsiders, yet the large park was open to the public and we made good use of it. On both sides of one of the paths close to the house, a row of statues had been bound in canvas to prevent bomb damage. To me, they looked like prisoners awaiting execution. Every time I cycled, with accelerated speed, along that path, I feared one of them would come to life and pounce on me. As the possessor of a bicycle, which my father bought me for my 14th birthday soon after we arrived in Waddesdon, I rode around the beechy Buckingham countryside, enchanted by the vast fields of corn, the haystacks, the grazing cows and the herds of sheep whose wool got caught in tufts on the barbs of wire fences.

One spring day, turning a bend, I found myself, unprepared, confronting a vast bank of daffodils. I had never before seen such an abundance of what appeared like wild flowers thronging an open space. When, later, I read Wordsworth's poetry for the first time I instantly recognised the similarity between his response and my own. Innumerable times since that spring so many years ago, "in vacant or in pensive mood", have I recollected this vision in tranquillity, "and then my heart with pleasure fills/And dances with the daffodils". When I began teaching English literature in Jerusalem and this poem was part of the syllabus, I waxed lyrical, expounding at length on what I had experienced a decade earlier, eloquently drawing a comparison between the impact the encounter had made on me and that described by Wordsworth. The class sat patiently listening to my euphoric account. When I had finished, one of my students, evidently giving expression to the response of the entire class, broke the spell by timidly asking, "Please, Miss Margaliot, what is 'daffodil?'" Only then was I made aware of the absence of this quintessentially English flower from the abundant flora of the Holy Land.

My love of English literature and, in particular, of the Romantics, developed along with my growing acquaintance with, and concomitant love for, the English landscape. We had an English teacher, Mr Deeming, with whom we at first studied the essays of Steele and Addison, which I found utterly boring save when they were dealing with Sir Roger de Coverly, but whose elegant and witty style I attempted to emulate in my own compositions. We also read Shakespeare's *Julius Caesar*, the set text for the Lower School Certificate. While we studied plot and characterisation, no mention was made of the moral dimensions of the play, the dilemmas with which the protagonists were confronted, the critical decisions they were called upon to take; the conflict between morality and political expediency. Despite its contemporary relevance, we were never called upon to consider how we ourselves might have reacted to the threat of dictatorship. How would and should one confront totalitarianism? Nothing was further from our teacher's mind than to relate the play to the contemporary context of the war.

In addition to Boots' lending library, Aylesbury had another source from which I could acquire reading material. Weatherby's, located in a back street, was owned by a true book lover, a man who delighted in bibliophile customers appreciative of his excellent stock and readiness to order anything not in stock. At the end of my first term at Aylesbury Grammar, I was pleasantly surprised to receive the sum of 15 shillings as a refund for my bus fares. Delighted, I stopped at Weatherby's *en route* home and for the first time purchased a book with my "own" money – the *Complete Works of Lewis Carroll* in the fine Nonsuch edition. On the bus ride home I discovered how much he had written apart from the two "Alice" books I already knew so well. So began a lifetime of obsessive book purchases, with which I built up a very impressive and eclectic library. In the 1980s, when we renovated our Jerusalem home, shelf-space was so drastically reduced that I was compelled to give away almost my entire collection of the English classics. It was like losing a limb.

In the sixth form, where English, together with History and French, became my major subjects, the abhorred maths and sciences gratefully left behind forever, I first became acquainted with Wordsworth and Coleridge, Keats and Shelley, Hazlitt and Lamb. We read them aloud, and at home memorised entire poems and portions of essays, many of which I remember to this day. After I had learnt Gray's "Elegy" I began visiting graveyards, reading the inscriptions on tombstones, fascinated to find some that recorded lives spent locally over 100 years earlier, moved to see how many children had not survived into adolescence.

Cycling in the villages around Waddesdon I saw the imagery of Keats's "Ode to Autumn" visibly embodied in the mellow fruitfulness of cottage gardens. In September, I picked pounds of blackberries from the fertile hedges around the village. Even at home, we were harvesting the apples from the tree behind our house. The plum tree outside the kitchen window supplied us with an abundance of fruit, which my mother learnt to bottle once she had made as much jam as our meagre sugar rations allowed. We had become landowners: gentlemen-farmers. My father, ever ready to experiment with new interests and occupations, and impelled by a desire to supplement what could be purchased either at the village grocery or, on market days, in Aylesbury, decided to go further than growing a variety of vegetables.

We had over an acre of land behind the house, a large part of which remained vacant even after we had planted potatoes, cabbages, marrows, beans and peas, celery and cucumbers, and even a strawberry patch. Thirty chickens provided a steady supply of unrationed eggs, as well as the joy of seeing little fluffy yellow balls break out of the shells and watching them grow. My father's enthusiastic embrace of farming unfortunately did not compensate for a lack of expertise. Encouraged by our success with chickens, he decided to purchase a pair of turkeys. They proved to be far more temperamental than the hens. No sooner had the hen turkey laid her first eggs than she flew up on to the roof of the coop my father had bought to house her and her mate. Higher than the chicken coop, its roof could not easily be reached. Unable to lure the bird down with either food or water, my father set up a ladder, hoping to catch her by the legs and bring her down by force. He reached the roof just as the bird hopped to the far end of the coop. Up went my father on the other side and away went the bird. Thus the battle of wills continued, my father reluctant to admit defeat, the bird determined to remain aloof, insouciant regarding the fate of her young. The eggs never hatched and the hen died of starvation but my father remained obstinate. New turkeys were brought in.

My father decided to branch out further. He bought a calf, which proved so fierce that my mother and I refused to enter the field in order to feed the chickens, and my father was forced to sell it. He went on to sheep, unaware that they have to be moved frequently from one field to another if they are not to develop foot disease. Smirking, our expert country neighbours observed these ventures, none of them ever deigning to advise my father before he made a purchase but never failing, after the event, to explain why he had been mistaken. This happened again when my father decided to dig a pool in order to raise ducks. No neighbour warned him that the ground was unsuitable and that, within a matter of days, the water would be absorbed into the porous local soil. Although the initiator of these investments in livestock, my father was not their caretaker. That task was left to my mother.

One stormy day I returned home from school to find her running out of the front gate to the stationer's shop a few houses down our street. I asked where she was going.

"I'm going for the ducks," she explained. These creatures had scrambled out of the pond and through the hedge into the stationer's back garden, where they were devouring his greens. Joining my mother, I helped her chase the birds, which obstinately refused to return via the hedge through which they had come. We had no alternative but to pursue them around the garden, pick them up, grasp them as firmly as possible under our arms and return them, one by one, to our own premises. No sooner had we successfully brought in one pair and set out for another than we found the first pair busily scrabbling through the hedge to reach the inviting greens. This pursuit continued unabated until my mother and I, drenched to the skin, decided to abandon the chase and await my father's return from town. The ducks bedded down for the night and the next morning, assisted by our handyman-gardener, my father succeeded in driving them back home, erected a wire fence between us and the sadly depleted greens, telephoned the slaughterer and, albeit reluctantly, abandoned duck-rearing. His decision came none too soon, for a few days later there was no water in the pond and we were left with only an ugly, swampy patch of ground.

The war years were among the happiest I spent in England. Not until later did I learn of the extinction of the Jews of Europe. I was unaware that among those murdered soon after the German occupation of Poland were my Uncle Mendel, his wife and my three comely black-eyed cousins. Since I belatedly learnt of this tragedy, I have felt considerable guilt at my own carefree existence at that same time. Although my father was better informed, he kept the knowledge from us. After the war, he adamantly refused to apply to the German government for "reparations". Nothing, he argued, could ever compensate for the horrors perpetrated by the Nazis. Willy, however, was bent on extorting even an inadequate, disproportionate repayment. After my father's death, he submitted a claim on my behalf. It was rejected. The grounds cited by the Germans were that my leaving Germany had resulted in my completing my studies two years earlier than I would have done had I not left my birthplace.

We were far away from the Blitz, though on one occasion a German bomber returning to base released a few incendiary bombs over the village, one of which landed in our front garden. We had spent the evening at Warmstone, my uncle's home about half a mile away, and had been followed, annoyingly, by Rip, his terrier, whom we tried in vain to shoo back to his own home. Soon after we had gone to bed, leaving Rip outside in the hope that he would go away, he began a frantic barking. My father went downstairs in order to quieten him. Opening the door, he found our front hedge in flames, Rip still barking and neighbours appearing at their windows to learn the cause of the commotion. The fire was soon extinguished and Rip gratefully admitted to the kitchen to spend the night in comfort, as a reward for so cleverly alerting us to peril.

Until 1944, when for several days convoys of army lorries passed by in an unceasing flow, announcing without a word the impending invasion of Europe, the village remained totally immune to what was happening elsewhere. Most of the evacuees, finding no suitable accommodation or employment in the village and its vicinity, returned to London or went elsewhere within months of arrival. Some, like my family, set up businesses in Aylesbury, or, like my father, from time to time commuted to London to keep up whatever business they had run there. I made new friends at school, growing close to my fellow pupils in the comparatively small sixth form. Many of our classmates had left at the age of 16, once they had, or had not, obtained the Lower School Certificate. Girls and boys, locals and Londoners, were now gathered in one class, though for most of the hours we spent at school we were divided according to our electives, the science pupils sharing virtually no lessons with those of us who had chosen the humanities.

Most of the time seems to have been summer, and many of those summer days appear to have been spent playing tennis (at which I became sufficiently proficient to play for the school in competition against visiting schools) and watching cricket, which I learnt to appreciate under the tutelage of our art teacher, Mr Harrison, who, an addict of the game, would take us out to sketch from the pavilion, interspersing his instruction with comments on the progress on the pitch. I read a great deal, particularly in the winter months, when the entire family sat in our living-room, snug and warm with an anthracite stove, listening to the radio, which continued to provide BBC staples such as the wonderfully comic *ITMA* (*It's That Man Again*).

Among the closest of my friends were two Londoners. One, Doris Lewis, was Jewish. She lived in Aylesbury, with her widowed mother and older sister, Lily. Doris, too, studied English and history. A perceptive and diligent pupil, her only hope of going to university lay in her winning a state scholarship that would cover the fees her mother could never afford to pay. This she duly did. Indeed, we

Londoners proved to be the brightest stars in the school's firmament. A number of us were determined to apply to the two most prestigious universities, Oxford and Cambridge, but Aylesbury Grammar School (like many grammar-schools, founded in the mid-17th century) had the odd and inexplicable practice of teaching Latin, once the staple of grammar-school curriculum, only in the first year of studies. Since Latin was a compulsory prerequisite for entry to the ancient universities, the school thus precluded acceptance to them. However, we were able to enlist the sympathetic help of two members of the staff who were themselves graduates of Cambridge: Miss Caldin and Mr Price.

Winifred Caldin was a Girton graduate. Of indeterminable age and far from attractive, she customarily held a protective hand in front of her mouth, as if apologising for her protruding teeth. She diligently kept abreast of contemporary research, interweaving the pages of the exercise book in which she kept her notes with material based on J.M. Thompson's innovative research on the French Revolution. Eager to help us attain our goal, she volunteered frequent additional classes, and greatly enlarged my knowledge and understanding of history. Mr Price, meanwhile, was an elderly roué, whom the authorities, presumably ignorant of his priapic propensities, had inappropriately entrusted with imparting Religious Knowledge.

Latin was not part of our curriculum and hence not included in our timetable. Although also a graduate of Cambridge, our headmaster declined to add to the expenses of staff salaries by paying for the teaching of a subject considered redundant. We therefore decided to bribe Mr Price – an inveterate smoker. Cigarettes were scarce but my father was able once every two weeks or so to bring a tin of 50 Players back from London. These we would surreptitiously purvey to Mr Price, who would arrange to meet us in a small room that was vacant after school hours. We would leave the cigarettes on a shelf from which he nonchalantly picked them up to put them, without a word, in the leather briefcase that appeared to contain nothing else. The only girls in our small class, Doris and I soon learnt never to sit too close to Mr Price or else to ensure that at least one of our male classmates accompanied us to the lessons. Mr Price, wont to tell risqué jokes, had a habit of placing a hand on your knee and then gradually sliding it up under your skirt. Too embarrassed and also too scared of offending him by commenting, we'd respond by edging our chairs away a few inches or making some casual movement that enabled us to escape the roving hand.

Once, travelling home on the crowded bus, I found myself wedged on the back bench between an elderly woman and a man who smelled strongly of alcohol.

Though he stared straight ahead of him I suddenly felt his hand on my knee. Just like Mr Price's, it gradually crept up under my skirt. I edged away but the hand pursued me, increasing its pressure on my thigh, groping inwards, attempting to force my legs apart as I desperately tried to clench them together. Panic-stricken, I turned to my female neighbour.

"What shall I do?" I whispered. "He's put his hand under my skirt." But far from coming to my aid, she grinned, shrugged her shoulders and muttered back:

"Oh, men, they're all the same." I decided there was nothing to do save take the same action as we adopted with Mr Price. I shook off the hand and planted my briefcase firmly between myself and the man at my side. Despite my wide range of reading matter, I was extremely unsophisticated and still totally ignorant of sexual matters. Romance was what I cared for and I never paused to reflect on what followed the clinching close-up kiss with which most films I saw inevitably ended.

At school, I formed a number of friendships with boys but, unlike others of my female classmates, I developed no reciprocal romantic attachments. My second "best" girlfriend was another Londoner, Dorothy Frost, who came from a middle-class family with none of the cultural richness from which I benefited. On Monday mornings, having (like the protagonists of John Osborne's *Look Back in Anger*) closely perused the more expensive ("six-penny") London papers, such as the *Observer* and the *Sunday Times*, as well as (in my own case) the weekly *New Statesman* and *Nation*, some of us engaged in discussion of the latest book reviews or the most recent films, or talked with a certain degree of informed expertise on the progress of the war and other political matters. Poor Dorothy, whose parents contented themselves with a cheaper tabloid, was inevitably left out of the conversation.

Feeling sorry for her, I offered to initiate her into the charmed circle of the cultured few by bringing her the appropriate sections of the Sunday papers and going over them with her during the lunch hour, when those of us who lived out of town partook of sandwiches in the school hall. While I had the advantage of a cultured home, Dorothy proved far more adept at what are now called "life skills". Greatly taken with a red-faced, strongly-built ox of a young man called Carter, who excelled at sports rather than academia, she took to arranging to meet him at the school gate as if by chance as he was leaving for the square at the town centre which served as a terminal for all the buses that radiated out to the surrounding villages. Although this frequently entailed delaying her own departure by an hour or more, while he completed his rugby or cricket practice, it ensured that they'd travel home together to the village where they lived, on the other side of Aylesbury to Waddesdon. Her admiration aroused the desired response in him. A year after we left school, she wrote to tell me of their engagement. The letter of congratulations I wrote back was my final communication with her.

With another classmate I maintained contact for much longer, since he, too, was accepted to Cambridge. M.P. (Martin Peter) Frankel had the distinction of being the son of a Member of Parliament and himself hoped to add the same initials to his surname as already preceded it. He had a freckled face, an undisguisably "Jewish" hooked nose, and, unlike the other boys, who invariably wore sports jackets and slacks, occasionally appeared at school in an elegant dark blue or grey suit. His father, Dan Frankel, a tailor by profession and a member of the Labour Party, represented the overwhelmingly Jewish working-class constituency of Stepney, where his main rival was another Jew, Harry Politt, a member of the small, radical Communist Party. Martin was staunchly left-wing, as were most of the Jews in Britain at the time, and he had no intention of concealing his political opinions. These were not, however, the predominant views of the conservative provincial society in which we now lived. Once, following the German invasion of the Soviet Union that transformed the Russians into Britain's allies, we pupils were enthusiastically singing the Internationale at a school assembly, as part of the repertoire of allied national anthems we had duly memorised in English translation. One of the teachers, who had sat through the Marseillaise and "Poland's might is not departed", abruptly and demonstratively left the hall, obviously finding this rallying cry of the downtrodden workers too much to swallow, allies or no allies.

Martin Frankel was a year older than me but in the sixth form, in which we spent our final two years of school, pupils of both years studied together and age became less of a barrier than before. Martin Frankel turned me into a public speaker. The school held regular debates, along time-honoured lines such as those in which undergraduates, many of them with political ambitions, engage at the university unions in Oxford and Cambridge. I had on occasion spoken briefly and far from memorably from the floor but one day I found myself chosen to second Frankel in proposing a distinctly political topic related to war crimes. At home, I composed a carefully argued presentation and, on the morning of the debate, showed it to him, hoping it would meet with his approval. It did not.

"This isn't a speech, it's an essay," he snarled and took my speech away to rewrite its arguments in a rhetorical style better calculated to arouse passionate feeling rather than appeal to the rational mind. Cowed, I delivered the speech that had been written for me, investing it with all the ardour that its style required. We won the vote with an overwhelming majority and I found myself surrounded not only by admiring fellow pupils but even by staff members, who for days complimented me on my eloquence. We were studying Rostand's *Cyrano de Bergerac* at the time and I experienced some guilt at resembling the handsome Christian benefiting from his ugly friend's poetic skills to win the hand of Roxanne. But Frankel never revealed that he, not I, had written the fiery speech. I continued to gain from this initial experience, gradually developing a no-less successful debating style of my own, which, however, like his, relied on dramatic emphases, repetitions, rhetorical questions and scornful satirical dismissals of my opponents' specious arguments.

How was it that, in a region where no Jews had lived until the outbreak of the war, there should nonetheless be virulent anti-Semitism? (The Rothschilds were not identified as Jewish by their tenants, most of whom in any case never came into direct contact with their landlord.) This question began to exercise me almost immediately after our arrival in Waddesdon, for I soon encountered preconceptions and prejudices founded on deep-rooted mythological stereotypes whose primativeness stunned me. In all seriousness, one of my neighbours, a girl younger than me, who waited with me every morning for the bus that took us to Aylesbury, asked me to show her where we Jews kept our horns. From her I also learnt that the entire village was convinced that we had built a munitions factory under the field behind our house. When I denied this allegation, she smiled slyly and said:

"Well, of course, you can't talk about it, can you? I mean, it's a war secret."
At school, frequent allegations were levelled at Jews as being black-marketeers. I felt helpless. Soon the insults and allegations became too much for me to bear.

One day, in the school grounds, as I was about to enter the building after the lunch break, two boys hissed "Dirty Jew!" as I passed them. I continued on my way trying to look as though I had not heard but when I reached the classroom and found Martin Frankel there, I tearfully told him of the incident. To my surprise, he marched out of the room without a word, returning only after the next lesson had begun. A few minutes later, the school secretary arrived, summoning me to the headmaster's study. Appalled, I wondered what I had done to warrant such a summons, which usually involved punishment or rebuke. In the study, I found myself face to face with my tormentors, who glared at me angrily. Mr Furneaux turned to them and uttered just two words.

"Now, apologise!" The culprits sullenly muttered a few indistinguishable words and suddenly I felt as though I were the guilty party. I began to dismiss the apology.

"It's not that I'm offended," I lied. "It's my people you've insulted." I could find no words to convey to them how pained I was. I knew they now hated me more than ever and that this conversation would serve only to exacerbate their loathing, since my "taletelling" (they were unaware that it was Frankel who had reported the incident) had got them into trouble. And sure enough, the harassment continued. The next morning, when I came into the library, which served as the sixth-form classroom, all my books had been swept off the shelf assigned to me. Pages torn out of my neatly-kept loose-leaf files lay scattered. I didn't dare complain, fearing that further punishment would only arouse fiercer responses. I was most afraid of physical attack. I had seen Chaplin's *The Great Dictator* and feared the possibility of being beaten up, having my head bashed against the school's stone wall, being waylaid on my way to the bus terminal, perhaps even being pushed under a passing vehicle.

Above all, I was troubled by the awareness that this attack on me was based on a distorted perception of our entire race. Naïvely thinking that increased knowledge would bring about a change of heart, I asked my father to bring me a supply of pamphlets published by the Board of Deputies of British Jews, which detailed the Jewish contribution to civilisation at large and to European culture in particular. These I left in conspicuous places around the library. Yet what were monotheism, the observance of a weekly day of rest from physical labour, a universal code of ethics, Einstein and Freud to these country louts? I doubt whether they even looked inside the pamphlets, the covers of which were soon defaced, the pages torn out and the entire stock eventually consigned to the wastepaper basket.

Defeated in my attempt at enlightenment, I shrank into a shell of self-protection, trying to efface myself, never to refer to my Jewishness, my religious beliefs and customs. Far from expressing pride in my identity, I tried as best I could to obliterate the differences between me and my English classmates. When in their company, I, as it were, detached my Jewish self, which I could express and gratify in the privacy of my home. I even began attending morning prayers, from which I could have been excused. Only with Doris could I be open and frank. This schizophrenic response to torment was one way of coping with the persecution resulting from being "other", "different".

My admiration of Frankel knew no bounds. He became the centre of the romantic fantasies that still constituted a virtual reality in my life. I had never totally ceased to live with an imagined alter ego – a witty, physically more attractive person, far more successful than me in winning the attentions of the opposite sex. As Lewis Carroll had written about my fictitious namesake, "This curious child was very fond of pretending to be two people", and my fantasies were even to me so vivid that they took on the truth of an alternative reality. As in my childhood, I was so convinced of this truth that I never conceived of myself as lying. I was simply living an alternative life.

At this time I became very close to my mother, who took a great interest in my school activities and devotedly helped me by dictating to me every evening the copious handwritten notes in which Mr Deeming summarised critical works such as those in the English Men of Letters series. These I duly typed, with black and red ribbon, to be passed around to my fellow pupils. While my mother thus fulfilled some of her own academic ambitions, which had been thwarted by the First World War, she took an equal interest in my extracurricular activities, vicariously enjoying and taking pride in my alleged social success. Every evening she would sit with me in the bathroom, while I washed, bathed or shampooed my hair, at the same time recounting what had taken place at school that day.

The basis of this narrative might have been truthful but certainly the embellishments, particularly the wishful thinking about the closeness of my relationship with Frankel, were not. Something about the way in which I described him and his actions recalled the characteristics of a young man of whom she had been particularly fond in her own younger years, and I think this helped her relive a rare pleasant time in her premarital life in Galicia. I had painted myself into a very tight corner by the time Frankel's departure for Cambridge in 1943 relieved me of the necessity of daily inventing new episodes in our ongoing love story but my mother's hopes of a more lasting relationship were further nourished by the correspondence we maintained during the year before I, too, went up to Cambridge.

In addition to debating, Aylesbury Grammar School developed other skills in me. We had a school choir, ably conducted by Mr Pope, the music master. We performed at school ceremonies and every year studied a major composition that we performed publicly before a paying audience. One year it was excerpts from Handel's *Messiah*, the next it was the "Spring" section of Haydn's *The Seasons*. In my first year we presented Taylor-Coleridge's little-known and rarely heard *Hiawatha's Wedding Feast*. I had not yet become a member of the choir. Instead, I was, with Martin Frankel, part of the percussion section, playing the triangle while he played the tambourine. My part, though essential to the sound, was comparatively small: it entailed counting a vast number of bars (at one point as many as 103!) while anxiously waiting for the conductor to bring me in with a nod in my direction. The next year I graduated to the choir, singing alto in *Messiah*. It was a relief to know that, even if I missed an entry, there were other voices covering my failure.

In drama I excelled, as I had in elementary school. I had natural acting ability and could easily enter the character I was portraying. Though I should have liked to play the romantic heroines, I found myself more often given the supporting roles, which, however, invariably required greater acting skills. Once, when the play we were performing was a sentimental thriller called *The Monkey's Paw*, I invested the role of a gossipy neighbour with a Cockney richness of humour that had the audience beside itself. I had been so successfully made up for the part that Mr Furley, the French teacher who knew me very well, failed to recognise me as I stood by the staff-room door on the day of the dress-rehearsal. He returned the friendly smile I gave him with a cold stare, hastening to come and apologise when he heard me, a few seconds later, speaking to another teacher and realised the voice was mine.

At my request, my parents came to the performance. There were several items on the programme, including a brief play in French, which helped maintain the school's scholastic reputation, though I doubt whether many members of the audience understood what was going on. I had neglected to inform them in which of the items I was performing and they arrived too late, to find a printed programme. When I went up to them at the end of the evening, expecting to be congratulated on my performance, which had earned a long round of applause on my exit and again at curtain time, I was flabbergasted by their response.

"You said you'd be performing in a play," my mother said reproachfully.

"If we'd known you weren't acting, we wouldn't have bothered to come," my father added.

"But I did perform!" I cried. "Didn't you see me? I was the neighbour. I was the one everybody applauded." My poor parents were appalled, because, not knowing that this was me on the stage and waiting patiently for me to appear, they had not paid due attention to what was going on and couldn't even recall my performance. Since they had put off coming until the last of the three performances, they never did see me or enjoy sharing in my *succès fou*. They did share in other, lesser occasions, however, for there were some that did not necessitate their travelling by bus to Aylesbury – amateur performances that took place in the village hall, in which I participated not only as actress but frequently also as author, for example, of historical pageants such as the one I later found featured in Virginia Woolf's *Between the Acts*, and playlets based on Jewish themes, which I and my Jewish girl friends performed on the appropriate festivals at The Cedars. Early in 1939, the Rothschilds had put this imposing residence, the largest house in the village, which derived its name from two great trees in its front garden, at the disposal of a Jewish boys' orphanage from Frankfurt, headed by the teutonically formal Dr Steinhardt. Several Jewish parents had seized the opportunity of saving their sons by sending them off together with the genuine orphans, who were comparatively few in number. At one of these little acts of mine, none other than the Rothschilds themselves were among the audience.

One of my early fantasies was calculated to express my academic rather than my artistic ambitions. During the fine, warm summer of 1940, back from Northampton, I played at "being at university". I invented a college called St Hilda's, unaware of the one that existed at Oxford. Out in the garden, with volumes of Arthur Mee's *Children's Encyclopaedia* spread in front of me, I diligently sat at a folding table, compiling notes about Greek and Roman divinities. I was being a brilliant student. It is now clear to me that these fantasy selves, including Martin Frankel's girlfriend, were compensation for a profound sense of inadequacy and inferiority that was induced by my awareness of not fitting the popular ideal of what a girl should be. I encountered this ideal not so much in real life as in the women's magazines I graduated to reading when we moved to Waddesdon. Even *Good Housekeeping*, which my mother purchased for its useful recipes and household tips, contained features on make-up, hairstyles and fashion.

Though the models of the 1940s were not yet as emaciated and anorexic as those that later came to dominate the profession, it was all too patently obvious that, while my brown hair gleamed and my complexion was clear of blemishes, I did not meet ideal standards. My bust was too small, my hips too broad. Even had my mirror not reflected the reality, comments like that of Willy Stern, which have haunted me throughout my entire life, actions like that of Aunt Stella in rejecting me as a bridesmaid, as well as many wounding comments on my appearance that she made later, combined to instil in me both an overwhelming sense of my own inadequacy and a comparable need to compensate. Such compensation might be accomplished by academic achievement, as became apparent after I had proved my mathematical prowess in the Lower School Certificate exam.

At the beginning of the following school year, my first in the sixth form, I was surprised to find Alan Fancourt, the school's unquestioned maths genius, who had come top of the class in all three of the exam's components, waiting at the crest of the hill that led from the bus-stop down to our school. Wheeling his bicycle alongside me, he first congratulated me on my results and then struck up a conversation consisting mainly of small-talk about the summer holidays, the coming school year and a variety of other matters such as might be considered of interest at this point in the school calendar. These topics provided enough material to keep us talking throughout the 10 minutes it took to reach the school gate, where of necessity we parted since there were separate entrances for the boys and the girls.

Assuming that this first encounter was purely coincidental, I was surprised to find Fancourt at the same spot the next day and the next, and every day thereafter until the end of the school year. Though we soon exhausted topics of conversation related to school, I learnt to ask questions about his family, hobbies and plans for the future. My satisfaction at having acquired so devoted an admirer was tempered by the fact that he was not the admirer of my choice but I nevertheless felt an at least temporary improvement in my self-image. This heightened self-esteem was, however, short-lived, as I found myself either a wallflower or relegated to partnering other girls at the school parties that now included ballroom dancing and this despite the fact that I was demonstrably, despite my weight, a nimble, skilled dancer. In the hope of encouraging one of the boys to dance with me, I whirled around the hall displaying my Terpsichorean talents with my perennial partner, a tall, anorexically thin girl from a puritanical, devoutly Christian family, called Hilda Biggerstaff, who seemed to release all her pent-up energies and emotions when we danced. Nothing aroused her as much as the fast tempo of "In the Mood", which Carter, a remarkably good pianist in addition to being a sports champion, played by ear with great verve.

When, towards the end of my first year at Cambridge, I found a "steady" admirer, an immature and illogical fear of being rejected led me to confirm and consolidate the relationship by over-rashly speaking about marriage and announcing our engagement. My parents were dumbfounded when I phoned to inform them of this over-hasty decision and my mother vehemently condemned it. Yet I felt a degree of triumph when I reported it to Martin Frankel, who only a few weeks earlier had kindly assured me that, although men of his age wanted to be seen with attractive young women, they would ultimately settle for intelligent women like myself when it came to marriage (the implication being that this would come years later). Being engaged meant that I no longer needed to worry about finding favour in the eyes of the opposite sex.

Apart from Fancourt and the male classmates such as Martin Frankel with whom I formed friendships based on common intellectual and cultural interests, I also had a boyfriend in the village, where I struck up a relationship with Herbert Tint, one of the inmates at The Cedars. For some reason into which I never inquired, Herbert attended a boarding-school in Bletchley, returning to The Cedars for the weekend twice a month. He soon asked me to go for walks with him whenever he came and we discovered many common interests in reading, music and films. I think he felt a certain superiority over the boys at The Cedars and that I somehow satisfied his needs to demonstrate that superiority vis-à-vis the others by showing them that he had a relationship with a member of the "superior" families in the village. All but one of the other boys had arrived in England after the age of 14, which at the time marked the end of compulsory schooling. They were employed in various capacities at the manor. There was only one exception. Undersized, extremely thin, red-headed, he too attended Aylesbury Grammar but because he was two years my junior we had no personal contact.

I met Herbert again by chance, sometime in the 1970s, when I caught sight of someone who resembled him seated at a table, facing me at a restaurant in Jerusalem. Curious, I went over to check whether I'd guessed correctly. I had. He was one of a group of professors of political science from various provincial universities in the UK and we exchanged news of our current lives. We did not, however, exchange addresses and I learnt no more of him.

On the other hand, with the "little shrimp," as I thought of him, I had a very different experience. In 1958, two young scholars from Yale University came to teach, each for one term, in the Hebrew University's English Department. They were a study in contrasts that soon aroused the amusement of the students. One, Harold Bloom, was a large, rumpled, raucous and very brilliant extrovert. The other, Geoffrey Hartman, was timid, reserved and never raised his voice, so that it was sometimes hard to catch what he was saying. Needless to say, Moshe and I extended hospitality to them and their wives. Early on in their stay, my study, with its book-lined walls, attracted the attention of Renee, Geoffrey's wife.

"How on earth did you accumulate so vast a collection?" she wondered. So I began to recount the history of my book-collecting.

"During the war I went to grammar school in Aylesbury…"

"Aylesbury!" she echoed, amazed. "But Geoffrey went to school in Aylesbury, too."

"When?" I asked

She paused for a moment before saying "1940 to 1942".

"No," I protested, adding very confidently. "There was no Geoffrey Hartman at our school."

"Oh, but his name then was Gert Heuman."

Now it was my turn to be amazed. Gert Heuman, the "little shrimp?" Excited, I went over to him and said, "I'm Alice Margulies". He gazed at me blankly. The name meant nothing to him. "My father used to run the High Holy Day services," I added. "Surely you remember us. We lived in the High Street. I used to come to The Cedars quite frequently." But it was no use. He remembered nothing. I tried to jolt his memory further, by vividly recalling his appearance in the French comedy performed on the evenings when I played the "Cockney woman". He had brought the house down, hopping around the stage, hands on stomach, pathetically shouting, "*J'ai mal au ventre! Jai mal au ventre!*" I reminded him of that, repeating the words. He had no recollection of his Waddesdon life. Except for one.

"I was always hungry," he said. "The big boys used to steal my food." Amnesia had obliterated all recollection of those bad days, of the orphanage from which he was able to escape in 1942 in order to join his mother, who had succeeded in reaching the United States and was able to obtain a visa for him.

I became acquainted with The Cedars primarily because the Steinhardts had two daughters, one of whom was my age, the other a year or so older. There were two additional young girls among the evacuees, both of them also refugees from Germany. One of them was a distant relation: her mother, who had died some years earlier, was the sister of my aunt by marriage, Esther, who had, like us, lived in Essen. It was natural that the five of us would form a kind of clique and equally natural that we would most frequently meet at The Cedars rather than at my home or in the small cottage rooms occupied by the other two families, who had not found (or had not been able to afford) houses to rent.

In addition to these meetings, my father's connection with The Cedars also brought me into contact with the residents there. Having organised and led the prayers for the High Holy Days soon after our arrival in Waddesdon, he had rapidly discerned that Dr Steinhardt, a typically semi-assimilated German Jew, lacked not only the knowledge required to give his charges an adequate Jewish education but even the desire to impart it. With his customary sense of personal responsibility, my father therefore offered to procure an appropriate teacher and also (presumably in order to overcome any possible opposition) to pay his salary.

At first, Willy and I also participated in these classes but it rapidly became clear that our knowledge far outstripped that of even the most talented of the Cedars boys and so Mr Kurenitz came to us every Sunday, to instruct us in what was his specialism, Hebrew grammar. Willy, having attended a Jewish secondary school, was proficient even in this and able to progress to more interesting material such as the Bible and even the classical poetry of the Middle Ages. In contrast, throughout the four years that preceded my departure for Cambridge, I was subjected to the repetitious conjugating and parsing, which I loathed, with only occasionally the relief of reading a few verses of the Bible. I tried as often as possible to cancel my lessons, pleading a headache or excess of homework to be completed by Monday morning but my father wouldn't hear of it.

Time passed. I was, on the whole, extremely happy. I had become close to Willy, with whom I shared not only a fondness for the same books and radio programmes but also a bedroom, where we chatted and exchanged jokes before falling asleep. We went for walks together and he helped me with my homework, when necessary. The range and depth of his knowledge never ceased to amaze me. A year after our move to Waddesdon, Willy left to study at the London School of Economics (LSE), which had, like a number of other London colleges, been evacuated to Cambridge. From there, early in 1943, he sent me the requisite forms for application to the two Cambridge women's colleges and so it was really he whom I have to thank for the fact that, in October 1944, I became a first-year student at Newnham.

Visiting Aylesbury Grammar to say goodbye before my family's post-war return to London, I discovered that none of the three evacuees (two of them Jewish) who had distinguished themselves by winning state scholarships, exhibitions or comparable university awards had been listed on the school's honour board. We were, to the last, foreigners, outsiders, even though, by failing to record our success, the school was depriving itself of the distinction of having enabled us to achieve it. It was an egregious example of provincial xenophobia and of cutting off one's nose to spite one's face.

Studies

I gained my first inkling of what I might expect if I were accepted to Newnham in the course of the train journey to the interview, in the spring of 1944.

With his customary concern for his family's welfare, my father had accompanied me to London to see me safely on the train to Cambridge. He had rejected my own inclination to seize the first available seat and, despite my protests, had continued walking along the platform, peering into every carriage until he found one in which a young woman about my own age, elegantly hatted and gloved, occupied a corner seat by the door. To my intense embarrassment, he leaned towards her and asked if she, too, were travelling to Cambridge for an interview. On receiving an astonished but polite reply in the affirmative, he told her my name and asked for hers.

"Isabel Quigley," she replied. It sounded like a character out of Dickens. I assume my own name struck her as equally – or even more – extraordinary. Having entrusted us to each other's company, my father wished us both a safe journey and much success, and stayed on the platform to wave farewell as the train moved off. I thus had a companion for my journey and we soon began conversing on various subjects related to the written exam we'd already passed. One of the questions on the "General" paper had required us to write about a work that we would take with us to a desert island. Having myself plumped for *Orlando*, which Willy and I had recently read and been puzzled by, I was completely taken aback by her choice: "Oh," she said offhandedly, "Dante's *Divina Commedia* – in the original, of course. Otherwise I'd finish it too quickly."

Not only had I never read Dante: I knew no Italian. Both were far beyond the limited range of Aylesbury Grammar School's curriculum. At the private school she had attended, my travelling companion had received individual tutoring to prepare her for Cambridge. How could I possibly compete with such a background? I realised then the vast chasm that lay between a state-financed grammar-school and the fee-paying British private schools. The difference between me and the other candidates became increasingly evident in the course of the weekend, which began with interviews on Friday. While I wore a navy-blue skirt and matching jumper that I myself had knitted, on the left breast of which my initials were embroidered in light (Cambridge!) blue, most of the other girls wore what the upper-class English then referred to as "coat and skirt", a one-colour two-piece, coupled with a matching blouse. When I commented admiringly on the elegance of one such outfit, in a very attractive blue-green tweed, the slightly surprised and dismissive response was, "Oh, this? It's just the school uniform." Recalling the ugly gymslips, the unflattering square-necked white blouses of BKHS, I felt totally humiliated. Here, in real life but in a far more sophisticated version, were the characters from *The Schoolgirl*, whose antics I had eagerly followed and envied.

When I went into the interview, the don examining me asked why I had chosen *Orlando*. I answered, quite truthfully, that what I would really have liked to take was the Bible but that – and Shakespeare – had been explicitly ruled out by the examiners. I refrained from adding that I might also have chosen Margolis and Marx's *History of the Jews* or, perhaps, Karl Marx's *Das Kapital*, which my brother was urging me to read. I explained that I had found *Orlando* hard to understand and thought that, in the seclusion of a desert island, and with little other reading matter, I might ultimately discern its meaning. I was particularly puzzled by the eponymous protagonist's sexual transformation from male to female. My interviewer seemed amused.

"Of course you know it's really about Vita Sackville-West," she half-explained, half-queried. No, I hadn't known that. "It's on the cover," she pointed out, taking a copy of the book from a shelf. Overwhelmed by embarrassment and feeling utterly foolish, I couldn't bring myself to confess that I hadn't purchased the book but borrowed it from Boots' lending library, where dust-jackets were promptly discarded when a new book arrived. I was certain I would not be accepted into Newnham, particularly given the competition. I'd met additional candidates at a cocoa-party hosted by a third-year student who was still in residence although it was the Easter vacation. At that encounter, my sense of being not only inferior but a real outsider was further strengthened. I was not only of a different class but (quite literally) of another nation.

The next day, profoundly dejected by what I was sure had been an ignominious failure to make a favourable impression, I toured the town, visiting the colleges one by one, traversing the meticulously maintained courts with their ancient buildings, opening the heavy oak doors that led into the halls hung with portraits of illustrious past students – Milton, Tennyson, Byron – the great and famous whose works I had studied and whom I so wished to emulate. I desperately hoped to be accepted and yet, at one and the same time, I feared it. The previous day's experiences had brought home to me all too forcefully that, in innumerable ways, I was not like the other girls. I was alien, not only Jewish but a foreigner, and though my flawless accent did not betray my foreign birth my ignorance of and inexperience in upper-class British traditions and mores would.

A month later, a letter arrived. I was, after all, finally admitted, though only as a "second-best", since another candidate had, to my mind inexplicably, chosen to accept a place at Oxford rather than Cambridge. My delight at having my wish fulfilled far outweighed the shame at not having instantly succeeded. In retrospect,

I realise that I never fully took advantage of being at Cambridge. The fact that I didn't make the most of my years there was in part due to the undemanding nature of the mode of studies, which consisted only of the writing of an essay for the weekly tutorial and, in my second and final years, participation in seminar-style classes for which there were few or no written requirements.

It was soon evident that the education I had received at Aylesbury Grammar School had been extremely superficial. While I had learnt to "love" a considerable amount of English literature, we'd been trained neither in critical analysis of the texts nor in discerning use of secondary sources, my teacher's approach being primarily biographical. Hence, although I knew numerous passages of Wordsworth, Keats, Shelley and Coleridge by heart, I was incapable of writing about their works – or those of any other writers – in the informed, analytical manner expected of us. There were vast lacunae in my capacity to comprehend and critically comment on texts. In consequence, I submitted woefully inadequate weekly essays and ended up with only a disappointing but totally justified 2.2 as my final result.

I cannot, however, blame only my lack of prior preparation for my failure. I didn't work hard enough to compensate for that lack. I dutifully attended a wide variety of lecture courses, some of them excellent, some exciting, a few dull and mediocre. I took notes diligently. I derived considerable pleasure and even insight from some of them but training in critical methods of reading primary sources and in the use of secondary sources was as absent as it had been at my school. The one important exception was the course on criticism given by F.R. Leavis, whose devastating and sardonic demolition of poems that for my English teacher at school had been virtually sacred were truly revelatory. But it was some time before Leavis and his close reading of texts came into my life and meanwhile I was drowning, yearning for help that didn't come. I well recall the dismaying response of erudite, timid Enid Welsford, when I asked her what I might read to assist me in comprehending the poems of Donne, who was the subject of a tutorial very early in my first term. After a few minutes of deliberation, she came up with an unhelpful reply:

"Why don't you just read Donne?"

There was a basic assumption at Cambridge that lecturers would present the fruits of new research, raw material in due course to be completed and published. Students were privileged to get a kind of preview, perhaps to serve as sounding-boards. Among the "Works in Progress" that I enjoyed was E.M.W. Tillyard's book on Shakespeare's History Plays (alarmingly, or pleasantly – depending on one's taste – free of footnotes), Basil Willey's erudite works on, respectively, 17th- and 18th-century thought, and Muriel Bradbrook's analysis of Ibsen. Miss Bradbrook, who later became Mistress of Girton and also Cambridge's first woman professor, always taught wearing a hat.

What I did benefit from at Cambridge were the social activities from which I gained life skills. Had I been more of an ant and less of a grasshopper, I would have derived much more than that intellectually and academically but there was neither adequate stimulus nor academic demand to encourage hard work and instil academic discipline. I would have benefited more had the Cambridge system been similar to that of most American universities, where – as I later learnt to my astonishment – students might be expected to read two novels for each session of their twice-weekly courses. In fact, when in the late 1950s tasked with giving a comprehensive course on "The Development of Shakespeare's Art", I, at times, asked the students to read three or four plays a week, particularly when these comprised a trilogy or even a four-play sequence, as in the History Plays. That proved to be excessive but a happy medium between such excess and the minimalism of Cambridge would have suited me perfectly, and would probably have led to better results than those with which I somewhat ignominiously graduated.

As it was, I seldom achieved illumination in tutorials, discussion groups or lectures. When I did, it was on the rare occasions when I was fortunate enough for one reason or another to receive a one-on-one tutorial rather than together with another student, as was customary. I can still recall the "shock of recognition" with which I reached true understanding of Browning's "Andrea del Sarto" only because Dorothy de Navarro led me through it step by step, line by line, in true heuristic manner, challenging me to perceive what was common to almost all of the speakers in the Dramatic Monologues in which Browning excelled: a sense of failure, of not having reached further than their grasp, of never attaining their ultimate goal. Perhaps these poems resonate so strongly in my mind because I now see them as applying to myself during this formative period of my life.

Fortunately, the Cambridge English Tripos stresses not only the literary creations of any one period but also the social background and the philosophy of the time. One major component of the exams at the end of each year was entitled "Life, Literature and Thought" of a specific period. Fascinated by the world of medieval England opened up by the lucid, enlightening lectures of H.S. Bennett, I achieved my best results in that exam. Ever since, in my own teaching, I have tried to convey to my students the social, philosophical and moral context in which an author was writing, and the way in which his or her works consciously or unconsciously relate to that context and are influenced by it. Hence my choice of a topic, when the time came to write my own doctoral dissertation, was "Renaissance Concepts of Honour in Shakespeare's 'Problem' Plays". In the course of teaching these plays – *Hamlet, Troilus and Cressida, Measure for Measure* and *All's Well that Ends Well* – I noticed how frequently the word "honour" appeared in the texts. This led me to a semantic analysis of the various definitions of honour that prevailed in Shakespeare's time. The conflict between these definitions and perceptions foregrounded the moral dilemmas that are central to each of the plays. All four of them hinge on the manifold and contradictory definitions of the concept.

In 1945, as the war neared its end, I became an avid theatregoer. The Old Vic was resident at the New Theatre in St Martin's Lane. Its stars included Laurence Olivier, Ralph Richardson and Sybil Thorndike, all of whom appeared in the course of one vacation in an impressive production of *Henry IV*. Olivier, who in Part I played Hotspur as a brash stutterer stumbling over his overheated words, succeeded admirably in bringing out the latent charm of this hotheaded rebel. In Part II, he contented himself with an unforgettable cameo as Justice Shallow, movingly conveying the comic mingling of mundane matter with the melancholy, perhaps unreliable reminiscences of an earlier, more virile self.

We had been charged with reading *Henry IV* and other plays in preparation for a seminar on Shakespeare the following term. When our instructor asked each of us what critical works we had read, I had to confess that while I'd read very little I had seen an illuminating performance. While this admission met with a stony look of disapproval, the ensuing discussion made it clear that I had derived more understanding from seeing the plays than I would have done had I merely read them. Although both John Dover Wilson's illuminating *What Happens in Hamlet* and Harley Granville Barker's theatre-based interpretations of Shakespeare had already been published, their enlightening contents seem not to have reached (or appealed to) my teacher. In my third year, studies finally became more integrated and interesting. In preparation for the paper on Tragedy, we had university lectures such as Bradbrook's on Ibsen, which were augmented by a college-based seminar for which the reading requirements ranged from *The Oresteia* to Strindberg and Ibsen. I hoovered up each week's assigned plays and discussed them excitedly with my colleagues. At last I had a satisfying sense of what university studies could and should be, how they can stimulate and challenge us intellectually, developing the mind and enriching the soul.

I also participated in a seminar on George Eliot given by Joan Bennett that required us to read all the author's works in chronological order. The only ones I already knew were *Silas Marner* and *The Mill on the Floss*, both of which had been recommended to me by Miss Burnham when I was 11. At that age I had of course failed to appreciate anything beyond their fairly simple plots. Now their psychological insight and moral earnestness became apparent. I came eventually to perceive the similarity between level-headed Tom and his impetuous sister Maggie, on the one hand, and, on the other, that between my super-rational intellectual brother and me. Joan Bennett had been born into a large, well-known, long-assimilated Jewish family, the Frankaus. One brother, Gilbert, was a novelist; another, Ronald, a comedian known for his risqué wit. She was married to the medievalist H.S. Bennett, whose historical-social approach I had found so inspiring in my first year.

When we came to discuss *Daniel Deronda*, Mrs Bennett adopted the same approach as F.R. Leavis in *The Great Tradition*, stressing the disparity between the Gwendolyn Harleth story and the Zionist idealism of Mordecai. The former she deemed excellent, the latter irrelevant and unconvincing. As an ardent Zionist, I wholly identified with Mordecai's passionate exposition of this messianic concept but didn't dare challenge Mrs Bennett. I feared I'd be unable to present my views cogently, and would end up dismissed by her and derided by my fellow students in the group, all of them men. However, among these was another Jew. English-born, Orthodox and Zionist, Aryeh Newman (aka Leibel) had none of my insecurity. To the surprise of the instructor and the students, he lucidly and eloquently set forth the basic ideas of the earliest, pre-Herzlian Zionists, with some of whom George Eliot had been personally acquainted. All that was now required of me was to nod in acquiescence as Mrs Bennett sat, speechless, with the bemused non-Jews waiting expectantly for the rebuttal that never came. (Leibel emigrated to Israel in the early 1950s and for a while, like me, taught English as a Second Language at the Hebrew University.)

The impact of subjectivity on interpreting a literary work was dramatically borne in on me some time after I arrived in Israel, when one of my acquaintances informed me that she was reading a Hebrew translation of *Daniel Deronda*. I waxed enthusiastic, citing the perceptive psychology of George Eliot's characterisation of Gwendolen. Some time later, the reader informed me that I must have been mistaken. There was no character of that name. It would seem that the translator, himself presumably an ardent Zionist, had found half of the work irrelevant.

In my time, Cambridge's two women's colleges were Newnham and Girton, the latter some way out of town. Not until 1948 could women officially obtain degrees and full membership of the University. Indeed, Cambridge was the last university in the UK to admit women to full membership. The exclusion had its positive aspects. With its students' entry into both the University Library and the University laboratories long forbidden, Newnham early on developed its own. In 1944 there was a combined quota of 500 students for both the women's colleges. A third, teacher-training college, Homerton, existed but wasn't officially part of the University. A popular saying, the stereotyping nature of which many of us greatly resented, ran, "Girton for brains, Newnham for brawn and Homerton for beauty". Newnham remains staunchly feminist, the sole Oxbridge college for women only. It still excels at sports but also has greatly advanced academically.

In accordance with our inferior status, the men tended to patronise the women, even though in terms of scholastic achievement many women far outshone men. We had, after all, undergone a greatly more stringent selection process. In many subjects, women gained better exam results, in this respect emulating some of the earliest women students, who were in their time not yet officially ranked in any class. With 28 men's colleges, there was a scarcity of women partners for the end-of-term dances held by many of the University societies and especially for the annual May Balls (held in June), which were the main social event in every college. For the latter, many male undergraduates imported female members of their family or friends of their sisters, making sure that they be as attractive and elegant as possible. I well recall my envy when a fellow member of the Jewish Society, a Second World War ex-serviceman, invited his London girlfriend, who daringly arrived wearing bright red tights and what for the time was a scandalously short skirt.

That is not to say that none of us was equally elegant. One of my contemporaries, Katarina Gavrilovich, of Yugoslavian aristocratic origin, enthralled me as I witnessed her stately descent down the staircase, resplendent in full ball regalia, wearing a blue-green gown of *changeant* taffeta, balanced on very high-heeled silver shoes and carrying a tiny pouch-shaped drawstring bag that matched her stunning dress, her hair piled high, held by two jewelled combs. This, I thought, must have been what Cinderella looked like when her fairy godmother outfitted her – an irresistible beauty. We were not encouraged to be vain. Our rooms had no full-length mirrors. If we wished to check how we looked, whether clothes fitted or petticoats protruded from beneath the hems of dresses, we had to resort to a public mirror at the head of our staircase. Exposed to the gaze and even comments of our fellow students, many of us either confined our self-inspection to hours at which we were least likely to encounter such responses or else entirely dispensed with it.

When, at the end of my first term, the time came for me to own an evening dress, Willy advised that it should not be black, white or red. I assumed that while the first and last of these might not be considered appropriate for a virginal 18-year-old, white was simply not practical. So my mother accompanied me to Dickens and Jones on Regent Street, where we ultimately and despairingly surrendered precious clothing coupons for an innocuous, pale-blue garment, which in no way flattered or even suited my flat-chested body. Some time later I lent it to a friend and noted that it looked much better on someone with a fuller bosom than I have been blessed with. From then on, I had evening dresses, like most of my clothes, made to measure.

At Cambridge and Oxford students come under the watchful eyes of two dons, both usually, though with some rare exceptions, members of one's own college. Tutors are officially *in loco parentis*, responsible for the general welfare and good behaviour of their charges, while supervisors oversee the fulfilment of scholastic requirements, including weekly meetings, for which written work is submitted. In the confusing manner typical of Cambridge nomenclature, whereby totally flat areas of the city are designated "Hills", these meetings are known as tutorials.

Newnham's Director of English Studies, Enid Welsford, was my supervisor. A tiny round ball of a woman, hair cut in an outdated 1920s bob, she scuttled like a mouse along the Clough corridors. If I opened the heavy Hall doors for her, she would duck beneath my arm to enter. She was kind and very erudite, never expressing highly critical judgment save in the gentlest and most hesitant of terms, often formulated as a rhetorical question: "Don't you think that...?" Her own area of expertise was the Elizabethan theatre, on which she had published two highly acclaimed works. She was a devout Anglican. In this respect she resembled my fellow tutoree, Peggy Williamson, with whom she would frequently embark on theological discussions in which I could play no part. However, when we came to study poetry that contained references to, or metaphors based on, the Old Testament, I could at last come into my own, deriving some degree of reassurance.

I was also able to ingratiate myself in an unexpected non-academic manner when Miss Welsford one day worriedly informed us that her watch had broken beyond repair. I promptly assured her that I could come to her aid. Two days later I presented her with a very attractive watch that my father had selected from the family firm's stockroom. She was duly impressed by the good taste and the speed we had displayed. When I visited her in 1950 she spoke disparagingly and despairingly of the profound ignorance of Christianity that typified the current generation of students. Attempting to analyse George Herbert's "Easter Wings" some had apparently not even known what Easter celebrated. She envied my good luck in having students who knew the Bible. I didn't share with her my own dismay on finding that they had no inkling of one of the most powerful passages in the Yom Kippur service. I'd discovered this distressing lacuna when I tried to teach the concept "simile" by citing the prayer in which God and God's relationship with the Children of Israel are compared consecutively to those between a craftsman and his tools:

> Like a stone in the hands of a stone-cutter…
> Like an axe in the hands of a wood-cutter…
> Like a web in the hands of a weaver…
> So are we…

To my chagrin, only the few religiously observant students in my class had an inkling of what I was referring to.

My tutor, Edith Chrystal, was in every way a contrast to Miss Welsford. Tall and gaunt, her white hair tied back in a pigtail that resembled a barrister's wig, her spindly legs encased, like Miss Welsford's, in heavy grey woollen stockings, she strode commandingly from her ground-floor room to Hall, where she gazed down imperiously from High Table upon the students below. She took her responsibilities seriously, with a sternness very unlike the gentle love that my parents, in whose place she officially served, showered upon me.

Miss Welsford and Miss Chrystal revealed a different and surprising side of themselves when it came to music. The former astonished me at a recital by Benjamin Britten and Peter Pears by jumping up and down in ecstatic applause, like the most excited of teenage fans of rock musicians in a later age. She stopped only when, after innumerable encores, the couple returned to deliver their positively final "No, no,/We ain't going to sing any more". One Sunday morning, I entered Miss Chrystal's room to pay my porter's fees in time to hear her speak with poetic rapture of the soprano's moving rendering of the final notes of Verdi's *Requiem*. Suddenly she was more human, an individual, not the representative of an institution.

My innate respect for rules deterred me from climbing into College after the gates had been locked, as a number of my more audacious contemporaries occasionally did. I was sure that if I did Miss Chrystal would be waiting for me on the other side. Indeed, on the sole occasion on which I defied regulations, my premonitions proved well-founded. I'd failed in my efforts to fulfil the weekly tutorial assignment. Ashamed to admit the truth, I decided to claim ill-health, a very severe headache, as an excuse. On this occasion, it was not Miss Welsford but another Fellow whom I was to meet. She sent me to see the nurse, who prescribed and administered aspirin, which I obediently swallowed. I had a ticket for a long-awaited concert that evening, at which Schubert's Octet in F-Major was to be performed, and I was greatly looking forward to it. But as I climbed the Guildhall steps to the auditorium a sharp admonitory finger tapped me on the shoulder. Turning, I encountered Miss Chrystal.

"Miss Margulies," she said, with a look of profound displeasure. "I understand you are feeling unwell. Kindly return to your room." I was too overwhelmed by guilt even to attempt to resist the order or to claim that the aspirin had proved an effective cure. Humiliated and angry, I returned to College and never again ventured to infringe rules. Henceforth, I abided by the arcane regulations that governed our comings and goings, our exits and re-entrances in the evening hours – rules which now seem utterly absurd and have, indeed, been discarded.

Not until 1969 did Britain grant men and women equal voting rights at the age of 18. Previously, one's 21st birthday was the date on which one obtained official independence – a moment frequently marked by being presented with a birthday-card or an iced cake on which appeared a key, the symbol of freedom to come and go as one pleased. Until then, one was subject to adult authority, which college tutors officially represented. For the men there was an additional, higher level of authority, that of the Proctors, who roamed the city accompanied by two agile, human "bulldogs", whose function it was to pursue and capture wayward students who had failed to be in by midnight. Since tardiness as well as absence from college grounds at night might lead even to "being sent down", as expulsion is known, only the very boldest or most dissolute of men would take the risk, preferring to find a way of climbing over the daunting walls that surround each college. While women weren't subject to the terrors of Proctors, college customs were far stricter than those that obtained at the men's colleges.

If we were going to be out after 8 pm, we had to sign an "Outbook", giving details of where we were going. If our destination was a man's room, his name and college had to be provided. We weren't allowed to stay in men's rooms after

10 pm. Newnham's main gate, guarded by the occupant of the Porter's Lodge, was locked at 11 pm. The time of our return would be duly noted in our Hall's Outbook. At the end of the term, we paid a porter's fee for the number of times that affable man had had to unlock the portals to let us in: threepence for 11 to 11.30 and sixpence for 11.30 to midnight. I spent a sizeable amount of money during my three years at Newnham. The reproving look on my tutor's face when I came to pay my dues at the end of each term made it clear that the frequency of my late returns, though not criminal, was nonetheless considered a form of delinquency.

A close friend of Willy's, a graduate student of law from London, rented rooms in town where he spent most of his weekends. I frequently visited him there on Saturday evenings. One Sunday morning I was summoned to Miss Chrystal, who sternly admonished me for infringement of the rules. Although I had been visiting a man, I had returned to college only at 11.30. Where had I been after 10 pm? Forgetting the rules, I innocently replied that I had stayed with my host till 11. I was then requested to divulge the identity of this host. The fact that he was not only a mature graduate student but a friend of my family helped assuage my tutor's fears.

Sex: one never used the word in referring to relations between men and women. Sex was something obscene, indecent, smutty. According to a well-worn cliché, it "reared its ugly head". While male visitors to Newnham were free to come and go throughout the day, their evening visits were strictly controlled. Their names had to be registered in a guest book kept outside our tutor's room, on the same table as the Outbook. After 8 pm we had to meet our guests at the main gate, accompanying them on their departure no later than 10 pm.

Like the guests whom they were accompanying, students who entertained men were thus subjected to the scrutiny of their fellows. This led to perceptible self-consciousness. Some strode confidently, secure in the knowledge that their guests were good-looking, gentlemanly, impressive. Others looked almost apologetic, as if they felt a need for approval not only of their guest but even of their own temerity in inviting one to their room. If one hosted men too frequently was one considered a promiscuous hussy? Was never hosting a man a sign of infirmity, an indication of one's being unattractive, of having nobody to invite? Little wonder that most women preferred to meet men friends outside College or that Newnham Walk, the short path whose abundant bushes and leafy trees offered dark shadows aplenty, was every evening lined with amorously entwined couples furtively snatching the last moments before midnight to make their farewells. Since the men too had to be in college by 12, bicycles were frequently purloined but invariably punctiliously returned the next morning, either by the borrower or by the vigilant police.

A passionate Latin admirer of one of my contemporaries found an original way of wooing her. Of aristocratic Spanish birth, he one summer evening enlisted a number of his friends to join him in serenading her. A Newnham abetter "signed them in". The sweet sounds of guitar and male voices filled the garden and brought us all to our windows. Bewitched by harmony, nobody in authority saw fit to rebuke anyone for what could in any case not be defined as a breach of rules. There were no relevant rules. Nobody had ever conceived that such an occasion might one day arise. At the end of the year, the suitor swept his bride off to Ecuador, which at the time appeared a very distant, exotic destination.

There were other, more blatant, breaches of rules of which the authorities were clearly unaware. We had to sign in at breakfast and dinner according to ancient tradition. This practice was referred to as "keeping nights", without a minimum of which one was not considered to have fulfilled residence requirements and thus could not graduate. Although leaving Cambridge without permission was forbidden, it was easy to sign in at breakfast, go off for the day and return by 7 pm. One of my contemporaries, Janet Ball, frequented the horse races at Newmarket. A close follower of breeding details and past equine achievements, she often returned with significant sums of money.

I encountered her in the late 1950s at one of England's stately homes, where she was, to my surprise, serving as an enthusiastic guide, extolling the tastes, manners and habits of the landed gentry. Since she had, as a student, expressed far-left views that were rare at Newnham, I found this career choice amazing and amusing: she seemed so thoroughly to enter into the spirit of British aristocracy. Perhaps her choice of History for her studies had implanted an appreciation of their style of living. Another History student, Jean Ward, regularly climbed into College after midnight. Tall and athletic, she easily scaled the stone wall that surrounded the buildings and always, prior to departure, prudently left the readily accessible window of the gents' toilet on the ground floor of Clough open to facilitate entry into the building. She was very blasé about her exploits, never boasting, simply reporting if she needed to explain her absence from an event or meeting that we'd expected her to attend. She was delighted when, on completing her studies, she was offered a post as buyer at John Lewis. Whoever interviewed her must have been as impressed as I was by her casual elegance.

If the now long-abandoned rules were intended to preserve our precious virginity, that end was probably most effectively served by fear of becoming pregnant. Female contraception was as yet unknown. Male contraception aroused associations of obscenity and lewdness: condoms, "French letters", were available only "under the counter", requested when nobody was within earshot. The general assumption appears to have been that since married men need not worry about impregnating their wives, the only customers for this merchandise must be either dissolute, promiscuous bachelors in pursuit of sensual indulgence with "loose" women or unfaithful, adulterous spouses. In either case, they were not the type with whom "nice girls" were or should be acquainted.

To this day, I cannot understand the logic behind the strict rules that Newnham imposed on its students. Their inefficacy was proven by the fact that during my three years in Clough two of my contemporaries became pregnant and were sent down. One of them married her "seducer", successfully completed her studies elsewhere and eventually became a lecturer at London University. The other was a slovenly, sluggish, fat and extremely unattractive student of Mathematics whose misdemeanour went unobserved until a late stage in the pregnancy, since we all (perhaps like her) assumed that she was merely putting on even more weight.

I often reflect on the impact that the cloistered life of a women's college must have had on its senior residents. I never saw any man visiting them, though I assume there must have been contact with male colleagues in other colleges or in their respective faculties. Certainly there was in-house conviviality: pre-dinner sherry and postprandial coffee and brandy in the Senior Common Room, where the fellows congregated before dinner and to which they retired after the meal. But what else? Living conditions in the women's colleges, as in the men's, were spartan, particularly in wartime. Unlike the ancient colleges, where rooms were located vertically on "staircases", ours were on corridors. The resulting impression was more that of a school than of a university. At each end of the corridors was a scullery where we could boil a kettle. Alongside these amenities were an inadequate number of toilets and bathrooms. In this respect we were better off than the men, who had to trudge to what they called the "bogs" for their ablutions. However, baths, as in wartime everywhere, were limited to a shallow five inches of water, the depth designated by a black line on the four tubs that served an entire corridor of 30 rooms. In the older buildings the weekly ration of a single scuttle of coal was insufficient to warm the rooms every evening during the winter months but in the more modern Peile Hall gas-fires had been installed and several of us frequently gathered in Estelle Levinson's room there to warm up.

The winter of 1946-7 brought bitterly cold weather. The Cam froze, enabling those who knew how to skate to exercise their skills, while simultaneously leading to numerous fractured ankles. Even though my mother had wisely insisted on my taking one of our warm European feather quilts, I shuddered whenever my feet reached the icy region at the foot of the bed. The thaw came just before the vacation, on an evening when end-of-term dances were being held. Willy and my boyfriend Sonny came up from London. As our taxi splashed perilously through the waters of the Cam that covered Silver Street Bridge we feared they might rise to submerge our feet. In precaution, I had borrowed oversized galoshes to cover my skimpy silver sandals, with the result that I flopped around like a seal before reaching the dance-floor.

Men had a set of rooms comprising a living-room and either one or two bedrooms, depending on the number of inhabitants. They also enjoyed the services of a female "bedder" or a male "gyp" who cleaned and sometimes cooked for them on the "en-suite" gas-stoves. My boyfriend was even taught ballroom dancing by his own worldly-wise servant, who had perceived how frustrated I was by his master's lack of that skill.

Since Newnham housemaids made their rounds only once a week, we were responsible for dusting and cleaning our own rooms. Furthermore, due to staff shortages, each of us was expected to perform certain weekly "housekeeping" tasks, which included library-dusting (at 7.30 am – an inhuman hour in the UK, when it is invariably still dark), gardening and a variety of other chores. With none of the gardening skills possessed by so many Britons, I applied for the dusting, in which I also supervised a team of my fellow students. Many of them frequently absented themselves, something I was far too law-abiding even to contemplate doing. In consequence, at least half of my fortnightly hour on duty consisted of running from room to room, rousing my reluctant subordinates. Since they reached the library only when the time allotted to our task had already expired, they were left free to proceed directly to breakfast. I thus learnt the often bitter lesson of responsibility.

During my first year I enjoyed the rare luxury of a set of rooms: a large living-room/study and a small bedroom. Like everybody else I hung my own pictures, reproductions sold *en masse* at Heffer's Bookshop. But I eschewed the ubiquitous Degas dancers and van Gogh cypresses, opting instead for contemporary works by Stanley Spencer, Walter Sickert and Duncan Grant. The *pièce de resistance* was a black velvet cushion cover I brought from home. It depicted the Wailing Wall, with black-hatted worshippers and a Hebrew inscription giving its name. This colourful handiwork invariably aroused considerable curiosity, providing me with opportunities to speak with pride of my racial identity. I also had an elegant *chaise-longue* and a unique bureau with faux-medieval carvings on its flap. Both of these I moved with me at the end of my first year, when the influx of graduate students from overseas resulted in two-room sets no longer being available to single occupants. The major attraction of the large new room I chose, located above the main entrance to Clough Hall, was its wide bow window, with a window-seat that overlooked the well-kept gardens that to this day remain the pride of the College, offsetting its dowdy Victorian exterior.

In 1998, those of us who had graduated prior to the granting of full membership of the University 50 years earlier were invited to attend the celebration of that long-delayed and hard fought-for achievement. I seized the opportunity of returning to my *alma mater* and was dismayed at what I found. Despite the continued beauty of the gardens, in which, unlike those of the men's colleges, everyone was permitted to walk on the grass, the buildings were dilapidated, the staircase leading to my old room sadly worn and scarred, the felt noticeboards tattered. Furthermore, the rooms that in my day had, like those of the men, at all times been kept open were now locked. Indeed, when I went into the centre of town to see the colleges I had so admired on my first visit, I found that even the dining- halls and libraries, to which there was once free access, were closed to the public, while most of the colleges even charged an entry fee. As I walked around the crowded town, I realised that the prime reason for this exclusivity was that Cambridge now draws hosts of tourists, from whom private property must of necessity be protected.

On the evening of 8 May 1945, I was desultorily playing table-tennis with a number of friends in the Old Lab, a neglected building at the back of the College gardens. Exams were over, the term was almost at its end. We were unable to concentrate on anything that required thought, reflection, even serious talk. Joan Sands was at the piano, endlessly and nerve-rackingly repeating the opening bars of Mozart's "Turkish March" – all that she recalled of that well-worn beginners' work. We knew that the cessation of war would soon be announced. The moment it came, our joy could not be confined to the College grounds. We set off on our bicycles, each one searching out friends with whom to celebrate. But merely finding another individual, in many cases someone not yet aware of the exciting news, was insufficiently satisfying. At such times one seeks a wider community.

As a result, I found myself not only with the president of the Jewish Society, whom I had gone to fetch, but with a large group of fellow members, all making for the centre of town. Soon we were dancing an elated *horah* round an outsized oak by King's College. Almost at once, others joined us, drawn by a similar need for public expression of joy. This necessitated a move to a larger space, nearby Market Hill, where the crowd formed a series of concentric circles, many hundreds of people rejoicing in the glow of the once-again illuminated clock face on the Town Hall. That night, few of us obeyed the rule of returning to College by midnight. To my knowledge, no sanctions were imposed. Presumably the dons themselves had been too deep in their own forms of celebration to notice the passage of time.

I indulged excessively in the innumerable social activities and cultural riches that Cambridge offered. Continental films at the Cosmo cinema, plays at the Arts Theatre. (Once I had a ticket to see Donald Wolfit's *King Lear* but turned back at the entrance, shrinking, panic-stricken, at the prospect of Gloucester's blinding.) Enchanting end-of-year lantern-lit madrigals on the river at King's, the lights and voices fading away as the boats moved slowly upstream. Dance was a rarer feature. I was particularly excited when Kurt Joos, who had escaped from Germany and taken refuge in Cambridge, announced a performance of his anti-war *The Green Table*. My parents, who had seen it in Essen, where Joos's company originated, spoke often of its powerful impact. Hurrying down Sidgwick Avenue, I was violently knocked over by a fast-pedalling cyclist, a fellow Newnhamite. Since I insisted on continuing to the theatre, she accompanied me. But on arrival there, I couldn't find my ticket, my head ached from the blow it had received and I was too dizzy to continue. I was suffering from concussion. Led back to Newnham, I was sent to bed by Miss Chrystal, who called my parents. The very next morning my father was at my bedside. It was not until 2006 that I saw *The Green Table*, in New York, performed by the American Theatre Ballet. Sadly, its harsh anti-war message was still relevant.

I subscribed to the weekly chamber-music concerts at the ideally small-scale, intimate Arts School. European artists were beginning to come to England, among them legendary figures such as the outstanding, nuanced performer of *Lieder*, Elizabeth Schumann, and violinist Fritz Kreisler, who amazed me by ceaselessly walking around the stage while he was playing. Among the "native" artists the ones that I found most memorable were the quintessentially English Pears and Britten, who hadn't yet attained universal fame.

On the last Sunday evening of my first year, I attended a performance in

King's College Chapel of Verdi's *Requiem*. My seat was behind the organ screen, on the other side of which, invisible to me, were the orchestra, soloists and choir. I had never before heard this operatically dramatic work and I still vividly recall my startled response to the ominous drumbeats that herald the "Dies Irae" and their sudden, spine-chilling later repetition, the trumpet call of *Tuba mirum*, the soprano's notes soaring up like swallows to the vaulted ceiling in the passionate pleading urgency of the "Libera Me". What crowned the evening and marked it all the more indelibly in my memory was the rare opening, at the end of the concert, of the western portal of the chapel, which bears the Hebrew tetrachordon. Still dazed by the power of the music, I saw, as I walked down the aisle, the unforgettable vista of the lawn leading down to the river, over which, under the final twilight rays of a dying summer sunset, like a Turner landscape, hung a very faint perse mist. The solemnity, mystery and spiritual elation of that moment will never be erased from my memory. On that evening I experienced an epiphany.

I attended the weekly debates of the Cambridge Union, an acknowledged training-ground for future Members of Parliament, civil servants and diplomats. Although women weren't admitted as members, we could, by invitation, sit up in the gallery, enjoying the verbal pyrotechnics, the wit and occasional wisdom of our male contemporaries, as well as some impressive opening speeches by well-known personalities from outside the University. I indiscriminately joined Societies: the Liberal Society, Fine Arts, Newnham's Debating Team. In the last of these, I excelled, several times delivering the opening speeches in debates against men's colleges that we invariably won. On one occasion, my dazzlingly witty and ingenious advocacy of the detective novel as superior to crossword puzzles won over an unexpected and unlikely admirer named Morton. A former major in the British Armed Forces, he sported a fine moustache and an impressive camel-hair "warm". He took to visiting me every Friday afternoon, just as I was hastening to dress before leaving for the Jewish Society. Once I was ready, he accompanied me as far as the entrance to the synagogue, where he bade me farewell. Occasionally he invited me to his rooms in Clare College, where he regaled me with stories of wartime activities and showed off photographs of his very beautiful sister-in-law. He was wealthy and something of an aesthete, and I never felt entirely comfortable in his company. I was therefore relieved when he transferred his attentions to a fellow Newnhamite. Also Jewish and like me born in Europe, she aspired to be embraced by the upper-class British world of which Morton was so clearly a member – a world in which I felt so out of place.

Jews recognise each other, no matter how hard some of us attempt to assimilate. In Hall we gravitated towards each other like swarming bees. Some of us had non-Jewish friends but my own intimate circle never included such "outsiders", with one exception. After the war, a number of South Africans were among the graduate students who began to arrive. Two of these, of clearly Semitic appearance, Dorothea Krook and Nora Reinhold (both of whom later became professors at the Hebrew University), joined our group. Their compatriot, Natalie Winch, proved more difficult to define. Though clearly not Jewish, she always sought a seat at our table and seemed to make few other friends. Several months elapsed before we discovered that her fiancé, Larry, of whom she frequently spoke and whom she incessantly cited, was a Jew – Laurence Lerner – who later became professor of English at Sussex University. This might well have been what prompted her sense of affinity with the "tribe".

From the end of my first year, my life beyond the College confines increasingly focused on the Jewish Society and its premises in Thompson's Lane. Here I attended Friday-evening dinners and Saturday-morning services, and guest lectures on Friday and Sunday evenings. Saturday evenings were devoted to our small Zionist study circle, at which I was among those who attempted to speak Hebrew, sang songs of the Zionist pioneers and discussed the philosophies of Ahad Ha-am, Leo Pinsker and of Theodor Herzl himself, the visionary of the Old-New Land of which we too dreamt. A good number of us did indeed ultimately fulfil those dreams. The Jewish Society was the major factor in my development as an activist, though my involvement in non-academic matters had begun at school. I further developed the skills of public debate, chairing meetings with elegance, diplomacy, efficiency and the mandatory Cambridge wit. I learnt the intricacies of a social organisation, with its manifold activities: handling accounts, conducting formal correspondence, proposing and persuasively arguing the case for controversial issues so as to ensure their acceptance by the society's members.

Among my own "breed" I felt none of the inferiority that still marked my relations with many of my non-Jewish contemporaries. Here I flourished and I was at home, admired and popular. At the end of my first term I was elected to the committee, and rose steadily up the ladder of positions via secretary and treasurer to the distinguished role of president, which I occupied in the Michaelmas Term of my final year. Along the way I also became active in the Inter-University Jewish Society, on whose behalf I attended the World Zionist Congress in Basel in December 1946 as a delegate to the Junior Congress.

In our synagogue, the women, though confined to four rows in a slightly elevated gallery at the back of the hall, were fully able to see and be seen. Perhaps that was why I felt no sense of exclusion and hence no resentment of the kind that irked me in places where women were relegated to realms more distant from, and clearly inferior to, those of men. However, when it came to leading the singing of traditional hymns at the Shabbat meal, I vented my indignation by proposing that women too be permitted to fulfil this role, despite the Orthodox prohibition against listening to women's voices. To my surprise, the motion passed with very little opposition, probably because too few of the men felt in any way bound by that prohibition. And so, the following Friday evening, I made history by being the first woman to lead. Unfortunately, the victory was marred. In my nervousness, I pitched my voice too high and, to my shame, had to readjust the key after the first two lines. But the precedent had been set.

During the weekend of my Newnham interview I became acquainted with the synagogue, which, uniquely, was owned and run by the University Jewish Society, and with the household of Dr David Daube, a lecturer in Roman Law. As one of the few Jews in senior academic positions, he was deemed suitable by the university authorities for the mandatory supervisory office of Senior Treasurer of the society, the person ultimately responsible for its financial probity. Dr Daube and his wife Helga had, like me, come to England as refugees from Nazi Germany but, unlike my family, they were "*echt Deutsch*", German citizens of the Jewish faith, as many such people frequently termed themselves. Although hospitable and welcoming, hosting a number of Jewish students for tea every Shabbat afternoon, they were also more formal than either us *Ostjuden* or even the average British Jewish middle-class families of my acquaintance.

The guests, often as many as a dozen, sat around the sides of the drawing-room, little tables with sandwiches and biscuits dispersed between them. Once all the guests had arrived, we filed into the hall, where a bowl and a pitcher of water provided the means for the washing of hands that traditionally precedes (or should precede) the partaking of bread. We dutifully recited the appropriate blessing, then returned to take our first bite of bread before resuming the conversation that the ritual had interrupted. Mrs Daube poured the tea (there was never any alternative, partly because coffee was even more scarce than the rationed tea) and Dr Daube handed each student a cup, politely but firmly refusing the help we offered. Conversation continued, at first in somewhat subdued tones, our host sitting at one end of the room while his wife sat at the other. I don't recall the conversation ever being truly animated. Most of the undergraduates present were, like me, inhibited as much by the unaccustomed formality as by Dr Daube's scholarly commentary on Jewish texts, such as those that had been read at the morning's synagogue service. This monologue he interlarded with forced humour, as if he were himself aware of the need from time to time to lighten the tone of the occasion.

In the final term of my second year, when I was elected Junior Treasurer of the Jewish Society, I had cause to visit the Daube household more frequently and less formally. Only then did I discover that beneath the Teutonic formality lay a genuine kindness, a friendliness that spanned the generational gap and a very keen sense of humour, even of the ridiculous, absurd, "shaggy-dog" kind that is so often considered uniquely English. From this I gathered that the formal tea parties were as much of an ordeal for them as for their guests. They conducted them not for their own gratification, but out of a strong sense of duty, something that his status as one of the university's very few Jewish academics required of them.

The Daubes had a young son, about seven years old, precocious as only the sole child of highly intellectual parents can be. During the Long Vacations between the years I was at Cambridge it became a regular treat for me and one of my male friends to take him and the daughter of another Jewish, non-academic couple punting on the River Cam up to Grantchester for tea in the vicarage orchard memorialised in Rupert Brooke's most famous poem. This conventional outing, so frequent an occurrence for increasingly blithe students, acquired an aura of real adventure when undertaken with two youngsters who did nothing to hide the renewed thrill they were annually experiencing.

Looking back, I think I assumed that at Cambridge I would never experience anti-Semitism comparable to that at Aylesbury Grammar School. What in fact I encountered was a version far more subtle, less crude, less uninformed, less conscious, at times seemingly unintentional. The sense of difference I had first experienced when I came to Newnham for my interview marked my relations with some of my contemporaries, particularly those from the wealthy "county" stratum of British society. One fellow student of English was Margaret, the daughter of the aforementioned Basil Willey, a meticulous scholar whose lectures I attended in two consecutive years while he was writing the books that established his reputation. There was no special personal relationship between us, so I was gratified to find myself invited to her parents' home one evening towards the end of our first term, shortly before Christmas. When I came upon her at the 1998 celebrations I lost no time in asking her a question, the answer to which I had been seeking in vain for 54 years.

"What was the game we played at your home when you invited some of us over one evening?" I inquired, still vividly recalling the embarrassment, confusion and humiliation that had paralysed me as all those present – Margaret's parents and siblings, the five or six other Newnhamites and a number of Professor Willey's Pembroke charges – suddenly began running round and round the large dining-table that stood in the centre of the room, engaged in something which, to my uninformed eyes, resembled nothing so much as the chaotic Caucus Race in *Alice in Wonderland*. All the participants were obviously cognisant of the rules. I realised they assumed that if I was there I must be equally knowledgeable. Nobody volunteered any explanation or directives nor inquired whether anyone needed them. Ashamed of confessing ignorance, I had pretended my leg hurt and stood aside, excluded from the boisterous jollity, hoping that by watching what was going on I might glean some insight and be able, belatedly, to join in. But the general confusion made this an impossible mission and I felt that I was in some way failing my hosts' expectations.

More agony was to come. After the game, as we were drinking cocoa, hymnals were handed out. Professor Willey seated himself at the piano and invited us to form a circle around him. As if they had already rehearsed, Mrs Willey, her children and the students instantly divided into four vocal groups and began harmoniously singing Christmas carols with which I was totally unacquainted. I opted to join the alto group, trying my best to follow the unfamiliar tunes. The others were too musically gifted to have failed to notice my helplessness but no one said a word. Finally, however, I was able to redeem myself. As the singing petered out, I asked our host whether he was acquainted with a very short, very beautiful Latin hymn in praise of God that our excellent music teacher, Mr Pope, had taught us. Discovering, to my delight, that he was not, I was able to find it for him. He sightread the notes; I sang the descant. He expressed appropriate admiration and thanked me profusely for having introduced him to the work. I felt as if I had in some way succeeded in making myself acceptable. Nevertheless, I was never again invited to the Willey home and I assumed that this was because I had proved myself a gauche outsider. In the years that followed, the painful memory of that evening frequently recurred. Now, over half a century later, here in a marquee outside the Senate House, champagne glasses in hand, Margaret and I were on a more equitable status.

"What *was* that game?"

Margaret was at a loss as to what I was referring to but after a brief description of what I recalled of the players' movements, she and others in the group around her simultaneously broke out with, "Oh, you mean ping-pong". Ping-pong?

98

Table-tennis? But I knew how to play that. It was my turn to look puzzled. An explanation followed: this was ping-pong "on the move", the entire group being expected to return the ball from one side to the other, while running around the table. No wonder I had withdrawn, perplexed, at the very outset. I'd never before encountered so much as a description of, or reference to, this strange game and couldn't possibly have understood its rules without an explanation – and that had not been forthcoming, considered unnecessary because everybody else in the room that evening had been initiated into the game in early childhood.

Throughout the process of my enlightenment, Isabel Quigley had been standing next to Margaret. She seemed extraordinarily pleased to see me. While I had from time to time since leaving Cambridge read book reviews she had contributed to the *Observer* and other London publications, we hadn't met since 1947. Now she delighted me by crying out:

"Oh, I remember your father. He was such a nice man! So kind." What a sobering corrective to my erstwhile sense of inferiority! I now realised the full the extent to which unpretentious genuine feelings can impress themselves even on strangers. "Just be yourself", my father often exhorted me. But of course first one must know oneself and once I was in Israel I did.

Because of wartime restrictions and a depleted staff, all students ate only in Clough Hall, one of the College's four dining-halls, which was therefore uncomfortably crowded at mealtimes. Many of the Jewish students, me among them, chose to sit together. One morning during my first term, arriving at breakfast later than usual, I found there was room only at what was known as the "Bottom Table", which ran parallel to High Table at the opposite end of the Hall, where the dons sat, and at right angles to the long rows of tables at which there were enough seats for the majority of us. According to an unwritten law that had early on been imparted to us, the Bottom Table was reserved for the *crème de la crème* of Newnham society – the "county" set, daughters of wealthy, sometimes titled, landowners, who – were it not for the war – might be participating in the London "season", perhaps even being presented at Court. They wore cashmere twin sets and pearls, had carefully polished (but unvarnished) nails and knew "everybody". Their brothers had attended famous public schools and as a result these young women were socially self-assured, acquainted with numerous of their brothers' former schoolmates, who were now fellow students at Cambridge.

Having no other option, I took my rations of butter, sugar and marmalade from the central trolley on which they were kept and seated myself at the sacrosanct table. All our ration jars bore identifying labels inscribed with our names. These I duly set out in front of me. Suddenly a beringed hand reached across. The young woman opposite me turned my sugar jar in order to decipher my name. "MAHgulies," she drawled haughtily. "That's not an English name, is it?" Although unlike her, I was perfectly capable of reading upside down and though (indeed, because) I knew her name perfectly well, since even at this early stage in one's Newnham career one already knew all the names of the select 20 or so Bottom Table set, I couldn't resist following suit. Reaching across the table, I turned one of her jars around and retaliated in kind: "O'Brien! That's not an English name, is it?" I'd scored a point but I never again ventured to sit at the Bottom Table.

I did, however, frequently sit at High Table, to which four undergraduates were invited each evening to dine with the dons. Usually, one's turn came once or twice a year but already in my first term I found myself listed with alarming frequency. The only other student thus singled out was Princess Aida Desta, daughter of the exiled Abyssinian emperor Haile Selassie. Like me, she was reading English and, since she occupied a room near mine, we had ample opportunity for meeting. We were also usually invited to High Table together. Once, when the tintinnabulations of the dinner gong had subsided and we were waiting for the dons to arrive so that we could ascend the dais, she asked me why, in my opinion, we were so frequently honoured. The only reason that occurred to me was that we were both considered out of the ordinary but while it was clear why this should be so in her case, I could conceive of nothing comparably complimentary regarding myself. So I muttered something non-committal, though I secretly thought that we were both regarded as strangely exotic: unknown quantities who aroused curiosity and therefore needed to be closely studied, like some rare species of tropical plant that had found its way into an English garden. I soon discerned the difference in attitude towards me and Aida, for while she was clearly respected and deferred to in a manner appropriate to her royal status, I was alternately subjected to a barrage of questions or ignored.

Those were the days of rationing but at High Table some species of meat occasionally replaced fish or pasta as the main dish. In my case, this in turn would be replaced by a chunk of yellow cheese, which was unceremoniously placed in front of me with a disdainful air by one of the few maids still in employment. Almost inevitably there ensued the following conversation between a neighbour and me.

Don: "Oh, Miss Margulies, are you a vegetarian?"

Me (hesitantly): "Not exactly. I only eat kosher."

Don: "Oh, how interesting. What does that mean?"

Me: "It refers to meat slaughtered and prepared in a particular manner."

Don: "Really! You must tell me more about it some time. Am I correct in assuming you are" – slight pause – "Jewish?"

Me: "Well, actually, yes."

End of dialogue.

On occasion, if the don on my other side had not overheard this exchange, it was liable to be repeated with a new interlocutor, while my embarrassment at being "different" continued to grow as my misery intensified. Nor was that the end of it. After dinner, the four students singled out for the honour were invited for coffee in their respective tutors' studies. Miss Chrystal was knowledgeable about Judaism. Her field was Semitic languages; passionately philo-Arab, she was in consequence profoundly anti-Zionist. At our very first meeting she had elicited from me the fact that my father was a leader of religious Zionism in England and she apparently felt it her duty to ensure that I had such dangerous tendencies, which I presumably shared, shaken out of me.

And so, after each of my command performances at High Table, as we partook of coffee in her room, she would deliberately turn the conversation to what was currently happening in Palestine. When Labour came to power, Ernest Bevin unexpectedly continued the policy of appeasing the Arabs by limiting Jewish immigration from Europe, turning away Holocaust survivors seeking asylum in Palestine. Zionist passions rose to a fury. Armed Jewish opposition in Palestine increased; settlers defied the British edict by helping to smuggle illegal immigrants into the country. In London, marches culminated in mass demonstrations of protest in Trafalgar Square and the loyalty of British Jews was sorely tested, often to breaking-point. I wasn't even British and my own loyalties were firmly, undividedly Zionist but I was too intimidated by authority to dare speak out against the hostile tirades of Miss Chrystal. Her animosity steadily became more pronounced, as she voiced her pro-Arab, anti-Zionist views, occasionally turning to me as if goading me to retort. I did my best to respond politely yet assertively but the awe with which I always regarded those in authority, combined with my inability in such circumstances to argue cogently in favour of a Jewish homeland, more often than not left me tongue-tied. I fear that Miss Chrystal might thus have triumphantly construed my silence as acquiescence.

Among my fellow students in Clough but one year my senior was Louise Cole. Having discovered that her maternal grandmother was Jewish, she had herself become "Orthopraxis" and was indeed, like so many "converts", far more pious than those of us who, to the manner born, wore our religion more lightly. Her totally assimilated parents, appalled at the direction she'd chosen, had asked Miss Chrystal to drive this nonsense from her mind. Hence when on one occasion Louise, who was a fellow guest, ventured to intervene in what was clearly harassment, the cold response was:

"Really, Miss Cole, I don't see what you have to do with this." In duty bound, I informed Miss Chrystal when I became engaged to a young man named Sonny Bornstein. "Sonny is not a name," she countered, leading me to confess that his given names were Israel Isaac. Unwittingly betraying my own stereotypical perception I went on to add that he was commonly referred to as "Sonny", since these patriarchal names did not suit him. Her sneering comment, clearly in reference to his markedly Semitic appearance, was, "Oh yes, they do!"

Imagine my amazement, therefore, when, on visiting Newnham in the summer of 1950, I found a Miss Chrystal who was not only friendly but positively pro-Zionist. This transformation, it emerged, was the work of a visiting Fellow from Israel: Pepita Ezrachi, a philosopher who was at the time in residence at Newnham, a woman of great charm and beauty as well as of intellectual power, had succeeded where Louise and I had failed. Undoubtedly, the establishment of Israel as a state had also played a part; post-Holocaust awareness of Jewish suffering couldn't be ignored and provided a convincing argument in favour of ensuring a homeland for this hitherto homeless, wandering people. Miss Chrystal's gushing admiration of Pepita and of all things Israeli verged on the embarrassing, as she repeatedly expressed her happiness at the fact that I was now living in this admirable country. That was my first lesson in "The Power of One".

23 July 1946. The leisurely, lazy Long Vacation, when students may, if they wish, take advantage of college and university facilities to study at will, free of the demands of lectures, seminars or tutorials. *En route* to breakfast, I follow my customary practice of perusing the headlines of the newspapers that are every day laid out for us in the Common Room. On the faces of the three fellow students who have preceded me are unmistakeable expressions of horror. As I move to join them, all three turn their backs on me: a gesture of repulse and rejection. But perhaps I'm being paranoid? I approach the table. The front pages of all the daily papers bear the identical photograph: the demolished seven-storey South Wing of the King David Hotel, the headquarters of the British Mandate Government. The shaven-off remains of the building, the debris, the dead bodies – all recall

London's Blitz. The bold, black headlines identify the source and extent of the brutality.

"Jews slay British civil servants." "Over 60 killed by Zionist terrorists." "Brutal murder!"

I'm known as the mandatory signatory of all Jewish Society posters that I pin on notice- boards throughout the College announcing those of our activities that are open to the public. I don't stay to read the full reports. The headlines suffice. I share in the guilt – and the shame. Without a word – what is there to say by way of explanation or justification? – I flee the room and hasten, breakfast uneaten, out of College. I cannot face any more accusing faces. The final count of the dead is 91. Many of them are Jews. This was the first in a series of Irgun, or IZL, terrorist attacks that climaxed in the hanging of two young British sergeants in retaliation for the execution of two IZL activists. To this day these attacks are perceived (and, by some, justified) as having hastened British withdrawal from Palestine and hence the establishment of a Jewish state.

Lacking British nationality when I first went up to Cambridge, I had at the beginning and end of every term to report my arrivals and departures at the local police-station. Although the constables who dealt with me were unfailingly polite, I felt like a criminal on parole, whose lenient sentence might at any time be revoked, to be replaced by more severe sanctions. Not until the end of 1946 were my parents and I finally granted British citizenship; I was then able to dispense with my Polish passport. That black document with its gold-embossed eagle was at the heart of a minor international incident that occurred in the summer of 1946.

For the first time, my parents and I had gone on vacation in Europe. For several reasons they chose to go to Scuol-Tarasp in Switzerland. A spa at which they would be able to take the waters, it had a kosher hotel and lay close to the border with Italy. The last of these factors was the most important, since my parents intended to meet my youngest aunt, Lotte, who had spent most of the war years together with her husband and young son in hiding in Italy. My cousin Alex, serving in the Jewish Brigade that steadily worked its way northward after the Allied invasion, had found them in a refugee camp. As soon as possible after our arrival in the Engadin region, we set off on a bus for the Italian border. Our fellow travellers, neighbours who knew each other, chatted away in the local Romansh language, which for us was even less intelligible than Swiss-German. One by one along the route they alighted as they reached the tiny hamlet or lonely house where they lived. Finally, we were the only passengers. The driver seemed surprised. It was obvious that we were a rare phenomenon. With gestures, he inquired whether we wanted to continue travelling. Perhaps he thought we had come on a local sightseeing trip. We indicated that we did indeed want to go on and so we proceeded to the border. The bus stopped. The driver motioned us to get off and as soon as we did turned around and drove off at such alarming speed that I feared he had abandoned us at the site of an accursed bewitchment.

There was nothing but a stretch of barbed wire to indicate that this was the border between Switzerland and Italy. We detected a narrow gap in the wire. Beyond it, a small, unimpressive guard-post displayed an Italian flag. A soldier who looked so young that he might have been newly recruited from among the local schoolboys came out of the hut, straightening his dishevelled uniform, surprised to see us. With a certain hesitancy, he took his place behind the table that stood near the barbed wire. Without waiting to be asked, we presented our passports. Those of my parents were duly inspected and promptly stamped but when my turn came the young soldier scrutinised the opening pages intently, occasionally looking up to scan my features as if to ascertain that the colour of my brown hair and eyes was correctly described, and that the photograph, distorted as passport photos invariably are, nevertheless depicted a face recognisable as mine.

Then, "*Parli italiano?*" I nodded, hoping against hope that the vocabulary I had acquired at Newnham during the previous summer's course in Dante and Boccaccio would prove adequate.

"*Polacca?*" he asked. The word was not in my lexicon but I recalled my parents referring to their non-Jewish neighbours as Pollacks. The appellation clearly didn't apply to me. I shook my head. "*Sei nata in Polonia?*" he persisted, assuming from my momentary hesitation that I hadn't fully understood his previous question.

"No," I said, pointing to the place of birth in my passport: Essen, Germany.

"*Dunque tu sei tedesca!*"

It was so categorical a statement that I felt considerable embarrassment in contradicting him.

"No. I was born in Germany but I'm not German." I'd switched to English, having finally realised that the summer course had not prepared me for altercation with the Italian military.

"Ah," he said thoughtfully, as if reflecting on what was to all intents and purposes utterly incomprehensible. He switched track. "*Dove vivi?*"

"I live in London, *Inghilterra.*"

"*Ah, sei* English" he pronounced it with a very long "e": Eeeenglish. But I had to disappoint him once more. I was in despair. Slowly pronouncing each word as distinctly as possible I said sadly:

"No. I'm not English. I just live in England."

A long silence ensued as he studied the passport, generously granted to my stateless parents by the Polish government-in-exile, then resident in London. Finally, overwhelmed by the lack of clarity, the contradictory details, he went off to find a more senior official. My parents anxiously waited to see whether I would be allowed to cross into Italy with them. The time at which we were to meet my aunt was fast approaching. She would be worried by our non-arrival, fearing some mishap. The officer, resplendent in a light-grey uniform sporting a number of ribbons that presumably represented medals, knew no more English than his subordinate but he wasn't prepared to reveal his ignorance. With an impressive display of self-importance, he too paged through my passport, and duly scrutinised both my face and the pages giving essential identifying data. Then, with a smile, he stamped the passport, handed it to me with a courteous bow:

"*Prego*," he said and added just one more word. "*Arrivederci!*"

Inheritance. We set off on a blue-gold Sunday morning with no clear destination, no defined purpose other than to escape from the sun-baked metropolis: a tightly packed carload of young people, freshly minted graduates, enjoying our last summer of freedom before settling down to income-earning responsibilities. We had no specific goal. We had bathing costumes and towels in case we reached the sea. We had an ample supply of fruit and sandwiches. We knew that wherever we went in rural England we would find a pub to quench our thirst. The South Downs came to mind. Box Hill resonated for those of us who knew Jane Austen's *Emma*. Never mind, we said, we'll see what crops up. We crossed the Thames and headed south-east, avoiding what was then, in the late 1940s, considered a highway and choosing instead the less-travelled lanes and byways lined with hedges where wild flowers grew surrounding peaceful pastures of calmly grazing sheep and cows. A perfect day for aimless ambling.

Suddenly, a signpost with the familiar emblem of the National Trust: Knole House. I gasped in excitement.

"We have to go there."

Willy, who'd been reading some of the same books as me, at once understood. He knew the connection to Virginia Woolf's *Orlando*. Knole was the ancestral home of the Sackville-West family, the home of whose inheritance Virginia Woolf's lover, Vita, had been deprived only because she was a woman. The loss had been a tragedy for her. Neither my brother nor I had possessed the essential background knowledge when we first read the novel, spellbound by the luscious prose, the twists and turns of plot, the bisexuality of the protagonist (Vita, of course). Knole was an essential part of *Orlando*. Now we had a chance of seeing it, of visiting it and traversing its rooms, courtyards, galleries and formal gardens.

Knole is a "calendar" house: 365 rooms, 52 staircases, 12 entrances, seven courtyards. It is surrounded by 1,000 acres of wooded land, part of it a deer-park. At its heart lies the original, oldest part of the structure, built in the middle of the 15th century, around which successive generations added layer upon layer of accommodation. The long gallery is lined with portraits of these Sackvilles. Here is, as Virginia Woolf saw, a history of England that covers four centuries and more. We came out to the park, sated: five young Jews, three of us not born in England, the others children or grandchildren of immigrants from Europe. We decided to picnic right there, in the inviting shade of an enormous oak whose ample trunk indicated it might well be as old as the house itself. I lay stomach down, my face cradled in my arms. Though it was well after lunchtime, I had no appetite. I breathed in the sweet scent of the grass. Unlike that of the London parks, it smelled fresh and untrodden. For the first time in my life, I felt intense envy.

"Who is wealthy?" asked our ethical fathers, rhetorically, replying, "He who is happy with his lot."

It wasn't true or at least at that moment it appeared not to be true. What we had seen was true wealth, the wealth not only of property but of continuity, of knowing not only the names of one's great-grandparents and their forebears but knowing what they looked like, what they wore, what corridors they traversed, where they mounted their horses, danced to the sounds of the timbrel, made love; being able to visit their graves, pray in the pews in which they prayed. And us? My father had his father's Kiddush cup. My mother lit her Shabbat candles in the candlesticks her mother had brought from Galicia. We had no photographs of the *shtetl*s in which my parents were born. We were fugitives, constantly uprooted, forever on the move. Willy and I even had a mother tongue that was not the same as that of our parents. Indeed, what was their mother tongue? Yiddish, which their non-Jewish neighbours, born in the same country, neither spoke nor understood? Polish, to which they resorted when they didn't want us to understand what they were saying; the language of "*Pas devant les enfants*"? Certainly it wasn't English, which rapidly became my mother tongue after we left Germany, while Willy continued to count in German, to find pleasure in classic and contemporary German literature. Yet he never was and would never describe himself as German. In Germany, we were *Ostjuden*. From after the Second World War, when we finally attained British citizenship, we were always British, never specifically English. I mystified the guard at the border between Switzerland and Italy when I presented my passport – and no wonder. It was Polish.

Oh, for the serenity, continuity and stability of the Sackvilles and of Knole. Vita, banished from her beloved Knole, deprived of her legacy because of her gender, could fall back on property initially less beautiful and certainly of lesser personal sentimental value: Sissinghurst, a manor house at which Queen Elizabeth once spent three consecutive nights. Even older than Knole, it had not been as well maintained, because it never remained for long in the hands of one owner, but Vita and her diplomat-author husband Harold Nicolson created there what is undoubtedly the most original and beautiful of English country gardens. It seemed a fitting place to which to continue our day in the country.

The gardens were in full high-summer flower, laid out like a series of rooms, each one with a "door", a gap in a hedge in between beds of tall flowers, through which one glimpsed a vista of a neighbouring room, as in a picture gallery. Its abundant lushness, the vast variety of colours and perfumes, the tranquillity (there were few visitors) were at one and the same time paradoxically exciting and soothing. And because the creative project of reconstruction and renovation had been undertaken only some 20 years earlier, there was no evocation of a centuries-long family saga. Here was something I could cope with emotionally, though never emulate. A little garden of my own, even a small back yard, a balcony, somewhere where I could tend a few potted plants. And where I could be happy with my lot…

In the summer of 1946, members of the Cambridge University Jewish Society decided to host a group of young DPs who had been brought from Europe by the Federation of Jewish Relief Organisations to live at a shelter in Mansell Street in the East End of London. We had by now learnt something of what had occurred in Europe during the war. A few Jewish ex-servicemen who had served there after the Allied invasion had begun to drift back to studies. But as yet we had only a glimmering of what is today widely known about the activities of partisan fighters, life in the ghettos and death camps, and the annihilation of European Jewry. In the UK many citizens were still engrossed in licking their own wounds, incurred during the Blitz and the massive air-raids, the rocket attacks and incendiary bombings that continued even throughout the last months of the war. In London the shattered houses left gaps like those in the mouth of a septuagenarian fast losing her teeth. As a privileged group studying at one of the most ancient universities, we felt impelled to perform some good deed for those who we knew had suffered in some as yet only dimly comprehended manner.

On a gloriously sunny Sunday, eight of us set out for the station to meet 15 boys who were coming from London. We'd decided that every couple of students would host three or four of the visitors during the morning hours, give them lunch and show them the beauties of Cambridge's colleges, perhaps take them punting and then, at 4 pm, before accompanying them to the station, we would all meet for tea in the rooms of the president of the Jewish Society. None of us had thought through the implications of this meeting of two very disparate groups, who had nothing in common save their Jewishness. We'd not foreseen what an odd-looking bunch they would be: of indeterminate age, with shaven or close-cropped heads, clothes that were clearly hand-me-downs that hadn't been chosen by their wearers and hung loosely on their thin bodies as if waiting to be grown into; distinctly continental and so non-British in appearance that we became objects of curious stares from others on the platform and later in the town. We'd not anticipated that none of our guests would be able to speak English nor, in most cases, to understand all but the most basic and minimal phrases, even when eked out by gestures and sign-language. Above all, we hadn't realised how complete their lack of interest in the sights of Cambridge would be.

I was fortunate in being able to speak German but almost every one of them came from Eastern Europe and a broken Yiddish was the closest they came to speaking something I could comprehend. In any case, it rapidly became clear that they were not to be entertained with polite conversation, sightseeing or punting on the Cam. They wanted to eat – preferably meat. Still rationed and scarce, this was moreover not available in its kosher form until the evening hours, when Livingstone's Restaurant opened. With some effort, we succeeded in persuading the owner of the restaurant to understand our plight and open up for lunch, at which the boys wolfed down sausages, chips and cabbage salad in gargantuan quantities, and with so total an absence of table manners that the cutlery remained unused. After lunch, to the amazement of the few women in our group, the boys, who stubbornly rejected our attempts to revert to the original programme of activities, drew aside the male students and entered into rapid, though mainly one-sided "conversation", with much excitement and gesticulation. From some of their gestures, I could see they wanted cigarettes – items that none of us carried about us and which, like meat, were a scarce commodity. Some of the men set off to find a shop where they might buy cigarettes but on a Sunday in Cambridge this too proved difficult and time-consuming, though ultimately successful. Each of the boys wanted at least one entire packet and some of them were visibly displeased at being given far less.

The confidential consultations resumed as I and my women friends stood by, despondent at our exclusion. Then I noticed an expression of shocked surprise on the face of one of my male colleagues, a helpless look cast at another of the students, shrugs of disbelief, in one case even horror, followed, very clearly and visibly, by appalled disgust. As our visitors lingered aimlessly I went to find out what was happening. With some difficulty and enormous embarrassment, the president of the CUJS revealed that the boys wanted to visit a brothel. Our male companions apparently knew nothing of the whereabouts of such an establishment or, if they did, would certainly not have confessed to such knowledge. With obvious discontent and clear disappointment on one side and acute embarrassment and disbelief on the other, the visit drew to a close. We drank our tea and ate our sandwiches in almost total non-communication one side with the other, the boys joking and chatting in Polish and we valiantly striving to make polite conversation in English. A few of us, including me, volunteered to take them back to the station, where we bundled them into the train waiting at the platform and with sighs of relief returned to our secure middle-class normality.

For me, the encounter proved a turning-point. I spent the remainder of the summer vacation volunteering at the Mansell Street hostel, where my task was to accompany a 14-year-old on his twice-weekly bus trips across London to the Maudsley Hospital. Nobody at the hostel bothered to tell me why he had to attend the out-patients clinic at what I vaguely knew to be a mental hospital. The boy appeared to be in excellent health when I came to fetch him. Paradoxically, it was when he emerged from the treatment that he looked in need of it. His hair stood on end, his eyes were wild, frightened and frightening, his speech more incoherent than ever, a babbling, unfathomable mixture of languages, dialects, abrupt phrases, short, sharp yet muted cries and occasional stifled sobs. I'd sit with him in the corridor for a short while, waiting for a return to some degree of normality before venturing out to the bus-stop for the hour-long journey to his "home". At a loss as to how to respond, I said nothing, made no comment on the transformation he'd undergone while he was with the doctor. Eventually I realised he was having shock treatment. Gradually, as a result of lessons at the hostel, his English improved slightly. We learnt to communicate in an odd mixture of Pidgin, Yiddish and broken German. We became friends of a sort but with no trace of intimacy.

Why did I have so slowly to surmise the context of the drama in which I was an actor? Why, I now ask myself, were we so ignorant of what the survivors had experienced before they reached a safe haven? What were they now experiencing as orphans, facing an unknown future in a strange country, with a new language, different customs, a different climate? We didn't dare ask. We lacked the appropriate language, literally and metaphorically. There was a certain reticence resulting, on the one hand, from not wanting to intrude, to open slowly healing wounds and, on the other, from fearing what we might learn. I felt the guilt of "There but for the grace of God…" That sense of guilt grew even stronger once I learnt, as I soon did, of the almost certain fate of my paternal uncle, Mendel, who, with his wife Rosa and their three daughters, had in 1940 returned from refuge in France to my family's native Poland. All had been shot to death when that was still the prime method of extermination employed by the Germans. One of those three girls was the same age as my brother; another was a year older than me. Worst of all and hardest to come to grips with, even today, was my growing awareness of a startling paradox: while the extermination of European Jewry was in progress, I was enjoying what were undoubtedly the happiest years of my adolescence, safe and secure amidst the natural beauties of rural England.

In 1946, as summer was turning to autumn, I already knew a little more about the concentration camps and the horrors of extermination than I had known when I first encountered the DPs in Cambridge. I saw numbers tattooed on the arm of a young woman who came from Europe as one in a group of Jewish students to visit London. I didn't know whether I would be intruding on her privacy, stirring memories of a terrible chapter in her life she would prefer to forget. For her part, did she think me unfeeling and unsympathetic for failing to ask? Or was she among the thousands of victims of persecution who, as I later learnt, preferred not to talk about the past? We fortunate ones who had been spared the horror were treading on very thin ice, blundering in a wilderness, a bewilderment of ignorance, from which we were at a loss as to how to escape. So we remained tongue-tied, silent, unquestioning, uncomprehending.

I had been a Zionist from early childhood. Since the age of about six, when I danced a lone *horah* round the kitchen table singing, "*Anu olim artza livnot u'lhibanot ba*".* I had known I too would one day "go up" to Palestine, to the Land of Israel. Now I made the fateful decision to go there as a social worker, rehabilitate people like these youngsters and assist them in becoming useful, committed citizens, fellow builders of a new Jewish state that, together, we would help bring into existence. To my parents' surprise and despite my father's well-

---

* "We are going up to the Land, to build and to be built in it."

meaning proposal that I spend a year in Europe perfecting my knowledge of French and perhaps also Italian, I applied to the London School of Economics, completed my final year at Cambridge in great impatience and went on to take a post-graduate degree in social work.

Towards the end of my first year at Cambridge, three of us who had come up to read English were invited to after-dinner coffee with Beryl Paston-Brown. A Newnham graduate, she had been enlisted to replace Dorothy de Navarro, one of the university's very few married women dons, who had just given birth. In the course of the evening our hostess mentioned that she would be glad to leave Cambridge and return to her London post at Goldsmith's College. Taken aback by this strange preference for an institution that did not even grant a bachelor's degree, we asked for clarification.

"It'll be a relief to go back to teaching at a place where students know why they're studying," she replied.

In 1945, her comment, with its implied criticism of our dilettantism, was incomprehensible, even offensive, but I realised its full meaning the moment I stepped through the portals of the LSE in Houghton Street. A few yards from the Strand and in the heart of London's theatreland, the building was undistinguished and functional. It lacked the beauty of the Cambridge colleges and was architecturally less attractive than even London University's King's College, which stands on the banks of the Thames not far away.

At the LSE there was an energetic purposefulness. A sense of determined urgency found physical expression in the way the students bore themselves. There was none of the sophisticated languor cultivated by so many at Cambridge. Here the men and women seemed always to be hastening from one place to another or standing impatiently at the doors of the library or classrooms, waiting to be let in so that they might occupy the choicest seats. Satchels and briefcases, disdained as too bourgeois in Cambridge, bulged with files and books. There was no imposed uniformity of dress such as the black gowns that male Oxbridge students were obliged to wear at official events, lectures and daily college dinners. Instead, there was a dazzling cacophony of colourful and exotic native dress. Saris, sarongs, dashikis, achkan jackets, dhotis and Kufi hats reflected the brown, black and yellow faces, the ethnic mix of the student body, indicating that a considerable number of them came from the far-flung corners of the British Empire, the ongoing vastness of which – still marked in red on maps of the world that continued to appear inside notebooks and diaries – loomed as if unassailable.

Ironically, many of these students returned to their native lands well-qualified to lead their countries to independence: they became fighters for freedom from empire. They were already deeply involved in political action, as indeed were the majority of the school's British students. Of these there were few who were not members or adherents of a political party, the choice being primarily between Labour and communist, as befitted a college established by founders of the Fabian Society. I had never before met a paid-up member of the Communist Party, though I assume there might have been a furtive few at Cambridge.

The LSE was based on a clearly defined socialist ideology. Among the senior faculty were men who had been instrumental in formulating that ideology and actively involved in creating some of the institutions that sought to improve the lot of the working class, to provide services and amenities that were generally available only to the middle and upper classes. Their ideological earnestness similarly infused the Students' Union. Unlike that of Cambridge, its debates were not intended to vaunt oratorical skill or wit, nor did they deal with frivolities. Here, men and women passionately addressed real-life issues. Egalitarianism was an explicit social goal, extending beyond the notion of equality of class and opportunities to equality of the sexes. There were as many women as men among the student body; but while there were numerous women academics at junior level, there were still few among the professors. Many of my fellow students had already worked for their living – an aspect of life that comparatively few Cambridge undergraduates had to contemplate before completing their studies.

The post-war influx of ex-servicemen raised the average age far above that of my contemporaries at Cambridge and the number of what were correctly identified as "mature" students was further augmented by the fact that many of them had come to earn degrees after years of professional work for which they now sought academic accreditation. Others were changing from one area of specialisation to another. The programme in which I was enrolled was designated a postgraduate certificate in social work, though the wartime hiatus had led the school to relax the prerequisite of a degree, accepting due professional experience as a temporary substitute. Of the original founders of the LSE, only one, R.H.S. Tawney, was still teaching there. I never studied with him but recall his emerging from the lecture-halls building on Mill Lane at Cambridge, a short, thin figure, to rebuke, in the mildest possible manner, a group of boisterous undergraduates, me included, who were making too much noise under the window of the room in which he was teaching. "That was Tawney," one of us said, awestricken, as we guiltily crept away. I was surprised. I'd expected this giant scholar to be as magnificently impressive in stature as he was in the writing of history.

One of the great theoreticians of the Labour Party did teach us. Harold Laski, a professor of political science, lectured extempore, always starting precisely on time and ending with equal punctuality, having delivered a perfectly constructed, lucid presentation of his topic of the day. With a fine sense of drama, he would from time to time histrionically punctuate his perorations by delicately raising a glass of water to his lips and taking a sip before delivering the climactic high point of his sentence. When he gave the final, brilliant, summarising lecture in a series that marked the centenary of the 1848 revolutions, the largest of all the halls was so overcrowded that his talk had to be relayed to two additional rooms to hold the overflow audience. I was in one of these similarly overcrowded rooms, where the audience sat as if entranced by Laski's capacity for seeing the "pattern in the carpet", the entire forest and not merely the individual trees, each of which had been well described and analysed by one after another historian or political scientist. Indeed, he dealt not only with the past but also with the future, in which he saw a lurking danger of totalitarianism no less deadly than National Socialism. He ended with the prophetic closing lines of Yeats's "The Second Coming", which chillingly refer to "that great beast, its hour come round at last", that "slouches towards Bethlehem to be born".

Another professor, Norman Ginsberg, who profoundly influenced me and had a more immediate impact on my professional development, was also Jewish but in every other respect differed greatly from Laski. He was quiet, slightly balding, with a fringe of grey hair. Calm and gentle, he did not so much lecture as talk to us in an almost conversational tone, encouraging questions and comments, to which he responded patiently. His introductory lectures to social psychology and social philosophy were well-planned and lucid but he was prepared to go off at an angle if he perceived from a student's question that he had not been fully understood. He seemed in all modesty to assume that the fault lay with himself rather than with the student. While I have an entire quarto file of notes from Ginsberg's courses, I have none at all from Laski's. Becoming acquainted for the first time, at first hand rather than through random discussion, with the theories of Freud, Jung, Adler, Melanie Klein and other pioneers and practitioners of psychoanalysis was exciting. Through them, I developed new insights into human behaviour, including my own, even more profound than those I had derived from literature. They added to my appreciation of the deeper meanings of texts I had studied, in particular the novels of George Eliot and Henry James.

I was inspired by my studies. An entire world of intellectual thought and political activity was opened up for me to contemplate and engage in. Whenever my fairly demanding lecture schedule permitted, I was in the library, or in the common room with my colleagues, a socially varied group unlike the Cambridge élite, often in a state of intense intellectual fervour. Like Keats when he first read Chapman's Homer, I sailed on wide oceans of knowledge I had never hitherto discovered. Intellectually, politically, culturally and socially these were the two most stimulating years of my life. I followed with enthusiasm and excitement the steady flow of legislation that created Britain's Welfare State. Walking down Kingsway from Tottenham Court Road, where the family car that carried my father and brother to work in Holborn dropped me off every morning, I would stop at His Majesty's Stationery Office to purchase the latest of the White Papers that detailed the new laws and services. They outlined a brave new world, one in which we – the younger generation of economists, planners, sociologists and social workers – would play a vital role.

As a child I had encountered beggars. They came to our door requesting alms. In tattered clothes, men sat on the pavements of shop-lined streets, cap in hand. Numerous permanently disabled ex-servicemen, sad survivors of what was still referred to as the Great War, blind, crippled, some with wooden stumps instead of legs or arms, hoped for pity from passersby. Some attempted to heighten their appeal by playing an accordion or singing tonelessly. Today, I think of them whenever I hear Schubert's mournful evocation of the organ-grinder in the snow. Now I became acquainted at close hand not only with the dire poverty, the sickliness, malnutrition and misery that lay behind the doors of houses in London's working-class districts and slums but also with the harsh and unsympathetic treatment too frequently accorded to inmates of orphanages, poor-houses and other institutions designed to keep society's outcasts, the "undeserving poor", out of sight. Numerous charities that presented themselves as enlightened, gentle and kind were in fact cruel. Touring one of Dr Barnardo's Homes for Boys, my fellow students and I were appalled by the punishment meted out to boys who wet their beds: the culprit was made to stand in a corner with the wet sheet draped over his head. Clearly, there was no understanding of child psychology, of the effects that the very fact of living in an institution, without parental love, must have on the youngsters. Since we were visitors, we couldn't make comments or suggestions. All we could do was resolve that, once qualified, we'd do our best to change such unfeeling systems.

My first summer assignment, even before I began formal studies, was to serve as assistant to a juvenile probation officer in a working-class district in south

London. On my first day in her office, prior to setting out on the daily round of home visits, she gave me a batch of files to peruse, each on one of the young offenders under her supervision. Many dealt with comparatively petty misdemeanours, such as theft or truancy. Some referred to family dysfunction, violence and assault. As I read the descriptions of conditions in the home, the number of family members of both sexes who shared beds, the unemployment or drunkenness of parents and older siblings, I was startled to note how many of the girl probationers referred to having been "interfered with" by one or another of their male relations. Ignorant and inexperienced as I was, I only gradually began to realise that they were in fact euphemistically referring to sexual harassment, assault or rape. Some of them, all under the age of 18, had already undergone abortions, which remained illegal until 1967. They were as much victims as offenders, helplessly trapped in an environment to which official sources offered little hope of betterment. Some were repeat offenders, who risked imprisonment if their continued misdemeanours became known to the authorities. The majority were trying as best they could to mend their ways, though uncooperative parents, unruly, unsympathetic siblings and hostile neighbours constantly conspired to set obstacles in their path to improvement.

A sympathetic and compassionate listener, my mentor at the south London office did her best to provide not only verbal encouragement but also practical assistance. Yet she was ultimately limited in her ability to procure the financial support that alone could have facilitated escape into a more congenial environment in which these young people might achieve salvation. Ironically it was sometimes only by confining them to borstal that one could ensure rehabilitation and emergence into employment and self-improvement.

The Family Welfare Association, at whose Hammersmith office I spent my long summer vacation, was more fortunate than the government-operated social services. While its most frequent *modus operandi* ultimately led to referring clients to the appropriate authorities, which its case-workers helped to identify, it was itself a non-governmental organisation independent of government funding. I soon learnt that the best and quickest way of achieving cooperation from my clients was by agreeing to grant the financial means to deal with the issue that had ostensibly led them to the FWA. Here, I was soon left to my own devices, with only minimal guidance from the two impressively competent women who ran the office, who quickly came to appreciate my rapid understanding of the work: initial intake-interviews, investigation of the circumstances that had led the client to apply to us, home visits, writing up and filing the fullest possible reports so as to enable whoever succeeded me to continue dealing with the case without interruption and without needing to repeat what had already been ascertained or accomplished.

I worked five days a week from nine in the morning until five in the afternoon, sometimes staying on in order to meet an applicant who for some reason was unable to come earlier. I visited lonely old ladies for whom my weekly visits constituted a rare contact with the outside world other than their brief daily chat with whoever was on duty delivering their meals-on-wheels – a task in which I occasionally joined other volunteers. One housebound octogenarian plied me with stale, dry and unpalatable home-baked aniseed biscuits, which she insisted I consume immediately, thus making evasion impossible. I intervened with hard-hearted landlords threatening their tenants with eviction if they failed to pay the weekly rent. I listened sympathetically to the tearful tales of women deserted by or divorced from husbands who refused to contribute child-support. I learnt a great deal about the "real world" that lay beyond my own limited boundaries.

My mother expressed consternation whenever I reported my activities. How could her daughter, so young and trained in virtuous middle-class Jewish behaviour, possibly cope with situations and people so unfamiliar to her? She became concerned about my moral and physical welfare, yet she was as proud as I was when I was able to report on the final interview with my FWA mentors. It was their practice to convey to each of the trainees, in a private conversation, the contents of the evaluation they would be sending to our supervisors at the LSE. They were unstinting in their praise of my work. As the senior of the two put it, "We thought at first that the speed with which you learnt the ropes and went about your work was a sign of superficiality but we soon realised you were indeed outstanding in your grasp of the problems and your ability to deal with them". At last I felt totally justified in having defied my parents' suggestions that I spend time in Europe to perfect my knowledge of French and Italian before taking up a career appropriate to "a nice Jewish girl" prior to her marriage. I had found my métier.

Nights at the Opera. "Most people live on food and drink," my father would say, "but Alice lives on theatre." Though his tone was indulgent, he would sometimes wistfully add, "Thank Heavens there's Shabbat. Then we can see her." He was right. I was stage-struck, intoxicated, an insatiable consumer of the cultural riches being served up all around me. The LSE is located just around the corner from Aldwych Theatre, down the road from the Strand and a short walk from Covent

Newnham College students in front of Clough Hall, Summer 1946.

By the lake in Emmanuel College, 1946.

With fellow students at LSE, 1948.

With Sonny Bornstein, 1946.

My beloved Hebrew teacher,
Shlomo Auerbach.

With Dalia Katz in Genoa, October 1949, being seen off for Israel by Willy.

Moshe on the cargo boat that brought him to Israel in October 1949.

Avalon Krukin in Paris, wearing my yellow raincoat.

In our Alfassi Street bedroom.

The Wedding, October 10, 1950. Standing with us are Uncle Alex and Aunt Stella.
Front row (l – r), Harry, my mother, Sadie and my father.

Listening to the Rebbe of Przemysl who had, thirty years earlier, officiated at my parents' wedding in Mannheim.

After the Chuppah.

Dancing with my father.

Harry and Sadie at Stansted airport, seeing us off to our honeymoon in Paris.

With the baguettes.

Moshe on the Arc de Triomphe.

Willy visits Jerusalem, Spring 1951.

With Yitzhak and Etty Rischin.

Back in Jerusalem after the wedding…   Photos by Gan Studio

In pensive mood. Early 1960s.   Serving in the IDF Rabbinate.

In Moshe's "hippy" period, 1973. (Photo Leonard Wolf.)

Teaching at the Hebrew University, caught on camera by my student Ran Eliraz.

English Department Purim Party, 1954. In centre, Adam Mendilow with Yehuda Amichai as Caesar at extreme right.

At Purim parties held by Moshe's place of employment: Indians.

Japanese.

Queen Elizabeth and Walter Raleigh, 1967.

Hippies.

Garden. Since classes ended at six, there was ample time to reach one's destination in time for "Curtain Up!" Tickets were cheap and while we would have to reserve them well ahead for Covent Garden, at all other theatres we could, already in the morning, book a little numbered stool that served as a proxy in the queue outside the box office, to be reclaimed shortly before sale of tickets began. We just had to hope that sufficient seats would remain and that we'd be among the lucky first comers.

Only for the highly popular Proms at the Royal Albert Hall, performed daily for two months each summer, does one have to stand in line for the cheapest tickets, which couldn't be booked in advance. These tickets didn't qualify the purchaser for a seat. Rather, as the very name of the series suggests, one had to stand or move around. Ushers promptly reprimanded anyone who dared to sit on the floor, save in the interval. Fortunately, the programmes were so stimulating that we rarely and barely felt fatigue. London's world of entertainment and culture had been kept alive throughout the war, though in a muted manner. Now it flourished, bursting forth in a great wave of interpretative creativity, a renaissance that produced some of the finest artists in the world. Resumption of international travel brought guest performers and even entire companies to reinforce native talent. Sitting up in the gods was cheap but on occasion entailed paying an additional albeit non-monetary price, as I learnt after a performance of Richard Strauss's *Salome* by the Vienna State Opera.

Driving back home from Covent Garden with my parents and Willy, who'd been sitting in better and more expensive seats, we were unanimous in our enthusiastic appraisal of the entire production. None of us had ever before seen or even heard the work. We were particularly bewitched by Ljuba Welitsch's passionate interpretation of the title role. Her flame-red hair and voluptuous body, the necrophiliac mixture of lust, longing and vengeance with which she crouched over the bleeding head of Jokenaan which Herod awards her after her seductive "Dance of the Seven Veils", and, above all, the powerful voice that soared above the orchestra – all these excited us beyond measure. One after another and sometimes all together, we babbled, bubbled, rhapsodising over what we had experienced. Then, as the initial flurry of emotion died down, my brother added, as if by way of final comment:

"And that moon!"

"Moon?" I was bewildered. "What moon?" Now it was his turn to be puzzled.

"What do you mean 'What moon?' Didn't you see it? It was there the whole time. How could you have missed it?" We eventually solved the mystery: I had been sitting too high up. The proscenium stage had obstructed my view of the upper part of the set. Only after we arrived home and I had taken my copy of Oscar Wilde's text from its shelf and read the detailed stage-directions did I become aware of the theatrical significance of the blood-red moon that slowly traverses the sky in the course of this drama of craving and revenge. Perched in the back row of the Upper Gallery, I had missed that element in the potent mix of music and movement. But what could one expect for two shillings and sixpence?

On another occasion even sitting in a better seat exacted a price, albeit of an emotional rather than financial nature. Long boycotted because of its association with Hitler and Nazism, Wagner's *The Ring of the Nibelungs* had its first post-war revival at Covent Garden in January 1948, with two great European singers, Kirsten Flagstadt and Hans Hotter, in the roles of Brünnhilde and Wotan. Willy bought expensive grand-tier tickets for the entire cycle. On successive evenings, beginning at the unusually early hour of 5 pm, the four excruciatingly long performances, physically trying for singers and audience, were punctuated by two intervals, themselves sufficiently extended to allow the wealthier spectators to partake of fortifying pre-ordered dinners served below the vast, impressive, glowing crystal chandelier of the bar. It was *de rigueur* to dress well when one had good seats. I wore an elegant new navy-blue suit and a white broderic anglaise blouse for *Das Rheingold*. I hadn't anticipated that those seated all around us, as well as those in the orchestra stalls below, would be in full evening dress. My brother's lounge suit, though tailor-made of fine cloth and well-fitting, stood out embarrassingly among the dinner jackets and black ties, while I squirmed under the disapproving, disdainful gazes directed at my inappropriate attire. We didn't belong.

Settling nervously into my seat, I noticed that the two elderly bejewelled ladies at my side were training their opera glasses at the Royal Box directly opposite. Following their gaze, I saw that the Earl of Harewood had entered, accompanied by a very attractive, dark-haired young woman. After extended scrutiny one of my neighbours turned to her companion and, in a voice oozing with contemptuous distaste, declared, "Her name is STEIN". She drew out the two vowels "Sty–en" as if to emphasise how foreign, non-Anglo-Saxon – and Jewish – the name was. There was no need to enlarge any further. I was relieved that they were unaware that the name of their neighbours was the even more unpronounceable Margulies.

The Earl of Harewood was already perceived as an aberration among the members of the Royal Family. While a prisoner-of-war in Germany, he had been "indoctrinated" with a love of classical music, especially opera, on which he was now sufficiently expert to have launched a new monthly magazine. Unlike his cousin the queen, who made only extremely rare appearances at Covent Garden, primarily when her royal duties demanded that she accompany visiting monarchs or heads of state, the earl appeared to have no interest in horses. His attachment to a foreign-born Jew (whom he subsequently married) marked him, too, as a misfit, like us. When I next saw the Earl of Harewood, at even closer quarters, he was standing at the head of the staircase of Edinburgh's Usher Hall, waiting like a host to receive friends, before a La Scala performance of Verdi's *Requiem*. He looked magnificent in a kilt, complete with sporran, knee-length socks and all the other paraphernalia of Scottish gentry, as to the manor born – more like the "real thing", these ladies would undoubtedly have thought. Ironically, the Steins had in fact converted to Christianity well before Marion met her husband-to-be. As with other German Jews, their conversion didn't in any way decrease the opprobrium and hostility of pure-blooded gentiles, who were in all probability relieved when the couple divorced and Harewood married a genuine Englishwoman from the ranks of the landed gentry.

Fortunately, there had been an earlier occasion on which anti-Semitism was noticeably absent. It lingers in my memory as a kind of counterweight to my recollection of the Wagner incident. In September 1947, the Vienna State Opera came for a three-week season at Covent Garden and I first became acquainted with Mozart and Beethoven sung in the original languages, live on stage. Such bliss! By way of exception, my parents invited me to join them in the stalls for *Don Giovanni*. It was the end of Shabbat and we arrived at almost the last minute. There was a perceptible buzz, some unusual, additional excitement among the audience. This evening a guest singer would appear in the role of Don Ottavio. As the lights went down there came an announcement: the guest would be none other than Richard Tauber, the tenor famed for his interpretations of Mozart, considered second only to the great Caruso.

Half-Jewish, Tauber had in 1938 fled Vienna, where he was one of the company's stars. In England, where no grand opera was performed during the war, he'd been reduced to producing and performing in a number of the operettas that were so popular in his native land. Unfamiliar to British audiences, these primarily drew nostalgic fellow refugees. Now, back on the stage of a grand opera house, Tauber was an ardent Don Ottavio, singing with perceptible emotion, drawing long, show-stopping applause after each of his two passionate arias. As he appeared for his final curtain calls, there were prolonged, repeated "Bravos". The audience was reluctant to let him go. When the entire cast came onstage to make their collective bows, they joined in the applause. Turning in elation to my parents, I saw tears in my mother's eyes and I recalled, as she and my father must have been recalling, their frequent listening to, and singing along with, the record we had in Germany of Tauber singing his most famous, sentimentally nostalgic signature song:

Wien, Wien, nur du allein,
Sollst stets die Stadt meiner Träume sein!...
Dort, wo ich glücklich und selig bin,
Ist Wien, ist Wien, mein Wien!

Vienna, city of my dreams...

That world was gone. In tune with its disappearance, Tauber the following week underwent an operation in which half of a cancerous lung was removed. The *Don Giovanni* of 27 September had been his final performance. He died soon after.

In December 1946, at the end of my term as president of the Cambridge Jewish Society, I went to Basel with my parents to attend the 22nd Zionist Congress. My father, a delegate representing the Mizrachi movement, had participated in the pre-war congress and was a member of the Jewish Agency's Actions Committee. We stayed at the Hotel Drei Könige, where Herzl had lodged in 1897 when, in the course of the First Zionist Congress, he had been immortalised in a photograph that showed him standing lost in thought or dreams on the bridge over the Rhine, next to the hotel. This first post-war, post-Holocaust convention of world Jewry was intensely emotional: it made us acutely aware of the horrendous extent and nature of the extermination of two-thirds of Europe's Jewish population, and its once flourishing culture. Unmediated encounters with survivors of death camps and partisans who had against overwhelming odds courageously fought Nazism forcefully brought home to me how fortunate we had been in escaping in time to the safety of Britain. Listeners sobbed throughout the roll-call of the destroyed communities and the horrifying numbers of their victims enumerated. Many of those present had, like my parents, lost members of their family.

120

Yet the suffering that had so recently afflicted our people did nothing to deter the various factions within the World Zionist Organisation from continuing their internecine wars regarding the future of the movement and its goals: a state on both sides of the Jordan, as the revisionists vociferously demanded, or contentment with only that part of the Palestinian land that lay to the east of the river; the nature of the struggle for statehood (should it include so-called "terrorist" activities against the British troops and civil servants who controlled the country and who were perceived as markedly pro-Arab, as well as against Arab insurgents themselves, or should it be conducted so far as possible by diplomatic means?); the most effective way of contending with the British limitation of Jewish immigration demanded by the Arabs, which entailed the interception of ships carrying survivors and confinement of those on board in camps in Cyprus.

Combined with personal rivalries (like that between the venerable president of the movement, Chaim Weizmann, who had successfully negotiated with the British to issue the Balfour Declaration in 1917, and David Ben-Gurion, who was the leading political figure in the Yishuv, (the Jewish population of Palestine), these highly controversial topics led to verbal attacks by one faction on another. Ideological and political differences, as well as clashes of personality, were destined to be a hallmark of the Jewish people, as they had been throughout our history. I was aghast at the violence, verbal and even physical, that marked the impassioned debate, most of it in the bastard language known as Congress-Deutsch, a mixture of Yiddish and German. I was appalled by the fact that Jews were fighting Jews, despite their common goal of establishing a Jewish state. And I was saddened by the fact that Weizmann, who had done so much to bring about the years of grace during which the British mandate initially ruled Palestine, was compelled to resign because of his "Anglocentric" point of view. His downfall struck me as every bit as tragic as that of Brutus or Coriolanus. His departure was especially hard to accept since nobody was elected to fill his place as president of the World Zionist Movement, thus creating a void of widely accepted leadership at a time of grave crisis in the annals of the Land and of the people.

Meanwhile, I was embroiled in my own controversies, as a delegate to what was termed the "Junior Congress", where a heated debate led me to take a firm public stance that was far from universally accepted in the movement. The issue at hand was what constituted *halutziut* – pioneering – and hence what the desirable attributes of those who wished to immigrate to Palestine were, at this time of restricted immigration and in the future, when an independent sovereign state was finally established. The commonly accepted ideal of a *halutz* was of a person who would work the land, transforming the barren into the fruitful. Hence, essential preparation for *aliyah* was by participating in a *hachshara* training programme, such as that which a number of my cousins had undergone before moving to Palestine, where they joined or helped establish a kibbutz, the collective commune based on the Marxist principle of "To each according to his needs; from each according to his ability". Although all the *kibbutzim* were economically based on agriculture, many of the members, including my cousins, had also acquired a skill that would be essential to the everyday operations of the collective: one had studied carpentry, another plumbing and yet another basic electrical engineering. Like most women, my cousin Hilde, the would-be dancer, trained in vegetable gardening and childcare.

Not only did I have no taste for collective life in which all property, including clothing, was shared; I also had no intention of taking up agriculture. I argued that the country needed professionals such as engineers, teachers and doctors, and also artists of all kinds, working in a variety of media to create a rich, stimulating culture such as had always characterised Jewish communities, even in the ghettos. Unwittingly, I was expressing the philosophy of the organisation, Professional and Technical Workers Aliyah (or PATWA), whose representative warmly seconded my argument. At the same time I was betraying the principles of the *Brit Halutzim Datiim*, the Union of Religious Pioneers, of which I was a card-carrying member. I found myself attacked by the representatives of my movement, who branded me a bourgeois traitor to their cause. Nevertheless, I stood my ground and was soon vindicated by my own experience, in the course of my first visit to Palestine a year later, during the Christmas vacation of 1947.

All but one of my father's family had succeeded in leaving Germany before the outbreak of war. Apart from one brother, who with his entire family emigrated to the US, all had reached Palestine, thanks to the immigration certificates my father — ironically, the only truly committed Zionist in his generation — had succeeded in obtaining for them. We arrived at Lydda after a long, gruelling journey that entailed stopovers in both Geneva and Rome. The as yet unpressurised aeroplane bumped up and down with such violence that all of us were so sick as rapidly to exhaust the supply of brown sickbags provided in the seat pockets in front of us. My father at once prostrated himself on the tarmac to kiss the sacred soil of the Holy Land. Throughout our stay he maintained and expressed in every word and gesture his elation and profound feeling of religious awe at being in the land so frequently referred to in Jewish prayer, in a country where feet trod on the same sacred ground as the great Biblical figures. After a lifetime spent in countries where Jews sought to conceal their religion, he was thrilled to see men walking home from synagogue wearing their *talitot* (prayer-shawls). Lydda airport was distinctly primitive: an unimpressive shed, with a counter running along one side at which sullen Arab customs officials insisted on opening and rifling through all our suitcases and, on the opposite side, the British immigration officers who assiduously checked our passports to ensure there were no illegal immigrants among us.

It was a strange transitional time in Palestine's history. Less than a month earlier, the UN had voted in favour of partition and the establishment of a Jewish and an Arab state within the borders ruled by the British Mandate. The vote (that many Jews thought would never have been favourable had it not been for the guilt implanted in the consciences of so many states by the Holocaust) would bring about the fulfilment of the Zionist dream. But there was an interim period, a kind of twilight zone, to be lived through before the reluctant British withdrawal. Meanwhile, the Arabs had intensified their armed resistance to Jewish statehood. Lydda was an Arab town. As we drove the short distance to the safety of Tel Aviv we were warned to keep our heads as low as possible, in case shots were levelled at us *en route*.

In Tel Aviv, the euphoria evoked by the UN vote of 29 November was still evident. There was a purposeful energy there. Houses were shooting up, sparkling white in the bright Mediterranean sunshine that heightened the blue of the ocean with an intensity never seen in England. I'd not expected the sun to be so blinding, the sky so cerulean, the sea so calm. For the first time, I fully comprehended the veracity of the Provençal works of the Impressionists, of Matisse, van Gogh, Duffy. The friendly informality was also refreshingly different from British stiffness. Nobody wore ties, hats or gloves. Shorts and open-necked shirts constituted the everyday garb for men of all ages. I was overwhelmed with happiness, not least because I discovered a new affinity with two of my older cousins: the beloved Alex, currently on leave from his kibbutz to study architecture at the Haifa Technion, and his younger brother Adolf (now known by his Hebrew name of Avraham) who, similarly released from his collective Kfar Giladi in the Upper Galilee, was studying at the movement's teacher-training seminary in Tel Aviv. I'd not known Avraham at all in Mannheim. Shy and reserved, perhaps because he suffered from a congenital limp, he'd never spoken to me on the rare occasions when he came home from the pioneer centre at which he was being trained as a plumber – an occupation then considered immeasurably more essential than teaching for the future of Jewish settlement in Palestine. Now we discovered a common love of art and music. He took me to a Saturday evening chamber-music concert at the diminutive Tel Aviv Museum, where the same programme was given twice in succession to accommodate as many as possible of those eager to hear it, and he went to great lengths to obtain a rare ticket to a Palestine Philharmonic concert at which Molinari conducted Beethoven's 5th Symphony.

Himself a gifted amateur artist, he later sent me a detailed analysis, with sketched illustrations, of the composition of van Gogh's "Starry Night", in response to my complaint (after seeing an exhibition of van Gogh's work in London) over what seemed to me its kitschiness. In all likelihood seeing this work reproduced on the walls of innumerable Cambridge undergraduate rooms had led me to perceive the painting as clichéd. In addition to developing an entirely new relationship with Avraham, I resumed acquaintance with the cousins who were nearer my own age, including those who had excluded me from their play in Mannheim. Because none of my uncles had found a source of steady income in Palestine and were, indeed, all dependent on their youngest brother Alex, the daughters had left school at the age of 16 to earn a livelihood. They were fluent in English and Hebrew, as well as German, which they continued to speak at home. Having attended commercial schools, they were also efficient in all aspects of secretarial work, including shorthand in both languages. While I had the advantage of a university education, I rapidly discovered that my cousin Margot (Miriam) was no less well-read and it was in fact on her bookshelves that I first encountered the works of the anthropologists Margaret Mead and Ruth Benedict. The oldest of my cousins, Edith, who was my brother Willy's age, was already married. She took me under her wing when I decided to buy some fashionable clothes – items that in England were still obtainable only in exchange for coupons.

For my mother it must have been a novel experience to meet the sisters-in-law who had in the past so tormented her. She now had a new identity, as the wife of a comparatively wealthy businessman who could afford to be extremely generous to his siblings. When he saw the scant number of chairs in the two-room apartment of *Tante* Etti, my father bought a new set of six that enabled the entire family to gather there. My hardworking mother found it surprising that my aunt Esther, who had also lived in Essen, was continuing her erstwhile practice of dressing formally to take daily afternoon coffee with her daughters at one of Tel Aviv's most esteemed cafés. Lack of money had rendered all the women skilful at smelling out bargains. Leather handbags could be freshened up; a twice-weekly "combing out" at the hairdresser maintained one's elegance; there were small wholesale outlets where clothing could be bought at bargain prices.

124

In addition to saving wherever possible, two families derived an income from letting one of the three rooms in their apartment. Every evening the living-room sofa was opened up to serve as a double-bed for the parents, while the two daughters in each household shared a room. The only reason why *Tante* Etti didn't have a lodger was that one of her two rooms was occupied by Hilde and her husband – an uncomfortable and undesirable arrangement that eventually led them to divorce. In comparison with this Spartan accommodation, our own modest suburban four-bedroom house took on palatial proportions. I assume that my parents, accustomed to reading and other intellectual pursuits, must have been taken aback to discover that the favourite leisure occupation of these same two families was card-playing, in which they engaged on at least two evenings every week and in which they expected my parents to join them. In retrospect, I find it strange that they didn't feel it necessary to spend the time either in reminiscing about their shared past or in catching up on the momentous events, personal and national, they had experienced since they had last been together.

My cousin Hilde, who'd fulfilled her dream of becoming a dancer and had attained considerable renown in comic roles at the opera, had married a talented but penniless artist who specialised in working for the theatre. He'd designed sets and costumes for the works in which she appeared. Unable to make an adequate living, he was performing at a café – the very same that my aunt and cousins frequented – asking patrons to come forward and draw a line of whatever shape on the large sheet of paper clipped to his easel. From that scant beginning he created an entire, amusing, cartoon-like drawing. The rapidity, skill and humour of his work brought gratifying rounds of applause. Our family, who'd come only because my parents had invited them to join us as their guests, were clearly impressed by the success of someone whom all of them had contemptuously dismissed as a ne'er-do-well. Even his formidable mother-in-law perceptibly softened her customary aggressive tone when she joined in congratulating him as he took his place at our table after the performance. Hilde beamed with proprietary pride.

British troops and the Palestinian police were still in the country, many of them resentful, angry and lusting to vent their hatred of the Jews, others fearful that Jewish "terrorists" might continue to attack British targets even though the desired goal of establishing a Jewish state was now clearly attainable. Yet others were bored, waiting impatiently for the day – the precise date of which was as yet uncertain – when they could go home. Although there were none posted in the all-Jewish city of Tel Aviv itself, I had several opportunities to encounter the

British. On Christmas Day, a day that, in Jewish townships, was in no way distinguished from others, we visited the coastal resort of Nethanya. As yet very small, it had a high street that served as the shopping centre running down to the sea and a number of modest villas located above the beach. Walking back from the beachfront to our car during the siesta hours between two and four when businesses were closed, we saw a group of inebriated soldiers standing outside a souvenir shop, one of them holding a large stone with which he was evidently about to smash the glass window. Unhesitatingly, my father approached him, told him we were from England, asked where he and his comrades were from, and undertook to contact each one's family upon our return to London. At once, the atmosphere changed, the boredom and anger were dispelled, and the soldiers and we went on our way, delighted by the outcome of the encounter.

Some days later, travelling by taxi to Haifa to visit my cousin Alex and his family, we found ourselves driving behind a British army lorry carrying a group of soldiers who had a machine-gun facing the traffic behind them. Our driver, anxious to be out of the way of danger, sought several times to overtake the lorry but each time found himself unable to do so because of oncoming traffic. The soldiers became increasingly tense every time the taxi returned. After the third attempt to overtake, they aimed the machine-gun straight at us, one of them poised ready to shoot if necessary. When the elderly man sitting next to the driver put his right hand into his inner breast pocket, the soldier prepared to fire but just at that moment the passenger extracted his British passport and waved it frantically, to show that we were not terrorists intending to attack. At once, looks of relief spread on all faces, as the soldiers waved back, cheering, while we, similarly, breathed sighs of relief at having been spared. For me, that episode served not only as an indication of the mutual fear that reigned in the country but also as proof as how readily that fear might be dispelled once there was a show of good will.

The widespread euphoria that from the first moment so impressed me was tinged with apprehension. Almost all the young Jews were members of the Haganah, the volunteer defene force that was the precursor of the Israel Defense Forces established together with the state in 1948. On my first morning in our Tel Aviv hotel, I was awakened by a repeated sound that to my London-trained ear sounded like the daily clip-clop of the milkman's horse. However, the sound didn't recede into the distance but continued, regular and undiminished, save when interrupted by an occasional call, the precise wording of which I could not discern. After 15 minutes, I could no longer contain my curiosity. I went over to the window and looked out on to what proved to be a quiet side street. Below me, lined up in the middle of the road, were two rows of teenagers, boys and girls in white shirts and blue shorts, each shouldering what looked like a broomstick. Facing them was a slightly older but still very youthful "officer", issuing the commands for their drill: "Attention", "Shoulder arms", "At ease", the staccato of each Hebrew monosyllable echoed by a sharp corresponding crack as the sticks hit the ground. When the Arab attack came, immediately after the Declaration of Independence on 15 May 1948, these were the men and women who took up what few arms Israel had and went out to confront armies with vastly superior equipment but lacking the patriotic fervour and self-sacrificial ardour of a people that had for too long been denied an independent state.

Built on the slope of Mount Carmel, Haifa was astonishingly beautiful. The old city, its population comprised mostly of Arabs, lay at sea level, while a modern road wound up to the peak, where my cousin's family occupied one of a small group of recently erected houses, the core of what later became the luxurious Ahuza quarter. As the bus ascended, I caught sight of the sea at every bend. I was enchanted. My cousin's wife, Miriam, whom I'd never met, had come to meet me in Hadar Hacarmel, a commercial centre halfway up the hill where the taxi dropped me off. My Hebrew wasn't yet good enough for a conversation; her English was only slightly more adequate. The sole language in which I could make myself reasonably understood was my broken German. As we chatted away, becoming acquainted, I was startled when the passenger behind me tapped me on the shoulder and, in an admonishing tone, uttered a phrase which I later came to realise was frequently aimed at those who chose to speak in a "foreign" language: "*Ivri, daber Ivrit!*" ("Hebrew, speak Hebrew!"). Chastened, I decided to remain silent for the remainder of the journey, while Miriam obediently spoke to me slowly in Hebrew, using the simplest, most basic vocabulary.

After spending the night in Ahuza, I moved down to Hadar. There my parents, who'd arrived a day later than me, had taken rooms in a pension owned and operated by a couple who'd immigrated to Palestine from Essen, where the husband had been a lawyer, at about the time that my father left for London. It was a very emotional reunion and my parents sat for hours with Mr and Mrs Koch, each side recounting what they had experienced in the tumultuous decade and a half since they'd last seen each other. The realities of pre-state Palestine were forcibly impressed upon us the next morning, as news rapidly spread of a massacre of Jews carried out by their fellow workers at the refineries in the port area. Word had it that the British guards had meticulously searched the Jews for unlawful lethal weapons but had permitted Arab workers to enter carrying concealed knives. The result was 39 Jewish dead. We stood on the flat roof of the pension to watch the funeral and saw the bodies wrapped in white shrouds, surrounded by a mass of mourners. I took a photograph of the scene, a souvenir of the Palestinian reality of bloody conflict between Jews and Arabs that five months later erupted into war.

Infected by the vitality and dedication of my contemporaries, and undeterred by the violence I had witnessed, I wanted to stay in Palestine, not even go back to London to resume my studies. Never before had I experienced such a sense of belonging. This was where I wanted to make my home. Impressed by my earnestness, Avraham took me to see some of the people in charge of social services in Tel Aviv. Every single one gave me the same advice: "Go back and finish your studies. When you are properly qualified, we'll be happy to give you a job." Disappointed by this rejection, yet cheered by the promise of future employment, I went back to the LSE and a new Hebrew teacher who'd teach me the conversational idiom I'd require once I was in my homeland – a vocabulary that hadn't been instilled in me either by the grammarian Mr Kurenitz or by my beloved Shlomo Auerbach, who read poetry with me, declaiming it as he marched around our living-room. It would be almost two years before I fulfilled my dream and "went up" to Israel to begin a new life. In that period, a bitter war was fought and 6,000 people, some 10% of the Jewish population, were killed, among them my cousin Avraham. Refusing to let his lame leg deter him, he'd insisted on joining the fighting and, unable to escape a Syrian ambush, had been brutally slaughtered in hand-to-hand fighting.

Back at the LSE I rapidly became acquainted with the considerable number of Jewish students who had come from Palestine to complete their academic education and professional training. We were all members of the LSE's Zionist Society, which included a number of philosemite gentiles. Once a week, we took our turn at the table at which college societies could display materials and sell literature presenting their specific cause. At other colleges and universities, the Palestinians firmly resisted all attempts to enlist them into the existing Jewish Societies. Despising diaspora Jews, they preferred in no way to be identified with us, perceiving themselves as a different, superior breed. Perhaps because I made no secret of my own ardent intention to go on *aliyah*, I succeeded in breaking through the barrier of snobbish hostility. As a result, there was rarely a Friday evening meal at which my parents failed to host one or more of them. My father delighted in practising his Hebrew and my mother in providing tasty home cooking to these visitors so far from their own homes.

128

Prior to my visit to Eretz Israel I'd discovered another unexpectedly passionate Zionist, one of my fellow students of social work. A Quaker, Frank Hunt had spent some time after the war with the pacifist Friends' Service Unit in a large DP camp in Admont, Austria. Frank had been almost as excited as I was when I told him, *en route* to one of our institutional visits, that I was going to Palestine in the Christmas vacation. Ultimately, he preceded me in going there once we had completed our studies. On arrival in Israel I found him with fellow Quakers working to alleviate the sufferings not only of the new immigrants living in one of the transit camps on Mount Carmel but also of the Arabs who'd remained in the lower city after the War of Independence. Unfortunately, this even-handedness didn't find favour in the eyes of the local Jewish population or the Israeli authorities. There was still strong anti-British sentiment. Precisely, the even-handedness fed the fear that the British volunteers were in fact perpetuating British anti-Zionist policies. Disappointed and depressed by this rejection, Frank and his colleagues left the country whose populace they had so wanted to help recover.

Among the Palestinian students were a number who became professors at the Hebrew University of Jerusalem. Prominent were sociologist Yossi Gross (later Ben-David), whose brother was killed in the War of Independence, Shmuel Eisenstadt, in due course a world-renowned sociologist, and Yona Rosenfeld, nephew of Israel's first Minister of Justice, Pinhas Rosen, who later headed the School of Social Work. Among the less distinguished students were two social workers, Bracha Svirsky and Batya Waschitz, who'd been sent by the Departments of Social Welfare in Tel Aviv and Jerusalem respectively, to acquire those in-depth professional qualifications that I'd been urged to attain before going on *aliyah*.

My closest relationship developed with Y. His father, like my own, was a member of the religious-Zionist Mizrachi movement and they'd become acquainted through serving on the Actions Committee. Although Y and I had been instructed by our fathers to look out for each other, we met for the first time quite by chance, at a gathering of the Zionist Society addressed by Max Seligman, a lawyer who'd defended members of the Jewish underground in Palestine when they were charged by the British for their "terrorist" activities. Sitting in front of me in a capacity audience was a very handsome young man, busily taking notes in Hebrew. After a while, when the (green) ink in his pen ran out, he turned to request mine, which I gladly lent. Only at the end of the talk, when we exchanged names, did we realise that both of us had finally found the person whom we'd been told to look out for. This began what proved to be a close friendship that lasted into my early months in Israel. We soon discovered a shared love of opera, music, art and theatre. This initially led to his joining Sonny and me on numerous successive evenings. He also became a regular Friday night guest at our home. My mother, who'd not overcome her distaste for Sonny, whom she considered socially inferior, at once saw in Y a more suitable match and though my father never expressed an opinion on the subject, he too clearly found Y congenial. Certainly, he possessed the social graces that gauche and undiplomatic Sonny so lacked.

My growing liking for Y was not the sole contributing factor to my breaking off my three-year engagement to Sonny. The strain of a prolonged sexually unconsummated relationship had also taken its toll. Although we now once again lived in the same city, we were seldom alone together. While he lodged with his married sister in south London, I lived in the north-west. As a result, even when only he and I went out together, unaccompanied by others, we parted at the Underground station. What lovemaking there was had become boring and completely failed to move me, physically or emotionally. Guilty at not being able to respond with any degree of passion, I was torn between loyalty and a desire for greater excitement, intellectual and romantic. In Y, I found a far more charismatic personality, and rejected Sonny's warning that charisma could be deceptive and superficial, like a charm that can captivate irrationally. Yet it was not only a failure of interpersonal relations that led me to make the break. A stronger impact came from an unexpected quarter: politics.

In February 1948 a communist *coup d'état* in Czechoslovakia, instigated by the USSR, overthrew the democratically elected liberal government. It brought about the suicide (if indeed it was such, rather than a defenestration) of Jan Masaryk, in mid-March. I was as appalled by the ruthless totalitarian methods as by the murder of a worthy, beloved leader, who was well-known and popular in Britain because of his service as foreign minister in the wartime government-in-exile. The use of brute force was the antithesis of the democratic principles on which I had been brought up and educated to believe in, and the victims were none other than the Czech people, who had only 10 years earlier been blatantly betrayed by Britain's policy of appeasement. Sonny had no such qualms. A quasi-communist, he saw nothing objectionable in the *coup* and even justified it. His insouciance came as a shock. I hadn't suspected how far to the left he had moved since the 1945 election that ousted the Conservative Party. Then, he'd voted Labour while I cast my vote for the Liberals.

Despite the acrimonious arguments that developed between us, it was some time before I could bring myself to reveal my decision to end our engagement. I was – and still am – a coward when it comes to saying wittingly anything that I fear might hurt others. For weeks I struggled to determine what would be the right course of action and, if it were indeed to be a break, how, when and where I could make it. What made it particularly painful was that I told him of my intention only in May, a day before the third anniversary of our engagement, when – with the approach of his final qualification for the Ministry of Defence – he began to talk about a wedding. I could delay no longer. Needless to say he wasn't convinced by my citing our political differences as the reason for my decision. As far as he was concerned I had betrayed him by forming a relationship with Y. Unfortunately, I couldn't in all honesty totally deny the allegation. I agonised over my motives, as well as over my actions. The standard of my weekly essays declined so sharply that my tutor, Nancy Sears, asked me what the matter was. Somewhat sheepishly, I told her about the break with Sonny, adding that I thought mine was a stupid reason for severing so long-standing a relationship. To my surprise – and gratification – she reassured me that the reason was in no way trivial.

"You cannot live an entire life with such vital differences in outlook," she said. In retrospect, I realise that only in the profoundly politicised environment of the LSE would a tutor pass such a judgment. I doubt whether anyone at Newnham would have been so perceptive, sympathetic and reassuring.

The Czech tragedy was not the sole momentous political event of my days at the LSE. The years 1947-8 also saw the gradual dismantling of the British Empire. Hindu India and Muslim Pakistan won independence on 15 August 1948 but the accompanying massacres boded ill for the region. Indeed, only five months later Mahatma Gandhi was assassinated. Someone announced the shocking news just as we were filing into class that Friday afternoon for our final lecture of the week. Instantly, the Indian students rushed out, panic-stricken. The rest of us were as if paralysed. How could one respond to such a crime? "Macbeth hath murdered sleep." Someone had murdered peace. Though we took our seats when the lecturer, Mrs Cockburn, entered, there was a marked restlessness in the room. Nobody could concentrate on "Theory and Practice in Social Work", not even our teacher, who, after a few opening sentences, burst into tears and abruptly, without another word, left the room.

Independence followed for Burma and Ceylon – more peacefully, since there was no religious enmity involved. But in Palestine, where nationalist and religious fervour stoked the flames within the country's borders, the UN decision on partition heightened the conflict that had already previously existed between

Arabs and Jews. Britain's continued implementation of its 1939 White Paper restricting Jewish immigration prevented hundreds of thousands of Holocaust survivors from rebuilding their lives in a new homeland. British Zionists responded angrily. I participated in a public protest against the inhumane policy, wielding the loudspeaker in a van travelling through suburban streets, calling on residents to join a march along the Strand to a mass rally in Trafalgar Square. A policeman stopped us to inquire whether we had a permit. Unaware that one was needed, we confessed that we did not but then went on to explain the humane basis of our action. Surprisingly – and fortunately – he found the explanation persuasive and we continued on our way, reassured. If we were stopped again, we could cite this earlier permission by way of precedent.

As armoured attacks on the Jewish population in Palestine increased in the months leading up to the Declaration of Independence in May 1948, the Palestinian students found themselves in a quandary: should they interrupt their studies in order to join in the preparations for the full-scale war that might follow independence or remain to complete their studies? Impassioned debates led to violent disagreements and broken friendships. Those who chose to stay felt compelled to explain their decision, somewhat lamely claiming that they'd be better able to serve the new state if they returned well-qualified to play a constructive role there. Unlike his younger brother, who was studying medicine in Geneva, Y remained abroad.

His decision disappointed me. I disapproved of his lack of patriotism. But ultimately my affection overcame that initial dismay and I soon found myself once again forgivingly going out with him almost every evening. From time to time, perhaps sensing that nothing permanent would develop from our relationship, we decided to break it off. Yet each time it was only a matter of days before one or other of us telephoned to set up a new date for yet another concert or theatre performance. Y failed the final examination and returned home without the Diploma in International Relations he had intended to earn. Ironically, this did not jeopardise his future. He at once obtained a post in the Ministry of Foreign Affairs. He was, after all, the son of Israel's first ambassador to Sweden. In the new state, connections were more advantageous than professional qualifications. When he left for Israel at the beginning of July, it was clear to both of us that I would soon follow. My implicit assumption was that we would then marry.

Homecoming

OCTOBER 1949 WAS one of the mildest and most beautiful Octobers I had experienced. For the first time in my life we were able for an entire week to take even our evening meals in the *sukkah*, the temporary dwelling in which Jews are bidden to abide in memory of their wanderings in the desert. In all previous years, we had had to sit huddled in our coats, an electric heater providing inadequate warmth. Usually rain accompanied the cold. This year was different. Two of my aunts came from Israel, my uncle from the US and there were jovial family gatherings around the table laden with the traditional dishes that my mother excelled in making. We jointly celebrated my 23rd birthday and my father's 59th. A few days later, towards the end of the month, I left for Israel with my brother in attendance to ensure that I travelled safely. A photograph he took on the train that carried us to Genoa reveals that, in what is now considered wholly incongruous fashion, I was wearing one of my elegant new two-piece suits, an angora sweater and pearls!

My parents came to Victoria Station to see us off. At the last minute, my mother, sobbing, asked my father, "Why are we letting her do this?" To which he memorably replied, "We raised her for this." I was to travel with Dalia Katz, whom I'd met two years earlier, when she visited England together with other Jewish students who were at the time studying in Europe. But Dalia, a brilliant but absent-minded chemist, had neglected to inform us of the time of her arrival from Geneva. We therefore stayed in a humble hotel close to the railway station, dutifully meeting every train that arrived from Switzerland. Finally, only hours before the time scheduled for departure, she arrived, self-possessed and unperturbed by the delay that had kept us on tenterhooks.

She and I were to share a second-class cabin on the SS *Filippo Grimani*. Among our fellow passengers were other Israeli students, who had returned to Europe in order to complete their studies after fighting in the War of Independence. Some of them had been Dalia's contemporaries at the prestigious Reali School in Haifa, where an excellent teacher had inculcated a thorough knowledge of the English language. Dalia herself had remained in Europe, engaged in gun-running – a dangerous task in which her beauty and aristocratic bearing undoubtedly helped her avoid suspicion. Unlike us, these young men were travelling deep below deck, in cramped and ill-smelling quarters. On the spur of the moment – either because he had been greatly attracted to Dalia during her visit to England or, as I now realise, because he might have wished he could continue with us to our ultimate destination – Willy decided to remain on board for the first day of our journey, at the end of which we reached Naples, where we were to remain overnight, waiting to take additional passengers on board the following morning.

Napoli! How infinitely more lyrical the Italian is, with its long, open "a" sounds than the English version. The reality, however, was far from romantic. Still showing clear signs of war damage, buildings unrepaired, pot-holes in the streets, it reeked of poverty. Rubbish was everywhere, homeless in tattered clothing lay on the narrow sidewalks. Rag-clad street urchins, their faces streaked with dirt, swarmed around us, begging for alms, clinging to our legs, impeding our progress, arousing a strange mixture of pity and revulsion. I'd never encountered such urban blight, even in the worst of London's slums. Sightseeing was impossible. What, after all, was there to see? The museum was already closed, Pompeii too far away. We escaped to the bourgeois calm of our ship, taking with us a straw-wrapped flagon of Chianti and an excessive quantity of the local nougat. Perhaps we hoped to assuage our guilt at being prosperous, at failing to respond with sufficient generosity to the imploring of the wretched mendicants.

The wine was consumed that evening, leaving us sufficiently intoxicated to forget, if only temporarily, the horrors of Naples. The excessively sweet and sticky nougat was soon consigned to the wastepaper bin in our cabin. Our next port of call, where we had only a short stay, was Piraeus, port of Athens. There, we climbed the Acropolis before returning to the ship. On board, we discovered that the newly embarked passengers were Jews from Greece and the Balkans, survivors of the Holocaust, with whom we shared no common language and who gazed at us in wonder at our clothes, which differed so vastly from their own tattered garments. I was overcome by awkward embarrassment, profoundly wishing to converse with them but unable to do so. These were precisely the people I hoped to be able to help integrate into Israeli society. Humbled, I suddenly felt in no way equipped to undertake this hubristic task. In addition to her friends in steerage, Dalia also knew – or was known to – a number of the first-class passengers. She was, after all, a niece of Israel Rokach, the mayor of Tel Aviv, and her mother was the editor of *Ha-Boker*, one of the country's major newspapers. On the final evening of our journey, I was invited to join her at the farewell party hosted by the captain. I was overawed by the identity of some of our fellow guests, whose names were familiar to anyone as acquainted with Zionist history as I was. Yet these idols proved to have feet of clay. They became inebriated, were excessively frivolous and, most embarrassingly, donned paper hats with which I was acquainted from British Christmas and New Year parties – definitely not what I had expected of Israel's "nobility".

I was relieved when we were able to leave early, ostensibly on grounds of fatigue. But instead of retiring to our cabin, we went up to the deck, where we encountered a very different form of celebration. The refugees were singing Hebrew songs and dancing a spirited *horah*, as if drunk – like the group we had just left. Their intoxication, however, was one of joy at the knowledge that the following day they would at last reach the destination of which they had dreamed. Once again, the song I had sung as a child, dancing around the kitchen table: "*Anu olim artza livnot u'lhibanot ba…*". Similarly inspired, in total accord with their delirious enthusiasm, I joined in the dancing that continued until we were all thoroughly exhausted. Throughout, the Israeli students had stood on the sidelines, looking on in what seemed more amusement than wonder. As I approached them, I heard one of them mockingly exclaim, in the German that was his parents' mother tongue, "*So habt Ihr euch das vorgestellt*" – that's how you imagined it would be. I felt as if a bucket of cold water had been thrown over me. It was my first experience of the disparity between the feeling of those of us who'd chosen to make Israel our homeland and those who'd had the good fortune either to be born there to parents who'd arrived earlier (some prompted not by Zionist ardour but by the impossibility of obtaining visas to other, more affluent destinations) or who had themselves arrived when they were still too young to have experienced a burning desire to go to the Promised Land. They couldn't comprehend the extent of our euphoric joy at the fulfilment of our dreams.

With Tel Aviv harbour too shallow to permit on-shore disembarkation, small boats came to take us to port. Trembling with excitement, I almost missed my footing on the rope ladder. With reassuring hands, Jewish porters steadied me and I landed safely, with an overwhelming sense of homecoming. Awaiting me were not only several cousins but also Y, who had come from Jerusalem to welcome me. I was to stay with my Aunt Lotte, who, with her husband Leo and their still- precocious son Gerd, had arrived from Italy as soon as the British departure enabled Jews to enter the country unimpeded. Their home proved to be in the same street as that where Y's grandmother lived, together with her recently married daughter and son-in-law – a strange couple, she a diminutive redhead, and he excessively tall and balding, both no longer young. They took me sightseeing in what had once been exotic Jaffa but now seemed little more than a deserted jumble of buildings. I wondered why they found this rundown town more interesting than the lively modern White City.

Tel Aviv now was, however, very unlike the one of December 1947. Where formerly there had been a plenty that contrasted sharply with the austerity in Britain, there were now food rationing, shortages of all kinds, reminiscent of the days of the war in England. Shops once abundantly stored were half-empty. Searching for a tea-set to give my aunt as a birthday present, I walked literally for miles before I found one in a dusty shop, on Allenby Street, far away from the more recently built northern section of the city where the streets, in so far as they existed, had been of unpaved sand when I visited two years earlier. The humid heat was oppressive, and I regretted having brought clothing suited only to the European autumn and winter. As soon as possible, I escaped to Jerusalem, where Y had rented accommodation for me.

November 1949. A narrow two-lane road winds its way up from the *wadi* between hills densely clad with pine trees. Scattered along the way lie wrecks of armoured cars – shattered and rusting. And on the crest of the hill, a town – yet another town just like the ones we've passed through on the road from Tel Aviv – only the houses are built of stone, they're more numerous and here and there are larger ones. Perhaps institutions of some sort? A hospital? An old-age home? We pass by a crowded market and then another row of low buildings and small shops. The taxi stops in a side street. All my fellow passengers alight. I remain sitting in the back seat.

"What about you?" the driver asks and I proudly reply:

"*I'*m going to Jerusalem!" He laughs.

"This is Jerusalem." This is Jerusalem? I'm stunned. I've expected something totally different. Misled by the maps that appeared in the *Times* almost daily during the War of Liberation, I've imagined a triangle similar to that formed in

136

London by Oxford Street, Regent Street and Piccadilly, with Bond Street connecting them. And here I find myself in a small town – a town divided, a frontier city, on the fringe, confined, immured. Walking down the Street of the Prophets you encounter an impenetrable bundle of barbed wire. At the end of bustling Jaffa Road, a high wall... "Stop! Border ahead!" Do you want to see a place that is unreachable? The Old City, for example? You climb to the roof of Notre Dame and see the taxis outside the Damascus Gate. Disappointing! Bethlehem? We march out to Ramat Rachel. But even on a fine day it's hard to make out a city of any kind. On the way from Rehavia to the town centre, a wall behind which lies the deserted city park protects us from the random shots of the Arab Legion. In the far distance one can dimly discern Mount Scopus, of which I've dreamt and sung throughout my life in the diaspora. On Hannukah, a menorah beams from there, one more light each night, a sign that we're still there, although none of us can reach it.

The exiled university is scattered among a number of Christian institutions: Humanities and Social Sciences at Terra Sancta, where I eventually teach; the Law School in Ratisbon; Medicine – Notre Dame. I wander from building to building until my department finally reaches the North Wing of the King David Hotel. The blown-up opposite wing is still in ruins. Street names in the city centre are confusing. Old timers refer me to Chancellor Street and Queen Melisanda. I can't find them because now they are called Strauss and Heleni ha-Malka. Of the British Royal Family only King George and Princess Mary still remain. On the other hand, some districts have no street names whatever: Talbiye, Katamon, Bak'a. There one has only two numbers, one of the plot, the other of the house, but with no logic whatsoever. The numbers don't help. Everything is jumbled. You have to ask the neighbours: do you know so and so? Where does such and such live? One isn't always successful in finding the person one is looking for and there are virtually no public phones. Who needs them when hardly anyone has a telephone at home? There are also scarcely any private cars. The few buses arrive at long intervals, passengers squeezed together like sardines in a tin. So we walk. We walk and walk – in the blazing sun, in the Jerusalem rain that comes bucketing down like sharp needles, turning to mud the innumerable streets that are still unpaved. We walk and on the way we greet each other. In Jerusalem all Jews are friends. Even kindly President Ben-Zvi walks, greeting everybody he encounters. At sunset the Jerusalem stone turns to golden pink. The city shines. True, a city divided, confined, immured – yet, in my eyes, perfect.

Y had rented a tiny two-room house for me in Rehavia. A low stone shed of a building in a quiet, unpaved lane, a short walk from his parents' home, it resembled the outhouses we'd had in Waddesdon. The lodging was sparsely furnished. The front room, into which one entered directly through an iron door, held a narrow bed and a wooden cupboard totally inadequate for the amount of clothing and bed linen I had brought. Beyond it, without any door to separate the two, was a second space, in which stood a plain wooden folding table and two chairs: the living-room. No pictures decorated the walls, nor was there a tablecloth. Further exploration led me to a narrow niche that held a sink and a marble draining-board, on which stood an electric kettle. There were, however, neither cups nor saucers, no cutlery of any kind. Finally, the bathroom and toilet, in which the bath with which I was familiar had been replaced by a shower.

Far from luxurious and not even very comfortable, these quarters nonetheless at first enchanted me. A bougainvillea in full purple bloom covered the front wall, the rent was low and, above all, it was a place of my own. Throughout the three remaining weeks of November the weather stayed warm and I felt no discomfort. But when torrential rains began to fall and the stone walls became icy cold, I returned one day to find that my landlady had removed the tall kerosene stove that should have been my sole source of heat, which I was in any case too ignorant and scared to use. I had also learnt from bitter experience that the water tank on the roof of the house, into which water pumped from the plains flowed only once a week, on Thursdays, was too small to hold more than a five-day supply of water, even if I confined my use to the scantiest of ablutions and two cups of tea or coffee per day. By Tuesday morning, the taps were dry. I began to understand why the landlady had preferred to move elsewhere but I hardly knew what to do. I hadn't yet found work, despite lodging inquiries with what proved to be every social-work agency in Jerusalem (there were only two) and my hopes of soon being financially independent were steadily sinking. When a man's face suddenly appeared at the glass pane of my front door one evening as I was about to undress, I decided that enough was enough.

I mentioned my dilemma to Y, hoping he would not think me either foolish or ungrateful. To my delight, his sister called on me the next day and asked if I would like to be a lodger in her four-room apartment. A tenant had moved to Tel Aviv, leaving only a few of his belongings, and she was certain he would be willing to relinquish the lease. So in mid-December, I moved to my new accommodation, which, in addition to a bed, held an ample wardrobe, a low coffee table, two armchairs, a bookcase and, facing the window, a large desk. I now had a comfortable home but still neither employment nor income.

Furthermore, it had become increasingly clear that there would be no marriage to Y, nor indeed was I any longer interested in one. On his home territory and under the strong influence of his snobbish class-conscious mother, he'd become more arrogant and when I finally succeeded in pinning him down for a tête-à-tête one evening when we were alone at his parents' home he accused me of having become coarsened by my intimacy with the Landman sisters. Since these two generous souls had issued an open invitation to spend time with them whenever I had nothing better to do and since their home had provided a welcome refuge on those Friday evenings when I wasn't invited elsewhere, I was shocked and angered. This was definitely not someone with whom I wished to share my life. I was happy that his work at the Foreign Ministry, located in Tel Aviv, provided a good reason for not seeing more of him.

Like most children in middle-class well-educated Jewish families in the diaspora, I was expected to learn Hebrew. While for boys the prime goal of such study was to prepare them for bar-mitzvah, the absence of any female equivalent for this coming-of-age ceremony leaves the rationale for it unclear. Possibly it was to enable us to have at least a rudimentary understanding of the prayers we were hearing or, even better, reciting, when we attended synagogue or listened to Kiddush at home before the festive Friday night meal. From the age of seven I attended twice-weekly synagogue-sponsored Hebrew classes. Although I could easily parse the opening chapter of Genesis, I never progressed much further, since every year successive teachers invariably, like the Torah readers in synagogue, began with *"Bereshis boro…"* ("in the beginning…"). Frustrated and bored, I tried to persuade my parents of the uselessness of continued attendance at Hebrew classes but they wouldn't release me from my duties and I, an obedient child, abided by their ruling.

Fortunately, release from this purgatory came when I was 11, in the form of membership in the Habonim Zionist youth movement. Instead of biblical text, we learnt the spirited nationalist terminology of the pioneers who were transforming the arid desert of Eretz Israel into an earthly paradise. *"Anu olim artza…"* we sang enthusiastically, ecstatically, as we danced our tireless *horah*. We acquired new vocabulary, though often in woefully mangled form, since we learnt by ear rather than by eye. More formal reinforcement was at hand. Two new teachers were hired by our synagogue. Mr and Mrs Harris were also ardent Zionists. While he was delegated to continue instructing us in classical texts, she was free less formally to supplement what we were learning. In consequence, I came to realise that some of the multisyllables that burst from my mouth in song were in fact composed of a number of monosyllabic nouns, verbs, adjectives and adverbs. The exotic, faintly Far Eastern *Adblidye* was, literally, a more prosaic *ad b'li dai* – never-ending – which in fact qualified the more familiar *avodah*, work.

War came. In a village 50 miles away from London, my Hebraist-Yiddishist father employed a teacher for an entire orphanage of Jewish boys, concerned for the Jewish aspect of the boys' education and overruling the mild remonstrations of the semi-assimilated director of the orphanage. The same teacher was to tutor Willy and me individually in twice-weekly lessons. Every single lesson by the grammarian Mr Kurenitz consisted of drilling us in the *binyanim*, the declensions of the verb. As a result, I became an expert in *poal, piel, pual, hifil* and *hitpael* but I couldn't utter a complete sentence. The nouns were missing. Escape came in autumn 1944, when I went to Cambridge. There I found a kind of reversion to Habonim in the form of a Zionist Study Circle whose fortnightly sessions of intellectual discussion always ended with nostalgic indulgence in the songs of the Second Aliyah. After the war, while I was still at Cambridge and the family back in London, my father engaged yet another teacher, for himself and my brother. Shlomo Auerbach's primary duty was to help them read contemporary Hebrew prose, such as that of Shmuel Yosef Agnon. During vacations, I too would be able to study with him.

Shlomo was in every possible way the opposite of Mr Kurenitz. Tall, rugged, with a craggy face, a large, prominent, knobby nose and invariably tousled greying hair, he loomed large in our drawing-room. He loved poetry and he knew by heart innumerable works by Bialik, Tchernikovsky, Rachel and others of our canonical writers. While I held the text in my hand, he'd pace excitedly around the room, declaiming fervently, passionately, employing the original Ashkenazi metre and pronunciation, which differ from those of contemporary Hebrew and give the works greater authenticity. If the poem had been set to music, he'd sing it in a deep loud baritone. I looked forward eagerly to my lessons with Shlomo. Infected by his immense enthusiasm, I came to know many of the shorter lyrical works by heart. He gave me his own copy of Bialik's *Vayehi Hayom* as a going-away present when I left England. Many years later, in the mid-1960s, when Israel was celebrating 50 years of the Second Aliyah, I listened enthralled to a nostalgic radio programme of pioneers' songs and joined in as Nehama Handel and other contemporaries sang them. I thought of Shlomo and how he influenced me, how he enriched me culturally and how he infected me with his love for Hebrew literature. Three days later, I learnt from my brother that Shlomo had died on the evening of the broadcast, just as I was thinking of him and in my heart thanking him for all he'd given me.

My sessions with Shlomo were incomparable and unforgettable but as the date of my *aliyah* approached I realised I still couldn't conduct a conversation in Hebrew. Anxiously I begged him to be more practical. He remained firm in his refusal to change our curriculum.

"Nonsense," he would say dismissively, then adding – with reference to what seemed invariably to be the subject of Lesson One in contemporary textbooks of spoken Hebrew – "you'll always be able to order tomato soup. But once you're in Israel you won't be reading Bialik and Tchernikovsky!" I knew he was right, yet shopping for food at the grocery store, ordering it in a restaurant or engaging in similar mundane matters seemed even more important than the classics at this critical stage in my life. So I began thrice-weekly lunchtime lessons with an Israeli (or, rather, a Palestinian-born) teacher, Ruth Cohen, who headed the BBC's Hebrew department. Stress was on spoken, conversational Hebrew and the acquisition of everyday vocabulary but always with insistence on using the correct grammatical form and gender (even with confusing numerals where rules are reversed). Something of Mr Kurenitz's strictures remained to guide me.

Although I frequently found myself having to resort to English during my early days in Israel, at least what I said in Hebrew was grammatically correct. It was many years before I learnt the correct grammatically incorrect, idiomatic Hebrew doggerel that must make all three of my teachers turn in their graves. Instead of *me'ayin*, *mieifoh* (whence), instead of *Ani hafetza*, *Ani rotza'h* (I want); *Puncher*, *Mesting* – derivations from English so distorted as to be unrecognisable; new coinages such as *halakh feifen* and *haval al hazman* (which literally means the opposite of its metaphorical meaning); army acronyms. I learnt "Hebrew as she is spoken". I continue to learn it from my best, most expert and beloved of teachers, my three generations of Sabra offspring.

Insider

Employment

UNEMPLOYED! "UNSALARIED", AS a modern American coinage more trenchantly puts it. In my naïveté, I'd never imagined it would come to this. After all, I'd arrived in Israel with a freshly acquired postgraduate certificate in social work from the LSE. But here I was, with credentials, recipient of the most glowing evaluations from the agencies at which I'd done the practical work required as part of my training, rejected wherever I went. I had hoped to work with new immigrants from Europe, the DPs as they were designated before the term "Holocaust Survivors" became the norm. In fact it was precisely my experience as a volunteer with youngsters of this population in London that had spurred me to move from English literature to an entirely different field.

I spoke and understood a number of European languages, including Yiddish, which I thought would enable me to communicate with my clients. Even my spoken Hebrew, though still far from fluent, seemed adequate to the tasks I would have to undertake. I was full of energy and eager to begin. But nobody wanted me. For one reason or another, I was deemed unsuited by the agencies to which I applied, of which there were only an inadequate few. Case work was my forte but it was hardly practised at the time. The hundreds of thousands of refugees who arrived from the Arab countries were indeed displaced but they required large-scale assistance in the inadequate transit camps in which they were temporarily "housed". Furthermore, they spoke no European language, while I had no knowledge of Arabic, Ladino or any of the Judeo-Arabic dialects in which they communicated. My qualifications were totally inappropriate; I didn't meet any of the required specifications. Rejected and dejected, I worried what would become of me.

"Don't worry, you'll find something," friends said. In fact, two of my colleagues from the LSE whose *aliyah* had preceded mine by a year had already abandoned social work because, lacking the money with which one usually won clients' confidence, they'd made no headway in improving the families' conditions or establishing relationships. "There's plenty of other work available," I was assured. "You just have to be patient and on the lookout for unexpected opportunities." One such arose on a Friday evening in mid-December, a month after my arrival in Jerusalem. The Landman sisters, one of whom had already switched from social work to employment by the Broadcasting Authority's Overseas Service, had, as was their wont, invited me to Shabbat dinner, together with other "homeless" immigrants. We were a motley group, ranging widely in age, country of origin, linguistic skills and wartime experience. Solly had captained a ship that brought illegal immigrants to Palestine. While studying medicine in Geneva, David had, like Dalia Katz, smuggled arms for the Haganah. Ze'ev had fought with partisans in Yugoslavia. And all the while I'd been safely cocooned at school or university. I was overawed by this fascinating "ingathering of the exiles".

Food was scarce, testing the Landmans' culinary inventiveness, yet the atmosphere was always congenial. We made Kiddush, broke bread, sang and talked, talked, talked... On this occasion, we were invited to after-dinner coffee one floor below, where the Landmans' eccentric Aunt Nelly lived, together with her husband, Sir Leon Simon. Formerly a high-ranking British civil servant as well as a scholar who'd published an excellent book on Ahad Haam, Sir Leon had originally been invited to serve as Chairman of the Board of Governors of the Hebrew University. When I met him in 1949, he was serving as its President. After hearing of my travails, he unexpectedly responded with a question, a remonstrance:

"But you've got a degree in English, haven't you?"

"Well, what good's that going to do me?" I asked despondently, wondering at the relevance of his query.

"We're desperately looking for teachers of English at the university," he replied. The university, which had been closed during the War of Independence and was now exiled from its home on Mount Scopus, had reopened a month earlier. For the first time, an American-style BA with numerous mandatory introductory courses and basic studies had replaced the original four-year specialised Masters programme. Of an unexpectedly large enrolment of 1,000 students almost all had elected English as the required foreign language. The three pre-war faculty members of the English Department could clearlyn't cope with such numbers. Taken by surprise, the university authorities were now scrambling to find qualified teachers. But teaching? It had never occurred to me that this might become my profession. Indeed, in my undergraduate experience, teaching was for various vaguely formulated reasons despised; the standard response by Cambridge students of the humanities to the question of what we planned to do after graduating had been "Anything but teach!" At first I demurred. I had none of the necessary qualifications. "Never mind," Sir Leon reassured me. "You'll learn on the job. The important thing is that you have a degree." He gave me the name of the head of the department, Mr Mendilow, and on my departure once again urged me not to neglect contacting him. I doubted whether I would be accepted but decided to keep my word.

On Sunday morning I delivered a note at Terra Sancta College, just around the corner from where I lived, at which the Humanities Faculty of the Hebrew University had found a refuge. I spelled out my scant qualifications, sceptical of the outcome. Nevertheless, the response was instant: a phone call from Mr Mendilow inviting me to meet him the next morning; a courteous, unintimidating English gentleman, exuding warmth and welcome, putting me at my ease. After a brief informal chat, during which he presumably garnered some impression of me as I did of him, he asked me to give a trial lesson of some 45 minutes at the Beit Hakerem High School, which I gathered was in some so far incomprehensible manner connected with the university. I could choose whatever topic I wished. I had two days in which to prepare.

What could I teach? I had no literature books with me. The "library" to which Mr Mendilow led me, housed in the abandoned Arab Umariya School in Talbieh, comprised a meagre dozen volumes that had been on loan to students before the war. One was a small edition of Shakespeare's Sonnets that had been found in the pocket of a member of the ill-fated group of 35 volunteers, the Lamed Hey, who set out to relieve the siege of Kfar Etzion. His face sagging with grief, Mr Mendilow handled it with great care, gently stroking the cover as he showed it to me. Clearly he'd admired, even loved, this martyred student: who had carried Shakespeare with him into battle. But the library was useless. I would have to improvise, play for time, hope for the best. I was frightened, overcome by a feeling of inadequacy and impending failure. I prayed for inspiration, toyed with a few (impracticable) ideas, finally decided on a strategy – a topic for discussion.

I took the bus to Beit Hakerem, then a distant suburb at the end of the number 12 line. Ignorant of the length of the journey and fearing I'd be late, I arrived far too early. A little row of small shops: a grocery, a sweet shop that also sold stationery and newspapers. Across the road, a barber. I stopped to fortify myself with a bun and a glass of *gazoz*, the popular fizzy drink flavoured with raspberry syrup. The school, affiliated with a teachers' seminary, was only a short walk away. Still too early, I was directed by the porter to the nearby, currently empty staff room. A bell rang and teachers streamed into the room, among them a tall, suave, well-dressed gentleman, speaking a carefully unaccented English, who at once introduced himself as Dr Pinhas Blumenthal. He was extremely kind. He assured me that the 12th-grade pupils were very intelligent, that their English was excellent (reflecting his own excellence as their teacher), that they were used to trial lessons by students and would undoubtedly collaborate with me to the best of their ability. Mr Mendilow arrived with Mr Morris, a short, rotund, apple-cheeked ball of a man, a world expert, as I later learnt, in the teaching of English as a foreign language. I was introduced to the class.

"This is Miss Margaliot," said Dr Blumenthal, helpfully adding that I had only recently arrived from England. I assume he intended this to arouse even greater than usual sympathy among the pupils. They rose to the occasion. Having chosen as my topic the question, "Why should we study literature?", I opened the discussion with what I hoped were stimulating remarks, as soon as possible encouraging the pupils to engage in a debate among themselves. At times I interjected provocative comments or questions. I drew on the debating skills I'd acquired at school and university. I knew how to keep the discussion going without its deteriorating into a free-for-all. In general I adopted a heuristic approach. To my surprise I enjoyed the experience, though I was greatly relieved when the bell rang to signal the end of my ordeal.

Back in the staff room, I was offered a welcome cup of tea, which I accepted with trembling hands. We sat down. For a few minutes there was an awkward, tense silence. Messrs Mendilow and Morris looked at each other. I tried not to look at them, gazing as if insouciantly around the room, taking in nothing of my surroundings. Then Mr Mendilow said:

"We'd like you to come and teach in the *Limudei Yesod* [Basic Studies] programme." It would be a part-time job, just over a third of the full-time 40 weekly hours. I was overwhelmed. In truth, I'd not expected such an invitation. Had I passed muster or was their need so desperate as to make them grasp at any passing straw? At once I felt panic rising. How would I cope? I knew no rules of English grammar, to which two of the four-weekly hours per class were devoted. Presumably I'd be able to make my way through the two hours of literature, though the lack of suitable texts would be an obstacle. I'd have to prepare stencils of poems I wanted to teach. No secretarial help could be expected. Fortunately, I was not the only newcomer. Another Englishwoman, a pre-state immigrant, Lily Lucas, already had some teaching experience and was ready to prepare classes together with me, though it might be a case of the (less) blind leading the blind.

I was to begin work on 1 January 1950, six weeks after arriving in Israel. Working at the university would, I thought, give me time to learn Arabic as well as perfect my Hebrew. Eventually, I'd become a social worker. But I never did change profession. I discovered that I loved teaching. Because I introduced a British-style system of individual tutorials, I established a warm relationship with my students, several of whom became close personal friends. I learnt that teaching is a most gratifying profession and that, if one relates to and engages with one's students as individuals, it is very similar to social work. Both require empathy, the capacity to listen and communicate, the ability to feel and express sympathy and affection. I now have the highest regard for those who practise the profession and who, like me, love it: there is no greater compliment than to be addressed as "*Morati*" ("my teacher") or greater satisfaction than to hear, as I have, a student say, "You changed my life". And it all happened by chance.

The English Department was in many respects unique. Alone of all the departments that constituted the Faculty of Humanities, it was utterly devoid of the vicious rivalries that elsewhere flourished so abundantly as to necessitate the illogical division of departments into numerous superfluous sub-departments. Thus Professor Duff's quarrels with Professor Peri gave birth to a Department of Romance Languages in addition to a French Department. Here, in turn, the rivalry between Professors Peri and Sermonetta led to yet another offspring in the form of an Italian Department. Professor Polotzky, a world-renowned linguist, so spurned his colleagues that the authorities deemed it wise to grant him an empire of his own, while his minions were either scattered throughout the Middle East, banished to Departments of Semitic Languages and Egyptology, or sentenced to eternal subservience in the lower ranks of the department of which he remained the permanent head. Similarly, Hebrew Literature had to be subdivided – medieval, modern and Kabbalah – in order to satisfy the egos of various faculty members. Even the undisputed master of Jewish mysticism, Gershom Scholem, wasn't immune from tyrannising his juniors, denying them well-deserved promotion.

The English Department differed markedly. This might have been because all three of its senior faculty members, so quaintly dubbed "Anglo-Saxons", were true gentlemen, invariably courteous even when they disagreed with each other; but above all because Adam Mendilow was a generous human being who never begrudged the success of others, and spent years encouraging and promoting his juniors. Since he was fully absorbed in teaching and administration, and because he was also an incorrigible procrastinator, the list of his publications was pitifully short and consisted merely of a few articles. Only very belatedly did he submit to his *alma mater* a doctoral thesis which was soon published under the title *Time and the Novel*. A breakthrough analysis based on various theories on the nature and definition of time, it has remained unique, a classic. Like John Livingston Lowes's *The Road to Xanadu* it kept me awake for an entire night, spellbound by the development of its arguments. New initiatives were welcomed at the department. At my suggestion, we adopted the Oxbridge tutorial system of meetings with individual students to discuss the written assignments they submitted. We established an Informal Club, which met regularly for extra-curricular activities that included poetry readings and folk-singing, and climaxed each year in a witty Purim *Spiel*, a topsy-turvy satire written and performed by our students that remained constantly good-humoured.

Among our students some became well-known Hebrew poets: Yehuda Amichai, Dalia Ravikovich and Dan Pagis. In an essay on *King Lear*, Yehuda memorably wrote that when he first read the play, "All the jars on the shelves in my mind fell off". All three, like many others, acknowledged that they'd learnt more about literature in our department than in that of Hebrew Literature. A number of our students, none of them native English speakers, eventually joined the teaching staff – a new, home-grown generation of scholars, critics, poets and translators. Adam was unfailingly supportive. As work on my doctorate dragged on far beyond the three years officially allotted – indeed, until well after I was married – he annually wrote to the authorities assuring them that "This year Mrs Shalvi will undoubtedly complete her thesis" and hence requesting just one more extension of my position. Such generosity of spirit was unknown in other departments. The comradeship between all members of the department was largely the result of the common bond of fellowship that he created.

In March, deep snow fell, knee-high. For several days Jerusalem was at a standstill. Food supplies were more than usually scarce. There was no bread. The only bakery in the city had no flour. Deliveries were in any case impossible. Accompanied by Ruth Landman, I tramped through the snow from one grocery store to the next but to no avail. There simply was no bread. The milkman who made daily deliveries, pouring the milk into the metal cans we set out, couldn't cart his wagon through the streets. But Jerusalemites were accustomed to shortages. The majority had lived through the siege, when dandelion-like *khubeiba* leaves picked in the fields served as a staple diet.

In the evening, a close friend of the Eynats, a highly eligible bank manager, like my landlord a native of Galicia, came to visit.

"There's a new café in the German Colony," he announced. "Let's all go there." Judith, then in the late stages of pregnancy, found the proposal preposterous. Pleading, he turned to me. "Will you come?" Yes, I would. My landlady, Judith, lent me a pair of galoshes and off we went, sloshing down what was then the lower part of King George Street, between Terra Sancta and the David Building at the foot of the hill. Apart from one beautiful round-balconied house on the corner of what is now Lincoln Street but was then merely a dirt path alongside the YMCA that enabled one to cross to the King David Hotel, there were no buildings on the left side of the road. A full moon shone bright in a clear sky, its light reflected in the deep, pure-white snow that blanketed the wide rocky expanse at the centre of which Montefiore's windmill rose like a displaced four-winged totem pole. The walls of the Old City glowed, one-dimensional as a stage set.

In the Germany Colony, a district deserted by its Arab inhabitants, the houses stood forlorn, here and there studded with shuttered shops. Pavements were non-existent, streets unnamed, street lamps rare and we had no clear idea of where we were going. Then, peering down a turning off the main road, we discerned a small shack from which came the sounds of an accordion. We headed for it. Inside, the air was steamy, the tables crowded together, snug and warm. This was Café Ta-ta-ta. The few couples who had preceded us were more Slavic than Semitic in appearance, the men with close-cropped hair, some of the women blondes with elaborate braids bound around their heads. Their drab clothes, bulky and outmoded, contrasted sharply with my elegant, pink, Ashkenazi raincoat. Our arrival caused a stir. Curious, slightly suspicious looks appraised us. Friend or foe? We took off our coats. The owner hurried towards us. Like his clients he was, it transpired, a new immigrant from Yugoslavia. All he could offer us was mulled wine.

Clearly encouraged by the unexpected advent of clients so different from the regulars, he hastily cleared a large space in the middle of the room. The accordionist, inspired by the entrance of more guests, enthusiastically struck up an infectious new tune and suddenly we were all dancing an ebullient polka, despite the cumbersome clomping boots and lack of food. Baked potatoes appeared as if from nowhere. Someone in the kitchen had been moved to action by the merriment. We had no common language. Delirious, all we shared was a joy of living, being young – the ecstasy of being in Jerusalem, in the snow.

April 1950. That morning he didn't go to work. This wasn't entirely surprising. For two days he'd been at home, suffering from chronic ulcer pains. But this morning was different. Far from looking haggard, he came into the kitchen, freshly shaven, hair combed neatly back, wearing a handsome dressing-gown in which I'd never before seen him. He was my landlord but also a friend. I wasn't simply a tenant: I was a member of the household.

On my return home one evening, he'd handed me an envelope that had arrived by mail from London, remaining to stand beside me in my room while I opened it. The express letter bore bad news: my father had suffered a second stroke. As I broke into tears, he embraced me in reassuring sympathy. Then he kissed me, on the mouth. The kiss winded me. I did not like it or want it. It was inappropriate, distasteful. Repelled, I pushed him away but not in anger, and thought no more about it. I assumed that it had been a spontaneous gesture of sympathy, a way of comforting me in my loneliness and helplessness, my longing for home and family, and desire to be by my beloved father. My cordial relationship with my "landlord" and "landlady" remained unchanged. We were all eagerly awaiting the imminent birth of their first child. Heavily pregnant Judith had abandoned the now too narrow marital bed in favour of a more spacious sofa in the living-room.

This morning she was at work. He and I were alone. We exchanged the usual bantering pleasantries. Then, he came closer and, suddenly embracing me so tightly that my arms were pinned to my side, pushed me against the wall, all the time kissing my face, cheeks and eyes but not my mouth. I didn't know how to react, what he expected of me. I felt uncomfortable, embarrassed, yet at the same time vaguely flattered. I'd never conceived of myself as the object of such desire. Still tightly embracing me, he slowly propelled me out of the kitchen. As if we were partners on a dance-floor, I followed his lead. I allowed myself to be led. I was in a trance, hypnotised, with no will of my own, passive. We exchanged not a single word. I can't recall any details of what happened once we were in his bedroom. I know I didn't undress. I remained wearing the pale purple woollen housecoat that people so admired, on my appearance in which so many had complimented me. What I do recall is a sudden sharp pain, followed by silence, before he said, "Go clean yourself up". Obediently, I went to the bathroom. My housecoat was stained with blood. He was still lying on the bed when I emerged.

"I wanted to make it easier for Y," he said nonchalantly, as if in explanation. And that was all.

The three of us – Judith, her husband and I – continued to live together in the same apartment in apparent amity. Ill at ease, I tried to avoid being alone with him, staying in my room when Judith was away from home, delaying my breakfast until they'd both left for work. On the rare occasions when I found myself alone with him in the kitchen, I tried to keep my distance. Once the baby was born and Judith on maternity leave, there were always others in the house, and I was able to relax and cease being on the alert. Some time later, when I was already engaged to the man I ultimately married, Y invited me to have coffee with him at the fashionable Café Europa. We chatted in some embarrassment. Our relationship had changed so radically since my arrival in Jerusalem half a year earlier. Then, impulsively:

"S seduced me," I said, without going into details. "He claimed it was in order to make it easier for you." Y burst into laughter. I don't know what response I'd been expecting. Horror? Disgust? Sympathy? Anything but this. I was in shock, revolted as much by the adulterous betrayal of a pregnant wife as by the way in which my own innocence and trust had been abused – and now this insouciant reaction. I felt sullied by a decadent, immoral society, the supposed *crème de la crème* of Jerusalem's snobbish veteran élite. Over the years, it is precisely this instant revulsion, immediately succeeded by anger, that has remained in my memory: that moment in the garden courtyard of Café Europa on Zion Square with the little string orchestra of middle-Europeans playing Strauss waltzes. That moment – and the recollection of the indelible bloodstain on my pretty purple housecoat. When I told Y the story I used the word "seduced".

Today, we call it rape.

Marriage and Motherhood

Allegro ma non troppo. "How did you two meet?" they ask, curiosity tinged with a *soupçon* of incredulity. I suppose we were indeed a somewhat incongruous couple. So it seemed at first even to him. But this is what happened.

In May 1950, the exiled Hebrew University was celebrating its 25th anniversary. Jerusalem was still somewhat of an outpost, divided between east and west. Festivities were modest. The opening event, held in the courtyard of Terra Sancta College, was of a formal academic nature. It was the only time that I saw faculty members in full academic dress. Augmented by distinguished scholars from abroad, they filed down the gangway to their appointed seats as we stood in respect. The Rector, Professor Simha Assaf, looking like a benign wizard, spoke about the newly inaugurated BA programme, memorably referring to the abbreviation as standing for *Ben-Adam*, an untranslatable term that might, imperfectly, be approximated by "a complete, decent, human being", a truly civilised person, a *Mensch*. I felt proud to be a part of this institution, albeit in a very minor role. The next evening, there was a "live newspaper". A highly popular form of cultural activity, it consisted of a number of short talks given by figures known for their work in any branch of intellectual or artistic activity. On this occasion, the panellists included world-famous philosopher Martin Buber and Kingsley Martin, the non-Jewish editor of the pro-Zionist British weekly, the *New Statesman and Nation*. In the absence of large lecture halls, Jerusalem's many cinemas provided venues for such events. In this case, it was the Orion Cinema in the centre of town.

My companion at the event was Avalon, an American woman of approximately my age, who was a fellow student at the university's intensive Hebrew language course. Angular, sharp-featured, abrasively sharp-tongued, at times tactlessly outspoken ("truth-telling", she termed it), she had "adopted" me or, one might say, forced herself upon me. Sitting in the gallery of the Orion, Avalon saw a trio of acquaintances entering the stalls. Uninhibited by accepted standards of appropriate public behaviour, she shouted down to them, calling them by name, standing up, waving her arms, beckoning them to come and join us. I cringed and wished I could dissociate myself from her but the people she was addressing acceded to her request (or her command) and came upstairs. They were a couple, a stoutish man whom I judged to be in his late 30s, and his slim and agile wife, whom Avalon introduced as Yitzchak and Ettie Rischin. But it wasn't Yitzchak and Ettie who captured my attention. Rather, it was the young, unnamed man accompanying them, whom Avalon apparently deemed unworthy of being introduced to me.

What are the clichés about love at first sight? I was bowled over. My heart stood still. Instantly, I knew that this was the man whose love I wanted to win and wanted to marry, with whom I wished to share my life. This was far beyond any physical, sexual attraction I had experienced. He was beautiful, young. His face

151

bespoke openness, candour, innocence, good nature; a cheerful, friendly demeanour. There was no putting on of airs or attempting to make an impression. He was simply there. And I wanted to be with him forever. But how?

I apparently made no impression whatsoever on him. Proof of this came two evenings later. A student of mine who'd been wooing me invited me to the concert by the Israel Philharmonic Orchestra that was yet another item in the festivities. In the interval, we went out to the foyer, this time of the vast Edison Cinema, which doubled as the city's largest concert hall. There, in a small group of what appeared to be students, was the object of my desire. Without hesitation, encouraged by the general informality of Jerusalem at the time, I went over and mentioned that we'd met earlier. Clearly, he'd forgotten the encounter but he responded politely, begging my pardon for not having recognised me. We exchanged a few more words, nothing that could increase my hope of continuing our acquaintance, and returned to the auditorium. At least I had learnt his name from hearing his companions address him: "Moshe".

After the concert there was a students' party, held in the dingy hall of a semi-deserted building near the no-man's-land between West Jerusalem and the Old City. An accordionist repeatedly played the ancient student anthem "Gaudeamus Igitur" but I was the only one who knew the words. It isn't a tune to which one can dance and indeed nobody seemed to have any intention of dancing. How different from the student balls I'd attended at Cambridge, even in the days of wartime austerity. The listlessness was depressing. Since my Hebrew was as yet not good enough for anything but the most elementary conversations, I was happy to find some of my own students among those present. Their English was far better than my Hebrew and they apparently sensed my malaise. Finally, in response to a remark of mine regarding the absence of dancing, one of them approached the accordionist to request a change of repertoire.

Immediately, there ensued first a waltz, then a foxtrot, then what is known as a "slow". A few couples took to the floor as I sat forlorn. I love dancing. My suitor, however, didn't know how to dance. But there, on the other side of the room, was the object of my love. This time, he did recognise me. He was alone. He asked me to dance with him. We made a perfect couple. He didn't know the "correct" steps but had a natural sense of rhythm, easy movement and the skill of leading gently but firmly. We talked as we danced. We became better acquainted, learnt a little about each other's reasons for being in Israel. There was an unspoken understanding that we would in all probability meet again but how or when remained unspecified. My student took me home and as we reached the gate swept me up and swung me around in the best Hollywood tradition. Nobody had ever done that before but it didn't further endear him to me. My heart was already elsewhere.

Andante. One of the pieces of information I'd gleaned about – though not directly from – Moshe was that he worked at Barclay's Bank and that he frequently went to have a late lunch with the Rischins, the generous, hospitable couple who had "adopted" him when they lived next door to each other in rented rooms on the other side of town, in Kerem Avraham. His route ran past my window. Every day I'd stand by that window opposite the Rehavia windmill at approximately the time at which he should be passing if he were going to the Rischins, hoping to catch a glimpse of him. He had a cocoa-pinkish straw hat that sat saucily tilted on the back of his head. He walked jauntily – a young man content with his lot. He seemed so vibrant, as if he were whistling his way through life: careless. Indeed, to be in that spring of independence in Jerusalem was intoxicating. Still I yearned to expand our acquaintance but as the Yiddish saying has it, "*Wie kommt die Katze über das Wasser*" – how does the cat cross the water? Help came from an unexpected quarter: Avalon, knocking at my door, demanding that I go for a walk with her. In vain I pointed out that I was busy at my typewriter, preparing stencils for the end-of-year exam – a slow and painful undertaking, given my limited typing skills and the ongoing need to apply Tipp-Ex lavishly in order to correct the numerous errors.

"Come with me," Avalon said, imperiously. "I've got somebody who can do these for you in 10 minutes." It was too tempting an offer to resist. I followed her to an elegant house in nearby Alharizi Street. Walking up to the first floor we heard music coming from a radio. The door was opened by Ettie Rischin, wearing shorts and a T-shirt, and wielding a duster. When she saw who her visitors were, she grabbed Avalon by the waist and whirled her around the large living-room in a lively polka that left both of them breathless. I stood by in wonder. Not a word had been exchanged.

Avalon explained the purpose of our visit. No problem. Within minutes Ettie, an amazingly nimble-fingered typist, had completed what for me was Herculean labour. There was time to have a cup of tea and become acquainted. At the end of the visit I was invited to Friday-night dinner. I had made a new friend and moreover one who knew Moshe. There was now a further connection, albeit tenuous, between us. I went to the nearby florist and ordered a many-coloured bouquet of large pansies to be delivered to 4 Alharizi Street. And sure enough, on Friday there was Moshe among the dinner guests. I was one step further to attaining my goal: we were moving in the same circle. Now how could I achieve greater intimacy?

Allegretto. Jerusalem was a small city. One encountered the same people over and over again – in cafés or restaurants, at cultural events, in the street. One began to assume one really knew these people, so one greeted them and soon they became one's friends. That's how it was with a number of us, all recent immigrants, most from English-speaking countries. We met, went out together – to one of the city's numerous cinemas or to a lecture or poetry reading. People lucky enough to own a gramophone would invite friends to come and listen to records. Once a week the YMCA held a concert of recorded music. Towards the end of a Shabbat afternoon spent in conversation, talk turned to what we would do that evening. Someone mentioned there'd be a chamber-music concert at Beit Ha-halutzot, where there was an appropriately intimate hall. We decided to go. Only Moshe demurred.

"I have to go home," he said. "I have to darn my socks." In those days of shortage, one didn't throw clothing away. But a man who darned his own socks was a rarity. I seized the opportunity.

"Tell you what," I offered. "I'll come and darn your socks tomorrow evening if you'll come to the concert tonight." And with total, well-based confidence in my own skills, I added, "I'm a very good darner". Moshe allowed himself to be persuaded. At the end of the second movement of the first composition that was played he turned to me and whispered:

"Don't you people ever clap?" I was aghast. What had I let myself in for? An adult from a civilised country who didn't know how one behaved at a concert? Never before had I encountered such a phenomenon. How could I possibly imagine myself living with someone so boorishly uninformed? I sat in emotional turmoil for the remainder of the concert, not encouraged by his lukewarm response to the evening. Nevertheless, I fulfilled my side of the bargain. I went to darn his socks. While I was thus occupied, he ironed his shirts, diligently, with impressive skill, folding each one carefully before finally placing all of them in a small wardrobe that was one of the few pieces of furniture in the room. Meanwhile, we talked – about ourselves, families, background, studies, the reasons for coming on *aliyah*. Despite significant differences – of age (I was two years older), education (I already had two degrees), occupation (I was teaching at the university, he was a clerk) and religious practice (he was far more Orthodox) –

we had a good deal in common. I loved his sense of humour, his not pretending to be anything other than what he was. His openness and what can only be described as innocence – everything that went along with his lack of sophistication – were a far cry from the qualities that characterised the men I knew, those'd encountered as a student at Cambridge or the LSE and those whose acquaintance I'd made since my arrival in Israel. We liked each other. We spoke a common language.

He escorted me back to Rehavia, buying me a falafel en route. And that was how it all began.

*Finale – Molto Allegro.*Contrary to custom and convention, it was I who proposed marriage. We'd been going out together for almost two months, relishing each other's company. We'd formed a bond of profound mutual affection. We had made love, and found both physical and emotional compatibility. We laughed at each other's jokes, even when they were corny and unsophisticated. One evening, when we were alone in his room – the only place where we could enjoy total privacy, despite the occasional prying of his elderly landlady – he surprised me by wistfully asking:

"What's going to become of us?"

"Why don't we get married?" I ventured hesitantly, fearing rejection. He reflected for a moment. Then:

"Good idea!" he responded. Two evenings later, when he escorted me back to my lodgings, he pulled an opal fraternity ring from his pocket and placed it on my finger. We were now engaged. I was due to return to London for the remainder of the long summer vacation, not only to see my parents but also to purchase equipment for the two-room flat they'd rented for me during their visit two months earlier. Located on the fourth floor, which was being added to a building in Rehavia, it was the perfect size for a young couple.

Recalling the painful consequences of thoughtlessly informing my parents by phone of my engagement, I intended this time to break the news in person, face to face. I was apprehensive. Aware of the anomaly of our relationship, and of the various indisputable disparities between Moshe and me, I knew they'd infuriate my mother – firmly entrenched in the conventional belief that a husband must be older, taller and wealthier than his spouse. I couldn't with equal certainty predict my father's reaction but even he might well be troubled at the prospect of my marrying someone in many respects so different from me. While I wouldn't be able to allay all their fears, I decided not yet to reveal the two-and-a-half year difference in age. Time enough for that inevitable shock. I'd stress his Orthodox religious observance – a characteristic I hoped might soften the blow.

My mother was angry. She flung recriminations at me: how could I, scion of a well-known and highly respected family, a graduate of Cambridge and the LSE, a teacher at the Hebrew University, marry a nobody from Brooklyn, a man without a profession who'd studied at a university of which nobody (including me) had ever heard? She wasn't impressed by the fraternity ring, though I assured her it was made of real gold. Refusing to be placated, dismissing all my arguments and impervious to my pleadings, she eventually grudgingly agreed to meet him once he arrived in London. However, this was not to be interpreted as indication of approval. On no account was he to be permitted to stay. A room must be rented nearby where a Jewish landlady could also provide a kosher breakfast. I waited anxiously, fearing Moshe might be offended by such a lack of welcome and, affected by the snobbish rejection, might change his mind, preferring not to attempt to break through the social barriers she was raising.

Fortunately, as I had hoped, my father, who accompanied me to the airport to meet Moshe, took an instant liking to him. Air travel was still comparatively rare, and airports were unsophisticated and utilitarian. After crossing the tarmac to the single building designated for arrivals, passengers emerged directly through immigration to the small arrivals hall in which we were waiting. Minutes after the announcement of touchdown, Moshe came rushing out, threw his arms around me, kissed and hugged me. After him raced an irate immigration officer, vainly trying to catch him by his coat-tails, demanding ID: passport, visitor's visa, proof that he had means not to become a burden on His Majesty's government. In his eagerness to see me and inexperienced in international travel, Moshe had simply ignored this formality. Seeing the passion with which Moshe embraced me, the official smiled indulgently and accepted my father's assurances that this was indeed a law-abiding though naïve young man, whose expenses would be fully covered by his hosts. My father was totally won over. Generous and open-hearted, he at once perceived that Moshe was no fortune-hunter, that we clearly loved each other and that I would find happiness with this spontaneous, unsophisticated innocent.

Less sentimental than my father, my mother was not so readily appeased. Not without some justification, she had pinned her hopes on a positive outcome of my relationship with Y, the handsome, cultured, well-connected student who never failed to bring flowers or a small gift whenever he came for dinner. He'd risen even further in her esteem since his father's appointment to a high-ranking

156

diplomatic position. It took her several years to perceive and acknowledge that Moshe's remarkable qualities were innate rather than a superficial veneer covering intense snobbery.

Pre-nuptial crises have been a staple trope in innumerable comedies. For those experiencing them, they are a nightmare of tension, misunderstanding and uncertainty so overwhelming that they come precariously close to causing a last-minute cancellation of the ceremony. Such was the nature of the 10 days that elapsed between Moshe's arrival and our wedding. Looking now through the little grey Jewish National Fund diary for that fateful year, I note an incessant whirl of family encounters, dress fittings, parties at the homes of friends, clothes purchase, evenings at the theatre, at a concert or out for dinner. "Registry office – collect licence", "Collect shoes", "Menuhin: Mozart, Mendelssohn, Schumann", "Moss Bros", "Austin Reed", "Collect wedding dress", "Collect wedding hat"… The most portentous of all the events is heralded a scant week before the wedding: "M parents due 7.45". Now close mutual scrutiny became inevitable. What would the two seemingly disparate parental couples find in common? If Moshe wasn't the spouse my mother had hoped for, would I more easily approximate to the ideal that his parents had presumably envisioned?

Moshe's parents were, like us, an odd couple, greatly differing from each other in temperament and behaviour. Sadie, American-born, was beautiful and quiet, gentle and unaffectedly gracious. "A real lady!" opined my snobbish English-born aunt (who never wholly resigned herself to having a Polish-born husband). Harry, who had arrived in the US from Minsk at an early age, was convivial, extrovert and loquacious – what Americans, using a term derived from the Yiddish, refer to as a *kibitzer*. By profession a travelling salesman specialising in men's clothing, he was experienced connoisseur of fashion and quality, a dapper dresser. At his insistence, Moshe reluctantly allowed himself to be led to London's most elegant shops, acquiring a new wardrobe of suits, formal shirts, ties, shoes and even an impressive camel-hair overcoat, all of which contrasted sharply with the T-shirts, slacks and shorts he had sported throughout the summer in Jerusalem. He was ill at ease, embarrassed at being the cause of what he considered extensive and unwarranted expenditure. Unaccustomed to giving orders, he let my father or brother give prior instructions to the friendly chauffeur who drove the capacious Austin my parents now owned, and who entered wholeheartedly into the excitement and enthusiasm that Harry expressed as they drove around the West End from one exclusive establishment to another.

Since I was busy with my own chores, Moshe and I met only in the evenings, in the company of others. There was no privacy. The sole opportunity for the physical contact we both longed for was when we went *en famille* to dinner at Selby's, a chic kosher restaurant that had recently opened, at which a three-piece band played dance music. No sooner had the music begun than we stepped on to the dance-floor to indulge in our customary amateurish mode of simply responding to the rhythms.

"No, no," said Harry, who had in his youth supplemented his earnings by working as a dance instructor. "I'll show you how to do it." I innocently assumed he would take Sadie as his partner and that we were to learn by watching. To my consternation, he took me by the arm and led me to the dance-floor. He indeed knew all the right steps but I had no comparable expertise in following them. I felt like a puppet being manipulated: resistant, inflexible. My distress was the greater not only because I knew all eyes were focused on us but because I was aware that I was disappointing him in this respect.

Fearing the consequences of revealing my and Moshe's difference in age, I continued to postpone informing my parents of this additional defiance of convention. I knew it would have to emerge at some point but I wanted to delay the inevitable disapproval for as long as possible. On this issue, Moshe's parents might prove as conservative as my mother. But truth will out – and not always at the appropriate time or in the desired circumstances. On the evening after Harry and Sadie arrived, my uncle and aunt joined us at our home to become acquainted. Alex, as sociable as Harry, delighted in our gregarious visitor's joviality, uninhibitedly plying him with questions about his background, family and profession. Some surprising data emerged, including the fact that Harry and Sadie had met when she came to take dancing lessons at the salon where he worked.

"When was that?" my uncle asked.

"Wait a minute," Harry replied, needing time to recall the details. "Let's see." He turned to his wife as being more likely to remember. "When was Moshe born?"

"1929," she responded.

There was a sudden brief silence, before Harry blithely continued his narrative, oblivious to the startled response of my family. I shrank into the low pouffe on which I was sitting in a corner of the room, wishing the ground would open to swallow me. Opposite me, my mother gave me the blackest of black looks. Even my father appeared shocked. So unaccustomed were they to such a divergence from custom that it hadn't occurred to them that Moshe's boyish appearance was indeed indicative of his young age. He was 21½ years old. I was about to celebrate my 24th birthday. Was this, I thought to myself, the unkindest cut of all? Needless to say, I was indeed scolded once the guests had gone but it was too late to prevent our marriage.

Many other embarrassments stemmed from the difference in customs between Europe and the US. These included the complex conventions of table manners. Moshe had already abandoned the illogical and awkward American custom of cutting one's meat with knife and fork in hand before setting the knife aside and switching the fork to the right hand in order to spear the food. Prior to dinner at my uncle's home I had instructed him in the complexities of "correct" table-laying: the array of cutlery and the order in which to use it, the types of glass, each appropriate to a different drink, the correct use of sideplates, the placing of napkins, with which one should dab one's lips before taking a sip from a glass, lest one leave a grease or even worse a lipstick-mark on the rim. Needless to say, he found the stress on such protocol ridiculous. Nevertheless he was chagrined to note that his father blithely disregarded convention.

Moshe was equally disconcerted to learn how he was to be dressed at the wedding. While I'd decided against a long dress as being unsuitable for future wear in Israel, he would be clad in the customary dinner-jacket, black tie and top hat. Although he looked superbly handsome and elegant, he felt as if in fancy dress. The item that evoked the greatest ridicule was the pair of white gloves that came with the rest of the outfit. Reluctantly, he put these on, only to be advised by my brother, who was fulfilling the role of "best man" with delicacy and understanding, that these were intended merely to be held, not worn. "It's crazy!" he objected. Nevertheless, he dutifully obeyed orders.

Inevitably, there came a point at which he could no longer tolerate the emotional and physical pressures. Matters came to a head on the Shabbat prior to the wedding, after he had been called to the Torah. It was "Shabbat Bereshit", the opening chapters of Genesis. Moshe read the chapters from the Prophets which follow the Torah reading, using the modern Hebrew pronunciation, rather than the one still customary in the Diaspora. There were murmurs of approval, followed by hearty cries of "Mazal Tov". Then Moshe disappeared. I went from room to room looking for him. He was nowhere to be found. Suddenly, it occurred to me that he must be feeling even more pressured than me. I, at least, was in my element. I had a premonition as to where I would find him. Without a word to my parents or his, I rushed off to his lodgings, where I found him, disconsolate and angry.

"I don't want all these people," he said. "I want to be with you!" I tried to reason with him: his father was anxious, guests were waiting, there would be unwelcome gossip, negative responses. He owed it to his parents to behave properly, not to disgrace them... In vain: he lay on the bed, sulking. Abandoning reason, I lay down beside him, hugged him and assured him that, come Tuesday, we would be married and, on Wednesday, flying off for our honeymoon, alone. Pacified, he relented and we returned to our duties. Harry looked at me with unprecedented respect.

Two clerics officiated at the ceremony. A study in contrasts, one was the venerable Hasidic Rebbe of Przemysl, who officiated at my parents' wedding in Mannheim, while he was *en route* to England. The other was the clean-shaven Anglo-Jewish Reverend I. L. Swift. He wore a white clerical collar that further emphasised the difference between him and the black-hatted rabbi, who presented us with a large silver Kiddush cup on which his name and title were prominently engraved.

We spent our honeymoon in Paris at the Joshua Reynolds, a small, elegant hotel at which Willy, an experienced traveller, had reserved a room for us. To judge by the benevolent smiles with which the receptionists greeted us, they knew we were newlyweds and we were duly ushered into a suite in which the dominant feature was an inviting outsize bed of burnished brass. Outside the leaves were turning yellow. The air was filled with an appetite-arousing odour of roasting chestnuts. Scorning the Metro, we walked for miles. We climbed the Arc de Triomphe and the Eiffel Tower. We took the train to Chartres and Versailles. Already familiar with Paris, I delighted in seeing the extent to which my unsophisticated husband shared my enthusiasm, how rapidly he developed an appreciation of art and architecture.

Moshe's observance of dietary laws far stricter than mine presented difficulties. There was only one certified kosher restaurant and the menu was far from typical of French cuisine. The welcome we received when the owners learnt we were from Israel didn't wholly compensate for the poor quality of the food. After our second visit there, with some pangs of conscience we cited the distance from our hotel as an excuse for not continuing to patronise the establishment. We offered some compensation by purchasing two outsize salami sausages and two bottles of kosher red wine. On the way back to the hotel, we bought baguettes, two cheap plates, knives and forks, and henceforth picnicked in our room. It was our first experience of keeping house together. We made abundant blissful use of the big brass bed. We were inordinately happy. The week in Paris proved an auspicious beginning to over 60 years of compatibility, creativity and compassionate companionship.

I became pregnant in May 1951. Moshe was ill with jaundice. In those days front doors were frequently left unlocked. When our family physician, Dr Spiegel, walked in unannounced and found us embracing (albeit fully clothed), he smilingly warned us that this was a highly contagious illness. Strict diet was prescribed, primarily fruit and vegetables. I set off for the greengrocer, wondering what I should find at this mid-season, when the winter citrus was no longer available, while the fruits of summer had not yet ripened. To my delight, I found cherries, the Hebrew name for which I didn't yet know. One of my students, ahead of me in the queue, kindly informed me that it was *duvdevanim*. When my turn came, I confidently asked for a kilo. The greengrocer looked at me in astonishment. It seemed that cherries, like virtually every other food, were rationed. I could have 250 grammes. I carried home the treasure, stoically denying myself the pleasure of tasting one of my favourite fruits.

In the summer, when I travelled to London to visit my parents, I went to see Dr Lindenbaum, who had attended my aunt throughout the succession of miscarriages she suffered before giving birth to her first child. After a very thorough examination, he assured me that the width of my hips, about which I had always felt so self-conscious, would ensure an easy delivery. Since at that time women sought as far as possible to conceal their pregnancy, I bought some pretty maternity clothes and also a copy of Grantly Dick-Read's *Natural Childbirth*, which determined me to implement the theory that he based on his experience with native women in Africa. Nobody in Israel was as yet practising ante-natal exercises, so I went by the book.

When I returned to Jerusalem, Moshe informed me that he'd decided he must volunteer for the army. As a US citizen he was exempt from conscription but felt that, since Israel was clearly the country in which he intended to spend his life, he should fulfil all the duties of a citizen. Military service was mandatory and the sooner he performed it the better. At the recruitment office, he was received with incredulity. An American volunteering to serve in the IDF was a rare phenomenon. Might he be mentally unstable? The authorities were ultimately persuaded of his sanity, since he was very soon inducted and, after gruelling basic training, assigned to the Military Police, where he was promoted to the position of investigator: a form of duty that requires mental skills rather than mere physical stamina.

I had a painless, unproblematic pregnancy. Indeed, I felt healthier than ever.

Moshe was away on military service, the winter of 1951-2 was bitterly cold and wet, rationing and food shortages limited one's diet primarily to the season's fruit and vegetables, yet I was happy. As a pregnant woman, I was allocated two eggs per week. I was discovering modern literature not included in the Cambridge syllabus; my new colleagues in the English Department, who increased in number and variety every year, were pleasant and stimulating. I enjoyed teaching and took all my midday meals at a pension, together with a number of faculty members from other departments. Avocado had appeared on the market, particularly good when spread on Israel's tasty black bread. My gynaecologist, Professor Sadowsky, was humane and reassuring. The nurse who worked in his clinic was a midwife who I knew would in due course personally attend on me.

Labour pangs began one evening when the English Department staff were gathered at my home for a reading of Blake. From time to time, my colleagues would notice a change in my facial expression, a drawing in and expulsion of breath as I practised the Dick-Read precepts. At the end of the evening, a young doctor friend came to spend the night with me. The next morning, she was replaced by Miriam Simhon, the midwife, who sat ceaselessly knitting, like Madame Lafarge, carefully keeping an eye on me and the progress of the labour. At one point, she impatiently burst out:

"The trouble with you English women is you're so controlled. You don't shout and scream. How's one supposed to know when you're having a contraction?" I tried to explain that screaming, if one were trying to conform to the rules of natural childbirth, was counter-productive but my Hebrew was yet inadequate to the occasion.

At about 1 pm Miriam, who had decided the time had come to go to hospital, went to telephone for a taxi and we set off. I'd not been prepared for either the enema or the cold shock of the razor that shaved off my pubic hair. The contractions were already coming with uncomfortable frequency. I was disconcerted to learn that Professor Sadowsky wouldn't be present, because his brother had died that day. Instead, Professor Bzizinsky, whom I'd never met, would replace him. All around, women were screaming, calling upon their mothers. "*Ima!* Oh, oh." Shrieks, sobs, agony. I tried to block out the sounds but it was impossible. Somehow I managed to convey that I wanted no intervention of any kind. I recall, as I lay on the delivery table diligently following the rules of breathing I'd learnt, hearing Professor Bzizinsky say in a tone of amazement, "Just like in the books!" It seems I was Israel's pioneer of natural childbirth.

The person who helped me most at that first delivery was David Scherr, a young immigrant doctor from England, who held my hand and allowed me to squeeze it as hard as I wished. At last – the final searing pain of the child's emergence, a burning sensation, which I interpreted as cutting. "Don't cut!" I yelled – in Hebrew, to my surprise. "We're not cutting," Bzizinsky assured me – and a second later I heard the baby, heard the midwife's "*Ben*": "Boy". In delight I echoed that cry – *Ben!* – and burst into sobs of relief. Later a woman who'd overheard my cry told me it had been clear I wanted a son, because of the tone of joy in my voice. The comfort of the first wash, as the nurse pours warm water over the shaven vulva; the concern when the infant is first brought to be fed – "Will I have enough milk?"; the sense of regeneration as one showers for the first time. A multitude of new sensations.

Like the Hebrew University, Hadassah Hospital, exiled from its Mount Scopus premises, was housed in a number of non-purpose-built premises. The maternity ward was in what had been the Anglican School. One long ward with about 30 beds housed all the women who had given birth or were expected imminently to do so. A totally inadequate two-cubicle shower and toilet served all of us. I soon learnt that if I wanted to wash in a clean space, I had to get up no later than 6 am. As a private patient of Professor Sadowsky's, I was put in a tiny two-bed cubicle at the far end of the ward but on a low truckle bed that lacked the apparatus for raising or lowering the body with which all the other beds were equipped. I accepted this accommodation meekly, glad at least to have a quiet corner. In the other bed was a gaunt Kurdish woman, who spoke little Hebrew and who received no visitors. All day long she lay, patient and silent, watching as various of my colleagues came to congratulate me, as vases of flowers filled the night-table. Each time a male visitor left, she would ask, "Husband?" and each time I would, sadly, have to say no, not husband, for Moshe did not come.

I had given birth at 5 pm on Tuesday. A neighbour brought telegrams from my family in England. I knew that the Rischins, our closest friends, who had been the first to learn of the safe delivery, had sent a telegram to Moshe in the army. Wednesday passed, Thursday passed. On Friday, the matron, making her daily rounds, persuaded my neighbour, who had given birth to her seventh child, an unwanted daughter (hence the absence of visitors), and who clearly yearned for one more day of rest in hospital, that she was needed at home for the Shabbat preparations. I tried to intervene on her behalf. Surely she could be allowed to stay till Saturday evening, after Shabbat. The matron was obdurate. There were always more births on Shabbat than on weekdays. There would be insufficient beds. And so, at 3 pm, a little girl arrived with a bundle of clothes to take her mother home. Her last words to me as she left were yet another repetition of what she had been saying at intervals for the past 48 hours – "*Lama lo ba?*", "Why doesn't he come?" To which she invariably added, sadly reflecting on her own fate, "*Yesh lach ben*", "You have a son".

I learnt a great deal through this pathetic woman and her experience, of the overriding importance in some cultures of bearing sons, of the lowly status of females, the way they are despised and rejected even from infancy. I learnt, too, of the institutional complicity in this dismal scale of values, of ruthless racial discrimination that overcomes compassion (for the matron would never have brought similar pressure to bear on an Ashkenazi woman), of the contempt in which new immigrants from the Arab countries were held by the European veterans.

By Friday evening, when a Shabbat calm lay over the maternity ward, my depression was intense. I'd heard nothing from Moshe. His silence and continued absence seemed wholly inexplicable. Surely they had given him leave for Shabbat, even if not for the birth of his son? As I lay anxious and dispirited – now in the standard hospital bed vacated by my Iraqi neighbour – unable to sleep, too tired to read, I heard the clump of boots and Moshe appeared, at last, in his uniform, smiling – totally oblivious to the distress caused by his delay. How could he have arrived so long after the beginning of Shabbat, when all traffic stopped? He had not just arrived. Reaching Jerusalem only a short while before Shabbat, and correctly assuming there would be no food in our apartment, he'd headed straight for the Rischins' home, where we frequently ate on Friday nights. Only after he'd washed and eaten had he walked over to the hospital, which was closer to their home than to our own. True, the telegram sent on Tuesday to apprise him of the birth had reached him only on Thursday, too late in the day to permit him to travel to Jerusalem. Hence his officer had decided he might as well depart together with all the others who were going on weekend leave. His explanation, like his behaviour, was totally reasonable but I was somewhat hurt by what seemed to me a lack of feeling – if not for the desire to see me, then at least the longing to see his firstborn. My response was, in fact, rather like that of my Iraqi roommate: "*Lama lo ba? Yesh lecha ben!*"

A Good Enough Mother?

Sitting at the dinner table one Friday evening early in 1970, shortly after I'd begun commuting to Beersheba at least twice a week, I asked my children how they felt about my being away from home so frequently. The question was prompted by a column that Katherine Whitehorn, a model of common sense, had contributed to the *Observer*, an article provoked by Betty Friedan's seminal *The Feminine Mystique* and the lively Women's Lib movement it had engendered in the US. With her customary perspicacity Whitehorn had queried the contention that career and family were compatible.

Micha, who was 16 at the time, responded with, "You're not always at home when you're needed", to which the eldest of my daughters, Ditza, almost three years his junior, added, "But when you are here, you're much more interesting than those mothers who're always cleaning windows". I welcomed Ditza's reassurance but in time I came to realise that I should have paid more attention to Micha's reproach. In retrospect, I'm painfully aware that, while I attained renown for my professional and public activities, I was a failure as a mother.

"What do you want to be when you grow up?"

Once I'd reluctantly abandoned my unrealistic ambition of becoming a philanthropist, my customary response to this frequently posed question was "an author". I later modified this presumptuous declaration: "a librarian". Anything related to books inordinately attracted me. However, from adolescence on, I added a rider: "I want to marry and have six children". Why six?

My conception of a happy family was undoubtedly inspired by the numerous books I read that portrayed the adventures of siblings engaged in a series of fascinating activities in what appeared to be a world devoid of mundane obligations, such as school attendance: *Little Women*, *The Treasure Seekers*, *Swallows and Amazons*, *Peter Pan*, *Mary Poppins*, *The Family at One End Street*... Parents seldom intervened. Indeed, they were largely absent or seldom referred to. With only a brother five years older than myself, rarely moved to have any intercourse with me other than a quarrel, I envied these fictional families and perhaps unconsciously longed to replicate them in my own adulthood. Six seemed an appropriate number, preferably evenly divided between the sexes. I forgot that specific ambition as I grew older, until I gave birth to my youngest child, when Aunt Stella reminded me of it. Unwittingly, I'd achieved my goal: three sons and three daughters, with an age range of 15 years. Where were the parents of those enviably blissful families of children's literature? Either dead, travelling abroad or presumably, though this was never mentioned, working for a living. Authors seldom felt a need to specify.

Reality is very different. Birthing is a natural process. Parenting is not. It is an acquired skill, at best a process of learning by doing. As the field of child psychology of which Anna Freud was a pioneer gradually expanded, so the number of "guidebooks" increased. Sometimes they were helpful, at others confusing and frustrating. My own "Bible" was Spock's *Baby and Child Care*, which was sensibly reassuring, with its motto, "You know more than you think you do". It recommended a balance between permissiveness (following the child's inclinations in matters such as food), and reasonable guidance and discipline. I consulted it frequently and implemented its major directives as diligently as possible.

My first failure in mothering was my inability to breastfeed. The overworked nurses at Hadassah lacked time and patience to encourage me to continue my attempts at nursing. No sooner did they discern my initial lack of milk (a not uncommon occurrence, particularly in the case of an inexperienced first-time mother) than they began bottle-feeding, from which, to my deep disappointment, I was unable to wean my firstborn. I proved no more successful after each of my later births, though I found a degree of consolation in cuddling my babies while they sucked at their bottles.

Because throughout the first two years after his birth I was able to concentrate all my teaching responsibilities into three mornings a week, I had ample time to spend with Joel. Storytelling and singing were our favourite pastimes. A large, abundantly illustrated *Mother Goose* served as the primary source for both activities and Joel, a quiet, docile child, rapidly developed a repertoire of rhymes. Wrapping him in a soft white woollen blanket, I would sit for hours on our balcony rocking him as we read and sang. He enjoyed my reading aloud for many years; until he began high-school I would each evening read to him from the English-language children's literature that exists in such abundance. Our evenings together are among his happiest memories of childhood. They also ensured an excellent command of English.

In contrast, my second son, Micha, was beset by misfortune even before he was born. The last trimester of my pregnancy fell in one of the hottest summers Israel had experienced. It was the first summer I spent there. The heat was unbearable. My feet swelled so painfully that on one occasion I had to remove my shoes and walk barefoot to the nearest taxi rank, to get home from the city centre. It was a miserable contrast to the well-being I'd enjoyed during my earlier pregnancy. Moshe's continued army service and subsequent absence from home heightened my distress. Though the delivery was as devoid of incident as the earlier one, Micha developed a rash in the lower part of his body that mandated postponement of his circumcision until he was a month old. He suffered from colic and cried bitterly after each feed. I engaged an acquaintance trained by Anna Freud who cared for him with great tenderness and unfailing patience – a substitute mother.

In 1955, at the suggestion of Adam Mendilow, who was eager to promote me to a more senior post in the English Department, I began research on a thesis topic that he suggested: the use of mythological sources in modern fiction. He transferred me from the English as a Foreign Language track to the department itself, to teach students doing finals in English. Although the number of teaching hours was reduced, I now needed to devote myself more to preparation. Hence the time I had to spend with my children was also reduced. Moshe, who completed his military service two weeks after Micha was born, was engaged in establishing Maoz, Jerusalem's first advertising company, in partnership with Yitzchak Rischin. He worked long hours and was rarely home in time to see the children before they went to sleep. Unprecedented pressure began to build up and, with it, frustration. Although we both enjoyed our work, we had too little time to spend with our sons or alone together.

In 1956, the UK Friends of the Hebrew University awarded me a bursary that would enable me to spend a year in England to further my research. We went off *en famille*, with Moshe planning to visit and learn from Britain's sophisticated advertising agencies. We rented a flat in Cambridge, hiring a cheerful, child-loving Irish maid, Peggy, to do the housework and, whenever necessary, to help care for the children. Joel began attending a nursery-school to which I took him each morning on my way to the University Library. Micha stayed at home, where Moshe, despite occasional sorties to London, became his principal caretaker. No longer colicky, he had become a jolly, friendly and charming child who amazingly developed inexplicable expertise in recognising and declaiming the names of every model of car that he encountered on our outings. Our bliss was abruptly terminated when it became apparent that Moshe was needed in Jerusalem. Although the city had comparatively few industries and businesses that required advertising, a significant number of them had responded favourably to Maoz's proposals. Yitzchak and an additional partner were unable to cope with the unexpected workload. At the end of September, after the High Holy Days and Micha's second birthday, Moshe abruptly disappeared from his life.

167

Before he left, we had already decided that we wanted another child and I soon found that I was indeed pregnant. Being a lone parent was tiring, especially at weekends, when Peggy was off duty. Willy came from time to time to keep me company, and in between his visits I occasionally went to stay with him and my mother, who showered her grandsons not only with hugs and kisses but also with delectable edible treats. When Israel went to war with Egypt at the end of October 1956, Moshe was at once drafted into reserve duty as the officer in charge of a burial unit operated by the IDF chaplaincy. Anxiously, I listened to radio reports, too distracted by worry to concentrate on my research. I was in any case finding the topic that Adam had, with the best of intentions, imposed on me, not to my liking. I loathed the winter cold. I wanted to go home.

Reluctantly, the Friends of Hebrew University agreed to continue disbursing my grant. At Chistmas, I introduced the boys to the singular events that accompany the season: Father Christmas at Harrod's and a pantomime. Then we returned to Jerusalem. Joel had forgotten his Hebrew; Micha had learnt to speak only in English. The excellent kindergarten Joel had attended had closed. It was hard to find vacancies elsewhere at this late stage in the school year. Unable to communicate with his old "friends on the block", Joel for the first (and only) time suffered nightmares, occasionally shouting in his sleep "I want to play!" Several months passed before I was able to return, reluctantly, to reading for my thesis. Ditza, who was born in June, was not welcomed by Micha, who took occasionally, in the absence of adults, to attacking her physically – acts that inevitably brought down severe rebuke and mild punishment.

While teaching a new course on Shakespeare's Problem Plays (*Hamlet, Troilus and Cressida, All's Well that Ends Well* and *Measure for Measure*), I was intrigued by the frequent references to "honour", a term that was clearly being employed in a variety of connotations. Wanting to learn more on this topic, I asked my colleague, Daniel Fineman, who had an encyclopaedic knowledge of literary criticism, what books he could recommend.

"Give me a day," he responded. The following day came his reply: "There isn't one. Why don't you write it?"

In 1958, numerous events marked the 10th anniversary of Israel's establishment. The Women's International Zionist Organisation (WIZO) announced a competition for Housewife of the Year. I was sitting working at the dressing-table in the comparative quiet of our bedroom, with my back to Moshe, who was ill in bed, when he began asking me a series of ridiculously simplistic multiple-choice questions.

"A friend unexpectedly phones to say she's coming to visit. Do you a) bake a cake; b) wash the living-room floor; c) dress elegantly and put on make-up; d) prepare a tray and wait for her arrival?" Absent-mindedly, I responded, slightly annoyed at this banal interruption of my reading. At the end, he said, "This questionnaire is the first stage in a Housewife of the Year competition. I'm going to submit it for you." I laughed, thanked him for his trust in my housewifely qualities and thought no more about the matter until, two weeks later, a student of mine who worked in news at Voice of Israel phoned excitedly to tell me that I had advanced to the second stage of the contest, which would consist of an unannounced visit by WIZO members, who would test the veracity of my responses and see for themselves how well I lived up to the initial positive image of my skills.

A morning of minor disasters. The pipe that drained the water from our primitive washing- machine had slipped out of the bathtub into which the water drained, flooding the entire surrounding area, including the entrance-hall. My "help" was out on her daily walk with Ditza. I was in the middle of preparing for a class I was to give that afternoon. At my wit's end, I seized pail and floor-cloth, took off my shoes to avoid soaking them and began as best I could to mop up. Then the bell rang and there were the WIZO "ladies", all well-dressed, all with the familiar coiffure of hair piled elegantly on the crown of the head. This was the "unannounced visit". Apologetically, I ushered them into the living-room, at the far end of which stood my desk, untidily stacked with books and papers. They asked questions about my family (three children); diet (I seldom cooked and rarely baked); hobbies (none); leisure activities (reading, cinema and concerts); and, finally, membership in women's organisations. Lamely, I had to confess that this was not a sphere in which I'd ever engaged. I noted the looks of disapproval they exchanged. Clearly, I wasn't an appropriate candidate for the final stage of this competition. Then, to my horror, they asked me to show them around the flat.

Engrossed in the task of hastily completing preparation of my afternoon lecture (part of a new, comprehensive and demanding course I was giving on "The Development of Shakespeare's Art", I had delayed making the beds in our bedroom. The children's room was cluttered with toys; the bathroom showed clear signs of its recent flooding. Half-washed clothes lay in the tub. Only the kitchen was fairly tidy, though there were still some dirty dishes in the sink, the remains of a late and hurried breakfast. The ladies took their leave and I returned to my desk. No prize for me! Never having expected to be a winner, I was not disappointed.

169

Yet two weeks later, the same devoted student phoned in delight to tell me I was among the 10 women who had been chosen for the final round of the competition. We were all to gather for a full day in WIZO's model domestic-science centre in Haifa. There, on the previous evening, we would be assigned our tasks and enabled to compile a shopping-list of items to be delivered the next morning. Two of the finalists, I and one other, were from Jerusalem. Before setting out for Haifa, we were invited to meet the mayor, Gershon Agron, who would cheer us on our way. He was clearly as surprised as I was to find me in the company of an ample-bodied, cheerful Kurdish mother of eight who lived in the new hilltop settlement, Mevasseret Yerushalayim, on the road to Tel Aviv. He asked the WIZO ladies how they had made their choice. What were their criteria? One of them explained that though I had fallen short of expectations in certain areas, what had most impressed them, in addition to my successful combination of family and career, was the list posted on my kitchen cupboard that enumerated the household tasks for each day of the week: Sunday – laundry; Monday – ironing; and so on to Thursday – shopping – and Friday – cook for Shabbat. This list indicated a most admirable model of planning and execution: a quality essential to good housekeeping they apparently found both rare and praiseworthy.

I was flabbergasted. I engaged in such planning quite naturally, just as I planned my courses. It would never have occurred to me to post the list as a memo to myself. It was there solely to guide my household help, who in time internalised the routine to the extent that, after a few weeks in service, they no longer needed to consult the list, which I didn't bother to remove. The demands of the Haifa finals were ludicrously unrealistic. Even the least sensible of housewives would never dream of performing the extraordinary tasks imposed on us. Divided into two groups of five, each group would spend the long day in two activities – one based in the kitchen, the other in the laundry – alternating at lunchtime.

My culinary task was relatively simple: to prepare full three meals for a family of four for an entire day. I knew a few simple recipes by heart, and included raw fruit and fresh salad, and I had brought the sharpest of knives from home to facilitate rapid chopping. While I was engaged in cooking, extensive table-laying, making mashed potato and other elements look appetising and attractive, one of my fellow competitors was preparing nothing less than a bar-mitzvah buffet for 24 guests. A mother of four from Haifa, she went about this daunting task in an impressively calm manner, as if it were the most natural thing to perform on a weekday morning. At the prizegiving ceremony, when she was declared the undisputed winner, we were also told that she carried out her household duties in similar composure each morning, before spending her afternoons making pottery in a kiln at the back of her house!

The laundering afternoon revealed clear cultural differences between the competitors. In the well-equipped, sparklingly clean laundry, we found a variety of appliances, ranging from the most advanced model of washing-machines to a paraffin burner on which stood a large, round zinc bowl – the utensils beside which women immigrants from the Arab countries traditionally crouched, bringing water to boil before immersing, scrubbing, rinsing and wringing the washing. The Haifaite made straight for the newest model, despite never before having set eyes on one of its kind. My fellow Jerusalemite headed with equal alacrity for the *pila*, as the zinc bowl was known. Reluctant to spend time figuring out the complexities of a new, more sophisticated model, I chose the machine that approximated most closely to what I had at home. I'd completed my tasks and was standing by the washing-line exhausted, scrutinising the fruits of my handiwork, when a jury of local WIZO members arrived. Anxious to share in the publicity, one of them insisted I take down my washing and reinsert it in the machine, next to which she posed with a large box of soap flakes, intently pouring them in. She was so busily engaged in facing the camera that the flakes fell on the floor and I was left not only to re-rinse and re-hang the laundry but clean up after her.

The first prize was £100 – a very substantial sum in those days. It went to the imperturbable contestant, whose buffet, tempting and appealing in appearance, was eagerly devoured by the judges. I was awarded the second prize, which at first seemed so trivial in comparison that when my journalist-student pointed the microphone at me to ask what I had hoped to win, I dolefully replied, "The money!" It consisted of a week's vacation in Herzliya. In fact, days spent quietly in the Sharon Hotel on the seafront facilitated the composition of a first draft of my doctoral thesis – an analysis of the four Shakespeare plays, which I hoped to expand to enable its submission before the end of the summer vacation six months later. However, when I eventually submitted it to my supervisor, the same Daniel Fineman who'd suggested I write it, he was dissatisfied. After an introductory chapter, in which I presented the extensive use of the term "honour" in the plays, I'd refrained from explaining the various meanings the word bore in their respective contexts. Dismissively, I'd written, "It is not my purpose to engage in close examination of the semantics of the term".

"You're wrong!" Daniel said. "It's precisely the semantics that you need to deal with." With his customary expertise, he presented me with an extensive list

171

of primary sources published in England, France and Italy between the 14th and 16th centuries, which, I eventually learnt, ascribed to the much-disputed concept a set of two dramatically opposed connotations. To read these works I again had to go to England, this time alone and for six weeks. I spent my days at the British Museum intellectually excited. It wasn't a blissful period in the lives of my children, as I learnt on my first morning back at home. I'd arrived late in the evening, when all four (Hephzibah, our second daughter, had been born nine months earlier) were already asleep. We left our bedroom door open, to be able to greet them when they got up. The first to emerge from the children's room was Ditza, on her way to the toilet. Seeing me, she said in a tone of the greatest astonishment, "What, you've come back?" It was clear that she had assumed I had gone forever. A colleague of mine later confirmed this sorrow for Ditza. During my absence, she'd seen Ditza sitting on the pavement, watching her brothers play with their friends. When the colleague asked her why she was sad, she replied, "*Ima*'s gone!" No: not a good mother.

Ditza wasn't alone. Micha had undergone a crisis of his own. Since he was to start first grade in September, I'd purchased all the necessary equipment – textbooks, exercise books, a well-stocked pencil case and a satchel – before my departure. The school, which Joel had been attending for two years, was in the centre of town, 20 minutes' walk from home. I'd assumed that since it was customary for a parent to accompany a pupil on this momentous day, Moshe would take him there and later bring him home. Only on my return from London did a shamefaced Moshe confess that since he had an important meeting that morning he had entrusted Micha to Joel, who was invariably reliable and responsible. However, on this particular occasion Joel, himself excited at entering a new class, had left Micha to his own devices. Having found neither his classroom nor a helpful staff member, Micha had walked home. The following day, Moshe, belatedly aware of his error, accompanied him and introduced him to his teacher, who insensitively scolded Micha for playing truant. Not an auspicious beginning to 12 years of schooling. Unlike Joel, who was a quick learner, diligent and conscientious, fulfilling all the requirements imposed by his teachers, Micha didn't enjoy school. He was too restless and had difficulty in memorising. Whereas throughout Joel's early years at school I'd sat learning Talmud with him, discussing Biblical texts he was required to analyse, I didn't do the same with Micha, nor did I have the sensitivity to discuss his needs or the patience to spend time listening to him as he stumbled his way through the chapters he was to learn by heart.

172

When the time came for him to switch to high-school, it was clear that the *yeshiva*-style establishment he was already attending was inappropriate. He was too much of a free spirit to fit into any of the religious schools that existed at the time but we finally found an understanding principal who was prepared to welcome him. But problems persisted. At every parents' evening, I was told that, although he was intelligent, he wasn't sufficiently diligent. Finally, the principal refused to promote him to 12th grade for the school-leaving exams, insisting he repeat 11th. We decided to move Micha to an "external" school for his final year.

The failure was, of course, that of the school rather than of a non-conformist pupil. I was tired of hearing the same refrain. "He's a competent student when he's interested," as he was in history, "but he doesn't make an effort." Micha, who never obtained his high-school certificate, over time became the most academically successful of my children: a perceptive and original literary critic, and an admired teacher, adored by all his students, whether at the experimental high-school he eventually headed or at the various adult-education programmes in which he taught Jewish philosophy and Hebrew literature. The transformation was largely the work of Judith, the remarkable woman he married, whom he had first met when she was in 12th grade. A year later, she left for the US, intending to study at Brandeis University. Then catastrophe struck.

When the Yom Kippur War broke out in 1973, Micha was in the early stages of his military service as a paratrooper. Based in the Jordan Valley, he had been appalled by the arrogance and insensitivity with which his colleagues treated the local population. He loathed injustice of any kind and was perturbed by the laxity with which his commanding officers related not only to wanton harassment of Palestinians but also to bullying and discrimination among the men. On parents' visiting-day, Moshe and I warily went to voice our objections to the officer in charge of the training camp. We told him about the beating-up of those whose failures to fulfil demands led to collective punishment for the entire platoon.

"Good," he said. "I'm glad to hear the boys are ensuring obedience to orders."

Two weeks into the Yom Kippur war, my 19-year-old son phoned to tell me that his platoon was being sent to the front line. For a tense three weeks we heard nothing from him. Moshe had been drafted and was once again, as in 1956, in Sinai with his squad of Orthodox men, identifying and burying the unprecedented and unanticipated, distressingly large number of casualties. From time to time, he relayed to me rumours related to Micha's possible whereabouts. Then I received a laconic postcard.

173

"I'm here just in my clothes," it read. "Everything else is gone." And the following day, Micha walked in, bedraggled and exhausted. He wouldn't tell me what he'd meant in that brief message. Determined to elicit even a little information, I began asking him about those of his colleagues I'd come to know and whose parents I'd met when we visited our sons. One of them, Moshe, was the boyfriend of Yael, a daughter of the professor I'd not been permitted to succeed as Dean at the University of the Negev. From time to time we'd exchanged what little information each of us had about the whereabouts of our loved ones. Now I began my enquiries with his name.

"How's Moshe?" I asked. Micha stared at me blankly.

"Dead," he said.

"And Aryeh?"

Again, "Dead."

And so I went down the list, overwhelmed with grief. Micha couldn't comprehend that I'd known nothing of what he and his comrades had endured. Only gradually did I learn that of his entire platoon only he and one comrade had survived the strategic blunders that led to the massive number of casualties, the obtuseness and obstinacy of commanding officers who failed to evaluate correctly the Egyptians' capacity to resist the IDF forces that in 1967 had so rapidly overcome the enemy. Micha had yet to confront a further ordeal: condolence visits to the families of his fallen comrades. We accompanied him on the first of these, to the parents of Moshe, where we found Yael and her mother among the mourners. With no prior greeting, Moshe's father leapt at Micha.

"Why did he die? How is it you're alive?" He seemed to assume that Micha had evaded death by not obeying orders. Micha was at a loss for words. Other visits proved no less traumatic. One mother, told the reason why he and his fellow survivor were visiting her, gazed at them in surprise.

"What are you talking about? What do you mean when you say he's dead? Look, he's outside in the garden."

Moshe, now an expert in printing and publishing, helped Micha compile and produce an elegiac booklet containing an individual tribute to each one of his slain companions. The entire Duvdevan company in which he had served was disbanded after the war.

Micha then had a breakdown. For 34 years he suffered from post-traumatic stress disorder, lovingly tended by his ever-patient wife. Married in 1975, they had three children.

"We can't invite friends over," one of them once matter-of-factly maintained, with no trace of resentment. "We have a mad father."

Micha cut himself off from his siblings, rarely attending family events. "And who didn't show up? Micha!" became a recurring sarcastic comment. Since he and his family lived in the apartment above ours, Moshe and I remained in ongoing contact. The trauma reached its peak in 1993, a short while before the 20th anniversary of the event from which it stemmed. Judith, normally calm, came down in untypically great distress. She'd learnt that Micha intended to go to Sinai, to the very scene of the disastrous attack he had survived, to immolate himself. She immediately contacted his commanding officer at the time, Joel Sharon, who had lost his legs and was wheelchair-bound. Sharon, who had directed a film entitled *Shellshock*, in which the major protagonist was coincidentally named Micha, asked to meet him that very evening and after a conversation that lasted until 2 am, alerted the IDF's chief psychiatrist. Micha was at once hospitalised at Tel Hashomer. Over the years that followed, he was in and out of mental wards, frustrated by the IDF's failure to recognise PTSD as a form of disability. Only in September 1998 did he feel compelled to agree to be interviewed for a long article in *Ha'aretz*, in which he detailed in full the military debacles that had led to his breakdown. The cure, when it at last came, was miraculous. Returning home from synagogue after the closing service of Yom Kippur in 2011, Moshe and I encountered Micha and Judith just leaving the house.

"Netta," they told us, referring to the older of their daughters, "has given birth to a boy!"

Micha was transformed. A doting grandfather who instantly established an intensely close relationship with his grandson Amos, he began once again to attend family events. He allowed us to kiss and hug him – acts he had strenuously avoided during the years of his illness. I felt as if I, too, had once again given birth to a son.

Late in the summer of 1958, shortly before the beginning of the school year, Joel developed mumps. A day later, so did Micha. Aware that this illness can cause sterility in adult males, Moshe scrupulously kept his distance. I did not. Very shortly after the boys' rapid recovery, I fell victim to the virus. What in them had lasted a mere two days kept me in bed with a high temperature for an entire week. The swelling didn't subside. I couldn't eat. Even drinking was painful. Moshe temporarily took refuge in the study. Isolated in our bedroom, I was overcome by boredom. I lacked energy even to read. All I could do was listen to the radio, which repeated a few highly popular songs *ad nauseam*. Incommunicado, I was intensely miserable. Once health was fully restored, I discovered I'd missed my period – a phenomenon unprecedented save when I'd been pregnant. All three of my pregnancies had been carefully planned so as to leave approximately two and a half years between them. Ditza, my youngest, was only 15 months old. Well, I thought, so be it and set off cheerfully to inform my friendly GP of the good news. Dr Spiegel didn't share my joy.

"That's bad," he said, a worried look on his face. "It's dangerous." I was flabbergasted. What could be the danger in bearing another child? Dr Spiegel summoned his wife. Though trained as a gynaecologist, she had no practice of her own but occasionally acted as his consultant. She knew me well and was aware that I'd been ill. "Shalvi's pregnant," her husband informed her. His use of my surname (which he often affectionately softened to "Shalvichen") added an official tone to the announcement. She, too, expressed alarm. Infection with mumps, she informed me, could result in brain damage to the embryo. The child I was carrying might well prove to be mentally retarded.

"That would be terrible, unbearable," she added. She knew all too well that of which she spoke. The Spiegels themselves had a mentally retarded son. Raised in a Swiss institution that specialised in educating youngsters like him, he had returned to Jerusalem as a relatively independent adult and was a familiar figure at IPO concerts, invariably sitting in the front row and uninhibitedly approaching the conductor to offer an affable congratulatory handshake. "You mustn't have this baby," she declared categorically. "It wouldn't be fair to you, to the child or to your other children." The Spiegels exchanged meaningful looks.

"You must abort," Dr Spiegel said.

"Yes," Malka added. "You must abort." *Abort!* To abort a child was to take a life. It was immoral. It went against nature. But would it be less immoral wittingly to give birth to a child that might never be able to lead a normal life? How could I condemn another human being to a blighted existence? Confused, struggling to make sense of what I was hearing, I burst into tears.

"But it's illegal!" I blurted out, as if that were the determining factor. My profound abidance by law, so deeply instilled in me by parents and tutors, seemingly led me to ignore other considerations. Malka sat down beside me. Putting her arm around me in soothing sympathy, she said:

"Don't worry about that," she said. "We'll help you. Nobody needs to know."

When urine tests confirmed the pregnancy, we decided to wait no longer. In a back room in the Spiegels' home, where he regularly received his patients, I learnt that there was a well-equipped operating room which I'd never before had occasion to enter. With their laboratory assistant at my side to hold my hand, the Spiegels delicately set about their task. I recall nothing save the excruciating pain as the womb was widened. Nothing I'd experienced in normal childbirth prepared me for it. To stop myself from screaming, I squeezed my eyes tight shut and clenched my teeth so firmly that the pain in my jaw distracted me from that in my vagina. Throughout the procedure, the Spiegels repeatedly reassured me:

"It'll soon be over!" "Only a minute more!" To me, that minute – if that indeed is what it was – seemed infinite. At the end, I was physically and emotionally exhausted. I never told Moshe about the abortion. In fact, I told nobody. I have never spoken of it. Yet, similarly, I've never forgotten it. Though I gave birth with my customary ease to three additional blessedly healthy, carefully planned, children, the thought of that unborn child still plagues me. Was it a girl or a boy? Fair-haired like Micha or dark like Ditza? As placid as Hephziba or wild, like Benzi? And would it indeed have been in some way abnormal or might it, despite our fears, have proved no less healthy than all its siblings? The questions can never be answered; the regret and guilt never wholly assuaged.

The physical conditions in which I gave birth steadily improved as the austerity and improvisation that marked almost all aspects of life in the early years of statehood gradually gave way to increasing stability. Micha and Ditza were born at Bikur Cholim, a purpose-built hospital erected in the centre of the city in 1925. By the time of Benzi's birth in 1963, the new Hadassah Hospital had been built in Ein Kerem, replacing its original quarters on still inaccessible Mount Scopus. With each move, wards became smaller, until only four women shared a room that had its own shower and toilet. The need to use these facilities before fellow occupants woke became less urgent. During the day, babies could sleep at their mothers' bedside. However, this sensible practice, which facilitates breastfeeding "on demand", was discouraged by the nurses, who preferred to have all newly born babies under what they apparently considered their own more watchful eyes, to be brought to the mothers at fixed hours but never during the night. Apart from the physical conditions, little changed. Wails of anguish still echoed around the delivery room, harassed midwives ran from one labouring woman to another and obstetricians still concentrated primarily on private patients like me rather than on the proletarian Sick Fund members. Above all, most women remained uninformed of the six-stage Lamaze practice, which resembles that of Grantly Dick-Read but is more detailed.

I had the good fortune to find a qualified instructor, the wife of my GP, whose classes I attended throughout the final six weeks of my last two pregnancies. She not only taught us the rules of relaxation and correct breathing but forewarned us of the inevitably difficult final "push", which requires breathing like a "panting dog". It works! I can still visualise the sunshine pouring through the window opposite me as I lay, contented and relaxed, with my newborn youngest child resting on the belly from which she had emerged a very short while earlier. Finally, I'd got it right. Could it have been the reassuring circumstances of her birth as well as the calm of mind that I maintained throughout the comparatively short time that elapsed between my arrival at Hadassah and her birth that led to her being the child most like myself? Named after my mother, Pnina was placid and calm. She is creative and artistic. Under Moshe's tutelage she became a talented graphic artist and for some time worked with him on his encyclopaedias. Throughout the years during which he was too occupied in his work to take time off to join me in my travels, she became my companion.

I had the joy of witnessing the development of her aesthetic tastes. She loves theatre as much as I do and can make critical comparison between several interpretations of *Hamlet* we saw. She was interested in fashion, and we spent time in London and New York, crossing from one side to the other of Bond Street or Madison Avenue, inspecting the shop windows that displayed the latest models. Her teachers at Pelech complained that she drew incessantly throughout lessons. She began studying fashion design when she completed her army service but rapidly discovered that this required not only artistic talent but an indispensable capacity to sew her exquisite designs. Alone of my children, she became a committed feminist and happily drew illustrations for the quarterly newsletters the Israel Women's Network published while I was its chairwoman. It seems fitting that today she and her family share my home.

Child number four, Hephziba, the second of my daughters, differs greatly from her older sister in both appearance and in nature: Ditza is dark-haired and black-eyed, Hephziba has a fair complexion and blue-grey eyes. When my mother fell ill on her final visit to Jerusalem, Hephziba would perch by her bed "reading" from a Little Golden Book that she had learnt by heart. "Her face is as beautiful as the shining sky of Israel," my doting mother would say, in Yiddish. Like Joel and Micha before her, Ditza began attending nursery-school shortly before the birth of the next sibling. Every morning I would accompany her, taking Hephziba with me and staying for a short while to see Ditza settling in, reassured by my

178

presence. One morning, my household help, who doubled as "nursemaid", burst panic-stricken into my study.

"Hephzi's disappeared! I can't find her anywhere."

Our four-room apartment had few hiding places. We searched under beds and inside cupboards. She was nowhere to be found. Noticing that the front door was slightly ajar, I concluded she must have left the apartment. We hastened to the garden that surrounded the house. No Hephziba. In increasing anxiety, we went out into the street, a dead end which served as the playground for all the children of the neighbourhood. In mid-morning the street was empty. It might have been my maternal instinct that led me to turn the corner to the little hill that led to the road, parallel to our own, where the nursery-school was located. There was Hephziba, happily serving as a living plaything – a walking, talking doll. Taking the hint, I took to leaving her there for two hours every morning.

Unlike her gregarious younger sister, Ditza was an introvert. When we moved to Bet Hakerem she refused to continue attending nursery-school, preferring to occupy herself in close observation and handling small objects she chanced upon. She might spend an hour watching ants laboriously bearing a straw from place to place. She searched for (but never picked) the first flowers of spring, the first almond blossoms. She collected tiny pebbles with coloured markings. She kept and lovingly cared for a white rabbit, weeping inconsolably when it died of lead poisoning after the railing of her balcony was painted. When an old house in our neighbourhood was torn down to be replaced by a modern building, Ditza rescued the wild cyclamen corms from its garden and planted them in our own, where they continue to bloom every spring.

Ditza played a vital role in Pnina's intellectual development. One evening at the supper table, four-year-old Pnina surprised us by describing in great detail how the eye functions.

"How do you know all this?" Moshe asked.

"Ditza told me," came the reply. It emerged that Ditza was systematically working her way through *Tarbut*, a children's encyclopaedia that had arrived in weekly instalments over several years, imparting its contents to a responsive pupil. Six children, all born to the same father and mother, yet each in innumerable ways different from the others. They remind me of the old advertisements for Heinz's "57 Varieties", with its accompanying adage: "Variety is the Spice of Life".

Throughout the years of our children's growing-up, Moshe and I were intensely engaged in our respective professions. Maoz went bankrupt in 1956. There were too few clients in Jerusalem. Jerusalem Pencils, Keter Plastics, the Jerusalem Shoe Company and Tara Cosmetics were all eventually persuaded to avail themselves of its pioneering service. The company produced sophisticated, high-quality, often witty advertising and publicity of a kind that had hitherto been unknown in Israel. However, the compliments the work elicited couldn't compensate for the clients' failure to pay their bills on time. For months, neither Moshe nor Yitzchak drew a salary, finally concluding that Jerusalem was not the place for a firm such as theirs.

Moshe took a special interest in printing and at once set about learning more. He studied for six months at the Hadassah-Brandeis School of Printing and apprenticed at a small firm that had done most of Maoz's printing. When Yitzchak was appointed head of the Israel Programme for Scientific Translations, he brought Moshe with him to devise, implement and oversee a method for efficient production of English translations of Russian scientific works with which the US government, alarmed by the unanticipated technological expertise demonstrated by the invention of the Sputnik, was anxious to become acquainted. Moshe originated a complex and extraordinarily effective process that over the course of each year ensured delivery of numerous works in a variety of disciplines, some of which (such as ichthyology and forestry) weren't widely known in Israel. Coupling Russian-speakers sufficiently fluent in English with Israeli experts in the respective scientific areas, he oversaw the compilation of texts that were then passed on to a team of skilled typists, equipped with the most up-to-date IBM electronic typewriters, who worked in shifts of eight hours from 8 am till midnight. Graphic artists were employed to create and delicately affix illustrative material, and the final product then went to offset printing and binding. The firm produced well over 1,000 texts, in most of which the National Institute of Science found little of interest. However, one of the works ultimately saved the US thousands of dollars, more than covering the cost of the entire project: a book on a method of cloud-breaking that could produce rain in drought-stricken regions.

Moshe had a capacity for working around the clock, taking only a short daily break to come home for a shower and what he referred to as a "cat nap". As the end-of-year deadline for finalisation and delivery of all the year's publications approached, he took advantage of this gift. Throughout November and December he was rarely at home. He later displayed the same exceptional ingenuity in devising innovative methods for printing and publishing when, again at Yitzchak's initiative, he went to work on the monumental *Encyclopaedia Judaica*, for which he introduced computerised typesetting to Israel.

In 1975 our respective roles in the household were reversed. After Sadie's sudden death in 1971, Harry had remarried – twice. First, he brought a blonde widow back from a visit to his sisters in the US. Lacking prior acquaintance with Israel and even a smatter of any language but English, she understandably had difficulty in adjusting to a culture and environment so different from those with which she was familiar. After only a few months of marriage, she requested a divorce. Not long after, on a second visit to the US, Harry met another blonde widow, who'd spent some years caring for her husband during his final illness. She, too, knew nothing about Israel and even seemed surprised to find that not everybody spoke English, and that foodstuffs looked and tasted different from those with which she was familiar. She was extremely unhappy. When Harry suffered a stroke some months after their marriage, she announced that she lacked the desire or ability to nurse a second husband. She returned to the US and Harry came to live with us.

Moshe had never taken a single day of sick leave. Finding that he had over 24 months of "vacation" due to him, he availed himself of the opportunity to leave his job and devote himself to caring for his father. At precisely the same time, I took up the position of principal of Pelech: I thus became the one who left the house early in the morning, returning late in the afternoon, often bringing work home with me. Moshe took over the household duties, discovering he enjoyed shopping and, especially, cooking. In contrast to my own limited repertoire of tried-and-tested main dishes that accorded with our children's still unsophisticated tastes, he began experimenting with more unusual fare, referring to the many cookery books we had accumulated over the years that I had rarely consulted. French, Italian, Indian and even Chinese dishes began to appear on the dinner table, precisely when our children, developing more sophisticated tastes, were prepared to welcome the innovative cuisine. Wanting to show off their father's culinary prowess, they invited friends to share the delicacies, oblivious to the guests' startled response to seeing a man wearing an apron. Moshe printed new visiting cards, in which he described his current areas of employment: Marketing, Home Economics and Transportation (the last referring to his function as the family chauffeur).

Excerpt from an e-mail received on 10 February 2016 from our oldest grandchild, Assaf:

I'm spending time in NYC continuing on my fundraising mission for my company.

I was sitting for dinner in a kosher restaurant and Rabbie Shteinzaltz [*sic*] was sitting next to me.*

I introduced myself and he said to me, "I talked today about your grandfather". I asked him – what did you talk about? And he said, "How he was so sure and secure about his manhood that he was happy to be the one staying at home". And said he remembered him from "Keter days". Thought you would like to hear!

Housebound, Moshe started to work as a freelance translator, editor and production manager, specialising in reference books. After Harry's death in 1982, he was able to devote more time to his occupation. Still working from home, he employed a staff that grew from one to five – all women – including Pnina, whom he taught the basics of her career as a graphic artist while he was engaged in producing a five-volume *Encyclopaedia of the Holocaust*, published by Yad Vashem and Sifriat-Hapoalim, which initially appeared in Hebrew in 1990 and, later, in English.

He was enamoured of reference books. Hardly a meal passed on a Friday evening without his consulting one or other of the vast and varied collection we had acquired over the years. No matter what the topic under debate, Moshe had a book for it. Becoming increasingly involved in my feminist activities and noticing the ever-growing literature on feminism of which we were apprised by the *Women's Review of Books*, he dreamed of producing a multi-volume "World Encyclopedia of Women". As he came to realise that this was too vast – and hence too expensive – a project, he whittled it down to the *Encyclopedia of Jewish Women*. Here, he was again innovative. Aware that a multi-volume hardcover work would be hard to market, he decided to publish it digitally in compact-disk form. He established Shalvi Publishing.

For five years, our home was once more a hub of activity. Again, a constantly growing number of devoted women worked in shifts from morning until late in the evening, precisely at a time when all the children (including Pnina, who, still unmarried, occupied a one-room apartment on the top floor of our house) were no longer living at home. I joined the team as assistant editor during the final two years before publication in 2006, proofreading and frequently revising every single

—

* Rabbi Adin Steinsaltz published a Hebrew translation of the *Jerusalem Talmud*, production of which began at Keter Press in 1965, when Moshe headed its printing press and bindery.

one of the entries. A labour of true love in which we were united, the *EJW* was the acme of Moshe's remarkable career in publishing. He was a model employer. He made a list of his employees' preferences, welcoming each one at the start of her shift with the appropriate beverage: tea (herbal or caffeinated), espresso, cappuccino, with milk frothed or plain... No wonder they all uniformly adored him, just as their predecessors at Keter had done. When he hosted a celebratory lunch on the completion of the gigantic undertaking, there were tearful expressions of gratitude and regret. My own response was one of relief: we would once again have the house to ourselves.

While my work in academia remained an ongoing source of income, from 1973 communal work rapidly occupied more and more of my time and my creative energy. Although innumerable hours of meetings were held at home, that time was not available for my children. Even Friday evening dinners, which had been the sole fixed time of the week that we regularly spent together in conversation and song, became occasions for entertaining the constantly increasing number of guests whose acquaintance I made during my travels. Shabbat-eve at the Shalvis was considered essential to the "Israel experience". Conversation was invariably interesting but those of my children who remained at home or were on occasion fellow guests lacked the fluency in English that could enable them to participate actively. We continued to holiday together but even four stimulating weeks amid the delights of Tuscany or England cannot compensate for 48 weeks of emotional deprivation.

I was not there to comfort them. Immersed in the pioneering activities of Pelech and the Israel Women's Network, I was not a source of the loving individual attention every child desires and needs. Frustrated, they sought other sources of attention and affection – friends, lovers and eventually spouses. Today my children reproach me for my neglect but I take a certain degree of (cold) comfort in the fact that they've learnt from their own negative experience and that they, in contrast to me, are not only model parents but equally dedicated grandparents. Only one of them, Pnina, has followed me into social activism. I'm far from wishing to imply that family and work can't be combined. Quite apart from the stunting effect that Betty Friedan diagnosed among well-educated, housebound women, economic considerations increasingly dictate the importance of shared income-earning. A variety of practices, some of which are already in effect in progressive countries, can facilitate the combination: two years of parental leave, shared by both parents; quality pre-school childcare; a long school day; nourishing school meals; flexi-time; job-sharing; working from home; return-to-work training… All of these would enable both parents (or a single parent) to devote an appropriate amount of time not only to their children, but also – as longevity increases – to ageing parents and other family members in need of physical and emotional support.

"W(ork) + F(amily) + C(ommunity) = WB (Well-Being)." I learnt this formula from a professor of sociology at Radcliffe. While this assumes an investment of time and energy in all three areas, it does not specify the optimal allocation of time to each one. The assumption, presumably, is that proportions will vary according to the age and specific needs of the caretakers and those in need of care. I erred in my undue, excessive, dedication to social causes at a time when mothering should have been my major focus. The numerous prizes and awards, tokens of the "fame" I achieved, are poor substitutes for what in Yiddish is called *naches* – delight, satisfaction. Ruefully, I contemplate the cryptic final lines of Robert Frost's tellingly entitled poem, "The Road Not Taken":

> I shall be telling this with a sigh
> Somewhere ages and ages hence:
> Two roads diverged in a wood, and I –
> I took the one less travelled by,
> And that has made all the difference.

A Postscript

When Member of Knesset Shulamit (Shula) Aloni, Amira Dotan and I once appeared together to speak on women's status before an audience of women in the south of the country, the inevitable question arose: "How do you combine your work with being the mother of young children?"

Amira, the first to respond, spoke of her husband's active role as a father but confessed that she was fully aware that this, combined with her high rank as Commanding Officer of the IDF's Women's Corps, led to his being derided as henpecked. In similar confessional mode, I revealed my guilt at being too frequently absent from home and family, relying excessively on a supportive spouse. To our consternation – and contrary to all principles of sisterhood – sharp-tongued Shula responded with withering contempt. "Children," she concluded, "can manage quite well without their mothers." Disconcerted by the unexpected mockery and reluctant to enter into a debate that might well result in further ridicule, Amira and I remained silent. The audience, delighted at Shula's wit, presumably interpreted our failure to respond as tacit agreement with her criticism.

When Shula died in 2013, I went to pay my condolences to her three sons. I sat for most of the time with the eldest, an educator well-known for his progressive views, which largely coincided with mine. Before I left, I plucked up sufficient courage to ask him what Shula was like as a mother. The question was unexpected: he reflected briefly before responding.

"She wasn't a good mother in the usual sense. She never took us on her knee to tell us stories or hug us. *Abba* did that. But," he added defensively, "she took us to the theatre and to concerts. *Abba* was always there."

When my parents came to visit me after my first Purim in Israel they realised that I was firm in my decision to remain in the country: my country. I had a responsible job and numerous friends. What I lacked was a home of my own. With their consent, I began looking for an appropriate residence, assisted in my search by Mr Weinberger, a kind, fatherly estate agent, who recommended purchasing a small flat in Rasco, a new housing project. Located on a hill only a short distance from Rehavia "as the crow flies", it was nevertheless isolated from surrounding neighbourhoods. Fearful for my safety, my parents objected to the remoteness and indicated their preference for a rental, rather than purchase. My mother may still have nurtured the hope that I would return to London.

Mr Weinberger then proposed a new apartment that was in the process of being built on the fourth floor of an existing house in Rehavia, Terra Sancta, where I taught, and within easy walking distance to the centre of town. At the suggestion of my landlady and her well-informed family, I took the plans to Ella Czapski, an interior designer from Berlin already famous for having decorated the Rehovot home of Israel's first president, Chaim Weizmann. Czapski was a short, sturdy, trouser-wearing lesbian. Her partner, known to all only as Frau Stern, was, in contrast, timid, thin and drooping, like the earrings she favoured. Czapski had a small shop off Ben-Yehuda Street filled with wondrous objects – old furniture, draperies, brass and copper utensils.

We took to each other instantly. She not only suggested some changes in the internal structure of the apartment but, at my request, began designing its furniture, immediately understanding the contemporary yet classical style that I like most. Initially intended as an unimaginative utilitarian three-room apartment, it was transformed into one in which there was a well-proportioned living-room and a slightly larger, longer bedroom, the latter with a half-room at one end, not separated from it in any way save by short walls on which low bookshelves were arranged, as they also were on two walls of the living-room. Both living-room and bedroom could be accessed from either the entrance hall or from the study, forming a fluid and convenient continuum.

It was in the exciting course of this planning that Moshe and I decided to marry. The first, unforgettable encounter between Czapski and Moshe caused me intense embarrassment. He arrived wearing shorts and a T-shirt, looking like a schoolboy. I noted Czapski's disbelieving response as he walked towards us where we stood waiting outside the Eynats' (my landlords') house. Could this be the person that I, a cultured, well-educated, sophisticated European, had chosen as my life-partner? Fortunately, his cheerful, easy-going manner won her over and in any case he made no attempt to influence our plans or interfere with them. There was no need to change anything on which we had already decided, since the metal single bed conveniently had an additional pull-out one underneath it.

I loved that flat. High up in the treetops, with a west-facing balcony outside the bedroom from which there was a broad and beautiful view over the as yet unbuilt-up hills beyond the Valley of the Cross. Compact, comfortable and aesthetically pleasing, it was much admired by all our friends. Every Saturday evening it was the setting for an "open house" to which no individual invitations were issued but which regularly attracted at least half a dozen people. The sole drawback was that the flat was cold. Although our wily and miserly *haredi* (ultra-Orthodox) landlord had added a storey, he had not augmented the central-heating system in such a manner as to enable it to serve us adequately. We had to resort to a kerosene stove, on which one could also heat up a kettle and thus provide the needed humidity.

Kerosene was sold by horse-and-cart vendors, whose approach was heralded by a bell and the call of *"Neft, neft"*. The method of purchase was that the homeowners came to the wagon carrying large cans capable of holding at least 10 litres. These were refilled on the spot. If the vendor was generous and the customers not too numerous, he'd agree to carry them to the purchaser's doorway. I didn't yet own a can and when the time came for me to purchase fuel, all I had was the empty bottle of Asti Spumante with which we'd celebrated our housewarming. With this in hand, I hastened down the steps and into the street, calling after the vendor, who'd already moved further on. He stared at me in disbelief when he saw the receptacle I'd brought with me and I was too embarrassed to know how to explain my idiocy in thinking it could be adequate.

We stayed in this first home for over four years. When our first child was born, his crib fitted perfectly alongside the half-wall between the bedroom and study but once our second son was born, in September 1954, the flat was clearly inadequate. In order to keep Micha's pram in our bedroom, we had to wheel Joel's crib into the living-room every evening, in the process considerably damaging the walls. It was time to look for something larger and more accessible. In any case, the absence of a space in the house entrance in which one could leave a pram had necessitated my heaving our massive English perambulator up 84 steps every time I took Joel out for a walk. According to my loveable obstetrician, this was actually very good exercise for a pregnant woman, helping her to develop the muscular strength required in childbirth!

Our second home was very near the first, in Benyamin Metudela Street, overlooking the entire Valley of the Cross as far as Givat Ram in the west. Every morning a shepherd led his flock from north to south, between the Arab villages that lay on the outskirts of the city. In spring, the olive groves of the valley were bright with poppies and cyclamen. Here we had four rooms: one for the children, a proper bedroom for ourselves and two additional rooms with only a ceiling-to-floor curtain serving to divide them when necessary. One served as living-room, the other as study. Our library had expanded considerably and bookshelves now lined all the walls from floor to ceiling. A major advantage of this home was that it was at the very end of a wide street, where all the many children of the neighbourhood – populated primarily by young couples like ourselves – congregated to play, forming fast friendships of which some have lasted to this day. But in 1959, as more houses were added beyond ours, traffic increased. When the bus route to town from the new Hebrew University campus was changed so as to run though our street, playing there became impossible, prompting us to move yet again, this time beyond the city to an outlying suburb dating from the early 1920s, with single-family homes built by the original owners, each of which had a large garden – many of them with fruit trees that justified the neighbourhood's name, Beit Ha-Kerem: House of the Orchard.

As with our first home in Alfassi Street, we purchased the new one in time to determine its layout. Again with the help of Czapski, who was undaunted by the initial opposition of the contractor to any proposals of change in his original plans, we devised a two-level four-bedroom apartment. Below, accessible by an interior staircase, were two more rooms – the master bedroom with its own bathroom and a large study. Because we were the first purchasers in a complex of three units each comprising two apartments, and since my brother had decided to purchase the upper of the two apartments that composed our "unit", we were able to ensure a front and a back garden. Like the original builders of our neighbourhood, we too planted fruit trees and laid out a large lawn at the front of the house, which in time became a favourite meeting place of all the children in the area. A shade tree near the low stone fence was designated the "neighbourhood tree" under which they gathered in pauses between games. After Moshe's parents immigrated to Israel in 1962, bringing a see-saw, slide and swings, the lawn itself became a playground for the younger ones.

The road remained unpaved until the late 1960s. Each winter a vast puddle gathered outside our house, the water accumulating as it ran down the slope opposite us. In the course of our first winter at our new home, as I sat working at my desk in the basement, I felt a sudden cold on my feet and, looking down, saw water flooding through the floor tiles. Our contractor had skimped on insulation and during the two winters that followed we occasionally woke up to find the study submerged. During our third winter, with a huge pond and a good deal of mud making it difficult to enter or leave the house, Moshe decided to take the matter into his own hands. Frequent appeals to pave the street having proved ineffective, he went to the relevant municipal department and angrily dumped a pair of extremely muddy boots on the desk of the startled official in charge. At the end of that winter, the road was paved. Berechyahu Street is now no longer the dead-end it was when we moved here in 1961 and today children in any case no longer play in the streets. Since it is one-way only, the sound of traffic seldom disturbs us. My brother's apartment, in which he in fact never lived, preferring one more centrally located once he came on *aliya* in 1996, was at first let but when our second grandchild was born to our eldest son, he and his family came to live there. We seized the opportunity of renovation, adding a one-room, self-contained flat under the tiled roof. It served several of our children in turn as a means of living independently while also close to all of the comforts of the parental home.

One by one, the children left home but this didn't result in greater privacy for Moshe and me. In 2000 he'd at last begun to work on the *EJW*. In 2005, the magnum opus was completed. Our house could revert to being a home. We decided to carry out much-needed renovation, installing a new kitchen and updating the "children's" bathroom… Moshe and I sought refuge for a few weeks with friends in New York. When we returned, we refurnished the four "new" rooms. I now had a sunny, south-facing study-*cum*-sitting-room, through the wall-length window of which I could again see treetops and watch a resident woodpecker at work carving out a large round cavity in one bark after another.

Moshe's office moved back to the third floor as he began a new project, still working with the most senior of his assistants. One room remained holding the *EJW* files and archives. We were able to host house guests.

Then this idyll too was shattered. Our youngest daughter and her husband, unemployed and barely making a living, moved in with us, together with their two young children. Again, no privacy. Shared facilities. Lifestyles that occasionally conflict. But still home. And much love and mutual support. Whenever people urged Moshe and myself to move to more compact quarters ("Why do you need so much space?" they'd ask, uncomprehendingly), my standard reply was always the same: "Our next move will be to Sanhedria, where we already have adjoining plots". This is where Moshe's parents and mine are buried. With his wonted consideration for others, Moshe chose this expensive site to make it easier for our offspring to visit all the graves at one time. With his customary foresight, he even provided instructions regarding the design of our tombstones and the texts to be inscribed on them.

Now he lies at rest there, the empty space beside him ready to hold my body in our last home.

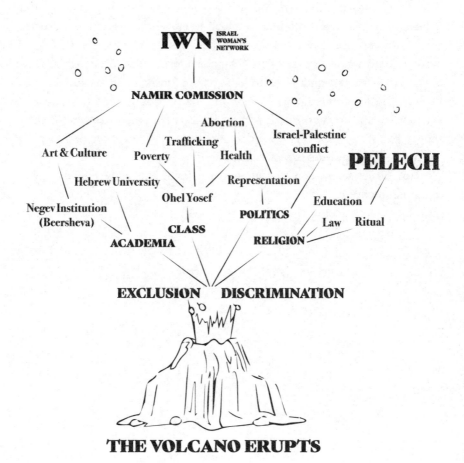

IWN ISRAEL WOMAN'S NETWORK

NAMIR COMISSION

Abortion

Trafficking

Art & Culture   Poverty   Health   Israel-Palestine conflict

Hebrew University   Representation   **PELECH**

Negev Institution (Beersheva)   Ohel Yosef   Education

POLITICS   Law   Ritual

CLASS   **RELIGION**

ACADEMIA

EXCLUSION   DISCRIMINATION

THE VOLCANO ERUPTS

The Volcano Erupts

LIFE IS A RIVER. A tired, clichéd metaphor, yet appropriate... We have our tributaries, the generations that precede us. The waters flow for many miles, sometimes smoothly, sometimes transformed into perilous rapids. Then they might diverge, forming numerous streams that all, ultimately, flow into the sea of the unknown. In my case, after childhood, adolescence, student days, first professional work, marriage and motherhood, a volcano erupted. It transformed my personal landscape, gouging into it a series of unplanned turbulent distributaries: feminism, education, religious rebellion, political activism and social reform. These formed a vast delta before gradually subsiding into a sunless, as yet unexplored sea of oblivion.

SHOCK!

Academia

"How would you like to set up a new English Department in Beersheba?" Adam Mendilow asked when he phoned me one day in the spring of 1969. I was taken aback. Three years earlier I'd been asked the identical question with reference to Tel Aviv. I'd rejected it out of hand because I was expecting my sixth child. Now my youngest was two years old, I had an excellent "nanny" and there seemed no objective ground for refusal.

191

"Would I be able to try to do something different?" I asked.

"Why not?" he replied.

I was tempted. I thrive on challenges, rarely weighing up the difficulties I might encounter. This opportunity to break away from a model that I perceived as outdated was irresistible. I consulted not only Moshe but my older children too. Nobody raised any objections, some were even encouraging. None of us were aware of obstacles or difficulties, nobody had a clear idea of what lay ahead, other than the fact that I would have to spend more time away from home. The older ones were as excited as myself by what was clearly going to be part of "making the desert bloom".

The BA programme at the Hebrew University had become stultified. Apart from a proficiency in English acquired in special EFL courses, students' acquisition of knowledge was limited to two, sometimes merely one, major subject. The class load was too heavy to allow time for reading between classes, so that in the English Department many students, particularly those who were also gainfully employed, attended classes without any prior acquaintance with the texts to be discussed. My dream was that in this new institution we might revert to the original vision of the BA degree when it was first introduced in Jerusalem in 1949: a wide range of general studies that would produce what the rector at the time had called a "*Ben-Adam*", a *Mensch*.

Indeed, the Institute of Higher Education in the Negev was from its inception novel, established jointly by the country's three senior universities: the Hebrew University, responsible for Humanities and Social Sciences; the Israel Technion in Haifa, which oversaw technology; and the Weizmann Institute in Rehovot, which went even further than overseeing a faculty in Beersheba by assisting in the establishment of a Desert Research Centre at Sde Boker, the kibbutz to which Ben-Gurion had retired. Once I had tentatively agreed to accept the offer, I went to meet Haim Beinart, whom the Hebrew University had appointed as Dean of the new faculty – a middle-aged professor of Jewish history, whose research and teaching related primarily to the fate of the *conversos* during the Spanish Inquisition. He was delighted that a senior faculty member like me was prepared to undertake establishing the English Department, and listened patiently and without demurral when I outlined the ways in which I wished to diverge from the Jerusalem curriculum.

Now began the practical tasks of recruiting staff and soliciting students. The first was soon accomplished. The Six-Day War had inspired a wave of immigration from the English-speaking countries and among the newcomers were young

192

graduates, albeit lacking teaching experience but with a good knowledge of English literature. Sharing my own eagerness to be involved in a venture that offered an opportunity to make concrete their Zionist ideals, they rapidly began to collaborate in hammering out details of the first-year courses we would be offering. I could supplement this small and as yet untried group with high-school teachers of English from Beersheba itself. Although they had no academic qualifications, they made up for that lack by the years of experience they had accumulated – experience that was extremely valuable, since our department would also be responsible for teaching English as a second language to students from all departments in the faculty.

As I'd anticipated, the students differed significantly from their contemporaries in Jerusalem. As I interviewed them they reminded me strongly of the classes I'd taught in my first two years in Jerusalem. Older, more varied in personal background, in many cases multilingual (though not fluent in English), they included Holocaust survivors and some who had been born in Europe to survivors living in the DP camps prior to *aliyah*. There were numerous members of the *kibbutzim* that surround Beersheba, as well as from the development towns established to absorb immigrants in the early years of statehood. For the vast majority of the applicants, this was a long-desired opportunity to study without the daunting expenditure of time and money demanded by travelling to the centre of the country.

Not only the students but also the physical conditions under which we worked reminded me of the good old days in Jerusalem. There was no campus. HIAS (Hebrew Immigrant Aid Society) House, a rambling building initially erected in the 1950s as an absorption centre for new immigrants, served as the headquarters where the offices of the administrative staff were located, leaving very little space for classrooms. Unlike Jerusalem, Beersheba had no Church-owned properties to rent. Instead, several shops nearby were turned into classrooms, entailing much movement from place to place – a particularly wearying task in the dry heat that obtains in the region almost year round. Yet despite the shortcomings, there was the buoyancy that so frequently characterises any pioneering project. Besides, many of the students – whether new immigrants or kibbutz members – were wholly accustomed to the makeshift, the temporary, the inadequate; it was the nature of their entire existence in the Negev. Compensation lay in what they were experiencing and accomplishing academically. Excited, eager, earnest and even exultant, they threw themselves energetically into their studies, eliciting a similar response from their teachers.

My ardour and efficiency rapidly elicited the admiration and even affection of the Dean, who increasingly sought my collaboration and advice. Fellow members of our faculty as well as those of others with whom I came into contact repeatedly elected me as their representative to the various bodies responsible for planning, development and oversight: the Inter-Faculty Council, the Senate and even the small but powerful Coordinating Committee, which comprised the three deans, the rector, the president and the CEO – all of them men and all but the last of professorial rank. Ultimately, I was even elected to the Board of Governors, where I rapidly learnt how powerless this august body of donors and functionaries (local and national) in fact was and the extent to which the wise counsel, particularly of well-known academics from abroad, was disregarded. In practice, only the Coordinating Committee possessed authority, though ultimately this too was limited by the need for approval of every major step by the Council for Higher Education.

Comprised entirely of senior faculty members from the country's major universities as well as members of the public who are appointed by the government, this omnipotent body is chaired by the Minister of Education, appointed to his post by the Prime Minister and invariably sharing the latter's politics. Few if any of its members were truly enthusiastic about the appearance on the scene of yet another institution of higher education. Only recently, and after considerable stalling, had they approved the recognition of the universities in Tel Aviv and Haifa. Now there would be yet another candidate for funding. Furthermore, due to the patronage of the country's three major institutions, the upstart in the Negev would undoubtedly decrease the number of their own new applicants – and hence their income. The conflict of interests led to the application of a tight rein on originality and innovation.

Nobody took the trouble to enlighten me on the complexities of Israeli academia or on the power wielded by its various components. Ashamed of admitting my ignorance and too shy to ask even my own dean for clarification, I contributed very little to the Coordinating Committee's proceedings, listening intently to the discussion and vainly struggling to formulate an opinion of my own. Fortunately, there was seldom a need to vote on any proposal and whenever there was, I waited to see what stand my dean took and meekly followed suit. My silence seemed to bother nobody; I was never explicitly asked to voice an opinion. I was, of course, the only woman member of this highest level of local authority.

Only once did I feel sufficient confidence to diverge from my code of silence. Seemingly disgruntled by a failure of some kind at the Hadassah Medical School,

Moshe Prywes had resigned his position as professor there and turned to Beersheba to promote his plan of establishing a Faculty of Health Sciences. The committee at once began discussing his proposals, devoting a number of successive meetings solely to this topic. Prywes envisaged an entity that would be unlike any that existed elsewhere in Israel. One of the most striking of his proposals was that students begin their studies in the hospital wards, gaining practical experience before continuing to the theoretical. He wished to launch this experiment at a new institution, one less hidebound by tradition than Hadassah, whose medical school had been inaugurated more than 20 years earlier.

My colleagues were startled by what they perceived as too radical a step but I was excited. They raised innumerable objections, ranging from financial difficulties and lack of adequate facilities to the threat of disapproval by the Council of Higher Education. Prywes persisted; refusing to be discouraged, he held his ground and I could finally no longer restrain myself. I raised my hand. Startled, my colleagues waited for me to speak. Their look of surprise was disconcerting but I was determined to make my case.

"Actually," I began, "there's a precedent to this approach of putting practice before theory. When I began studies in social work at the LSE, I had to spend five weeks working in the field even before the beginning of the first year." Social work? Had I actually studied that? Why my presence in the English Department? Bewilderment replaced surprise. Fearful, I held my line. "Work in the ward enables the teachers to judge whether the applicant possesses the human sympathy, empathy and readiness to listen the profession demands. And it enables the students to decide whether this is really what they want to devote their lives to."

Prywes beamed at me approvingly. My dean's face reflected admiration. The others appeared not to have comprehended the import of my maiden speech. They might still have been so astounded by the very fact of my speaking they hadn't heard the content. I can't claim to have been responsible for the committee's final half-hearted and reluctant acquiescence. It's far more likely that they simply wanted to proceed to other matters, each according to his own priorities.

Prywes's approach proved successful. Within a short time of its inception the Medical School became the most popular in the country, attracting outstanding students, few of whom dropped out before completing their studies. I don't recall ever again uttering a single word in the remaining half year of my membership in the committee.

That lack of active participation was a far cry from the major role I played in discussions within and about my own faculty. In the meetings of department heads, all of them my peers in terms of responsibility though not of seniority, I had no inhibitions. Confident in my knowledge and experience, I freely expressed my opinions and presented proposals on everything related to our goals, practices and future development. I was respected; I was heeded; I was influential.

My vision of the university as a whole and, more specifically, of our faculty's role in giving that vision concrete expression remained as it had been before I first agreed to become actively involved. Still unaware of the limitations imposed by the Council for Higher Education, I made increasingly radical proposals, finally suggesting a total restructuring of our entire faculty so as to increase interaction and collaboration: a symbiosis between the various departments. Out of the individual "trees" that each of them represented, I wanted to create a forest that would enable our students (and even our faculty) to perceive the totality of western civilisation and culture, as well as the role played by Judaism, Jewish thought and even Jewish practice in the creation of that culture. The sharp divisions between the departments should be eliminated, the frontiers abolished. My holistic approach was in sharp contrast to what had recently occurred in Jerusalem, where the long-combined faculties of humanities and social sciences had been separated from each other.

Grudgingly, only a very few of my colleagues voiced agreement in principle, daunted by the need to rethink the syllabi and reorganise the curriculum of their respective departments. Even those who personally acquiesced doubted they could win the approval of their respective department heads in Jerusalem. They were also deterred by the amount of discussion and collaboration such a change would necessitate.

I was promoted to the rank of Associate Professor at the beginning of 1971. All but one of the others struggled to produce a list of publications that would make them eligible for tenure. Two who had not yet completed their PhD theses were still considered very junior in their "home" departments, where they were teaching nothing but adjunct courses linked to a lecture by someone their senior. I'd been astonished and outraged early in my term of office when the Dean revealed to me that he viewed the institute as a place of interim employment for gifted graduate students at the Hebrew University until such time as they qualified for a position in Jerusalem. *My* intention was to develop a faculty composed of people who already lived in the Negev or explicitly declared (and in most cased carried out) their intention of settling there.

With Joel in the garden at Sonia Gardens, Summer 1952.

On the bed in Alfassi Street.

Joel aged two.

With Micha, born September 1954, and Joel.

Joel and Micha in Cambridge, Autumn 1956.

With Ditza in 1959.

With Ditza, Joel and Micha 1958.

With Hephziba (1963).

The family in 1965.

In our garden in Beit Hakerem.

The children.

With Willy.

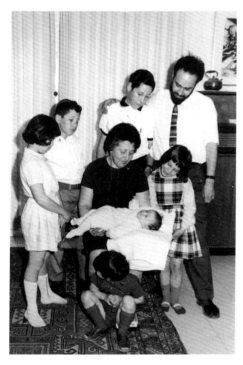

Pnina is born, January 1967.

Pnina and Benzi, 1974.

In the Sukkah with Harry and Sadie seated on the left, Joel standing behind them. Seated at the front (l – r) Pnina, Ditza, Hephziba and Benzi on Micha's lap.

All the family 1970.

With our "clan" on the front steps of our house, 1998 (Photo Debbi Cooper).

Celebrating my 80th birthday with our children, their spouses and offspring.

At the garden gate.

With (almost) all the grandchildren and their offspring celebrating my 90th birthday, October 2016. (Photo: Debbi Cooper)

Encouraged by the support of Professor Nathan Spiegel, an elderly Holocaust survivor on the verge of retirement who headed the Classics Department and shared my belief that "nothing human is alien" to us, I persisted in my quixotic attempts at persuasion. The Dean, however, voiced such strong opposition that my few supporters were soon dissuaded. I became increasingly aware of his opposition but undiplomatically persisted in my attempts at persuasion. Obstinacy led to downfall.

In the spring of 1973, the Dean officially announced his resignation from the post, prompting a search for a suitable successor. At the close of the next meeting of the Coordinating Council I was invited to join the other members at lunch. The unexpected invitation stemmed not from my being deemed an equal in seniority but from the offer of a ride back to Jerusalem made by the even more senior and world-renowned scholar from Jerusalem whom the Council of Higher Education had appointed as supervisor of the Beersheba "offspring". Rather than having to wait in some corner of the makeshift campus at HIAS House, I found myself at the city's most expensive restaurant, sharing a table with six men, all of them older than me, one of them (the CEO) a recently retired IDF officer.

From the first I felt out of place. My discomfort increased when the informal opening exchanges between my companions took on what was for me a distinctly unpleasant form: a series of jokes that grew bawdier, as if they were competing with each other in salaciousness. Except in literature, I've always found such humour distasteful. Women are the butt of the jokes. It's misogyny. I didn't join in. I sensed that I was being tested: was I "one of the boys", sophisticated and sexually experienced, or was I, despite my marital status, uninitiated, ignorant rather than innocent, a prude, a prig? Profoundly embarrassed, I writhed in my chair, all the while studiously scrutinising the menu as if I hadn't yet decided on my choice. I did my best to avoid their gaze. The first course arrived and with it a change of topic: the proposal of candidates for the position of Dean.

Now I was even more taken aback. Few of the men whose names were mentioned (needless to say, they were all men) had what I considered the necessary qualifications. None had as yet served in any capacity at the institute, nor could they be presumed to have any knowledge of its unique structure and the complexities of the collaboration between its three very diverse entities. When the meal came to an end no candidate had as yet been identified. The search would continue.

On the way home to Jerusalem, my "driver" asked for any suggestions I might have, names I'd refrained from mentioning since I wasn't present in any official capacity. As I had only a very few additional candidates to suggest, he soon turned to other topics, including some related to his own field of specialisation – Crusader history – in which he was expert. The informality of our conversation came as a delightful contrast to the fraught luncheon experience. Only when I returned home and recounted the events of the day to Moshe did we simultaneously come out with our identical conclusion: "You are/I am the obvious person for the job". I lost no time in presenting my candidacy to my "driver", phoning him the very same evening to arrange an early meeting. He expressed no surprise, despite the fact that we had just spent over two hours together – ample time in which to convey whatever I had to say. He suggested lunch the following day. Another lunch! Though joking would be inevitable, at least it would be witty. Nevertheless, I took the precaution of immediately clarifying the agenda.

"*À propos* yesterday's discussion, I'd like to submit my candidacy for the position of Dean," I said unhesitatingly, in a low voice. He said nothing. Thinking he might not have heard me above the clatter of dishes in the Faculty Club, I repeated the sentence more loudly. Again, he remained silent, while I sat awaiting a response. A minute must have passed before he spoke.

"You should present your candidacy formally," he advised, expressing no opinion of his own. "You have to speak to the decision-makers. I really have no say in the matter." Given the previous day's discussion, I knew he had more than an equal say. His word would carry infinitely more weight than that of any one of my fellows in Beersheba, although they were far more familiar with my accomplishments. He remained studiously neutral.

Because Moshe encouraged me not to desist, I set off on a round of the most humiliating encounters of my life. I had never before needed to solicit support for a candidacy of any kind. Quite the contrary; as was true of my position as head of the department in Beersheba, I had frequently been requested to stand for an office for which I had not even contemplated applying. That had certainly been the case not only at my high school but also at Cambridge and the LSE, at both of which I'd been elected chairperson of more than one society. On this occasion, my fate lay in the hands of my seniors in age and status, some of whom – including the Rector of the Hebrew University, a mathematician – I had never met and who in all probability knew nothing of substance about me or my achievements. I was daunted. The very thought of blowing my own trumpet was alien to my nature. I went to each meeting in fear of being rebuked or even mocked for my pretensions. The misgivings were well-founded.

The Rector's secretary must have listed our meeting on his daily agenda: he'd either not consulted that list or, immersed in more important matters, forgotten it. I waited uncomfortably while he completed the task in which he had been engaged when I was ushered in. As if his mind were still on other things, he said nothing, waiting for me to begin the conversation. He had a thin face, an austere expression. I was struck by the contrast with his plump older brother, a jovial professor of Hebrew with whom I was friends. Turning slightly in my direction, he sat in Sphinx-like silence, one hand covering the lower part of his face, obscuring mouth and chin: inscrutable. He waited for me to speak. I half-stammered what, over time, became a recurring opening sentence:

"I'd like to present my candidacy for the position of Dean in Beersheba." I went on to cite some of my qualifications for this position. No response. I added a few details about the English Department and its successes, briefly referring to the staff and the students – subjects on which I could speak with greater enthusiasm than about myself. Still he said nothing. I waited in silence, not knowing what further information I should venture to provide. Panic-stricken, I wondered what more was expected of me. What, if any, was the purpose of this torture?

Finally, he lowered his hand, turned back to the papers on his desk and said nothing more than "Thank you. *Shalom!*"

I was dismissed. I withdrew abjectly, bitterly debating with myself as to whether I should walk backwards, as in departing from a deity or a monarch. Since he was again absorbed in his work, the caustic gesture would in any case go unremarked. Yet I remained unshaken in my goal. While final approval would have to come from the Rector, he would surely seek the opinions and recommendation of those who, while subservient to him in rank, might be presumed to be reliable judges of my abilities.

I proceeded to the next office-holder on my list: the newly elected Dean of the Faculty of Humanities at the Hebrew University. A colourless professor of history reputed to be an extremely boring lecturer, whom I had never known to participate in any faculty discussion, I believe he had been elected to his exalted position only because, this being a time of financial cutbacks and hence imminent dismissals, nobody else had been willing to stand. He was as yet ignorant of what was going on in Beersheba, yet when I again began by citing my reason for coming to see him he interrupted me. In a tone of disbelief he proclaimed: "But you're a woman!" I was incredulous; it had never occurred to me that my sex might prove an obstacle.

"Why would that matter?" I asked, but he gave no answer, instead perusing the *curriculum vitae* I had submitted to his secretary when I made the appointment. Like the Rector, he gave no indication of assent or rejection.

"I'll be in touch with you once I've spoken to your dean. I need more details."
Again I was dismissed. In all, he seemed surprised that anybody, either male or
female, should desire appointment to so onerous a task. He proved not to be alone
in his opinion of female capabilities. The identical sentence constituted the instant
response of all three of the dignitaries at the Beersheba Institute: the President,
the Rector and the CEO. I couldn't believe my ears. At least one of them hastily
added an explanation: they were looking for someone who would reside in
Beersheba and I, married to a man who worked in Jerusalem, would surely not
be able to accede to that demand.

"On the contrary," I answered him. "My husband and I have already
discussed this and he, in fact, is prepared to be the commuter." His turn to be
shocked. So domineering a woman might prove disruptive, dictatorial, less
obsequious than I had so far appeared in the meetings in which we had both
participated. Unlike the Jerusalem functionaries, these three Beersheba colleagues
did know that I possessed at least some of the necessary qualifications. Yet none
of them granted me a positive sign of approval or support. Though increasingly
discouraged and despondent, fully aware I would not be appointed to the position
I sought, I realised that I had to speak to the incumbent whom I had hoped to
succeed. This was the encounter I most dreaded, aware of the hostility I had
aroused by repeatedly demanding reform.

Without waiting for me to begin the conversation, he shot an angry
accusation:

"I've never encountered such blatant lobbying, such shameless self-
promotion! Never in all my life. You should be ashamed of yourself!" The
accusation proved more than I could bear. In the first place, his contention that
I was unique was totally inaccurate. I myself had frequently been lobbied by
colleagues seeking my support. But far more painful was the fact that I had in fact
been advised that such action was mandatory. I had not initiated it of my own
accord. Then came the unkindest cut of all. "I once saw you as my obvious
successor," he said caustically, "but your behaviour has been despicable. It has
proved you are totally unfit for the job."

I burst into tears. Far from eliciting sympathy or compassion, my distress
aroused yet another sneering pronouncement:

"You see, you're just like all women!"

Needless to say I was not appointed to the position. Yet my humiliating
experience led to a profound change in my perception of gender equality in Israel.
I had for the first time encountered discrimination such as was non-existent in

the English Department in Jerusalem; Adam Mendilow was not only scrupulously fair but profoundly concerned for the academic welfare of his staff, always exerting himself on our behalf, without exception giving all of us a sense of security and moral support. Now I had encountered a very different reality. Was I alone in this? Was it a purely personal matter or had others encountered similar prejudices and preconceptions? In the course of the weeks during which I went from one male superior to another, I occasionally reported on the unanticipated outcome to some of my women colleagues in other departments in Jerusalem.

Each reported similar discrimination in promotion. All had been bypassed in favour of a male colleague. The criteria applied to women were more stringent. The process, if and when it was begun, took longer and more frequently ended in rejection. Post-doctoral fellowships were seldom granted to women. If they were – and if the fortunate recipient decided to spend the year researching abroad – the sum allocated was less than that which men received. The nepotism law which forbade the employment of husband and wife in the same department constituted yet another obstacle to their advancement, since the men, unimpeded by motherhood, invariably not only completed their doctoral dissertations more speedily but also accumulated a longer list of publications qualifying them for appointment.

The list of impediments seemed interminable. Yet the most shocking and totally unanticipated revelation was of sexual harassment: a phenomenon that was more widespread than any of us, including the women subjected to it, had imagined. None had reported it, even to their female colleagues. The victims blamed themselves; perhaps they had in some way unwittingly provoked the unwanted solicitations? Had their behaviour, dress, posture, speech and make-up encouraged the men in question to assume that they themselves sought a sexual relationship? They were trapped between submission to the men's unwanted advances and their own ambitions – the desire for the high grade they knew they deserved. This, however well-deserved, had been – or was in danger of being – denied them. None confessed to having succumbed to temptation. Colleagues were left to draw their own conclusions.

Two of my friends, Galia Golan and Frances Raday, like me Associate Professors, agreed that collective action was needed. By way of the grapevine that exists in every institution, we called a meeting of women from all departments. Scores attended. They listened to the data we had already accumulated, adding others of which we were as yet ignorant. The most egregious, wholly illogical and unwarranted discrimination was fiscal: the male survivors of deceased female employees were awarded a lower pension than widows of male employees! Since all of us, irrespective of sex, contributed equally to the pension fund, the discrimination was against women, though men were the ones directly affected. Armed with an impressive list of complaints, the three of us requested and were granted a meeting with the three most powerful men in the institution: the President, a new Rector and the CEO – yet another retired IDF officer.

They received us warmly. Refreshments were served. It was like an informal encounter between friends. In due course we began the "business" part of the meeting. Successive items all met with an identical response from all three men: "I didn't know…", "We weren't aware…". One might have thought they existed on a different planet, so ignorant were they of the practices that had for years been the norm in the institution they headed. Presumably none had examined, let alone queried the practices. Their ignorance was genuine, their tone apologetic. By the end of the meeting we had elicited a promise of reform. Justice would be done and equity established.

Only one complaint fell on deaf ears: the least logical of all the forms of discrimination – that of pension inequity. That would be too costly, the CEO maintained. I pointed out that expense would not be as great as he feared. Actuarially, women were known to live longer than men; hence the number of beneficiaries would be lower. There were far fewer female than male employees. In any case, I argued, the discrimination was unjust. He held his ground. Many years were to pass before this wholly justified complaint was addressed and amends made.

We didn't raise the issue of sexual harassment. We were too embarrassed. The term was not yet in common use. Nobody believed such a phenomenon existed, certainly not that it might serve as an obstacle to the advancement of women in their profession. Why should any woman object to a compliment, a friendly arm round her shoulder, even a welcoming or parting kiss? On the contrary, such show of collegiality should surely be encouraged. Even over a decade later, when the law against sexual harassment and discrimination in the workplace was enacted, the same arguments were again trotted out, this time to no avail. Nobody, not even the President of Israel himself, would be immune to complaint and prosecution.

Promises are all well and good but how does one ensure implementation? How does one eradicate long-held assumptions? A few of the injustices could be rectified through new regulations. Directives from above might affect lower-ranking decision-makers but a mindset that derives not only from personal prejudices or preferences but from centuries-old social conventions defies reform and innovation. The absence of women in decision-making forums meant that there was no one sensitive to gender-based discrimination. We needed "watchdogs", whistle-blowers, affirmative action. Before we departed from the President's office, we elicited a promise that a senior woman faculty member would be appointed as ombuds(wo)man to whom women, both faculty members and students, could turn for help in addressing injustices.

How crucial the involvement of a feminist was in preventing such injustice was borne out by the proceedings at a meeting of the subcommittee whose responsibility it was to sift initial proposals for promotion to tenure at the Negev Institute. I was one of the four Hebrew University faculty members on this subcommittee – the only woman and the only one familiar with the institute. Our mandate was to scrutinise the individual files of those whom department heads had recommended. Our own recommendations would then be forwarded to a more senior committee. If this was also approved, the candidates' CVs and copies of their publications would be sent for external review by an expert at another university, invariably one outside Israel. This snobbery at times constituted an insurmountable obstacle. Save where Jewish studies were concerned, referees fully competent in Hebrew were few or non-existent. The subcommittee's verdict thus carried great weight. If we considered a candidate as lacking the necessary qualifications, he or she would be doomed to rejection.

We had over 30 files before us. Some contained more than one letter of recommendation. At first, we looked carefully at every document. Our verdicts were almost always unanimous. When there was some disagreement, brief arguments offered by one or other of us served to persuade those who differed. However, as time passed, my colleagues grew impatient. We were tired. The chairman cut short discussion. Decisions were, to my mind, sometimes made too hastily – an almost cursory verdict of thumbs up or down. The mere number of publications was becoming too vital a factor – one that could be determined at first glance. Similar attention was paid to the length of time over which the publications appeared. I knew from experience how long an interval might elapse between submission of a manuscript, the initial response it elicited from an editor or publisher, and the date of publication. But I raised no objection. I didn't want to be perceived as a troublemaker.

Inevitably, once the time factor was introduced, there followed reference to the candidate's age. Was this a child prodigy of some kind or would he, if promoted, have only a short period remaining in which to teach? Preference should clearly be given to the young. Again, my own experience led me to question the decision: I had been 36 when I completed my doctorate. In the course of the previous 11 years, I had given birth to two daughters; I was already the mother of two sons when I began my research. All my male colleagues in the English Department who began working on their theses at around the same time completed them well before I did. Hence, although I was their senior in terms of years of teaching in the department, they received tenure before I did.

My travails came to mind while we were discussing chronologies, yet I remained silent. My personal decisions regarding motherhood would be of no interest to my colleagues. However, I changed my mind when, among the last three remaining files, we came to the first – and only – woman candidate, Dorit Padan-Eisenstark.

"Only five articles," one of my colleagues pointed out.

"All in Hebrew," added another, disdainfully.

"And she's 50 years old!"

That clinched it. The file was ignominiously rejected. Although I knew Dorit well and greatly admired her, I could not deny the facts. I felt I had no grounds for querying the decision. I bit my tongue. Two files remained. The first of them was that of an instructor in the History Department, whose area of specialisation was the Holocaust. Two members of the committee were personally acquainted with him. Not only did they heap praise on the originality of his research and the excellence of his writings; they referred to the fact that he was himself a Holocaust survivor, that he had fought with the partisans, arrived alone in pre-state Palestine, joined a kibbutz, served in the Palmach during the War of Independence and finally begun studies at a mature age. His publications were few and all in Hebrew. Without a word of demurral – indeed, with murmurs of wonder and admiration – his candidacy was approved.

I could no longer contain myself. I requested that we reconsider Dorit's file. My colleagues demurred. There was no precedent for such a request. Besides, it was late and we were tired. I insisted. Either because they were so intent on ending the meeting or because they respected me sufficiently not to deny my outrageous request, they acceded to it. They opened the rejected file. I launched on my argument, fuelled by indignation at the preposterous discrimination. Together with her mentor, Rivka Bar-Yosef, Dorit had pioneered women's studies in Israel. Her findings had been startling and illuminating. She had definitively detailed the gender-based discrimination in the workplace, the lack of promotion of women, the unwarranted wage differential. She had even exposed the lack of equality in *kibbutzim*, where women were constantly relegated to the service sectors of childcare and "catering".

The originality and quality of her publications more than compensated for their comparative paucity; they were in fact equal in number to those of the candidate of whom my colleagues had unanimously approved. Because the data she had accumulated related only to Israel and her sources, such as they were, solely in Hebrew, Dorit had also so far written and published only in that language. And yes, she was no longer young. But she had established the country's first programme of women's studies in the department of Behavioural Sciences in Beersheba, which she had headed since its inception. Finally – this was my trump card – though not a Holocaust survivor, she was a war widow whose husband had been killed in action in the Six-Day War, leaving her as sole provider for their three children. I concluded by firmly asserting that I would retract my approval of the previous candidate if my colleagues refused to submit Dorit's file for further consideration.

Whether they were persuaded by my impassioned defiance or, alternatively, did not want to jeopardise the chances of the "survivor", whatever the reason, they acceded to my demands. I felt profound satisfaction that justice had been done. Dorit never learnt of her promotion. On a snowy day, when the roads were slippery with ice, she was killed in a road accident *en route* to Beersheba. Devastated by the loss, I found some comfort in the fact that I had in some way contributed to her children's receiving a more generous pension than they would have done had I not intervened on her behalf.

In 1996, with a woman president newly at its head, the Ben-Gurion University of the Negev bestowed an honorary degree on me. In my acceptance speech, for the first time I publicly revealed my experience at the same institution 23 years before. The audience was astonished. Alone among Israel's now numerous academic institutions, the BGU each year punctiliously honours an equal number of men and women.

The Hebrew University lagged behind Beersheba in recognising Women's Studies as a legitimate academic discipline. The ignorance and obliviousness that we had encountered when we met our university's male directors led Galia Golan to devise and propose a comparable department at the Hebrew University. Women colleagues eagerly responded, volunteering to develop courses related to their respective disciplines. The proposal had, of course, to be approved by the

Faculty Council, in which men were a vast majority. In the course of the protracted struggle to establish the department, its advocates – me included – encountered fierce sexist opposition.

"Who ever heard of men's studies?" was one of the many comments that conveniently overlooked the exclusion of "Her-story" and the works of women writers and female researchers. Numerous wearying discussions at meetings of the Faculty of Humanities and Social Studies finally led to a compromise. The resulting diminished unit of Gender Difference Studies (rather than an entirely autonomous department) combined existing courses with a minimal number of new ones, given by veteran faculty members who had, like me, developed a feminist approach to their fields of expertise. Reading Simone de Beauvoir, Germaine Greer, Kate Millett and Susan Brownmiller prompted me to reinterpret texts I had taught for many years.

Teaching Chaucer, I discovered hitherto undetected subtleties in the portrayals of the Wife of Bath and the Prioress: the fate of both these women was determined by social mores and conventions rather than by their own desires and longings. In my doctoral dissertation, I had written about the Renaissance concepts of honour that dictated male modes of action and reaction in a period when that term was variously and often contradictorily defined. That had led me similarly to consider the way in which women's honour was conceived and to the discovery that, in contrast to the widely varying interpretations of the term where men were concerned, women's honour was equated solely with chastity. In that vein, I wrote an article entitled "'Honour' in *Troilus and Cressida*", which was published in *Studies in English Literature* in 1963. Eight years later, in the light of my newly acquired insights, I became aware that Shakespeare's characterisation of women was infinitely more subtle. That led me to a total revision of my earlier narrow, negative interpretation of Cressida, whom I now perceived as the victim of a military society in which women, though seemingly idolised, were in fact no more than helpless objects of male sexuality and lust, to be surrendered in political bargaining when "honour" (in its sense of "prowess on the battlefield") was at stake.

In 1972, I delivered a paper presenting this interpretation at the annual conference of University Teachers of English, under the title of "Sexual Politics in *Troilus and Cressida*". The paper met with incredulity and ridicule. Even my much-admired thesis supervisor offered the dubious compliment of comparing me to Maurice Morgann, the subject of his own innovative research on an 18th-century critic known primarily for an interpretation of Falstaff that was based on the assumption that he was a real human being and not merely a fictitious though engagingly round character in a work of imagination. To this day I am uncertain whether the comparison was intended to be complimentary. I returned home in a state of extreme self-doubt. Given the negative reception, perhaps I was indeed pursuing a phantom. Moshe's familiarity with the play was insufficient to enable him to offer anything more specific than the customary reassurance. "Trust your own judgment." Only some weeks later did I receive professional validation. At a chance encounter, a colleague from another university told me he had been thinking about my paper and added, "I believe you really have a point!"

In June 1973 I began work on a book on Shakespeare's female protagonists. Publishers expressed interest. It was a hot topic. In October, the Yom Kippur War broke out. Moshe and our two oldest sons were all at the front and Shakespeare's women seemed, at least temporarily, irrelevant. In addition, I now had my duties as Head of the Languages and Literatures Institute to attend to. These proved more time-consuming than I had assumed, particularly since I was, as was my wont, bent on introducing changes and reforms. My manuscript was laid aside, doomed never to be completed.

I didn't abandon my feminist approach to literary analysis. From 1980 until my retirement 10 years later, I gradually developed, refined and restructured an annual course on drama on and by women, initially entitled "Women, Love and Marriage in Drama". I took the liberty of beginning with Chaucer, comparing the impression of the Wife of Bath and the Prioress that we derive from *The General Prologue* with a subtly corrective one that emerges from their respective tales. In the latter I perceived the women as yearning for lives very different from those to which they have been doomed. Hubristically, I continued in chronological order to the modern period, ending with Harold Pinter's *The Homecoming*. Over the years that followed, I annually revised the list of texts, concentrating increasingly on the modern period.

Beyond the discovery of an entire new genre of theatre, the most illuminating aspect of these courses proved to be the class dynamics. In the first year, my class comprised some 20 women and one man. Although he was one of the most brilliant students in the department, his exceptional intelligence and breadth of knowledge did not, to my mind, justify either the awed, even cowed response of the women or his monopoly of class discussion. In vain did I address direct questions to individual women or turn a pleading gaze in their direction when I wanted their input. With few exceptions, they remained silent, presumably fearing the scorn they might evoke in their male classmate should they venture an opinion.

207

The second year was worse. There were now three men, two of them Palestinian school principals from the West Bank, in their 40s, studying for an MA degree. Their society's culture, patriarchal and patronising, was still largely based on a strict distinction between the respective roles of women and men, the former being almost exclusively domestic. Women's liberation was foreign, the sexual permissiveness of mid-20th-century western society anathema. They were firm in their beliefs, unhesitating in expressing their opinions, relentless in asserting the correctness of their worldview, albeit in as yet imperfect English. As far as they were concerned, *The Taming of the Shrew* was an excellent guide to the correct method of dealing with a rebellious wife; they perceived no hint of irony in Katherine's final speech of submission. In every class, they laid down the law firmly and at length. Fear of being considered racist or contemptuous of another culture kept my class tongue-tied. Nobody dared venture a contradictory opinion once the opening judgment had been emphatically delivered by one or other of these men. It was left for me to try, as diplomatically as possible, to present counter-arguments.

However, when we came to the modern period, the Palestinians began to flounder. Edward Albee's *Who's Afraid of Virginia Woolf?* floored them completely. They had no clue as to what was going on, could not understand the American idiom or the complex shifting relationships between the four characters, or the underlying fantasy that sustained the marriage of George and Martha. Even when I spelled it out for them explicitly, they failed to realise that the child who was killed off had never existed. Suddenly their earlier dogmatism evaporated and in most of the last few classes of the year they remained utterly silent, frequently revealing by the expression on their faces the extent of their shock and revulsion at the decadent 20th-century mores of contemporary playwrights.

The third year of teaching the course was utterly different. My class was composed entirely of women but so varied in age, and ethnic, national and cultural background as to present a veritable cross-section of Israeli society. There was a 19-year old American spending her junior year abroad and a highly cultured Israeli, of European origin, slightly older than me. There were full-time students and some taking advantage of the Hebrew University's new policy of admitting non-students to audit individual courses. There were single women, married women, mothers and widows. Some were already divorced, others in the process of disengaging themselves from unhappy unions. Never before had I encountered a group so rich in life experience, nor one so ready to engage in what I consider

208

the optimal mode of analysing and evaluating a text: by bringing one's own experience to the reading and interpretation, while at the same time opening oneself up to the text in such a way as to let it increase and deepen one's understanding of that experience. Every week I came home, elated, to report to Moshe what had passed. I think there are few such satisfying experiences for a teacher as that which I enjoyed the year I had an all-female class.

In the fourth year, when the course was reduced from two semesters to one, I pared down the time-span covered and the amount of reading material, teaching exclusively plays by 20th-century women dramatists I had never previously taught. The texts were contemporary and little-known and never performed in Israel or, to my knowledge, outside Britain. Most of them were revisionary in nature, radically challenging in subject matter, in format (forget about the classic three-act structure!) and in language: demotic street slang, even local dialect, non-chronological presentation of events sequenced like the flashback of cinema, distinctly feminist and revolutionary.

Debbie Horsfield's *The Red Devils Trilogy* charts the lives of four young Mancunians, from ardent fans of Manchester United to adult achievers; Caryl Churchill's chronology-defying *Top Girls* brings together contemporary women and antecedents real and fictional from different cultures and times; Pam Gems's sad, funny, gender-bending *Aunt Mary*, the eponymous hero of which is a transvestite; Maureen Duffy's *Rites*, a chilling variation on Euripides's *The Bacchae*, set in a public lavatory, in which the victim of the frenzied lynching proves to be a woman. While the rejection of social norms was in many respects comparable to that of the Angry Young Men of the 1960s, the accompanying subversion of theatrical conventions was startlingly original. I had no problem in eliciting discussion. A dynamic interaction – between the readers and text, me and the students, and the students themselves – left all of us, after each class, with a sense of enrichment. Relaxed, fearing neither hostile criticism nor uncomprehending sneers, we would talk freely, continuing well after the allotted hour and a half, until the next class knocked at the door and put an end to the animated discussion.

Once again, there were two men in the class: one a shy, young Israeli Arab, who occupied a seat in the back row and never once spoke up. I refrained from calling on him, fearing I might cause embarrassment. The other was blond, handsome and gay, originally from South Africa, who sat bright-eyed and alert in the front row, took an active role in discussion and revealed, by the enthusiastic expression on his face, that he found the course illuminating and exciting. As in previous years, I began the first class by asking students to describe a personal experience that could not have occurred had she or he been of the opposite sex. This man reported that during a recent visit to his homeland he had purchased a pair of purple suede shoes. One day, as he was walking along Jaffa Road in the centre of Jerusalem, he passed a group of teenagers waiting at a bus-stop. When he had gone a few yards further, one of them called after him, "Hey you! Come back here." Obediently, he retraced his steps, whereupon the same young woman pointed to his feet and informed him that "Men don't wear purple shoes!"

The female students were young and self-confident, and we all derived not only much pleasure but also, I believe, benefit from the course. At the end of the second semester in 1990, I bade farewell, thanked the class for their exhilarating collaboration and revealed that this had been my last class at the Hebrew University. They were disconcerted by the announcement. My South African student accosted me in the corridor afterwards.

"You can't stop teaching!" he admonished me. "You've changed my life." It almost led me to change my mind about retirement. For a brief moment I thought about reversing my decision but the counter-arguments overcame the lapse in resolution.

There were diverse reasons for my early retirement from the Hebrew University. The most obvious and most readily admissible was that I had completed 40 years of teaching. Although they had brought me much happiness, I now felt fatigued enough to warrant a more leisurely life, even if that led to a reduction in income.

There were two additional reasons. The first was a financial crisis in which the institution found itself, having vastly overspent on constructing the new campus. In order to balance the budget, numerous as yet untenured young teachers were dismissed. In our department, all the victims were our graduates. Like me, dismayed at the prospect of losing our gifted colleagues, Ruth Nevo (who had joined the department one year later than myself) also decided to retire. We were certain that our posts would cover the expense of at least four of our former students. We were mistaken: the positions were reallocated to other faculties, so that our own department suffered a double loss, of senior and junior staff.

Distance proved a decisive factor. Instead of the 20-minute door-to-door walk through a *wadi* where the changing flora continually fascinated me, I now had a 50-minute bus ride of unreliable frequency. After four consecutive hours of teaching, the waiting in line and crowding into a packed bus was the burden that broke the camel's back. Helpful as always, Moshe became my driver in both directions, interrupting his working hours. This was clearly not a desirable solution and taxis proved too expensive.

I had been uniquely privileged to visit Scopus even before the Six-Day War. Shortly before Passover in 1955, Adam asked me if I'd like to join the convoy that went up once every two weeks, to change the small force of Israeli "police" (actually soldiers), whose presence there had been assured by the terms of the Armistice Agreement of April 1949. What a question! I jumped at the opportunity, even though I would be in the midst of the preparations for the most demanding of Jewish festivals. Indeed, the convoy would be carrying a large supply of *matzoth* and other Passover-related food for the forces on the mountain. Since the armoured bus in which we travelled had only narrow slits in lieu of windows, we saw tantalisingly little of the landscape. In addition to Adam and me, there were some half-dozen others, among them the female director of a library at an American university and Norman Bentwich. Norman's father, Sir Herbert, had brought his family of eleven children to live in Palestine in 1929. Norman, who had served as Attorney General under the British Mandate, was on his way to pay his respects at the family cemetery, located on the lower slopes of the mountain. Our armoured car stopped there to let him alight. Bentwich was going up to visit his family's graves, located on the lower slopes of the mountain, where our armoured car dropped him off.

The "campus" itself was surprisingly small – a number of scattered buildings, few save the National Library higher than one storey. All was silent. Time had stopped in the spring of 1948. Posters on noticeboards announced Purim parties that were never held. It was as if a spell had been cast. As in the story of Sleeping Beauty, this precious spot was waiting to be awakened. In the library, we stopped to gaze longingly at the stacks of books, still so scarce at the new location on Givat Ram. The visiting librarian opened one of the catalogue drawers and gently ran a hand over the cards it contained, as if she were stroking a beloved child. I noticed that she had tears in her eyes. Defying prohibition, Adam hastened off to the English Literature shelves, stuffing a few small volumes into his pockets.

And then we went up to the round tower that crowns the building, from which the Hanukiah had beamed every year. There was the astonishing study of Yehuda Magnes, the university's first president. Windows all around. A breathtaking view. On one side, the Old City of Jerusalem, the Temple Mount with the Golden Dome of the Rock shining in the sunlight. On the other – a barren wilderness, without a spot of green. The divide between ancient civilisations and a void. How brilliant and visionary a choice for a new seat of learning, a realisation of the Zionist dream of resettling the land. Throughout my years at Cambridge and the LSE I had dreamed of standing at this spot. The sounds of Avigdor Hameiri's plaintive, yearning song resonated within me: "For hundreds of generations I dreamt of you, of the merit of seeing the light of your face…".

The reality, when it came 20 years later, proved vastly different. Resembling a fortress designed to withstand any future conquest by an enemy, the new campus was densely covered with various massive buildings, each with its own interior design. The one that housed the Faculty of Humanities was the most irrational and confusing of them. The ground floor was Floor Three. Eight sets of staircases led from one storey to the next. Each set had its own colour. Frustratingly, each staircase was illogically divided into two "branches", both of which ultimately led to the identical spot. Halfway up from the ground floor, two short sets of stairs diverged but whichever one chose twisted, Escher-like, to the same point. Moshe helpfully drew little arrows on the walls to guide me to the Dean's office.

"I resent having to make unnecessary decisions," my colleague Shirna Kissilevitz complained. She was not alone in feeling frustrated and aggrieved. Her feelings were shared by all our colleagues in the Humanities. At the first faculty meeting, held in the only (octagonal!) lecture hall large enough to hold all members, Bezalel Narkiss, the head of the Art Department, proudly informed us that he had been able to foil a Ministry of Education plan to award the Israel Prize to the architect responsible for this horror. To add to our misery, when the first heavy rains fell, buckets had to be placed strategically around the building to catch the water that dripped through the roof.

On Givat Ram, the chairperson of the English Department, alone among the staff, had a private room. Now everyone, from the rank of associate professor, had one, while more junior faculty members shared rooms, in couples or foursomes, according to rank. Gone were the common staff room, welcome urn and comfortable armchairs that facilitated convivial encounters between lectures. The automats that dispensed tasteless coffee or watery cocoa were a poor substitute. We met each other only when we went to collect our post at the boxes outside the English Department office. My colleagues welcomed the change. Many moved their entire libraries up to their rooms on campus. I did neither. My room had a superb view over the Old City, comparable to that which had so impressed me on my first visit 20 years earlier. But the sterility and the lack of camaraderie combined to instil a sense of alienation I found uncongenial. I preferred to concentrate on the social issues that had come to take up an ever-increasing amount of my time.

SHOCK!

Class

1949. Shabbily dressed beggars line Jerusalem's main streets, hovering around bus-stops, accosting passersby, sitting patiently on the curbsides, hands outstretched for alms. Sometimes an enterprising exception offers combs, toothbrushes, haberdashery for sale. Many of them go from door to door, begging for clothes, food, money. Old or young, male or female, almost without exception they are "Oriental" Jews, some veterans of the pre-state period, others – the majority – immigrants who have arrived from the surrounding Arab countries in the first year of independence. They are an integral part of the Middle Eastern urban landscape.

The new immigrants initially lived in transit camps – *ma'abarot'* – tent cities that provided the barest of shelters. In Jerusalem, there was a large "camp" in the Allenby Barracks, corrugated-iron huts abandoned by the British forces. The canvas tents in the south and west of the city were by the mid-1950s almost all replaced by jerry-built housing projects, long rows of three-storied buildings, where families with six, seven or even more children were crowded into two or three small rooms. New districts grew up on the edges of Jerusalem. Old, infrequent buses carried passengers tightly packed to the centre of the city, where most shops were located. In the new districts only small greengrocers opened, providing the most basic, severely rationed products.

This was a world of which I had only the barest awareness and no first hand acquaintance whatsoever. Given that I had originally come to Israel to be a social worker, my ignorance is explicable only by the fact that I was already myself comfortably cocooned in the secure, familiar, middleclass, European life of Rehavia, where culture and camaraderie compensated for material shortages. I belonged to the Ashkenazi pseudo-élite who wittingly or unwittingly relegated

213

the *olim* from Arab countries to a lower social and economic status, and subjected them to various forms of discrimination. Until the Palestinians replaced them after 1967, these were our hewers of wood and drawers of water, a rich source of cheap labour.

Ohel Yossef. Before 1948, Katamon was an Arab section of west Jerusalem, distinguished by its handsome villas, large gardens and dignified appearance. Alongside these, the British had built attractive apartment houses, each with four or five flats on no more than three floors. The scene of fierce fighting and heavy losses in the War of Independence, the buildings were requisitioned as abandoned property in order to house Jewish refugees from the Old City. Apartments and villas alike, they were sub-divided into smaller units. Dignity gave way to ramshackle closing-in of balconies, unlicensed additions of prefabricated outhouses and washing-lines on which laundry continually fluttered.

Beyond this old quarter, a new one, misleadingly named Katamonim, was hastily erected: long, ugly rows of over-populated buildings, linked like railway carriages, with multiple entrances and little public space surrounding them. Two blocks, 8 and 9, in an overcrowded hive on Bar Yochai Street, were particularly notorious: poor, crime-ridden, drug-infested enclaves, so degraded that neither social workers nor police officers would venture to approach them unaccompanied by a colleague.

In 1974 I was initiated into this world of poverty and crime by Dr Louis Miller, whose wife Joyce was a close friend and university colleague. Louis, who had served in the Royal Air Force during the Second World War, immigrated to Israel to fight in the War of Independence. Tall, broad-shouldered, with a Clark Gable moustache, he was an impressive figure. His speech was slow and deliberate, perhaps to ensure that his Hebrew be correct; he rarely raised his voice. He commanded instant attention and respect. At the time the head psychologist at the Ministry of Health, Louis was profoundly concerned with the fate of the boys and young men in the Katamon community. Dropouts from school, they had little hope of improving their economic condition. They turned to drugs, theft and violence. Most of them were already known to the police; some had served short prison sentences. Many of them, as I later learnt, were routinely held in custody over Shabbat, to prevent violence at football games, where supporters of the competing teams invariably came to blows. All of them were sons of illiterate or semi-literate parents who had arrived in Israel as part of the huge wave of immigrants from Arab lands.

In an attempt to help these youths escape a pattern of antisocial activities born of resentment and anger engendered by the various forms of discrimination to which they were subject, Louis had brought in Yossi Alfi – an actor and director of Mizrachi background – to begin working with some dozen of the youngsters, using an as yet little known tool, psychodrama or, as it was also called, community theatre. This enabled the young men to vent their antisocial feelings by acting out their experiences.

Amazingly, a year's devoted activity with a dozen youngsters resulted in a startlingly stark drama. It was entitled *Joseph Goes Down to Katamon*. The première in summer 1973 was attended by parents and neighbours. Raw and impassioned, it initially engendered a certain degree of pride but this was overwhelmed by the anger aroused by a scene that graphically presented a gang rape in prison. Indignant parents interrupted the performance, demanding that their sons leave the stage. The entire adult population viewed the content as atypical, intensifying the social stigma by which they had for so long been tainted: "You're blackening the entire neighbourhood!" they shouted.

Unfazed by their parents' indignation, the actors interrupted the performance in order to respond. "You can't bear to watch this. But we experienced it." Amid the shouting from both sides, Yossi Alfi proposed that the argument be postponed until after the show had ended and this was indeed what happened, not only at the first performance but at all subsequent ones, by which time both sides had learnt to present their respective arguments more calmly and reasonably, and the adults had, it seemed, come to understand and appreciate the humiliations their sons had undergone. In the eyes of their contemporaries and juniors, the cast of *Joseph Goes Down to Katamon* had achieved heroic status. They basked in the admiration. Soon afterwards, they had an opportunity to build on it.

During the Yom Kippur War, they organised activities for younger children in the bomb shelters of the tenement referred to as *shikunim* – games, competitions and charades in which they could communicate the acting skills they had developed. They also discovered their own leadership abilities. Their success aroused an ambition to expand their work to embrace the entire community of Blocks 8 and 9. They decided to found a neighbourhood organisation, Ohel Yossef – Joseph's Tent – to shelter all the residents. With this ambitious aim in mind, they turned to Louis, who had throughout retained his unofficial position as mentor. Louis was aware of my enthusiasm for theatre, evinced in collaborating with Joyce on a student production of *Measure for Measure* in 1964 and, three years later, on a brilliantly innovative *Twelfth Night*. He also knew of my social-work training and interest in social issues in general. Hence he approached me with a request to head the public committee that would determine policy, based on the needs, requests and proposals of the residents, and would guide and evaluate activities. I agreed. Although brimming with ideas, the cast of *Joseph* were as yet ignorant of organisational structure and process, unaccustomed to financial management and fundraising. But they were willing and anxious to learn and listen to practical advice, even though this sometimes involved tempering their impatient inclination to bring about instant revolution.

In addition to the founding members, the committee I headed comprised local residents, men and women aged between 25 and 63, municipal social workers whose "beat" included this area, delighted at being finally granted entry to it. There was one other "public figure" like me: Dr Bolle – a dignified gentleman who headed the Ma'aleh state-religious high-school, a veteran institution, which had been uprooted from its home in the centre of the city and dumped in this unsavoury location, presumably in order to draw more pupils from the Katamonim – a move that unfortunately led to the departure of middle-class Rehavia pupils but without attracting the locals. A true *yecke*, a German Jew with impeccable manners and infinite patience, Dr Bolle generously opened the school's doors to the organisation, repeatedly repairing broken windows, repainting walls defaced by graffiti and replacing vandalised furniture.

At Ohel Yossef we learned to appreciate each other's virtues and respect differences. For both sides, the collaboration was enlightening, exemplifying the principle of *Kol Yisrael Haverim* – "All [the people of] Israel are friends". But it soon became apparent that not everything could be achieved by volunteers. Professionals were needed, especially to coach children in after-school hours. Hence, money too was needed, and I soon discovered that the municipality in fact had a budget for precisely such activities as we were planning and engaging in. It had never occurred to the powers-that-be to consider the Katamonim as suitable candidates for official funding. When they did finally agree that we qualified for help, since we met all the criteria, including numbering public figures on the board of directors, some funds were allocated but not (as I discovered by carefully scrutinising financial documents I elicited from the municipality) the sum to which we were entitled. With evidence in hand, I set out to confront the head of the Youth and Education Department, a deputy-mayor of Jerusalem known for his brusque toughness. I accused him of swindling the deprived of the city out of its due. Reluctantly, he agreed to release the entire sum. I was greeted as a heroine.

While few of the adult men of the district remained for long on Ohel Yossef's *ad hoc* committee, the women not only continued to attend meetings regularly but also grew in number. Sharing their sons' desires to bring about radical change, they had never before found an appropriate framework in which to realise those desires. Now they had one.

In addition to fulfilling commonplace household tasks, many women were able to find work as servants. What little money they earned was handed over to their husbands, who were in charge of shopping at the market but played no other role in housekeeping. No accounts were rendered regarding expenses. The women carried a double burden: work at home and work outside the home. They were, of course, also charged with childcare. Hence they welcomed an opportunity to work close to home, bringing pre-school age children with them. Spirited, intelligent and highly motivated, with a wealth of life-experience that more than compensated for lack of formal education, they not only participated enthusiastically in committee meetings but created a subsidiary activity that brought them unprecedented income, and, with it, prestige at home and in the community. At their initiative, we elicited municipal funding to convert an abandoned prefabricated hut into a kitchen, where some dozen women, utilising skills inculcated from an early age, baked traditional Moroccan sweetmeats they later sold.

The "Women's Kitchen" in Katamon rapidly became a tool for more than income-earning, developing into a popular clubhouse, where the women gathered to chat in whatever free time they had.

"Why don't we add some education?" The question came from Shoshi, a young social worker assigned to the district. We set about recruiting professionals who spoke about child-rearing, nutrition, and hygiene. "We can't cope," was a frequently heard, though reluctantly expressed, complaint. "My husband won't let me handle money. He goes to the market himself." "There's no room for all the children." "So much laundry!" "It's always noisy." The women freely raised their issues. Hesitantly, one of our guest lecturers suggested birth control.

"Perhaps your husband should use condoms?" she asked, reluctant to phrase the suggestion more emphatically in the imperative. The women burst into laughter. The very idea of expecting an Israeli male – and especially one of Mizrachi origin – to control his sexual urges sufficiently to enable such a practice was too ludicrous to contemplate.

"You Ashkenazim!" they mocked. "You don't know what you're talking about!" "If I suggested that," one of them specified, "he'd beat me." The fear of violence seemed even greater than the fear of getting pregnant once again. Indeed, the bruises on faces and limbs testified to the use of physical force. Ignorant about female contraception, which was (and still is) unavailable in health clinics, the only method of preventing giving birth they knew was abortion. "Children are a blessing!" was the refrain of a well-known song, the irony of which escaped the poor.

The Katamon women's helplessness, the ruses to which they resorted in order to keep their husbands unaware of the aborted pregnancies, the financial hardships they incurred by surreptitiously paying for the abortions out of hard-earned income as domestic servants and their total unawareness of the many health risks involved, appalled Shoshi and me but there was too little that we could do to eradicate deeply engrained prejudices or to bring about enlightenment.

When a new neighbourhood went up on the edge of the Katamonim, more spacious, better built, intended for a slightly more affluent public, resentful Ohel Yossef leaders decided to act. They organised a squat in the new apartments and refused to budge until they received firm promises for better housing in another part of the expanding city. It took some time before these promises were fulfilled. In the meantime, the area around Blocks 8 and 9 was cleaned. A small garden was planted, where ceremonies were held on Memorial Day and Independence Day. New, larger bins gradually led to a decrease in the amount of rubbish thrown into the streets. The residents began to take pride in their little neighbourhood. At the end of 18 months of determined effort and skilful action, Shlomo Vasana, the most charismatic of the young leaders, wondered aloud what would happen when he and his fellow founders left.

"But why would you leave?" I asked. He stared at me.

"We're going into the army!" It was the first time I became aware that these remarkable young men were only 18 years old.

In 1977, the Jewish Agency partnered with Jewish communities abroad to launch Project Renewal. They allocated a vast sum of money for a grandiose scheme aimed at helping the Israeli government engage in a wide-ranging programme of urban renewal, in the so-called development towns that had been established after 1948 and in the neighbourhoods that had, like the Katamonim, been hastily erected. Suddenly a great deal of money was available and it was to be administered to a large extent by the local communities themselves.

A delegation of the Katamonim women came to see me. They had been pushed off the committee, replaced by men who had never in any way been involved with Ohel Yossef. They asked me to attend the general meeting of local residents that was soon to be held. I did and was appalled at the undemocratic mode of conducting what could hardly even be described as a discussion. Rather, it was a series of rulings, "decisions", fiats, laid down by a local henchman, a Likud activist who seemed unaware of the work of the previous three years. The successors to the founders of Ohel Yossef apparently found it expedient to collaborate with him.

The women tried to speak up, to present programmes and projects which they felt would improve the quality of life of the residents: childcare facilities, playgrounds, parks… They were never given a chance to present their proposals. Finally, I felt I had to step in. I requested the right to speak. The chairman looked at me for a moment, then said:

"Who are you, anyway?" A collective gasp greeted such *lèse-majesté*: "A Pharaoh who knew not Joseph!" I was too embarrassed to cite my contribution and that of my colleagues on the advisory council. Fortunately, others did so and I was allocated three minutes. From my experience of giving brief radio talks, I knew that one could get a great deal said in so short a time. I marshalled my arguments carefully and succinctly. I could have saved my breath. The chairman wasn't listening. And so the women remained excluded from decision-making. Their needs were not taken into account when the time for financial allocations came but a great deal of money found its way into the pockets of the newly empowered Likud "bosses" who had, in every part of the country, brought in the local, mainly Mizrachi vote that swept the party into power for the first time, ousting the left-wing majority that had ruled Israel since the founding of the state and even earlier.

Yom Kippur 1973. Something shocking and unprecedented is afoot: motor traffic – on this holiest of days, when even the least observant of Israelis never travel. Cars are moving. A motorcycle spurts off. Walking home at the end of the lengthy *Mussaf* prayer that ends the morning service, we are horrified to see, outside the little Sephardi synagogue at the end of our street, an army truck. Young men are hastening from the building, piling into the vehicle. Our second son, Micha, currently on leave from his paratroop unit, has hurried home before us and is already in uniform, heading to a customary collecting point at Binyanei Ha-uma, not far away.

As we reach our house, the upstairs neighbours, who listen to Army Radio, the only station that functions every day of the year, tell us there's been an Egyptian attack in Sinai. Anxious but not knowing what to do or is expected of us, we rest and return to our congregation for the final Ne'ilah service, the last chance for forgiveness before the gates of heaven are closed. Only later, after sunset, do we learn the extent of the initial disaster: the surprise attack, cunningly planned for a day when Israelis would be least on the alert and prepared to fight. Many of the men serving on the Suez Canal are religious. Today they are not wearing boots, only slippers. This is how they were taken into captivity. More blows were to follow. The fighting continued for two and a half weeks; 2,656 men were killed in action and 314 taken prisoner. Moshe, once again an officer in charge of a unit entrusted with identifying and burying the dead, had taken out his uniform, "just in case". In the event, he would be wearing it for almost a year.

Men are recruited – all those eligible for reserve duty, aged 21 to 55. The economy grinds to a virtual standstill. Food delivery is affected. There are no women truckdrivers and in any case trucks have been requisitioned. There is minimal public transport. The all-male cooperatives have over the years adamantly refused to accept women into their ranks. Elderly men are brought out of retirement. At the Tadiran factory, which, *inter alia*, manufactures equipment for the IDF, machines stand idle: 80% of the staff are women but not one is a mechanic. Mechanics are at the front, like the buses. Similar failures occur everywhere.

Abruptly and painfully we become aware of the absence of women from all but the lowest ranks of essential services. Other than biology, the sciences and technology are not considered appropriate fields of study for girls and women. Neither parents nor teachers encourage them to enter these fields and the girls themselves rarely think of doing so. True, there's a woman Prime Minister, Golda Meir, but she's the subject of obloquy and blame, responsible for a failure of government and a lack of foresight that led to our being caught off guard: more proof that women aren't fit to occupy public office.

SHOCK!

The Namir Commission

The beginning of the school year. Busy in my office trying to iron out the innumerable problems of timetabling that inevitably emerge despite the most meticulous attempts to prevent them, I was interrupted by a phone call. My secretary apologised.

"It's the Prime Minister's office," she explained. "I thought you'd want to speak to them."

The caller identified herself as Ora Achimeir.

"I'm calling on behalf of Member of Knesset Ora Namir," she added and went on to explain further. Namir had been invited by Prime Minister Yitzhak Rabin to chair a commission on the status of women in Israel of which she, Ora Achimeir, was the coordinator. She went on to describe its purpose: to propose legislation and administrative changes designed to improve the social, economic and political status of women. "Unfortunately," she added, "there are no reliable data available." Hence the initial stage of the commission's proceedings had to be fact-finding. This, in turn, could in many instances be achieved only by direct contact with those sectors of the population directly affected by current conditions. "We're looking for representatives of the lower-income sector," she concluded. "I understand you might be able to recommend someone."

Two candidates immediately sprang to mind. One was Betty, the spunkiest, most opinionated and articulate member of the Ohel Yossef neighbourhood community. The other was Sarah, Betty's faithful "shadow", less outspoken but also a fund of common sense and life experience. They were among the initiators of the "Women's Kitchen" that had been set up as part of the rehabilitation of Katamon. They were both intelligent and committed, their feminist consciousness aroused by the educational activities in the "Kitchen". Both could make a unique contribution to the discussions. Having made my recommendation, I hesitantly added a request:

221

"Could I be co-opted to the commission as well?" I was profoundly concerned with matters related to the status of women in Israel.

Within a week my letter of appointment arrived. I was to be on the Women and Family Committee. My experience in education and communal organisation had been ignored, seemingly outweighed by my being a working mother of six children. Betty and Sarah refused the invitation extended to them, either because they were intimidated by the thought of mingling with a group of people different from themselves or because they were sceptical as to the likelihood of any concrete results emerging from the discussions. I, on the other hand, welcomed the opportunity not only to learn more but also be involved in what had the potential to shape new policies.

For well over the year initially anticipated, I experienced a profound, intense enlightenment. So did Ora Namir, who initially perceived the commission's target population to be the the socio-economically disadvantaged. As far as learning was concerned there was no significant difference between the members of the commission: it was an eye-opener for the radical feminists no less than for the veteran members of the long-established, conservative women's organisations and even for the Members of Knesset. Without exception, we became more fully acquainted with the details of women's lives in Israel, and the nature and extent of discrimination to which they were subject.

There were close to 100 members on the commission, a group so diverse that the majority were unacquainted with each other. Sixteen were men, without exception professors, doctors or rabbis. All the current women MKs – six in number – were included. Their party affiliations ranged from Geula Cohen on the nationalist right to Shula Aloni on the liberal far-left. Despite the unbridgeable gap between their respective political agendas, these two were close friends. Most of the women who had not been re-elected were also included, some of them profoundly resentful at having been ousted. Many of them were kibbutz members of the old school, their socialist-egalitarian ideologies seemingly frozen in the mid-1950s.

The commission's function was to present to the government "social, cultural, educational, economic and legal means of advancing equality and partnership between women and men in every aspect of life in the country". It was to recommend actions intended to create such equality. Finally, it was to propose practical measures calculated to advance the rights of women and eliminate gender-biased discrimination. A tall order!

Together, the members constituted a plenum, which met once every month,

222

each time to discuss the findings and recommendations of one of the nine committees to which the members had been assigned according to their area of expertise: education and professional training, women's status in labour law and social security, representation and involvement of women in public and political life, image and communications, women's role in the family, public services, women in the workforce, women in distress and women in the defence system. The appointed chairpersons of the committees served under Ora Namir as a steering committee, with Professor Yehezkel Dror, an expert on public policy, acting as advisor. Each committee was assigned a research assistant-*cum*-coordinator responsible for collecting data, summarising relevant bibliography, inviting expert "witnesses" to appear before the committee and herself meeting those unable to attend committee meetings.

The chairwoman of our committee was Nitza Shapira-Libai, a lawyer and Labor Party stalwart, whom Rabin later appointed to be the first advisor to the Prime Minister on women's affairs. Of the nine members, two were men: one a rabbi who rarely attended, the other a lecturer in social work at the University of Tel Aviv. Radical Marcia Friedman was counterbalanced by an Orthodox communal worker. In addition there were a Christian Arab doctor, Mary Mishour Hadad from Nazareth; Matilda Gez, a Labor MK in three former Knessets who had not been re-elected; two social workers from different parts of the country – and me, listed as a faculty member of the Department of English Language and Literature at the Hebrew University, to all intents and purposes an anomaly.

Blatantly missing were the data and perspective of the Mizrachi lower classes, which Betty and Sarah could have provided. These were, however, presented at a meeting we held in Ramat Gan with a group of women similar to those of Katamon in social and economic circumstances, educational background and family status, all aged between 19 and 22, already mothers of at least two children. Frustrated, hopeless, ignorant, illiterate, lacking in skills, lonely, frightened, cowed, they longed for help to escape their miserable lives: skills of literacy and numeracy, vocational training – anything that would enable them to enter the workforce. And if they were indeed fortunate enough to find employment, they needed childcare. One hesitantly referred to family planning and contraception. She mentioned the pill. Another retorted she'd been told this was dangerous.

All the women members of our committee were gainfully employed. We were also the mothers of children, some young, others nearing adulthood and military service. Hence it was not surprising that the first subject we decided to tackle was the "double burden" of combining income-earning and home-based duties. It

223

was a topic on which we had firsthand experience. In most families, the need for adequate income necessitates gainful employment of both parents. At the same time, women traditionally bear prime responsibility for housekeeping and childcare.

I was the only one in our group who had the good fortune of being married to a man who practised egalitarian sharing at home. Hence I proposed that all laws regulating employment relate to both men and women. I was taken aback by my colleagues' responses to what they obviously considered an unattainable goal. Some of them queried the very desirability of so subversive an arrangement. Marcia, the only one who agreed with me in principle, fell in the same category as me: we were both deemed uninformed aliens. Unlike me, however, she couldn't cite her own marriage as one exemplifying the ideal of collaboration. Hitherto unaware of the extent to which our household was atypical, I counted my blessings and said no more.

It was clear that systemic change was essential if we were to achieve greater equality of the sexes. Most of us were aware that a few enlightened nations had already adopted measures designed to ease the "double burden". Those measures were based on an assumption that home-making and parenting constituted an enterprise in which two partners must be equally engaged. So what was required? we asked ourselves. We recommended parental leave that would enable fathers to be free to share in childcare; a longer school day; low-cost school meals; shorter school vacations. In 1977, even the most radical among us were still far from proposing more advanced practices such as flexitime, job-sharing, work from home and paid leave, not only on giving birth but also for caring for elderly parents or other dependents.

It would be many years before the paradigm change of sexual revolution in the west that marked the 1980s impacted on Israel. In 1977, when we referred to "single mothers" we were thinking of unmarried or divorced women. A single-sex union between two women, one of whom might give birth with the help of some form of artificial insemination, was inconceivable. Homosexuality and lesbianism, abominations in the eyes of the Orthodox, were acceptable to the more enlightened sectors of society but were considered abnormal.

Lack of awareness and a failure to adapt to changing conditions led to the sharpest and most acrimonious conflict in the plenum. An impending critical Knesset vote that kept the parliamentarians away resulted in there being a majority of "radicals" at a plenary session at which we were to determine our stand on the employment of women on night-shift, for which employers had (until 1988) to request permission from the Ministry of Labor. Marcia Friedman cited evidence that indicated that employers showed no compunction in requesting – and had no difficulty in obtaining – permission for women to work in arduous and low-paying occupations, as nurses or telephone operators. Yet when it came to the new field of computer-related occupations, a growing area of employment in which night-shift workers were paid 150% salaries, employers were not requesting permission to employ women. Our committee's recommendation was that no night-time work should require special permission or, if such permission was considered essential, the onus for applying for it would fall on the employee rather than on the employer. No significant opposition was raised. Our vote carried the day. We were therefore taken aback when, at the subsequent plenary session, without any warning, Ora Namir announced that she intended to accede to a request for a re-vote to accommodate those who had been absent from the previous meeting.

There was no precedent for such an action but no objections were raised. None among the more progressive members of the plenum was prepared for the concerted onslaught on our resolution led by the Labor MKs and the Histadrut members who, on this occasion, were present in full force, indignant and hostile. One of them with great passion cited women's long fight to obtain the International Labour Organisation ruling of 1919 that provided the protective measures we so wantonly sought to sweep away.

"True," Marcia responded. "But the ILO has rescinded that measure. Things have changed. What once was revolutionary can become hidebound and irrelevant." Her argument failed to persuade the old guard. They stood their ground. Our original, progressive vote was overturned – an indication that even women themselves were not yet keyed for sexual revolution.

Childbirth, planned parenthood, contraception, cessation of pregnancy: that highly charged complex of issues was the only one on which the members of our committee came to virtual blows.

Our discussions were held at a critical point in the national debate on abortion. The sole objection I had 20 years earlier instinctively voiced in response to my doctor's unequivocal proposal to abort – that it was illegal – was at that time a valid one. The Spiegels' reassurance was equally well-founded. Abortion was illegal under a law dating to the days of the British Mandate, a law that had never been enforced. Among religious Jews, no matter of what ethnicity, it was anathema. Yet the sole case in which a doctor had been charged after performing an abortion was when his patient bled to death. He was prosecuted for

225

manslaughter. Not until the mid-1970s did the Knessset address the issue, passing a bill based largely on a traditional halakhic principle: seek life. Judaism prioritises the mother's welfare. In accord with this compassionate approach, if a tragic need arises to choose between the mother's life and that of the infant, the mother's will always take precedence, even at the very final stages of childbirth, when the foetus is viable.

A law passed in 1975 legalised abortion on the basis of age (if the mother was under 17 or over 40 years old); if the pregnancy was the result of a forbidden relationship such as rape or incest; and if the physical or mental health of either the mother or the child was at risk. In all cases, permission had to be granted by a panel of five, composed of doctors and social workers, with the optional addition of a rabbi. The procedure had to be performed during the first 12 weeks of pregnancy. Fully aware of the inevitably explosive nature of the debate we would have, Nitza Shapira-Libai wisely postponed it to the very end of our discussions. To ensure as full as possible an attendance, she sent out the date and agenda well ahead of time. For the first time, all the members attended.

Conflict was inevitable, given our substantial differences in religious belief and practice. Each side sought to persuade its opponents of the righteousness of its own cause. The rabbi fired the opening shot. Quoting scripture, "Increase and multiply!" he said. "That's what God commanded. It is a SIN not to bear children!" He cited a rabbinical decision that ruled that contraception was permissible only once a couple had produced at least two children of differing sex. Nothing else would ensure pro-generation in years to come. Mary Hadad, like most Arab Christians a Catholic, fully agreed with him. Marcia, needless to say, expressed a diametrically opposed view.

"Women have the right to decide for themselves, the right to control their own bodies. You can't force a woman to bear a child she doesn't want." Nitza, equally radical, fully supported Marcia. The rabbi's ire was again roused.

"We lost six million in the Holocaust," he shouted. "You want to kill more Jews."

"And you want to kill more women!" Marcia shouted back, startling us by her vehemence. "Women aren't just wombs! They're human beings, just like you!"

Other members of the committee, like Nitza, favoured reinstating the 1975 law. The Orthodox social worker refrained from expressing an opinion, presumably torn between obligation to follow rabbinical edict and her intimate acquaintance with the women who were victims of the current law.

I sat silent, tormented by inner conflict. I knew that my fellow feminists expected me to come to their aid. Indeed, one part of me did perceive the justice of their argument. Women should be free to choose and determine their own fate. Yet I couldn't overcome my revulsion at denying life to another human being. Lamely, I attempted to evade the prime issue. Instead of expressing a view on abortion itself, I referred to the importance of sex education, the importance of fully available contraception, the importance of avoiding unwanted pregnancy. Finally, I went so far as to propose that women should give birth even to a child they themselves did not wish to raise, then offer it for adoption. Thousands of childless couples were eager to adopt. Marcia and Nitza gazed at me in disbelief.

"You can't be serious," Marcia said, incredulous.

I couldn't confess my own experience. The rabbi looked at me approvingly.

"Very sensible," he said, embarrassing me by assuming I fully agreed with him.

Perhaps emboldened by my indecision, others expressed similar reservations. In the end, we had to agree to disagree. In her report to the plenum, Nitza was compelled to confess failure to achieve consensus.

In 1978, when Ora Namir finally submitted the two-volume report with the commission's 241 recommendations, the government was no longer that of 1976 and the Prime Minister to whom she submitted them was not the one who had appointed her and us. Though Menachem Begin, who had been elected in 1977, was famed for the courtesy with which he related to women, equality of the sexes was not an issue that unduly concerned him. The death-knell of the Namir Report was sounded when, on the occasion of its festive submission, he responded by saying that he had so high a regard for women's opinions that he did nothing without first consulting his wife.

In 1988, the Israel Women's Network conducted a follow-up survey to establish how many of the commission's recommendations had been implemented. We discovered that a mere 32 had and 39 partially: 160 had been ignored. Yet at that very time there was undeniable evidence that momentous change had taken place and that Israeli society was engaged in a process of social transformation that might eventually ensure the equality of opportunity, reward and status that the members of the commission had sought to bring about. Consciousness-raising groups and women's centres were established. Women's studies or gender studies were introduced. Both the country's first shelter for battered women and a rape crisis counseling service, were opened. A Women's Party participated in the Knesset elections of 1977.

SHOCK!

Religion

Law. Among the Jewish values my parents instilled in me was the pursuit of justice. Injustice angered me: I was appalled by racial discrimination. I chafed at the unwarranted power that wealth bestows, abhorred the very notion of slavery and subjugation. By word and deed, I tried as best I could to counter them. I didn't anticipate encountering gross injustice in Judaism and Jewish law. I certainly didn't expect to find it in the rabbinical courts which in Israel have sole jurisdiction over all aspects of personal law: legitimacy, conversion, marriage, divorce.

"I shall never forget that sight," my *Tante* Etti said, as we sat in the garden of the pension where she spent the summer months to escape the humid heat of Tel Aviv. "She stood with cupped hands outstretched, her body trembling. A little woman waiting for her husband to give her the *get*," (the bill of divorcement." The "little woman" was her Aunt Peche, whose husband had requested a divorce).

"But why was he divorcing her?" I asked, puzzled. I was unaware that there had been breakdown of marriage in our family.

"She was barren. Bore him no sons." This seemed to Etti sufficient reason. Despite her pity for the rejected woman, she accepted the legal ground for the divorce. "Better for her to be divorced than to be an *agunah*. That was the worst fate that could befall a woman. We had some of those in Skalat."

"*Agunah*." I had heard the term, which literally means "anchored". It was the title of a novel by the Yiddish writer, Chaim Grade. The anchored women were those unfortunates whose husbands cast them off without giving them a divorce. At a time when many men emigrated from the *shtetl*s to escape poverty and seek their fortunes elsewhere, the wives remained behind, abandoned, waiting in vain to be sent for. In innumerable cases, the money for the fare never arrived. Neither widowed nor divorced, the *agunot* couldn't enter into a relationship with another man without being labelled adulterous. Any children they bore would be considered *mamzerim*, bastards, themselves beyond the pale of the Jewish community, outcasts. My aunt's compassion moved me. I was glad that the *agunah* phenomenon no longer existed.

I was mistaken. The instrument of my enlightenment was Penina Peli.

Described in one obituary as the "mother of Orthodox feminism", Penina was a passionate advocate for women's rights within Judaism. She believed that freeing Orthodox women from discrimination was essential to the redemption of the Jewish people. Daughter of one Orthodox rabbi and married to another, Penina had received an excellent Jewish education. She could cite chapter and verse to support views which were widely considered heretical. In the early 1970s she tempestuously began challenging notions as to what was and was not permissible for women. In contrast to me, Penina was fully aware of the injustice that characterised the *batei din*, the religious courts that in Israel have the exclusive right to determine that a divorce must take place. She had learned of the abuse to which women were subjected, of the way in which the judges angrily accused women who refused their husbands' often outrageous demands for exorbitant bribes, the forfeit of financial support, child custody and property.

With another Orthodox feminist, Sylvia Mandelbaum, a recent immigrant from the US, Penina established Mitzvah, an organisation that aimed to help women trapped in the labyrinths of the religious courts. At first, the most the two could do was accompany their "clients" to the innumerable, frequently hostile hearings, giving moral support and comfort to counter the verbal abuse hurled at them. Eventually, they concluded that they had to appeal to the highest authority, none other than the Chief Rabbis themselves, who head the country's entire state-funded rabbinical establishment. Perhaps because I was personally acquainted with the previous Askenazi Chief Rabbi, Shlomo Goren, to whom Moshe had served as aide-de-camp throughout two and a half years of his military service, Penina asked me to accompany them. It proved to be the first of many fruitless meetings, which received no media coverage and hence drew no public attention.

However, I had been enlisted to the ranks of the Fighters for Justice. In order to be armed adequately for such an encounter, we sought rabbinical guidance, initially turning to two Orthodox rabbis whose publications indicated that they would be sympathetic to our cause: Ze'ev Falk, a professor in the Law Faculty of the Hebrew University, and Eliezer Berkovits, a Holocaust survivor who had recently come on *aliyah* after serving as the greatly beloved and widely respected rabbi of a large Orthodox congregation in Chicago. Both men had published books and articles on Personal Law. Both were sympathetic. They willingly expounded on their interpretation of rabbinical law – one that was clearly more consistent with modernity, more sympathetic towards women and far from the outdated misogyny that reigned in the religious courts.

Encouraged by the response from these two experts, Penina and Sylvia requested a meeting with both the Chief Rabbis. As the weeks passed, they sent occasional reminders to the director of the rabbis' office. Finally, he succumbed to their nagging. A time was fixed. Penina, Sylvia and I set out together, to beard the lions in their den. They might have thought that, having participated in the meetings with our experts, I would be able to contribute to the discussion. I doubted I could but I hoped there might be strength in numbers. I needn't have worried.

After what seemed an interminable wait in the outer office, we were ceremoniously ushered into the spacious room where the two functionaries sat, one on each side of an imposing desk. Each wore his well-known "uniform": one, a black suit and stiff, wide-brimmed black hat, the other in a richly embroidered robe, with an imposing turban crowning his head. No sooner had the clerk uttered the word "*agunot*" than one of the rabbis sternly interrupted him.

"There are no *agunot* in Israel," he said. "We have no such problem." Penina attempted to respond by describing some of the cases in which she was involved. "You don't know what you're talking about. There are no *agunot*! These women just refuse to accept the rulings of the courts. In fact, it is they who are to blame!"

There was truth in his allegations: in strictly legal terms his contention was justified. *Halakha* defines an *agunah* as one whose husband is missing, cannot be found and might no longer be alive. This ruling might be applied in the case of a husband who had travelled abroad and not been heard from for many years or a soldier pronounced "missing, believed killed in action". Throughout the ages, rabbis have been scrupulous in efforts to track down the men concerned. Today, the same meticulousness characterises the identification of those who fall in battle.

The women whose case we were attempting to plead were not *agunot* but rather *mesuravot get*, women refused divorce. In Jewish law, a *get* is valid only if a husband of his own free will places the bill of divorcement in his wife's willingly outstretched hands. Should the husband refuse to perform that act, the correct term is "*mesurevet get*". A woman could refuse to accept the *get* but it was seldom in her interest to do so, since she would be forfeiting alimony and risk losing custody of children. The husband could obtain permission to take a second wife, while any relationship on which she might embark would be considered adulterous. We had not sufficiently comprehended the distinction between an anchored wife and one denied divorce. Penina tried in vain to counter our detractor's argument. A hand was raised in a gesture of dismissal.

"There's no more to be said," she was told. Undeterred, Penina persisted, citing our experts. Their names were like a red rag to a bull. "Falk!" came the angry response. "He's not Orthodox!" "Berkovits? Who's he?" Falk was indeed un-Orthodox. Though strictly observant, he was a model of openness and tolerance. At his funeral many years later, his only son recounted how his father would every Shabbat take him to a different synagogue, including the then barely nascent Reform and Conservative congregations, in order to instil the basic concept of "These and these are the words of the Living God". When it came to Berkovits, the issue was different. His publications were in English. While Sephardi rabbis frequently lack fluency in that language and are, in any case, reluctant to consult or cite non-Sephardic sources, the Ashkenazi Chief Rabbi might legitimately have been expected to be familiar with publications in English.

Throughout the proceedings, Sylvia, like me, remained silent, though not for the same reason. Lacking fluency in Hebrew, she was unable to follow the exchanges. My own deficiency was in knowledge of *Halakha*. Penina had no alternative but to desist from her attempt at persuasion. Though temporarily defeated, she and Sylvia persisted in their efforts to free victims individually from the bond of a dead marriage but they proved unable to bring about comprehensive reform. To this day, unjust discrimination against women remains the norm, not the exception. Thousands of Jewish women worldwide remain in bondage.

SHOCK!

Judaism

Judaism is patriarchal. In Scripture, women are depicted primarily in their biologically determined role of wives and mothers. Failing to give birth to sons was considered as failing to fulfil the natural function that stems from God's curse on Eve: to bring forth children (in the Hebrew, sons) in pain and to be ruled over by her spouse. Of the four matriarchs, only the unloved Leah is exempt from difficulty in procreating. Miriam and Deborah are acknowledged as prophets but they are the exceptions. From the time of the Exodus, women cease to play a central role in the national saga.

"The honour of a king's daughter is wholly within." "Woman's voice is an abomination." "A man who teaches his daughter Torah is teaching her profanity."

Rabbinic Judaism is misogynistic. *Halakha* restricts women's lives, excluding them from the three "houses" central to Jewish life: of study, prayer and justice. As daughters, sisters and wives, women have no independent standing in the community. The duties mandated for women are family- and household-related: kindling the lights that usher in the Shabbat and holy days; observing family purity; setting aside a portion of bread dough to commemorate the tithe paid to the High Priest in the Temple. All are based on the assumption that adult Jewish women are married and engage primarily in household matters. From all time-related commandments, such as praying at specific times of day, they are exempted. Over the centuries what may have begun as a benevolent exemption based on awareness of the primacy and demands of home-making hardened into strict prohibition. Women who defied the rules were condemned as *mordot*, rebels.

Ritual. As a child, I accompanied my mother to synagogue on holy days, sitting with her in the women's section, separated from the men by a barrier. Sometimes there were curtains of varying thickness; sometimes merely a wooden lattice-work fencing. The synagogues we frequented in London had what were rather grandly referred to as Ladies' Galleries, a nomenclature possibly intended to compensate females for the fact that visibility and audibility were limited to the front row. Because that was where our seats were located, I was privileged to see the top hats of the *gabbaim* (wardens) in their box facing the congregation and to witness imposing ceremony: the removal of richly decorated Torah scrolls from the ark, the procession accompanied by kisses – some ardent, others perfunctory – of the male members, the raising of the scroll at the conclusion of the reading and, on Yom Kippur, the awe-inspiring prostration of the rabbi and cantor during the *Mussaf* service. I could see the *Cohanim* go up to stand at the altar heads shrouded in prayer-shawls, though I was careful to cover my eyes during their blessing lest, as my mother and grandmother warned, I be blinded by the glory of their countenance. In short, I was a spectator or a minor member of the chorus, certainly not a major protagonist.

On one occasion, I decided to be more active.

By *Sukkot*, the Feast of Tabernacles, 1945 my awareness of discrimination against women in every area of civil life and society was already heightened by knowledge of the hostility and harassment that had attended their efforts to attain higher education. My first year at Cambridge, where women were in a distinct minority and excluded from membership of élite entities such as the Union, had further sharpened my resentment but I had not as yet applied that resentment to my religious experience. This innocence was about to be challenged.

Every *Simchat Torah* my father would walk for miles to attend the Rejoicing of the Law celebrations at the small synagogue, the *shtiebel* of the Rebbe of Premycyl.

"Come with me," he proposed. "You'll enjoy it," he assured me, assuming that I would share his own enthusiasm. Located on the ground floor of the rebbe's home, the *shtiebel* was a far cry from the synagogues we customarily attended. There was no Ladies' Gallery, only a windowless room that could, at best, accommodate the half a dozen women who arrived on Yom Kippur. Apart from me, the only females in these tight quarters were the rebbe's twin daughters, dutiful girls considerably younger than myself. Assisted by her three older daughters, the *Rebbetzin* hastened to and from the kitchen, ensuring a lavish supply of her celebrated onion biscuits and pickled herring. Fuelled by innumerable bottles of *Schnapps*, singing was loud, dancing energetic, the agility of even the stoutest of the men amazing. The joy was infectious. I too felt an urge to celebrate. Yet here I was, excluded and deprived. Emboldened by indignation, I invited the twins to join me in a circle dance of our own. We too would celebrate.

"No, no, we mustn't," they demurred. "It's only for men."

"You're wrong," I responded. "Wasn't the Torah given to women as well as to men?"

Either they were persuaded by the logic of my argument or overawed by my superior status as a student at a prestigious university. Whatever the reason, they agreed. As we danced, we sang. Our joy was short-lived. Within minutes, the beadle appeared. Furiously, in the sharpest of condemnatory terms, he scolded us for our daring immodesty. He bade us desist at once from this licentiousness. Chastened and humiliated, we obeyed but I remained resentful and in later years found various excuses for not accompanying my father to the "Rejoicing" of a Law that so blatantly discriminated between men and women.

SHOCK!

Education

"Pelech": A spindle. The word appears in a derogatory manner in the derisive dismissal of a misogynist Talmud sage who contended that "Women's wisdom is solely in the spindle."

Considering the controversy that surrounded Pelech throughout so much of its history, it comes as no surprise that there is a measure of disagreement even regarding the date of its founding. There are those who claim the school was established in 1966 when the Rosenblüths first rented a flat in Jerusalem's Bayit Ve-gan district, a quiet suburb near Mount Herzl, and began teaching a small group of 14-year-olds, including their younger daughter. Others maintain that the more correct date is September 1967 when, following the territorial realignments that resulted from the Six-Day War, Reb Sholem, as he was universally known, persuaded the Ministry for Religious Affairs to let to him an abandoned building on the slopes of Mount Zion, in what had previously been No-Man's Land. It was there that Pelech launched its highly unorthodox activities, seeking to attract ultra-Orthodox girls from the Beit Ya'akov network, and provide them with a much wider range of program of secular studies and more in-depth Jewish studies than those available at Beit Ya'akov.

Gemara (Talmud) was from the first a compulsory subject at Pelech, though explicitly prohibited to girls from the ultra-Orthodox community and even in state religious schools taught only to boys. Natural curiosity, far from being stifled for fear it led to religious scepticism, was actively encouraged, even when it led to study of topics normally taboo in ultra-Orthodox circles. Little wonder, therefore, that within five years of opening Pelech was being boycotted by the very community that it had set out to enlighten, while simultaneously attracting ever-growing numbers of daughters of well-educated "modern Orthodox" families, many of which were headed by well-known academicians, members of the free professions and community leaders.

Soon after the Passover vacation in 1975 I received an unexpected phone call

234

from Pnina Rosenblüth. "The inspector is coming to visit. Would you be prepared to sit in on some of the classes with him?" she asked. "I'll be too busy teaching myself and I think somebody should accompany him, don't you?" "Why me?" any sensible person might have responded. But I knew all too well (or so I thought) why I'd been chosen for this dubious honour. In fact, I had brought it on myself.

Three years earlier, at the same season of the year, I had toiled up the steep path through the Valley of Hinnom to the crest of Mount Zion where, just outside the Old City walls, there were a number of dilapidated buildings that had from 1948 to 1967 stood unoccupied in No-Man's Land. I was on my way to the Pelech High School for *Haredi* Girls.

Ditza, our eldest daughter, had been miserable and underperforming at the Evelina de Rothschild School, the only one considered suitable for girls of her background and capabilities. I wholly sympathized with her desire to leave the school, having myself been deeply disappointed by its dismal educational outlook – or lack of one. Worried by the low grades she was receiving, Moshe and I had attended an evening at which, as is customary in Israel, parents went from teacher to another to discuss their offsprings' progress. Ditza's chemistry teacher, who had given her a particularly low grade, was hard put to identify our daughter. "Is she the one with curly hair?" he asked. The history teacher's comments were even more disturbing, though she was at least able to identify the pupil in question.

"She's alright when she has to think for herself," she admitted grudgingly, "but usually she seems out of touch with what's going on in class." I suggested that perhaps the pupils should more frequently be called upon to "think for themselves," though this would of course also make greater demands on the teacher.

Moshe and I had been to see the principal to voice our dissatisfaction. An elderly man, close to retirement, he proved to be totally unaware of advances made in educational theory and practice during the mid-20th century. His major concern was that the pupils ultimately pass the standard matriculation exams. He failed to see the difference between accumulation of factual knowledge and what should be the ideal outcome of schooling: the ability to explore, evaluate, analyse, deconstruct, deduce, understand – a collaborative process in which the teacher was the facilitator but not the final arbiter. In vain did we elaborate. Moshe and I had left, wondering how, in the absence of Orthodox schools for middle-class pupils, we could further our gifted daughter's education. Ditza had her own solution ready.

"Pelech," she pronounced, firmly.

"But it's *haredi*," I remonstrated. "We're not *haredim*."

"I don't care," she responded, defiantly. "It's a good school!"

I went to see for myself. Climbing up Mount Zion, I passed several teenagers, each in the school's dauntingly Orthodox uniform of long sleeves and long stockings so inappropriate for a hot khamsin day in Jerusalem. Each was bent over an exercise book or folio pad, oblivious to the few passersby, writing rapidly, seemingly intent on accomplishing whatever her task was. When I entered the cavernous hall, I was greeted warmly. I was already acquainted with Pnina. Plump and rosy-cheeked, a kerchief always wound around her head in defiance of the constantly changing fashions of headgear of Orthodox women, she looked more like a Polish peasant than the excellent veteran full-time teacher of English at a secular Jerusalem high-school that I knew her to be. In contrast, Reb Sholem was wiry, short, sharp-featured, the grey hat perched perilously on the back of his head giving no clear indication as to which specific sector of Orthodoxy he subscribed to.

What were these girls doing out in the sun? My first enquiry elicited a surprising explanation: since the school practised the honour system, pupils were permitted to sit wherever they wished during exams, on the understanding that there would be no cheating. Breaking of rules was known to be prevalent in other schools; sometimes teachers even colluded with pupils in order to achieve good grades, thus satisfying the demands of the Ministry of Education and so attracting good families. Impressed by Pelech's exceptionally enlightened approach, I was further captivated by details of the wide-ranging curriculum the Rosenblüths proudly presented to me. However, the incident that ultimately persuaded me that this was indeed where I would like my daughter to be educated involved one of their pupils. A member of my synagogue, I knew her to be modest, intelligent and courteous. We greeted each other.

"You know Rachel?" Reb Sholem asked, as if surprised at my acquaintance with so unimpeachable an ultra-Orthodox girl. He then told me that for part of her assignments for the final matriculation exams, she was writing a paper on Christian symbols in the novels of Graham Greene. Christian? Graham Greene? At a *haredi* school? This openness was beyond belief. After that I had no objections to Ditza transferring to Pelech, which she did in 1973.

Unfortunately, 1973-4 was not a good year. Pelech was not spared the distress the entire country suffered during and in the wake of the Yom Kippur war. Classes were disrupted for weeks. Some of the male teachers had been wounded, others had long periods of reserve duty. Against his will, Reb Sholem was compelled to bring in women, whom he normally spurned because they were "constantly giving birth". But with their husbands away and children to care for, few of these were available. There was chaos.

The school was also bankrupt. Not yet accredited and hence unqualified for financial or other support from either the Ministry of Education or the Jerusalem Municipality, it also lacked donors. No accounts were kept. Salaries were unpaid or paid "in kind", as in "You need a new suit. Go to X and have one made and I'll cover the cost." Worse still, furniture was old and tattered. There was no library. Impressive educators but the poorest of administrators, the Rosenblüths elicited the sympathy of some of the parents, me included. We formed a committee. We arranged meetings with senior officials at the ministry and the municipality, many of whom had been alienated by Reb Sholem's contemptuous manner.

Then came the final blow. In May 1974 a terrorist attack on a school in Maalot, which resulted in the death of 22 pupils, made us painfully aware of the dangers emanating from Pelech's isolation outside the Old City walls. To intensify the need to move, pupils and principals arrived one morning to find the school's sparse and outmoded furniture piled outside the padlocked building, which had been illegally taken over by the neighbouring Diaspora Yeshiva. A frantic city-wide search for new quarters led us to a small house in Bayit Ve-gan, whose elderly owner agreed to let the ground floor and one room on the upper floor, where she continued to reside, filling the building with pungent odours of highly spiced foods, and occasionally venturing forth to demand greater quiet and decorum. These were totally inappropriate premises but our classes were small: the 12th grade comprised 10 pupils, while no other grade had more than 20. One small room doubled as "library" and staff-room – a combination made all the easier by both the extreme paucity of the library's holdings and the minimal staff.

A month before the move, the Rosenblüths abruptly announced their intention to close the school. They could no longer afford to invest in it, nor could they afford to work there full-time. But above all they cited as the major reason for their decision the "infiltration" of enlightened modern-Orthodox families and the steep decline in the number of *haredi* applicants. This was no longer the school they'd intended it to be. Aghast at the decision, the parents sought to avert disaster. Several of us, particularly the recent immigrants from the US, experienced in fundraising, undertook to organize an event that would bring in

237

some much-needed revenue and I rashly volunteered to help with administration, the principles and practice of which were alien to both Pnina and Reb Sholem. After much pleading, they agreed to postpone their retirement for another year. Official recognition bringing state support was essential. A delegation comprising several of the more distinguished parents set about requesting it. Their efforts proved effective. The Ministry of Education would look into whether the school met with official requirements. The ministry's regional inspector would visit to determine whether Pelech qualified for recognition. I was to accompany him.

I was impressed by the quality of the teachers as well as by the pupils, who were eager, responsive participants, clearly enjoying the classes. The atmosphere was relaxed: a model of collaboration between teachers and taught. Emerging from the last of the classes, the inspector and I were met by Pnina, to whom we conveyed our enthusiastic and complimentary comments. Presumably because he knew that the Rosenblüths jointly headed the school, the inspector innocently turned to Pnina and asked with whom he should in future be in contact on matters regarding Pelech. The answer, to my consternation, followed without a moment's pause:

"Professor Shalvi," said Pnina, not looking me in the eyes.

And that was how, in the spring of 1975, I became principal of Pelech.

As the Rosenblüth's abdication became known, members of the staff who shared Reb Sholem's religious views informed me that they would no longer teach at Pelech. Although Pnina at first agreed to continue teaching English, she later changed her mind and I was left with a pitifully inadequate staff. I could however offer no tempting full-time positions. Fortunately, new candidates appeared, some seemingly unaware of the change in the nature of the school, which the *haredi* community had publicly ostracized by posting condemnatory placards in the districts where they lived. I recruited a former student whom I had dissuaded from continuing to strive to attain a Ph.D. degree and who had instead followed my advice to continue to be a successful English teacher. I begged elegant Madame Avichail, a model of French-inspired elegance, to stay on and she acceded to my request. So did Hananel Mack, the most outstanding member of the staff. A miraculous survivor of the Yom Kippur War who had for some time hovered between life and death, he was both learned and emotionally intelligent – an all-too-rare combination. Hananel was adored by his pupils and I found in him a tactful guide on what was both desirable and permissible.

Classes remained small. The ultra-Orthodox pupils who no longer applied had been replaced by only a few daughters of families like my own. The 9th grade numbered a mere 16, my younger daughter among them. It included two from Beit Ya'akov whose enlightened parents lived in comparatively tolerant Bayit Vegan. The 12th grade had only eight pupils, since Reb Sholem had the previous year summarily expelled almost the entire class because he considered the pupils incapable of passing the Bagrut matriculation exam. So pronounced a failure would not only be an indelible stain on Pelech's reputation but also an indication that the school was unworthy of accreditation, which is dependent on pupils' success in the final examinations.

Undaunted, I flung myself into fulfilling my self-appointed ambition to turn the school into a model of what I hubristically saw as the ideal education: one that would equip pupils to eventually function as informed, committed and engaged members in a modern, democratic Jewish state that granted equality to all its citizens "irrespective of race, religion or gender," as our Declaration of Independence put it.

With that goal in mind I sought to make the curriculum more immediately and recognizably relevant to the contemporary social context and social needs. I devised new courses, adopted innovative practices, magpie-like picked up ideas from a wide variety of sources. I read Carol Gilligan's *In A Different Voice* and found in it reassuring confirmation of my own belief in differential teaching methods for girls and boys. I followed the suit of my friends David and Hanna Greenberg, who had established a school near Boston that practised truly democratic modes of self-governance, granting pupils rights that are normally considered solely those of the staff.

"Only connect." E.M. Forster's epigraph for *A Passage to India* was my educational guiding light. I sought to show pupils (and teachers) how ideas, ideologies, areas of knowledge, even individuals, interact, intertwine, interlock – how the disparate trees of cognition combine to constitute a forest of knowledge and understanding.

Seeking to learn from Best Practices, I mercilessly dragged the senior teachers to visit such schools all over the country as had a reputation for innovation and excellence. The British Council funded a study tour of the UK, arranging for me to be hosted by a variety of schools considered innovative. Nowhere did I encounter anything as original and exciting as Pelech. In fact, ours soon became the school to which visitors came in order to encounter methods so unprecedented as not to be found elsewhere in Israel.

To my great good fortune, I had taken up my post at the most auspicious of times. David Pur, the founding headmaster of an innovative school at Kibbutz Givat Brenner and a great believer in, and advocate of, open, pupil-centred education, had just been put in charge of secondary education at the Ministry of Education. As a result, a major reform had been launched, abolishing the traditional "sets" of specialization that compelled 9th-grade pupils henceforth to choose between humanities and science and granting greater autonomy to schools that wished to implement innovative courses. I was doubly fortunate in finding young teachers who had not only completed a degree at the Hebrew University, but had also studied education at the newly-founded Kerem Institute, which shared Pelech's ideal of combining Jewish and general studies. They were fully prepared to respond to my challenges of innovation.

Delighted to find a principal who shared his views, Pur gave me every possible encouragement and support even when I faced criticism from officials in the Religious Branch of the Ministry of Education. Within three years, Pelech was accredited as one of the (then) only two officially recognised "experimental" high-schools in Jerusalem. We were in the good graces of the Ministry of Education and beginning to be grudgingly appreciated by the head of the Jerusalem Municipal Education Department, who nevertheless continued to maintain that we were an elitist, all-Ashkenazi, discriminatory institution.

Unfortunately, when I began working at Pelech I was insufficiently acquainted with the niceties of Orthodox Judaism as these find outward expression. I had, albeit reluctantly, adopted a more modest form of dress: no open neck, sleeves at least to the elbows, skirts reaching to four inches below the knee. My beloved frocks and elegant pants suits hung unused in my wardrobe. After trying on a variety of headgear, I baulked at covering my hair, citing other observant women who remained similarly hatless in defiance of the rabbis who had long ago defined a woman's hair as – like a woman's voice – an abomination.

Other strictures with which I was inadequately acquainted led to a series of confrontations with a trio of male teachers of Jewish Studies who were graduates of Mercaz Ha-Rav, a yeshiva that was considered most in accord with the views and practices of the modern-Orthodox community. My ignorance was the cause of conflict between myself and this trio.

By 1977, I arrogantly assumed that I had accumulated sufficient knowledge about the role and status of women in Judaism to enable me to lecture and to present a critique on the topic. My maiden public foray into the field was in 1977, during my first visit to the US. "Women in Judaism" was the topic of an address

I was to deliver at what was at the time the only congregation in Palo Alto – an easy-going, multi-denominational group, headed by a gentle Orthodox rabbi who had studied in Israel.

I found myself at an astonishing event, of a kind I had never before encountered: a bat-mitzvah ceremony, in the course of which the 12-year-old protagonist not only read the entire weekly portion of the Torah as well as the subsequent chapter from Prophets, but also delivered a brief Dvar Torah, a commentary on what she had read.

I was overwhelmed. What I was witnessing was so contrary to what I was about to describe as being Judaism's customary discrimination against women. Nevertheless, I delivered the address I'd prepared, adding my profound admiration of what I had just experienced and complimenting not only the young woman and her family (all the female members of which had been called to the Torah), but also the congregation as a whole on their progressive – even revolutionary – stand.

To my surprise, my remarks were greeted with loud applause. I assumed this to be the customary American way of responding to a guest speaker. It was only at the reception that followed that I learnt that this was in fact the first time such an egalitarian ceremony had been held and that it had been preceded by a lengthy and not entirely friendly debate with the rabbi. I felt some remorse at having sided with the rebels. I had, as it were, bitten the hand that fed me (metaphorically: I was not receiving any remuneration for my address). Generously, the rabbi complimented me on what I had said. His wife was less forgiving. During lunch at their home, she made her own opposition to both the celebration and my address very clear.

Upon my return to Pelech, I seized the first opportunity to relate what I had witnessed and to express my admiration for the "heroine" of the event. I hoped my account might stimulate some of the pupils to follow her example.

However, not only were my own excitement and enthusiasm not reflected in the pupils' response; rather, it elicited a caustic comment from one of the male teachers of Jewish studies, whom I knew to be a lover of classical music.

"In an orchestra," he said firmly, "when the violinist plays the notes composed for the violin and the trumpeter plays the notes composed for the trumpets, there is harmony. But when the violins play the trumpets' notes and the trumpets play the notes of the violinists there is discord!"

He needed to say no more. His message was clear. Male was distinct from female and any attempt to alter the millennia-old distinction (and subsequent discrimination) was anathema, sacrilegious undermining of Jewish law, Jewish tradition and Jewish values.

I learned never again to express my heretical views on the inferior status of women in Jewish ritual within the confines of Pelech.

A little later in 1977 I encountered a phenomenon that was utterly new to me: a religiously observant woman seemingly as knowledgeable in Talmud as the male members of my staff. A recent arrival from the United States, Beverly Gribetz had already heard of Pelech's reputation as the only girls' school at which Talmud study was obligatory. She applied for a post and I was delighted at the thought that at last our pupils would have a role model. I offered her a part-time position, inviting her to give a course on Women and *Halakha*. Beverly rapidly opened up new vistas of halakhic rulings related to women, raising questions regarding rules and practices our pupils had never before been called upon to examine critically.

Others did not share my delight. Among the staff there was soon unrest. A mere two weeks into the school year, a self-appointed delegation of the three male Jewish Studies teachers demanded that I instantly dismiss Beverly: "She is not Orthodox," they asserted. "She studied at the Jewish Theological Seminary which is" (they could hardly bring themselves to utter the profanity) "Conservative!"

My defence of Beverly's religious bona-fides finally made them relent, but only partially. They insisted on a meeting of the entire staff, whom I invited to my home, ostensibly for a social gathering that would enable the veterans and newcomers to become acquainted. We settled into a circle, each person prepared to introduce him/herself not only by name but by a few identifying remarks. When Beverly's turn came, the tone and content changed. One by one, the three accusers fired questions at her, some of them so basic as to be ludicrous.

"Do you keep meat and dairy separate in your kitchen?"

"Do you attend synagogue every Shabbat?"

"What are the various blessings one says, according to what one has consumed?"

And so on.

While I felt increasingly uncomfortable at the openly hostile tone of her prosecutors, Beverly remained cool, calmly answering each question. After half an hour of grilling, the questioning ceased. As the meeting broke up, the three self-appointed judges approached me. Admitting she was religious, they still insisted on her dismissal: "We can't have our girls thinking one can attend a Conservative institution and still be Orthodox." Unswayed by the illogic, ignorance and intolerance, I decided I would disregard their demands. The three inquisitors submitted their resignation, effective at the end of the school year, causing no little damage to Pelech's reputation through the rumours they spread about my own unfitness for the position of principal and the questionable nature of Pelech's so-called Orthodoxy. Beverly stayed at Pelech until she went back to the US to complete her doctoral thesis in Talmud. Then she returned to Israel and founded the Tehilla School for Girls.

Spring 1979. I was in Milwaukee, serving as scholar-in-residence for the first time in my life. It was only my second visit to the United States and I was still unfamiliar with the niceties of American Jewry, the distinction between Orthodox, Modern Orthodox, Conservative, Reform.

At Friday night dinner at the home of the rabbi and his wife who were hosting me for the weekend, I found myself surrounded by additional rabbinic couples, all of them apparently halakhically observant, yet all of them mocking the excesses and absurdities that have increasingly come to characterise Orthodoxy. It appears that one of the major current injunctions from the Council of Sages is against *negiyah*, physical contact between males and females. Like my fellow guests, I well recalled my days as an adolescent in the religious-Zionist youth movement Bnei Akiva, where we all danced with arms on each other's shoulders in the rousing hora without, so far as I could tell, any undue sexual arousal. I was taken aback by the levity regarding certain rules, regulations and practices that increasingly govern stricter Orthodoxy. The mockery and irreverence amazed me. Not what I'd expected from a group of rabbis. I was puzzled both as to what to expect and what was expected of me the next day, when I was due to speak at the morning service.

Some clarification followed. I would be speaking at the annual Women's League Shabbat. The topic had been determined months earlier, when my visit was first scheduled: "The Status of Women in Judaism and in Israel".

Arriving at the synagogue, I discovered that the women members would be holding their own service, apart from the men and in a separate hall, not in what is known as the sanctuary. Some of the women were wearing *talitot* (prayer shawls), a practice I considered a male prerogative. I sat bemused as the service began. Women were expertly leading the prayers. The entire congregation was

243

obviously well-practised in the Shabbat service. The singing was joyous, the atmosphere festive. A special occasion, for women only.

A Torah scroll had been allocated to the women. The reading was impressively flawless, arousing my wonder and admiration. Suddenly, I found myself approached by the "warden". Would I accept an *aliyah*? I struggled to find the correct response. I had for some years been preaching and teaching the need for greater equality between the sexes in everything pertaining to Judaism, but I had been doing so in an Orthodox environment, limited by halakhic considerations. I was an object of acute criticism by the Orthodox establishment in Israel. I had obligations towards Pelech. On the other hand, I yearned for inclusion in the spheres from which Jewish women are traditionally excluded. I looked around. There was not a single man present. At least I was not defying the ban on mixed worship. There was also nobody who might reveal my delinquency "back home". I agreed, gave my Hebrew name and was called up to the Torah. I resisted an attempt to place a *tallit* around my shoulders and used the Torah girdle in place of *tzitzit* with which to kiss the scroll. I chanted the appropriate blessing in a shaky voice.

Then – there was the script in front of me. I cannot remember what the *parsha* was. I was oblivious to the content. All I saw were the black letters on the yellowing parchment; the silver "hand" moving inexorably from word to word. I trembled with emotion. The tears came and I sobbed uncontrollably: sobs of joy at being granted the privilege of the moment; of anger as I realized that I could have had this revelatory experience 40 years earlier had I been a male. Recovering equanimity, I recited the final blessing. Looking up, I noticed for the first time the faces around me – amazed, startled, questioning, sympathetic. Tears were in the eyes of some of the older women sitting close to me, perhaps the only ones present who recalled their own exclusion and the hard-won struggle to be counted. The younger ones obviously saw nothing remarkable in what they had witnessed – just an elderly lady being emotional. Over what? Since I had not as yet been formally introduced, very few of those present knew anything of my Orthodox background, of the discrimination, the depravation to which I had been subjected in all matters religious. For me, still standing at the table where the Torah scroll lay, there was a lack of completion. I was reluctant to return to my seat. Something indefinable was still missing to mark this for me momentous experience.

Suddenly it came to me. Instinctively, I uttered the first words that came into my mind – the blessing for anything that is new:

244

"Blessed art Thou…who has kept us in life, and has preserved us, and enabled us to reach this moment." *Shehechyanu!*

My next "indiscretion" was to request the military authorities to send a woman officer to explain the nature of women's service in the Israel Defense Forces and its compatibility with religious practice. This was directly opposed to the school's initial policy of forbidding military service for women. It was also counter to official rulings on the part of the religious branch of the Ministry of Education, which on this issue, as on others, abided by the edicts of the Chief Rabbinate.

Again, I was faced with teachers' threats of resignation; again I refused to buckle under. None other than the commanding officer of the Women's Corps chose to come to speak to our 12th grade. Teachers crowded the classroom, anxious to hear her words, in order, no doubt, to rebut them. However, the content and manner of her address were so eminently reasonable, so considerate of the beliefs and practices of our pupils and their families, that not only were my opponents disarmed, but a major change occurred in the behaviour of our graduates, of whom well over eighty percent came to choose service in the IDF. The remainder elect a full two years in the voluntary National Service framework, devotedly serving both country and community.

A major innovation in Pelech's programme of studies was a 4-year programme of Total History. It combined the traditional coverage of political and social events, with study of concurrent literature, philosophy, art and music. In 10th grade, this comprehensive 10-hour-a-week course dealt with the Middle Ages and early Renaissance. What better place than Jerusalem to study the Crusader wars, to illustrate and make concrete the clash between the three monotheistic faiths? Each of them had left visible evidence of their presence in the heart of the Old City: the Western Wall and ancient synagogues, the Church of the Holy Sepulchre and numerous monasteries, the majestic golden-domed mosque on the Temple Mount. I suggested that the staff include tours in the lessons. They were startled. Surely *Halakha* forbade entering a "heathen" place of worship? I was taken aback. This was a prohibition of which I was entirely ignorant. It seemed to me based on superstition rather than Biblical or rabbinical law.

I decided to consult a rabbi. Since Jewish practice allows one to "make for oneself a rabbi", I could choose one that I assumed would support me. The obvious choice was Rabbi Aharon Lichtenstein, the head of the yeshiva in Efrat, holder of a Ph.D. in English literature from Harvard, a man steeped in both

Jewish learning and western culture, who had immigrated to Israel a few years earlier.

To my dismay, not only did he forbid visits to "heathen" sites, but informed me that in Europe it was the custom for Jews to spit and cross the road when they encountered a church. My parents had at no time done this, though they never visited the medieval abbey in Essen. I had clearly made the wrong choice of rabbi. There were no tours to sacred sites other than those of Jews.

My "errors" led the parents, with the best intention of maintaining the image of Pelech as a "religious" school ("*haredi*" had been dropped from the name as no longer appropriate), to appoint a halakhic supervisor, in order to avoid future debacles. They elected Rabbi Zev Gothold, a European who specialized in Jewish art and was known to be open-minded and liberal. Unfortunately, although he and I agreed on major issues, he did not find favour in the eyes of the pupils, very few of whom consulted him. Probably sensing that he was *persona non grata*, he did not stay long at the school.

There followed a search for an appropriate replacement. The choice lighted on Jonathan Blass, a recent immigrant from the US, an ordained rabbi, whom I had employed to teach Talmud. When the increased size of our library warranted employment of a professional, he introduced me to his wife. The first act on which the couple decided was to place all works of Biblical Criticism on the top shelf, where they were not only inaccessible but even concealed from the prying eyes of our pupils. This act should have alerted me to the couple's excessive zeal in removing all possible temptations of heresy. Unfortunately, it failed to do so.

Jonathan was delighted to assist me in the selection of candidates for entry into the 9th grade, the major element in which was a personal interview aimed, inter alia, at determining the degree of the candidate's observance of religious rules. Finding his standards far too stringent, I insisted on accepting girls whom he considered insufficiently Orthodox. Offended, he and his wife both resigned. Unbeknownst to me, he sent a letter to the parents of all the candidates who had been accepted, warning them that Pelech was not strictly "kosher". A few of them at once cancelled their application. This was doubly unfortunate: not only was the school's reputation unjustifiably impugned but in addition there was financial loss, since among these parents were some of the wealthiest, who had begun to support Pelech even prior to their daughters' acceptance.

Nor were my trespasses solely religious. I had also transgressed political norms that were increasingly prominent in the religious sector of the community. I had permitted our pupils to meet their Arab counterparts. Worse still, I had myself participated in a comparable encounter with Palestinian women. Three teachers who lived in the Occupied Territories immediately submitted their resignation, unpersuaded by my account of how this face-to-face encounter had utterly transformed my own political views.

I had already several times been reduced to tears by the ongoing attacks on my unorthodox views and actions. Each time my family comforted me. Each time, a considerable number of the pupils (all daughters of more moderate parents) posted statements in my defence on the school's noticeboard. A press report in the local Jerusalem weekly published a false report on my dismissal. Wishful thinking?

The Street of the Kings of Israel stretches along what was for many years the dividing line between Jewish and Arab Jerusalem. The length of its name reflects the metaphysical distance between the points that lie at either end. To the north is the ultra-Orthodox Jewish neighbourhood of Mea Shearim, where immodestly dressed women who venture to infiltrate are verbally abused and sometimes physically assaulted by men scuttling about wearing garb identical with that worn by their forefathers in eighteenth-century Eastern Europe. At the southern end arises the noble edifice of Notre Dame, a Catholic monastery that categorically excludes female membership. And beyond that lies modern Western Jerusalem.

Originally an unpaved footpath, the road was created in the late 19th century, together with the New Gate, to enable Christians to pass from the New Jerusalem into the Old City without being molested by Muslim residents. It is lined with handsome buildings that originally housed Christian establishments of one kind or another – chapels, churches, convents. After the foundation of the State of Israel in 1948, when few Christians remained, many of these buildings were requisitioned by the government to house ministries or other institutions.

Among these is the Ministry of Education, which occupies no fewer than three buildings, including an incongruous replica of Florence's Palazzo Vecchio that initially served as the Italian Hospital. In a more modest, even nondescript, neighbouring building are the headquarters of the Department of Religious Education, the goal of my leisurely wandering one fine spring morning in 1989. Poised midway between anachronistic Mea Shearim and modern Jerusalem, its geographical location symbolizes an inner conflict within the Department itself, between close observance of often outmoded *Halakha* and Modern Orthodoxy's more enlightened interpretation of Jewish law.

247

I was responding to an invitation from the head of the Department of Religious Education, a modest, gentle man, whom I knew well and with whom I had a warm professional and personal relationship. I had been summoned at very short notice, without being informed of the purpose of our meeting, nor had I bothered to enquire. I assumed it would be related in some way to the experimental curricula we were developing, in which he had once expressed interest. Hence I was unprepared for the accusatory content and the aggressive tone of his opening remarks. In no way directly related to the fulfillment of my duties as principal of a school which, under my leadership, had attained renown for innovation and excellence, they were a lengthy diatribe against my so-called "political" activities.

What in particular irked my superiors and aroused their ire were my blatant public attacks on the Chief Rabbinate for its discrimination and dereliction of duties in dealing with issues of divorce, and my participation in dialogues between Israeli and Palestinian women, "the enemy". As head of both the Israel Women's Network and the Israel chapter of the International Coalition on *Agunah* Rights, I had organized and led demonstrations against the misogynous rabbinate, had appeared on television, been cited in the press condemning the failure to address the plight of these "anchored" women. I had attended an Israeli-Palestinian women's dialogue in Brussels, which was incorrectly cited by the Israeli media as a meeting with members of the PLO. Such actions were unacceptable, unforgivable.

Taken aback by both the accusations and the vehemence with which they were being uttered, I responded by explaining my motives for these so-called offences, stressing why both equality of the sexes and peace with our neighbours were of the utmost importance, not only for me personally, but for maintaining Israel as a just and democratic state. Admittedly, although I refrained from preaching to my pupils, I presumably served as a living example with which they could, if they wished, identify, but I never imposed my views on them.

My rebuttal seemed to fall on deaf ears. No counter arguments were forthcoming. It was like talking to the wall. My interlocutor sat expressionless as I pleaded my case. As if programmed by his superiors, he repeated the order: I must at once cease these activities and undertake never more to engage in them. And then came the ultimatum, so extreme that it left me, in my turn, speechless: Either I desist from these "nefarious activities" or the Department would withdraw accreditation from the school.

A short pause, during which we both sat in silence. Finally, I said I needed time to weigh my response. As he rose to escort me to the door, he stopped and suddenly came to life, to his old, familiar self. Putting his hand on my arm, in plaintive tones he said, "You're making my life at home very difficult for me. My youngest daughter wants to attend your school, just like her older sisters did. They and my wife are furious with me. But after all, I can't send my daughter to a school from which I've had to withdraw accreditation."

I felt immense pity for him. The poor man was simply obeying orders, orders that went against his personal inclination.

So I did him a favour. Rather than give up fighting for the causes so dear to me, I soon resigned from Pelech. His youngest daughter was now free to attend the school of her choice and I was free to go my own way. Both he and I had won, but at considerable cost to us both – and, in particular, to the school.

Winding my way back along the Street of the Kings of Israel I no longer had any inclination to meander. The buildings seemed antiquated, memorials to what was once a lively neighbourhood. Many of them, shuttered and with gates locked with rusty chains, looked unoccupied, unused. The few shops were shabby, the goods they sold dusty, uninviting. All seemed forlorn, hopeless. I quickened my pace, anxious to return to the vibrancy of the Newer Jerusalem, its bustling streets, its crowded cafés and modern brightness — an atmosphere more friendly and accommodating towards reform and progress. I never again set foot in the Department of Religious Education.

"My girls" I call them. Today they are everywhere and in every profession, but especially, to my delight, in education, spreading the philosophy and practice of Pelech, setting up more "branches" of the school outside Jerusalem, where there is now even a Pelech School for Boys – the strangest application of the caustic comment on women's wisdom that the Rosenblüths wittily adopted as the name for the unique school they established. Two alumnae currently serve as Pelech principals – one at the High School, the other at the Junior High, which is located in the old building on the top floor of which (next to the roof which once served as the site of both daily prayers and the monthly General Assembly), I once had my modest office. They are judges, doctors, university lecturers, curators, business executives. They are bearing out my contention that no area in life should be closed to you just because you are female. Above all, they have modernized Modern Orthodoxy.

"Pelech" is no longer solely the name of a school: it is an educational concept.

*

I recall one examiner who came to my office on emerging from the oral examination that tested pupils' knowledge in Talmud. First, astounded, he congratulated me. "They are just as good as the boys at the Yeshiva High Schools!" he said and then went on to tell me that when he had asked one pupil why she was studying Talmud, she had replied matter-of-factly "So that I can sit and study it together with my husband."

"My girls" have done more than that. Applying their knowledge and their "different voice", they have created an entire movement, reforming traditional practice by applying feminist principles. They created a feminist organization of their own. "Kolech", Your Voice, they called it, urging Orthodox women to speak up for themselves. Two of them have been ordained as rabbis. A third, who prefers to refer to herself as a "Woman of *Halakha*", is consulted even by male Orthodox Jews on matters relating to women. A constantly increasing number of congregations not only allow but encourage women to lead services. My own remarkable rabbi is a Pelech alumna who has created a uniquely egalitarian congregation in which all men and women enjoy equal rights and privileges.

Surveying how feminism has affected Israeli society, one is compelled to admit that the greatest revolution has occurred in Modern Orthodoxy. Not only have the women themselves "come a long way"; they have carried their communities in their wake.

Echoing the Psalmist, I say "I sowed in tears, but I am reaping in joy."

SHOCK!

Status

In the 1984 Knesset election women voters for the first time outnumbered men and the average educational level of women voters (as measured by the number of years of schooling) exceeded that of men. Nevertheless, the number of women elected decreased due to the foibles of Israel's electoral system, whereby one votes not for an individual but for a party list, in which the placing of candidates is determined by personal ties and influence rather than by ability, achievement or promise. Women are thus at a distinct disadvantage, since these ties are to a very large extent formed during military service and an individual's worth is unduly determined by military-career criteria that automatically militate (literally as well as metaphorically) against women. There was clearly little chance that there would be a significant number of women in the cabinet, no matter whether it was Shimon Peres or Yitzhak Shamir who would be charged with heading it. Indignation and resentment were especially paramount among feminist activists and women in academia.

At the same time as the under-representation of women in Israel's government body had become a fact, what was simultaneously making itself felt was a burgeoning feminist awareness of the inequities inherent in Jewish law and practice. For others, sociological issues were at the heart of the matter: how to deal with the exclusion of women from the public spheres of Jewish life, religious and secular? An unanticipated spark soon ignited a slowly burning, growing awareness into action.

Late July 1984. A clear, pleasantly cool Jerusalem summer evening. In the vicinity of the President's Residence an unduly large number of pedestrians were hastening towards the modernist building of the Van Leer Institute, half hidden behind thick shrubbery. Inside the building a large auditorium was already packed with an audience comprised primarily of women of all ages. Sitting on the steps, standing in the aisles, they resisted the ushers' attempts to limit their numbers. The organisers of the event, all men, were taken aback by the unprecedented size and the pugnaciousness of the audience. Never before in the 20 years of the annual US-Israel Dialogue held under the auspices of the American Jewish Congress had they encountered such a phenomenon. The opening nights, which the public at large could attend, had always attracted a sizeable audience in addition to the 30 or so invited participants from each side of the ocean but there had never before been such a palpable buzz.

For the audience itself, the reason was clear. The topic to be discussed this year was "Woman as Jew, Jew as Woman: An Urgent Enquiry". But beyond the relevance of the topic lay the identity of the American opening speaker: Betty Friedan. Friedan had had a major impact on the status of women and, more particularly, on women's awareness of the inequalities and discriminations to which they were subjected. On an earlier visit in 1971, Friedan had encountered resistance to her theories but in the intervening 13 years those of us who had at that time rejected her contentions had ourselves experienced discrimination. We were now not only older but also wiser.

When Friedan stepped up to the podium, at once passion was in the air: anger, outrage, rebelliousness; an unsparing, scathing attack on the male establishment; a diatribe against discrimination in every sphere of society and specifically, in this case, within the Jewish establishment in the United States; a call for radical change. In the United States women might have "come a long way, baby", but so much still remained to be done. And here in Israel the feminist movement was in its infancy. Where to start? According to tradition, the American Jewish Congress discussions during the three days that follow the opening are held behind closed doors. The rule was seldom challenged and when a rare individual request was made to be present at one or another session, permission was readily granted. But this time the customary announcement that discussion would continue in camera caused an uproar. Women demanded free access throughout, though they were prepared to be spectators and audience rather than active discussants. No way, said the AJC local director, David Clayman. It's against the rules. What rules? This isn't a game; it's our life. Stalemate.

Then I spoke up and suggested a compromise: closed-circuit television. Whoever wanted to see and hear the sessions could do so in the comfort of the Van Leer lounge, well-furnished with sofas and armchairs, while the intimacy of the Dialogue could be maintained. And so it was. Some sessions drew larger audiences than others. "Women in the Workforce", apparently relevant to many professionals, attracted a considerable number, as did "Women in Politics". Although every session began with a sometimes too academically dry presentation of current research and its findings, discussion invariably turned to ways of improving the sorry situation. In this way, the 1984 Dialogue, already so different from its predecessors, also differed from them in that it was accompanied by practical proposals.

I chaired the final session. It was on "Women and Religion". The speakers were, respectively, Blu Greenberg, wife of an Orthodox rabbi, who at the time still maintained that Orthodox *Halakha* did not conflict with feminist aspirations to equality of opportunity and status – a position she later greatly modified; and Shulamit Aloni, the vehemently outspoken opponent of the Israeli rabbinical establishment, and, in particular, of its monopoly and sole jurisdiction over all aspects of personal status, including legitimacy, marriage, divorce and inheritance. The ardour with which she spoke, the cogency of her arguments and her

252

undoubted knowledge of Jewish sources held the audience in thrall. But something even more dramatic was to come. For as she reached the end of her presentation, the doors burst open and scores of women, the largest number as yet to have been in the lounge, streamed into the auditorium, demanding a say in the proceedings: shouting, shaking, weeping.

I was at a total loss as to how to respond to these passions. Duty-bound to call for order, I did not have the heart to staunch the stream of emotion. I knew that these were the real-life victims of rabbinical courts, the "chained or anchored women" to whom Shula had referred. The urgency of their incoherent demands spurred sympathy and demanded a less formal, more humane response. I called on a number of them to come forward to relate what they had experienced. Their stories confirmed the truth of all the accusations that had been levelled against the unjust, misogynist rabbinical court system. I doubt whether anyone among the invited participants, or even of the general Jewish public in Israel and the Diaspora, had ever been fully aware of the extent of the personal suffering experienced by the women denied divorce.

Trapped in non-existent marriages, unable to remarry, unable to bear children with another partner since the child of such a union would be a bastard, often left with no financial support, denied justice by unfeeling judges who had spent all their lives in all-male company and were unaware of, or unmoved by, the women's needs and suffering, the intruders demanded real change, a different system, a different government, an end to rabbinic monopoly. Filled with a mixture of compassion for these victims and revulsion at the heartlessness of the courts, the invited participants sat overwhelmed, not knowing how to proceed. Helplessness seemed to paralyse us. But Friedan had the answer.

"You've got to put your bodies where your mouths are!" she proclaimed, challenging us to action. We took up Friedan's gauntlet. Having intended to summarise our findings and post them in the lobby, we had the basic materials for banners. Rapidly we wrote succinct slogans in outsize letters. Some of us drew up a written statement enumerating our specific demands in greater detail. We knew that at that very moment, at the nearby King David Hotel, Shimon Peres, head of the Labor Party, and Yitzhak Shamir, of the Likud, were negotiating who was to be the first in the position of Prime Minister. We also knew that in the recent elections women voters had for the first time outnumbered men.

Preparations completed, we proceeded casually to the hotel, a large group of women – perhaps tourists? – enjoying the sunshine, admiring the impressively noble Arab architecture of Talbieh. As we approached the hotel, a press photographer unexpectedly took photos of us, so there is a record of myself in the forefront, flanked by Nitza Shapiro-Libai and Galia Golan – a Sovietologist who was to play a major role in the fight to establish a department of gender studies at the Hebrew University. At the hotel there were no guards. This was the time before maximal security sealed off meetings of VIPs from the hoi polloi. We entered the elegant lobby undisturbed. We unfurled our placards. "More women in the government." "Equal work, equal pay." "'No' to Rabbinical Rule." Taken by surprise, the hotel manager and staff tried to evict us. They were soon joined by henchmen of the two party leaders. In vain did they try to persuade us, at first gently, then with increasing anger and veiled threats, to go away and be "good girls". We stood our ground. We insisted on meeting the two men and demanded to know their whereabouts.

In the course of the next hour, aides of increasing seniority came and went, still insisting that there was absolutely no possibility of our meeting Peres and Shamir face to face, recommending that we entrust them – the emissaries – with a list of our demands, promising they would be delivered. We continued to stand firm. Since members of our group, ensconced in the lobby's armchairs and sofas, were already consuming copious cups of coffee and even indulging in snacks, the manager of the hotel was no longer insistent on our leaving and we ourselves were determined not to yield. Finally, a message came. The gentlemen were prepared to meet a delegation of three. It was up to us to decide which three. For what was for me no obvious reason, I was at once designated to head the trio.

"Alice, you go!" Coming I know not whence, the first cry was taken up by others. There seemed no escape from the responsibility. However, I was free to choose my companions. What angel was it that guided me that day? It was certainly not a deliberate, thought-out policy that made me pick Tamar Eshel and Yael Rom, neither of them from my own academic circle nor even personal friends of mine. Unlike me, they had years of political experience but currently bore a grudge against their respective, opposing, parties. I had no party affiliation and nobody knew how I voted.

The three of us were led down to the lower depths of the hotel, where there are a number of meeting rooms. We were told to wait in the corridor, which was devoid of any kind of seat. Once again, we stood and waited. An hour passed. We grew increasingly impatient and angry at the delay. Finally, I suggested that each of my colleagues send an identical note to her party leader. The note read: "It is largely because of women's votes that you are here today. We demand you meet us." Whether they were persuaded by this message or because they wanted a break in their negotiations, the ploy proved effective. Within minutes, there were the two party leaders, all smiles and oozing bonhomie, seemingly oblivious of the fact that they had kept us waiting for hours.

We wasted no more time. I took out the sheet of paper on which we had listed our demands, beginning with that for greater representation of women in the government. Because an official announcement regarding the premiership was expected that day, numerous journalists were present. Microphones were pushed towards me. Cameras flashed. Afraid I'd mispronounce a Hebrew word, my hands were shaking. Instantly I felt Yael and Tamar, on either side of me, holding me firm, supporting me. Emotionally and physically strengthened, I became more confident, my voice stronger, the tone more emphatic.

"We, representatives of the women of Israel and of US Jewry, herewith demand…".

Peres and Shamir continued to smile. They nodded their agreement. They would certainly bear these demands in mind. They would heed our complaints. The next government would be different. There would be legislation and administrative action to reform and ameliorate women's status, to right the wrongs to which we had for so long been subjected. Reassured and relieved, we returned to the lounge, where rapturous euphoria now reigned. We had met the challenge of Betty Friedan. We had won. We had stood our ground. We had been heard. We had even encountered good will. Victory!

As the women crowded around us, excited, congratulatory, my colleague Frances Raday, lecturer in law at the Hebrew University and feminist litigator, turned to me and said:

"This is what we need, Alice. A non-partisan lobby for women's rights."

"Right," I acquiesced in my customarily impulsive manner. "Let's do it!"

But how to set about it? I'd never before found myself in the position of having to initiate the establishment of a feminist organisation. Little did I know what such an action entailed, nor did I dream what would result from my initial enthusiasm. Yet I realised that if I myself did nothing, nothing would follow. No benefit would derive from our week-long discussions and there would be no significant practical results to our hard-won encounter with the leaders of the new government. Although I was still teaching full-time at the university and maintaining the pioneering activities of Pelech, I would have to find time to become actively involved in furthering equality between the sexes countrywide.

SHOCK!

Gender Discrimination

It was the beginning of August, the month in which Israelis go on holiday. Only in September did I invite the Israeli participants in the AJC Dialogue to an informal meeting. Approximately half of them attended, most of them from academia and the free professions. We unanimously decided to establish a non-partisan organisation which, unlike the veteran Naamat (the working women's association) World International Zionist Organisation and Emunah (religious nationalists), would not offer services such as childcare but would focus on advancing women's status via consciousness-raising, litigation and legislative advocacy – appropriate modes of action for a group of well-informed and determined feminists like us. We had an agenda, broadly based not only on the demands that emerged from the Dialogue but also on the ill-fated recommendations of the Namir Commission, on which some of us had served. Our overall goal was equality of the sexes in every respect: representation, status, opportunity and reward. In all of these, gender was never to be held a determining factor, save in so far as it could lead to affirmative action and the abolition of inequities.

There was some discussion but little disagreement before we decided on an appropriate name for our body: the Israel Women's Lobby. (In English the final noun was misleadingly translated as "Network", ostensibly because we were warned that "Lobby", perceived as a political concept, might make us ineligible for tax-deductible donations from abroad.) We composed a motto: "For Justice and Equality". We eventually even devised an emblem: a little flower, the crown of which was in the form of a Magen David, its angles softened into roundness, its stem the biological emblem of the female. We were anxious to stress that "Israel" did not imply exclusion of non-Jews. A similar inclusivity marked our mission statement: "We aim to unite women and men in Israel who identify with our ideal of ensuring it be a country of true equality and justice, in the spirit of our Declaration of Independence".

256

Word of our initiative spread, and more and more women requested permission to come along. They too were almost without exception members of the free professions, primarily from academia. I found myself *de facto* chairwoman. Our meetings were highly informal, even improvisational, open to all who cared to attend. The only participants who had practical political experience were Yael Rom and Tamar Eshel. Tamar, as a former Member of Knesset, had been an invited participant in the Dialogue. Yael had in her standard aggressive manner pushed her way in, vociferously criticising the predominance in the Israeli contingent of women from academia and "Anglo-Saxons" — in our case mostly one and the same. After a third frustratingly fruitless meeting, these two political veterans asked to meet me. I invited them to my home. They expressed sympathy and condolences on our group's failure to turn theory into practice.

"You've really done a splendid job in getting things off the ground," Yael said.

"An excellent group of women," Tamar agreed.

"But" – I waited for the reservations – "the trouble is you have no political experience."

"And a lobby, after all, is political," Tamar said.

"You saw how we succeeded in eliciting a response from our party leaders," Yael added.

"So what do you propose?" I asked, aware of my political shortcomings. I began to feel they might be right: I knew nothing of the workings of the Knesset, with which Tamar was so familiar, nor was I acquainted with the internal intrigues endemic in the various parties. Their response was ready.

"We'll gladly take over." Sensing my hesitation, Tamar hastily added:

"You could be Honorary President and we would just be chairwomen," evidently unaware that I care nothing for empty titles. I was on the verge of surrender when I caught sight of Moshe peering round the door at the far end of the room, facing me but invisible to my visitors. Frowning, wagging his forefinger at me, shaking his head from side to side in vigorous warning, he made it clear that I must on no account acquiesce in this putsch. I thanked Yael and Tamar for their concern and their willingness to take responsibility. I asked for a few days. So meek was I that they left duly convinced that they had attained their goal. They must have been taken aback by my rejection of their offer a week later.

I scrupulously remained unidentified with any political party, while constantly stressing my total commitment to IWN's liberal ideals. Determining our agenda was an essential preliminary step. Numerous widely varying issues had to be addressed, all of them seemingly of equal importance. How to prioritise? And what modes of action were available to us? We had called ourselves a lobby but we had no idea how one practised lobbying. We had direction but as yet lacked method. As for our shortcomings in the field of parliamentary politics, it was David Clayman, the director of the AJC's Jerusalem office, who came to the rescue. An experienced lobbyist in his own right, David undertook to instruct us in the basic principles of his craft. First, our utopian wish-list needed refining: specifics had to be spelled out and concrete proposals formulated, and we needed allies at both ends of the electoral spectrum.

We began with the politicians. There were at the time merely 10 women MKs. To most of them we had no access or prior connection. What we had was largely negative, dating back to the mid-1970s, when those of our group, including myself, who were members of the Namir Commission found ourselves often at loggerheads with the majority. The non-partisan among us had proven far more revolutionary than even the most supposedly radical MKs, except Marcia Friedman, an immigrant from the United States whom Shulamit Aloni had co-opted from the Women's Party to join the Civil Rights list. Nevertheless, since it was imperative we enlist them, we decided to invite all 10 MKs to a meeting at my home.

It wouldn't be easy to convene so unique a gathering. We were not yet sufficiently established for the MKs to feel in any way obliged to attend. Galia Golan, a member of the Labor Party clearly perceived as left-wing, was delegated to approach Shula, whose initial response was that politically she had nothing in common with Geula Cohen. However, she ultimately reluctantly acceded to Galia's relentless urging. We had netted our first catch. With her name as bait, I next turned to Geula. A tempestuous ex-"terrorist" who had switched allegiance from the Irgun Zvai Leumi to the more extreme Lohamei Eretz Yisrael (Fighters for the Land of Israel), Geula had been imprisoned by the British and was now a member of Herut. Not in any way associated with feminist or women's organisations, she asked who else of her Knesset colleagues would be attending. Despite their dramatically opposed political views, she and Aloni were close friends. Hearing that Shula would be there, Geula responded with equal readiness. She proved a vital catalyst. Hesitantly, aware of my anonymity in politics and with a strong sense of insecurity, I approached the remaining women MKs. As soon as I informed them that these two "extremists" would attend, several others fell in line. We learned an important lesson: nobody likes to be excluded. In the event, we had six guests, though Shula had soon to leave to attend another meeting.

As we settled down over refreshments, some of the MKs levelled suspicious glances at us. We were an unknown quantity. They also displayed an understandable coldness towards political rivals. The traditional "leftists", two of them members of most relentlessly Marxist *kibbutzim*, felt vulnerable in the company of their political opponents. "Terrorist" Geula Cohen was equally anathema because of the longstanding bitter feud between the Lohamei Eretz Yisrael and the mainstream Hagana. Eventually, the official part of the meeting began. I opened it by asking in what way we, a non-partisan group of intellectuals, could be of help to them: what plans and dreams did they have which we might help to further? We offered to assist in whatever way seemed appropriate, but first we needed to know their goals. Despite the political differences between these women, they all appeared discomfited by my offer. Clearly they had assumed they would be asked to help us, yet here the tables were turned.

Geula was the first to respond. Passionately, she asserted that our primary goal should be greatly to increase the number of women in the Knesset.

"At least 30% of the total," she declared. None of her colleagues had expected Geula, of all people, to be so radical in her demands. Not to be outdone by a right-wing extremist – she wasn't even a socialist! – the members of the Labor Party and the even more left-wing Mapam not only supported Geula's proposal but added further issues, including some that later emerged at our "town hall" meetings. Others now spoke up, referring to work opportunities, equal pay, childcare.

The enthusiasm of the MKs that ensued was heartwarming, though I must admit that, on our part, there was some surprise, not to say disappointment. Their agenda seemed limited and provincial. In contrast, in academia a decade of research and the development of women's studies had furnished the IWN founders with data, information and insight. It now became clearer than ever that none of this had permeated to either the political sphere or, as we were soon to discover, the public. Systemic change was an unknown concept. Our guests were ignorant even of terminology. The concept of "gender" as distinct from "sex" was new to them, although on this score there was a legitimate excuse: there was as yet no Hebrew equivalent.

Yet if we attempted to enlighten the female MKs so early in our relationship, we would arouse resistance and resentment. We contented ourselves with diligently recording their suggestions. We undertook to do everything in our power to support the legislative proposals that one or all of them might bring before the Knesset. We would provide data, appear as experts at the committee stage of discussion, perhaps help bring the issues to public attention via op-ed pieces, promote their initiatives. By the end of the evening all was amity: allies in the battle for women's liberation. The IWN now had friends in high places. We would keep our side of the bargain. By way of *quid pro quo*, we would request their support for those, probably far more numerous, reforms which we ourselves initiated.

Our next goal was to increase the level of public support. We felt we needed corroboration of our views, as well as greater exposure among Israeli women whom we hoped to represent. I thus spent a considerable amount of time addressing meetings all over the country. Some of these we ourselves initiated, turning to local branches of the established women's organisations and requesting that they convene an audience. Others were the result of interest on the part of groups of women in various sectors, such as the kibbutz movements, who wanted to learn more about the status of women in Israel, though not necessarily because they felt in any way impelled to be involved in making an impact on that status or changing it. I became the IWN's ambassador-at-large. I spoke in cities large and small, sometimes to audiences of 100 or more, sometimes to a mere handful, my twofold aim being to raise awareness of discrimination and to clarify what were the dominant issues of concern to the country's female population, urban and rural, Jewish and non-Jewish, religiously observant and secular.

It was in the nominally egalitarian *kibbutzim* that I encountered as high a degree of acceptance of the status quo as among the religiously observant. In both cases, the women had internalised the traditional biologically based division of roles. I valiantly attempted to persuade my listeners that difference need not lead to discrimination, exclusion or inferiority. The kibbutz women, convinced they already enjoyed total equality, tried to rebut my arguments. Yet even they had ultimately to admit that the range of occupations available to them was limited, restricted to the customary "Three Cs": cooking, cleaning and childcare – but on a much larger scale. Grudgingly, they admitted that boys were permitted to take driving-lessons in order to drive tractors; the girls, who did not engage in agriculture, were not. With only a pitifully few exceptions, no woman had ever held the powerful position of kibbutz secretary or treasurer.

The readiness with which women acquiesced in their own inferior status proved to be a major obstacle. Had they been browbeaten for so long as to make them believe that theirs was a God-given natural condition, based on physiology? In Israel's fertility-obsessed, family-centred, conservative culture, the unmarried, the childless, the lone women hardly merit attention. And so I traversed Israel,

On the roof of Pelech with parents and staff.

With Esti Feshin at Pelech. A successful entrepreneur, Esti is now a Board member of Pelech.

The Pelech library.

Four generations of Pelech principals. Seated with me: my predecessor Pnina Rosenblüth and Shira Breuer, my successor. In front, Sophie Pfeffer (left) and Rachel Tzur, currently heads of the High School and Junior High respectively.

Summer 1992. Hosting newly elected women members of the 13th Knesset.
(l – r) Naomi Chazan, Tamar Gozanski, Dalia Itzik, Esther Salmovitz, Yael Dayan and Anat Maor.

Marching to the King David Hotel, July 1984 flanked by Tamar Eshel on left and Nitza Shapiro-Libai.

Presenting our demands to Shimon Peres (left) and Yitzhak Shamir.

Seated between Naomi Nevo (left) and Yael Rom, with (l – r) Naomi Chazan, Frances Raday and Roberta Reisman.

Summer 1996. With members of the 14th Knesset. (l – r) Naomi Blumenthal, Tamar Gozanski, Anat Maor, Marina Solodkin and Naomi Chazan.

Burning ketubot, the standard marriage
contracts which give the husband
"possession" of his wife.

Planting the first sapling in the Women's
Grove in the Judean Hills with Dafna Izraeli.

Protest at the Central Post Office
in Jerusalem.

"Greater love hath no man…"
Moshe provides shade at a demonstration.

In 2009, even the living room became my office.

At the Masorti Movement's Women's Annual Study Day at the Schechter Institute
of Jewish Studies, 2012.

Closing ceremony of Project Kesher's first gathering, Kiev 1993. (Photo Joan Roth)

With fellow Israel Prize Laureates and functionaries on Independence Day 2007.

With E.M. Broner, a writer and feminist pioneer instrumental in introducing radical innovations in Jewish women's religious ritual.

New York-based feminist philanthropist Barbara Dobkin: the first to appreciate the importance of both Pelech and IWN and an ardent, generous donor to both.

Moshe's favourite photo of me in what he referred to as my "gentle fighting mode".

With my friend Sally Gottesman and her children (l – r) Ezra, "Little" Alice and Charlotte. (Photo: Debbi Cooper)

Today, in my Jerusalem Garden of Bliss. (Photo: Debbi Cooper)

becoming acquainted not only with *kibbutzim* of all parties, with small historic towns such as Petach Tikva, Hadera and Zikhron Yaakov, but with often capricious public transport. I also became familiar with a wide range of women whose sole common trait was a uniform unawareness of the current inevitability of discrimination and inequality. As I invited the audiences to voice their concerns, it became clear that the IWN was fulfilling the much-needed functions of consciousness-raising and empowerment. But we soon learned that action has its price.

For some time, we had no office space other than my home, where we regularly held lively discussions on policy, plans and activities. We had no funds apart from a modest but helpful start-up grant from the AJC. Rightfully proud of the unanticipated and unprecedented outcome of the Dialogue, the organisation's leaders instructed David Clayman to give us an initial sum of $5,000, the help of his staff and the use of office equipment, which included photocopying and fax machines. Clayman also appointed one of his staff members, Janet Sherman, to serve as our treasurer. Given our limited financial resources the latter function was rather that of bookkeeper. As the scale of correspondence grew, it was clear that we needed a secretary too and, ideally, a small office, to which women could come with their problems and proposals: a resource centre. As the number of participants in public events increased, we needed to rent halls. We needed money. We were advised to seek overseas support. I had already achieved something of a reputation as a public speaker, having since the late 1970s been frequently sent as emissary to the United States by the Jewish Agency, the World Zionist Organisation and the Hebrew University. My major topic, where it was appropriate, was The Status of Women in Judaism and/or in Israel. These speaking engagements now gave me an opportunity to refer to the IWN, its goals and its achievements. Sometimes I was able to follow up my public appearances by meeting with individuals, many of them prominent, wealthy women, who appeared potentially to be — and in most cases indeed became — sympathetic and generous supporters of IWN.

Overseas travel was tiring and entirely dependent on invitations from abroad. We were therefore delighted to learn that there was a new potential source of support in Jerusalem: the New Israel Fund. This gave the IWN encouragement, financial and moral, introduced me to potential donors at meetings to which I was accompanied by a member of the NIF's US staff and had speaking engagements arranged for me. Ultimately we became recipients of a generous core grant that freed us from the obligation of submitting a new request each year. Had it not been for the NIF, the IWN could not have achieved what it did. We became Israel's outstanding organisation for women's rights. "Great oaks from little acorns grow"; or, as Herzl memorably exhorted his generation of Jews and inspired future generations, "If you will it, it is not a fable".

Both fundraising and the desire to enlist more members mandated public relations, the initial form of which was a periodical newsletter. The first edition, published in February 1986, a mere eighteen months after the establishment of IWN, testifies to the extraordinary multiplicity and variety of our activities.

The newsletter prominently featured the issue of *iggun* (women denied divorce) which had gained prominence in our "town hall" meetings. Among our earliest initiatives had been the establishment of two sub-committees mandated with preparing halakhically-based solutions to this problem. One consisted of lawyers, both male and female, the other of rabbis and scholars of Jewish law, among whom was a sole woman, Hannah Safrai, the first woman widely acknowledged as an expert in *Halakha*. Together, these committees had compiled a list of five solutions to the problem, ranging from the preventative measure of pre-nuptial agreements to the most extreme, rarely implemented measure of annulment.

The Rabbis again denied the very existence of the problem challenging me to provide proof to the contrary. By the time of the second meeting, we already had such evidence. Initial data derived from an alliance we had formed with Daniella Valency, founder of provocatively named "Prisoners of the Religious Courts". She had a list of dozens of women who were "anchored", though few of such long standing as herself, who had already been in this state of limbo — neither truly married nor divorced — for fourteen years. When our committee came to present the requested data, they also brought with them a list of five halakhically sound solutions. All were summarily rejected.

Reflecting the extent to which we perceived Orthodox *Halakha* as a major obstacle to equality between the sexes, we held a study day on Women in Judaism, held in Jerusalem in July 1985 to coincide with the Jubilee Convention of the (Orthodox) Rabbinical Council of America.

Fortuitously, the week's Portion of the Law included the story of Judaism's first feminist revolt, the claim by Zelophad's daughters that they not be disinherited solely on the grounds of their father's having left no male heirs. This unprecedented demand for equal rights left Moses in so great a dilemma that he turned to God Himself for guidance. The unequivocally positive (and in Hebrew

262

markedly succinct) response was: "The daughters of Zelophad have spoken justly." I made this the text of my opening remarks at the session that preceded the simultaneous workshops that dealt respectively with personal status and divorce; women in public prayer; Torah study for women; and the image of women in Jewish sources. We held the event at the Laromme Hotel where the rabbis were staying. Only two of them responded to our invitation to attend the study day. However, a greater number of their wives, did attend and we took this as a welcome sign of openness to the new winds of change that were beginning to blow even in the Orthodox sector.

The first reference in a feminist context to "Zionism as a form of Racism" (a stand officially adopted by the UN General Assembly in November 1975) appeared in the "Declaration of Mexico" which encapsulated the proceedings of the First World Conference for Women. In that document, the Jewish national movement was equated with "colonialism, foreign occupation, apartheid and racial discrimination in all its forms". Given this hostile denial of Zionism, the Israeli government, together with the major Jewish women's organisation, the International Council of Jewish Women, were wary of cooperating with the UN on gender equality and failed to respond adequately to global expectations in the increasingly important realm of women's status.

Five years after Mexico, only a small official delegation represented Israel in Copenhagen at the Second World Conference. Composed of the customary representatives of the country's mainstream women's organisations and including Leah Rabin, wife of the Prime Minister, its members were not only uninformed but also – even if only subconsciously – ill-disposed towards feminism. Not only were they ill-equipped to respond to the repeated equation of Zionism and apartheid; they were similarly incapable of presenting the burgeoning of a local feminist movement of which they were themselves either unaware or contemptuous. It was left to the Jewish women from the US who attended the parallel NGO Forum to come to the defence of both Israel and Zionism.

On her return journey from Copenhagen to the US, Phyllis Chesler, a devout Zionist already well known internationally because of her pioneering work, "Women and Madness," was a guest at my Friday night dinner table. Shaken by what she perceived as not only anti-Zionism but also the anti-Semitism inherent in both the official and non-governmental proceedings and resolutions, she voiced her disappointment and dismay at the inadequacy of the official Israeli response.

Nobody had informed our delegates of either the findings or the recommendations of the Namir Commission. It was as if Israel had marched in place for five years.

As the date of the 1985 UN conference that launched the Decade of World Women approached, I felt impelled to ensure IWN's participation in the event to be held in Nairobi. Our members, well-versed not only in the status of women locally but also in developments in feminist theory and practice internationally, would be able to sway the opinions, if not of all participants, then at least of feminists.

Our motives were not wholly altruistic. By appearing on the international scene, we also hoped to ensure greater public and governmental awareness of our work and hence recognition of our ability to provide up-to-date information and advocacy. IWN's findings and recommendations would carry greater weight, even with national decision-makers.

Hence, we rapidly organized a panel entitled "Mobilizing for Equality," for which we enlisted our U.S. colleagues Belle Abzug and E.M Broner, as well as Amina Rahman of the Urban League, all of whom were already scheduled to attend the forum of NGOs that takes place simultaneously with the official UN proceedings. They agreed to join our own members, political scientists Galia Golan and Naomi Chazan, and Ester Eilam, a founder of Israel's Feminist Movement. Aware that Naomi Chazan's expertise in African Studies would be invaluable in establishing good relations with women from that continent, we lobbied to have her included in the official delegation. Objections were raised on the grounds of inadequate funding. I overcame this problem by raising money to cover all her expenses. Naomi fully justified her inclusion since she was undoubtedly instrumental in having the troubling Zionism is Racism equation deleted from a UN document after it was first adopted in 1980. In addition, we used some of our meager resources to engage two young Jerusalemite women graphic artists to produce a series of eye-catching posters incorporating photographs of our various advocacy endeavors.

Immediately upon their return home, we invited the entire Israeli delegation, including the members of the establishment, to participate in a debriefing session at the Van Leer Institute, where they excitedly conveyed their impressions of the Nairobi proceedings. Held in the same hall in which the cataclysmic AJC Congress Dialogue had opened the previous year, the event was attended by over three hundred women and was in itself an indication of the interest and enthusiasm that the Network had generated in less than a year's activities.

*

Equal Opportunity. Very soon after its founding, IWN took up the case of one of its founders, Naomi Nevo, versus the Jewish Agency, the country's largest employer, second only to the government, which discriminated between men and women with regard to the age of compulsory retirement. While men could continue working to the age of sixty-eight, all the while accruing larger pensions, women were compelled to retire at age sixty- three.

Naomi had immigrated in 1948 and completed her doctoral studies in Israel. She delayed taking up a career and was in her late fifties when she began field work as an anthropologist at the Jewish Agency. Now aged sixty-three, at the height of that career, considered an expert in her area of research, she was being forced into involuntary retirement. She was represented by Attorney Frances Raday, who had won a settlement granting equal retirement age to women professors at Hadassah Hospital. The Court ruled in 1990 in Naomi's favour. In the meantime, Frances, together with what she describes as "two wonderful ex-students of (hers)," Neta Ziv and Rachel Benziman, IWN's staff lawyer, had launched "a decade of feminist legislation," which began with a successful cooperation with women MKs and government lawyers that resulted in the 1987 Equal Retirement Law.

More significant and far-reaching than the case of Naomi Nevo was that of Alice Miller vs the Minister of Defense, in which Neta and Rachel again collaborated.

An exemplary high school graduate, Alice Miller was granted deferral of military recruitment in order to enable her to study for a degree in aeronautical engineering which she completed summa cum laude. In 1993 she applied for acceptance to a fighter-pilot training course – the first woman to do so. Although she already held a civilian pilot licence she was rejected solely on grounds of being a woman. Among those to whom she turned for help was MK Naomi Chazan, who had already earlier submitted a draft bill to equalize the terms of military service of men and women. Naomi in turn enlisted two young lawyers, IWN's Rachel Benziman and Neta Ziv of the Association for Civil Rights in Israel. Both enthusiastically seized this opportunity to apply their feminist principles on Miller's behalf. The case became a cause célèbre since it challenged innumerable presumptions regarding the qualities required of Israel's fighters, among whom pilots were considered the crème de la crème.

A major dilemma which confronted the appellants was that of the undeniable

265

physiological difference between the sexes, predominant among which was that of child-bearing and child-raising. One needed therefore to prove that fulfilment of these natural functions need not necessarily detract from the contribution women could make, which would be of no less value than that of men. Rachel and Neta succeeded in obtaining a court order to elicit classified information on the average length of men's service and the amount of time they spent on leave in the course of twenty years of such service. Comparing these with the amount of time during which child-bearing women might absent themselves, they proved that there was in fact no difference. These findings effectively clinched the case. In 1995, the Supreme Court of Appeals found in Miller's favour and she was permitted to take the stringent tests that all volunteers for pilot training undergo. The customary half-hour psychological interview that follows was in her case extended to well over twice that time. At the end of it, Miller's application was rejected on the grounds that she was "excessively motivated". Miller accepted the outrageous verdict with much grace, declaring that she had at least cleared the way for other women. Naomi Chazan's proposed legislation finally passed the Knesset in 2000. Today women are to be found everywhere, though still not as combatants on the front lines. Tellingly, Neta Ziv ends the very detailed article in which she presents and analyses the Alice Miller case in full, with reference to two photographs of women, both of them with the rank of Lieutenant Colonel in the IAF, one of them is embracing her two young children, the other with a baby several months old in her arms.

IWN was bent on ensuring maximum media coverage of this unprecedented case in order to raise public awareness of the IDF's discriminatory policies and practices, of which the Air Force's out-of-hand rejection of Alice Miller's request was merely one example. We decided to enlist the support of leading public figures, including President Ezer Weizman himself, a former commander of the Israel Air Force. Weizman was well known not only as something of a womanizer, but also as a male chauvinist of the first order. It was he who coined the boastful motto "The best [men] go to be pilots", to which popular culture, encouraged by the pilots themselves, added the rider "The best girls go to the pilots".

Weizman had been cited as contemptuously dismissing Alice Miller's demands with a rhetorical query: "Have you ever seen a man knitting?" Nevertheless, he received us most warmly. We were plied with refreshments and engaged in general chit-chat, while he focused his gaze on the youngest and most attractive member of our delegation. Finally, with our allotted time running out, I broached the subject of Alice Miller, while one of my colleagues unexpectedly produced a photograph of her son, an IAF pilot, sitting peacefully in the garden knitting! This trump card served like a red rag to the bullish president. Impassioned, trembling with rage, he burst out with "A woman can't fly a F-16! I can't fly a F-16!" Realizing that this was the involuntary admission of a no longer virile man we tactfully ended our visit.

SHOCK!

Art and Culture

In Israel only a few women poets were well-known, primarily among the literati. Those that were, such as Dalia Ravikovitz and Yona Wallach, through their lifestyles achieved a notoriety that led to frequent, predominantly unflattering references in the gossip columns, rather than appreciation of what is now acknowledged as their genius. Women were never the winners of prestigious literary prizes nor did they constitute a significant number of winners in any other of the many categories in which comparable prizes are annually awarded. Indignant at the lack of appreciation of women authors and out of a desire to bring their very existence to public awareness, in 1986 Moshe encouraged me to "do something" – raise the self-esteem of Israeli writers. Thus challenged, I decided on an international conference of women writers. At the outset, I had no idea of either the vast amount of administrative work or the funding that would be required for so hubristic a scheme. Like Everest, "it was there" and without any prior consultation with my colleagues, I set out to conquer it.

We drew up as comprehensive a list of invitees from as wide a range of countries as possible. We wrote to publishers and embassies for information and recommendations. Rashly, I over-generously offered assistance in covering airfares and promised accommodation in Jerusalem. The Jerusalem Foundation and Mishkenot Sha'ananim, which was established precisely to host visiting cultural VIPs, proved responsive to my call for help. We lacked funding. Estimating that the cost would be approximately $60,000, I approached potential donors. Convinced that I would be jailed as a debtor, Moshe kindly assured me that he would visit me in prison. I grew despondent as the date of the conference approached and requests for assistance with fares mounted. Finally, while on a visit to New York, I found I was still short of $20,000: help to cover the shortfall came from two unexpected quarters.

Someone referred me to Mira Spektor. A poet married to a wealthy right-wing political activist closely connected to Likud and Menachem Begin, she invited me to her home. We took an instant liking to each other. At the end of two hours of conversation that leapt from topic to topic, Mira pulled out her cheque book and handed me $10,000. Though encouraged by the unanticipated generosity, I remained despondent. I was due to leave New York that night and my mission remained unaccomplished. I still had one appointment before the flight: with my old friend Avalon Krukin. As soon as we met, I poured out my sense of failure and fears for the success of my enterprise. To my astonishment, Avalon solved the problem.

"I'll give you the rest."

The Women Writers Conference proved a highlight in the IWN's activities. Shimon Peres, the most cultured and best-read of Israeli politicians, and Jerusalem Mayor Teddy Kollek agreed to speak at the opening, for which the Van Leer Institute, its auditorium filled to capacity, was once again the setting. As the week progressed, women from every country read from their works at the Mishkenot. Apart from a few "stars" of international standing, such as Grace Paley and Marilyn French, the majority were unknown not only in Israel but outside their own country. Unanticipated revelations prompted generous expressions of appreciation. And there were unexpected crises. A participant from Indonesia, which has no diplomatic relations with Israel, had neglected to apply for an entry visa and was stranded in Hong Kong. My made a hasty appeal to the Foreign Ministry, elicited a gracious response, enabling her to attend the final sessions. Suitcases were lost in the process of transferring from the Mishkenot Sha'ananim to hotels. I was overwhelmed, not by the crises, but with delight at the unanticipated outcomes of the encounters.

The Israelis who had virtually no work translated into English, felt empowered. Ruth Almog, a novelist and critic whose essays today appear almost weekly in Israel's major newspaper, *Ha'aretz*, told me that for the first time in her career as a writer she had a feeling of self-worth. This was a salutary counter to the remark made by Yehuda Amichai, one of Israel's most distinguished poets, when I encountered him in the lobby. Like a number of other male visitors, he didn't bother to enter the small hall at Mishkenot Sha'ananim where the readings

268

were held. He had come solely to meet Grace Paley, who – together with Sana Hassan, the Egyptian author of *Stranger in a Foreign Land* – drew the most media attention.

"Why women writers?" Amichai enquired, contemptuously.

Shulamit Har-Even, in a public session held at the Van Leer Institute, challenged Marilyn French's claim that there is a distinct difference between the writings of women and those of men. She sought to prove her point by revealing that she had herself published works under a male pseudonym, and that nobody had detected any difference between these and her other books. Marilyn responded by questioning the astuteness of our (predominantly male) literary critics. Perhaps there had been no difference in style since the author was one and the same? I doubt whether Shulamit was converted to a more distinctly feminist understanding. Augustine Zycher, who had earlier produced a film which for the first time revealed the malfunctioning of the rabbinical courts, interviewed each of the participants, against the background of the gardens surrounding the Mishkenot. Today, the historic films languish in the IWN's archives, their celluloid gradually cracking.

Esther Broner revived ancient pre-Mosaic customs related to the entire range of female experience by devising a moving ceremony to close the conference. At the festive lunch that followed the final session, came a series of Shofar blasts. "Everybody out!" Esther commanded and we had no choice but to follow her as, like a Pied Piper, she led us to the cloisters that surround the central courtyard of the Faculty Club of the Hebrew University.

"Women who have been in exile from one another, dispersed throughout the nations, are now themselves a nation!" Esther triumphed, adding "Everyone, write the word 'Writer' in your own language on the poster." How and when had she enticed staff and volunteers to conjure up the abundance of cardboard, the numerous scissors, the coloured pencils, the sticks of glue which she bade us use? Enchanted, we obeyed. "Now, everybody sing with me."

Mesmerized, we followed instructions, learning a modified version of the classic Hebrew hymn of praise to solidarity: "How good and pleasant it is for women to sit together."

In English, French, Spanish, Flemish, Danish, German, Dutch, Japanese, Hungarian and a medley of other, even more exotic languages, each participant took her turn in leading the others in a multi-lingual rendering of the song.

"Hair symbolizes power," Esther declared. Each woman cut a lock of hair from the head of a colleague, gluing the locks to a large board – blonde, brown, black, red, curly and straight.

269

And then, the grand finale.

"Miriam took her timbrel out and all the women danced…" she sang and, thrusting a tambourine in my hand, impelled me to lead a snake dance, winding between the pillars, forming smaller circles, on and on, exuberant, boisterous. Finally, as we stood, breathless, Esther proposed an oath.

"If I forget thee, O Jerusalem Conference of Women Writers, may my pen lose its point!"

Hugs, kisses, even some tears – of joy or perhaps of sorrow at the thought of parting. No similar conference has been held since then.

Margaret Drabble and Mary Gordon had both already visited Israel. I invited them to dinner on Friday night. Margaret's first husband had been a Jewish actor, Clive Swift. Margaret revealed that even after their divorce, his mother continued her practice of phoning Margaret and the children every Friday to wish them a pleasant weekend. This was a welcome counter to the negative stereotype of the Jewish mother that emerges from the works of so many Jewish male writers.

SHOCK!

Media

The relegation of women to a minor role in Judaism and also in the secular Jewish state was reflected in the country's print and electronic media. We soon discovered that this distortion was particularly evidenced in television. Early in its existence, the IWN had incorporated a Media Research Unit, founded and headed by Dina Goren, a university lecturer in communications. At her initiative and under her direction, we devoted a month to monitoring and analysing TV's approach to gender. The aim was to quantify the number of women acting as presenters of programmes, featured in news programmes and/or participating in the talking-head discussions that proliferate in Israel. Using a guide that Dina designed, members were to take note of the topics these women were expected to address, the time allotted to women in comparison with that enjoyed by men in the same or similar programmes and the extent to which they were interrupted in mid-speech. As far as other Israeli-made programmes were concerned, we wished to establish the roles in which women were presented.

Almost 100 viewers participated in the research. Unsurprisingly, the findings confirmed our pessimistic preconceptions. There was not a single woman among lead presenters. On the rare occasions when a woman was invited to participate in a newscast, it was either on a topic that was women-related (hence considered of little consequence) or on other minor matters, never on items of national or international importance. There were no women commentators or producers and it was also clear that the few women who were permitted to appear on the screen had to be attractive. In dramas, women appeared almost exclusively as either homemakers or victims.

As a result of these findings we established watchdog committees to scrutinise print and electronic media as well as advertising, in order to facilitate prompt responses to sexism and discriminatory practices. Many of the protests we submitted to advertisers were effective. However, the Israel Broadcasting Authority, of which Israel television was a part, proved impervious to our protests. At the public presentation of the research results we held at the headquarters of the Journalists Association in Tel Aviv in 1986, the Head of Television, Haim Yavin, responded to a question as to why there were no programmes specifically for or about women by confidently asserting that Israel television didn't cater to any minority audience. He seemed genuinely amazed at the hoot of laughter mingled with indignation that greeted this; after all, we knew (what he appeared to have forgotten) that there were programmes specifically for children and for Arabs – populations far smaller in number than women.

We decided we had to meet him, to make him aware of the data and to urge reform. As a former student of mine at the Hebrew University, he greeted me with the respectful address of "My teacher", while my companion, Rachel Ostrovsky, one of the founders of *Noga*, the country's first feminist periodical, similarly addressed him, reminding him that she had taken a course he gave at Tel Aviv University. Either because of these relationships, he listened attentively to our presentation, finally responding with "*Mea culpa!*" and an undertaking to initiate changes as promptly as possible. He was as good as his word. That same evening, when he was presenting the main newscast, he reported on the results of a basketball match in the Women's League: a first in the history of the Israel Broadcasting Authority. We seized the opportunity of being inside the IBA building to speak to some of the women employees. All complained of unequal

271

pay practices, their confinement to lowly tasks and the virtual impossibility of promotion. When we urged them to organise and demand equal status with that of men, they were appalled. To do so was to risk dismissal.

Haim Yavin had referred us to Yair Stern, the Head of News Broadcasting, over which Yavin had no control. Stern proved a far tougher nut to crack. When we were finally granted an interview, he not only kept us waiting but received us with his feet propped on his desk, leaning back in his tilted chair – a pose which he retained throughout the half-hour he accorded us, during which he evinced not the slightest interest in what we were attempting to convey. Indeed, after Rachel, a very attractive blonde, had completed presenting our findings, the sole (and startling) response he directed to her was:

"You know, you have beautiful eyes." Realising there was little hope of attaining anything even remotely resembling Yavin's acknowledgement of guilt, we curtailed the meeting and left.

Stern's obliviousness to the importance of due news coverage of women-related matters was borne out in 1989. Anxious to bring the plight of *agunot* specifically to the attention of Knesset members, whom it might move to promote legislation designed to limit or propose alternatives to the extent of rabbinical power, we held a conference at the Knesset to which we invited MKs and members of the public. The event was ingeniously planned. In a series of brief presentations, personal stories related by *agunot* would alternate with proposals for reform formulated by lawyers and halakhic experts. When I arrived, I was delighted to find Ya'akov Ahimeir, TVs primary news presenter, sitting in the vestibule. I assumed we were to receive major coverage in that evening's telecast.

"I'm so glad you've come," I gushed. He looked at me blankly. We had never before met and I hadn't begun by introducing myself.

"I don't know what you're talking about," he replied. I began to describe our event but he cut me short. "I'm not here for that," he interrupted – and said no more. I was dismayed. Having learned from bitter experience the importance of media coverage and being aware of the need for a prior approach to those responsible, I had the previous day telephoned Rafik Halabi, editor of that day's TV news, who cordially promised to report on the event. What had happened? Where was the correspondent who had been delegated to cover the event? No representative of Israel Television arrived. Yet the conference proved more dramatic than we had anticipated. The personal narratives revealed the hopelessness and helplessness of the victims. They aroused not only sympathy but also indignation and resentment at the failure of the rabbinate to implement measures that could alleviate the suffering – measures which were lucidly and eloquently presented by the experts.

The undoubted star of the day was the wife of an Orthodox Yemenite named Yihye, to whom she had unwillingly been married at the age of 14. For close on 30 years he had refused to grant her the divorce that a court had approved. Comfortably ensconced in prison, where he had been appointed to the respected position of Warden of the Synagogue, with all physical needs provided for and no need to earn a living, he persisted in his non-compliance with the ruling of the rabbinical court. His wife was left in the limbo of being neither married nor divorced, unable to enter into another relationship, and solely responsible for maintaining herself and their daughter. Her story evoked tears. The pitifully few women MKs who had taken the trouble to attend were overwhelmed by the evidence of a situation of which they had been unaware. For the first time, they were learning about and empathising with the tragedies of anchored wives. As the drama intensified, Galia Golan rushed out to Ahimeir. She tried to persuade him to join us. Surely this was newsworthy material. But he refused to be moved. He had been sent to cover a decision that was to be reached by one of the Knesset committees and he was not to be sidetracked. There was no TV coverage of our event.

I phoned Halabi to voice my disappointment. Angrily, I reminded him of his promise. I demanded an explanation and an apology.

"It's a matter of policy," he explained. "I like to leave our viewers feeling optimistic". Hence the final item had been about a new French film, *Red Lips*. "It's directed by a Jewish woman," he pointed out, assuming that this rare fact would be adequate compensation for having failed to keep his promise. As I write this, some 40 years later, women are playing a significant and highly admired role in television as producers, investigative reporters, editors, film-makers and lead news presenters in prime-time TV.

SHOCK!

Health

It's 1991 and the Gulf War is at its height. Rockets are falling all over the country, though fortunately not in Jerusalem. A delegation of five, we have an appointment to meet the Minister of Health. We firmly resist his secretary's attempt to postpone the meeting and wait patiently for the minister to appear. Ultimately we are admitted and the minister, Ehud Olmert, asks us what is the purpose of the meeting.

"We'd like to talk to you about women's health." He seems taken aback.

Bewildered, "Women's health?" he asks. "What's the difference between women's health and men's?"

Now it is our turn to be taken aback. We had not anticipated so vast a lack of understanding.

Then, "Well, women give birth," I offer, lamely.

A pause.

At last, "So what is it you want to talk about?" he enquires, providing us with the opportunity of presenting our case to the highest authority.

We should not have been surprised by Olmert's ignorance. The founders of IWN had initially been similarly ignorant. It had not been on the agenda of the Namir Commission which, dealt solely with the restrictive legislation that severely limited the cessation of pregnancies.

Only in 1986, when a small group of health workers, headed by Michal Schonbrun, brought it to our attention, did we realize the relevance of the subject to our agenda. In the course of their work, they had become increasingly aware of the failure of the country's HMOs to take into account those aspects of health that are specific to women. No authority seemed aware of differences in morbidity. Statistics and other data vital to correct treatment were indiscrete according to gender; no differential treatment was practiced. Since most women were themselves unaware of their uniqueness, they not only failed to ask correct questions but even felt guilty at having complaints and

274

demands different from those of men. Maintaining that women were over-sensitive and hysterical, doctors expressed these feelings in offhand, superficial diagnosis and over-frequent prescription of anti-depressants and other placebos. Deterred by their unsympathetic manner and ineffective treatment, women ceased consulting physicians and remained untreated, sometimes with fatal consequences.

Wholeheartedly embracing their cause, IWN established a Health Task Force, becoming a pioneer in its awareness of, and response to, the general ignorance and neglect of women as a discrete category in every aspect of health, whether physical or mental.

In 1987 we began operating a comprehensive women's health service: An information hotline that referred women to doctors known to be sensitive and sympathetic to women's physical and mental needs was supplemented by a support unit whose members offered to accompany women to health appointments.

Two years later, Michal, together with sociologist Amy Avgar, devised a pilot Leadership Training Programme to develop a core group of women health professionals who would collaborate in advocating for changes in the health system designed to meet women's needs. The first of these courses was held in the north of Israel. Deliberately targeting as varied a range of participants as possible, we succeeded in drawing an applicant pool of close on sixty, of whom twelve Arabs and thirteen Jews were selected. When I attended the "graduation" ceremony, I was moved by the enthusiasm, excitement and sisterhood that the course had engendered, as well as by the immense appreciation and gratitude that the (Arab) director of regional health services expressed in his congratulatory speech. Such collaboration was still unusual.

Among the dismaying data uncovered by IWN's Research and Resource Centre were two that related specifically to the health of ultra-Orthodox women. Not only was there a higher rate of breast cancer in this sector; its members also suffered to a greater degree from eating disorders – a phenomenon which was virtually unknown and medically unrecognized in Israel. The high rate of breast cancer proved to be largely a result of the women's reluctance to consult male doctors, on grounds of modesty. If and when they did finally overcome that reluctance, the disease was frequently in too advanced a stage to be successfully treated.

The suggested solution to this problem was two-fold: more women technicians had to be employed in administering mammography at HMOs located in religious districts and more women had to be encouraged to avail themselves of this service. The latter goal could be achieved if rabbis collaborated by stressing Judaism's emphasis on the importance of preserving human life. We enlisted Dr. Claire Davidson, a profoundly religious Jew who successfully rallied rabbinic support. Michal's team members were equally successful in persuading HMOs to train and employ more women technicians. In consequence, the breast-cancer mortality rate among ultra-Orthodox indeed declined. Eating disorders proved more difficult to overcome. Since meals are so central an element in the practice of Judaism and women are the main providers of those meals, they are often from as early as Wednesday of each week obsessed with Shabbat-related shopping, cooking and baking. That obsession in turn generates either an aversion to food that leads to anorexia or binge-eating, both equally damaging to women's health.

IWN did not confine itself to ensuring a systemic change in all aspects of women's health. We also addressed ourselves to legislation. In the late 1980s we began lobbying for passage of an "informed consent" bill which would obligate physicians to explain all treatment options to patients who risked losing a body part. At the time, women undergoing biopsies for breast cancer were required to sign a consent form giving the physician full authority to decide on treatment, including mastectomy, in a one-step procedure.

Only in 1996 did the Knesset pass a Patient's Right Law. It had taken a long time to overcome physicians' resistance, but we had been fortunate in finding an ally. Boaz Lev, assistant director-general of the Ministry of Health, proved receptive to our demands, inaugurating a Steering Committee on Women's Health. At the same time, the Israel Centre for Disease Control, which is part of the ministry, established a division on women's health, appointing a woman supervisor – whose salary, however, was initially to be covered by IWN!

Our meeting with Olmert in 1993 was prompted by the Knesset discussions then being held regarding a proposed Health Insurance Law which would define the contents of the "basket" of services to be provided by HMOs, funded by the Ministry of Health. These criteria totally ignored both women's lifecycle and the unique ailments to which they are prone. We advocated for inclusion of contraceptives in the health "basket". In this we were unsuccessful. Israel's policy is dictated by an obsessive psychological insistence on maintaining Jewish plurality in the country. There is no funding for the birth control that is of such vital importance, especially to the poorer section of the population. Expensive fertility treatment is permitted and covered until the mother has, if she wishes, successfully given birth to two children. The physical and psychological stress that women endure in the process is considered as fully compensated for by her awareness that she is fulfilling not only a personal but also a national mission. We demanded fair representation of women on the Health Council that would compile the list of criteria. We even came armed with a list of suitable candidates, several of whom were, passed over in favour of better known but less well-informed male doctors.

"You win some, you lose some!" On the whole, our victories exceeded our losses. Today, every hospital in Israel has an out-patients department dedicated to women's physical and mental health, staffed by the ever-increasing number of women qualifying for the medical profession.

SHOCK!

Trafficking

On one of my increasingly numerous visits to New York, Kathleen Peratis, a member of the Board of Directors of Human Rights Watch, made me an offer I could not refuse. She would fund a project, to be headed by a young American lawyer, to investigate the nature and extent of human trafficking in Israel. The lawyer in question, Martina Vandenberg, wrote the following report:

"It began in the Israel Women's Network Resource Centre in Jerusalem. Nestled next to the bookshelves, metal filing cabinets overflowed with news clippings. One thin folder, labelled "Trafficking," contained just four articles. A short item from an English-language paper reported that a large group of young, Russian-speaking women dressed as nuns had arrived at Ben Gurion Airport from Moscow. The authorities, suspicious, determined that the "nuns" had been trafficked into Israel for forced prostitution. Another clipping showed a police official holding dozens of passports retrieved from Haifa's harbor; traffickers had dumped the passports into the water after meeting women from ships arriving in port. Like the fraudulent nuns, the young women hailed from the former Soviet Union and Western Europe.

The year was 1997. No one believed that human trafficking could flourish in

Israel. But the random tidbits in the files led to a six-month investigation and what began with a thin file ended up on the front page of the New York Times.

The investigation included more than fifty in-depth interviews with police, prison officials, senior officials of the Ministry of Interior, criminologists, sociologists, and victims of human trafficking. Together with IWN researcher Noga Applebaum, I travelled throughout Israel, asking about a spike in the number of women from the former Soviet Union trafficked into Israel's commercial sex industry. They followed research protocols and methodologies that I had developed in Russia as a consultant for Human Rights Watch. With Applebaum conducting interviews in Hebrew and I in Russian, the IWN team gathered overwhelming evidence of a disheartening reality: hundreds of women, possibly even thousands, had been trafficked into Israel for forced prostitution.

The women themselves reported that they had travelled to Israel in search of a better life. Many had responded to newspaper advertisements in their home countries. Believing they would find legitimate jobs, they instead found themselves held in forced prostitution. While some of the women were willing to engage in voluntary sex work, they did not know – and could not have known – that they would be forced to provide commercial sexual services, around the clock, for little or no pay. Stripped of their passports, guarded by traffickers, and subjected to physical violence, they had little or no hope of escape. Many of the victims told us that they had been sold as chattel, sometimes more than once. The price that brothel owners paid for the women became the victims' "debt." They were told they could not leave until they had paid the purported debt in full. Their only source of funds: illicit earnings from forced prostitution.

Encounters with law enforcement authorities brought only additional suffering. The authorities treated the women as criminals. Women who tried to report their abuse faced arrest and prosecution. After several failed attempts to interview trafficking victims held in brothels in Tel Aviv, IWN petitioned the government to permit researchers to visit women at Neve Tirtsa prison. Prison staff, sympathetic to the women, provided the researchers with unfettered access.

The women's stories reflected horrendous abuse and exploitation in Israel. Many were mothers whose paramount goal was to send money to the children they had left in the former Soviet Union in the care of elderly, impoverished grandparents. Trapped in prison, the women dreamed of returning home to their families. They were told by prison officials to call family members, friends or acquaintances in Israel who might help them purchase a plane ticket home. As often as not, they called the only number they had: that of their trafficker. Some

traffickers actually bought tickets for women to return to their home countries...
only to re-traffic them immediately upon arrival. Traffickers added the cost of the
plane ticket to the victims' ever-growing "debt" and sent them back overseas to
re-enter forced prostitution.

The IWN published a report, "Trafficking in Women to Israel and Forced
Prostitution." While it was still in draft form, I flew to Moscow and provided an
advance copy to Michael Specter, a reporter for the New York Times. Specter
travelled to Israel and wrote the story, which appeared on the front page of the
New York Times on January 11, 1998. The article, titled "Traffickers' New Cargo:
Naïve Slavic Women," provoked outrage. Madeleine Albright, en route to Israel
for meetings with Netanyahu when the story broke, requested that talking points
about human trafficking be faxed to her airplane.

The first to draw attention to human trafficking in Israel, the report prompted
hearings before the Knesset, legislation, and an increase in services provided to
victims. In 2000, Amnesty International published a report on trafficking of
women to Israel showing how little progress the country had made in combating
this scourge. Amnesty titled the press release accompanying the report, "The
Israeli Government Must Stop Human Rights Abuses Against Trafficked
Women." In 2001, the US Department of State ranked Israel as a "tier three"
country, one taking insufficient steps to combat human trafficking.

The Israel Women's Network, along with a coalition of other non-
governmental organizations, continued to advocate for better services for
trafficking victims. The coalition also broadened the Israeli discussion to include
forced labor as well as forced sexual services. The situation today is widely
believed to be better; Israel is now ranked as a "tier one" country. While it is
unlikely that human trafficking has been eliminated altogether in Israel, the IWN's
early research and advocacy exposed the abuse, creating immense pressure for
change."

The unfortunately widespread association between new immigrants from the
Former Soviet Union and sexual promiscuity created an entirely false perception
of them as being freely available for sexual intercourse. We received complaints
from women who, upon applying for jobs, had been openly propositioned by the
potential employer: employment would be conditional on her consent to accede
to his demands for sexual "services."

The victims turned to IWN's Hotline for help. Realizing that providing moral
and legal aid ad personam would not bring about radical change in public opinion,

we published an alternative calendar, comparable to the "pin-ups" that decorate all workplaces whose employees are primarily male. Each photo bore not only the name of the model but also a full account of her academic and professional achievements. Widely publicized and distributed, the calendar served as an appropriate antidote to vilification.

SHOCK!

Israel Defense Forces

The Alice Miller case had been a significant landmark in the struggle for women's rights in Israel. At IWN, we were already well-versed on sexual discrimination in the armed forces, since some of us had been enlisted by Amira Dotan to serve on an advisory committee to support her efforts to open up to women a wide range of military occupations that were restricted to men.

Like myself, a number of the group had never served in the military because we arrived in Israel at too advanced an age to be recruited. In order to enable us to become acquainted with IDF practices, Amira arranged a series of visits to units that were to all intents and purposes closed to women, save for their role as clerks.

Ultimately, Amira and her immediate successors proved extremely successful in their insistence on the inclusion of women in all units of the IDF. Since the late 1990s women have played an important role in every branch of the IDF, even serving in combat units on the front lines at times of war.

IWN's involvement in the topic of women's role in the military led, ironically, to an unanticipated turning point in our organizational development. Many of our members had become active in dialogue encounters with Palestinian women in an effort to achieve the mutual understanding essential to peacemaking, at which male politicians on both sides were proving unsuccessful. For us, military service was not as ideal a goal as it was for the majority of Israelis, particularly among men. We would have preferred an abolition of compulsory service and its replacement by volunteerism. We were certainly not anxious to promote equal conditions of service for women in combat units.

Nevertheless, we were aware that equality of responsibility for national security was an essential prerequisite for the achievement of equality in civilian life. As we all knew, an impressive military record was a key to higher status in civilian life: officers who had continued their service beyond the mandatory period and had retired at a comparatively early age advanced far more rapidly than their female coevals. In Knesset member Naomi Chazan's memorable metaphor, men could "parachute" into politics. Any party would be happy to have a major-general (res.) on their list of candidates for the Knesset. Even in civilian life, military rank was an important element in one's CV.

Since military service appeared an essential sine qua non for women's advancement, what should be IWN's policy? Compulsory service identical in length and nature to that of men? Voluntary service only? Together with men or in a separate Women's Corps, such as currently existed?

We decided to hold a debate with both Amira Dotan and Tali Shahak-Lieder, at the time the country's only female military correspondent. Word of this debate spread far and wide, though we had not publicized it. I noted with surprise and delight that many of those present had never before attended any of our meetings.

The debate was heated. Amira perceived the Corps as serving a dual purpose: advocating for, ensuring and enhancing women's roles and status in the IDF, while also representing women's interests in all cases of discrimination or sexual harassment.

The wide difference of opinion between the speakers elicited passionate expressions of both support for, and opposition to, one side or the other. Since the initial purpose of the meeting had, been to enable IWN's committee to reach a decision on the stand we should adopt, I foolishly decided to take a vote. I do not recall which way it fell, but I all too well recall the unfortunate outcome for our organisation.

Either because the decision was not to her liking or because she was more organizationally experienced than I was, Yael Rom immediately perceived my error, indignantly querying why I had not clarified who in fact was eligible to vote. I had failed to take into account the numerous participants who had never before been in any way connected to our activities, nor had I declared that this was a straw vote, rather than one that would be in any way binding so far as further IWN action was concerned.

I was nonplussed. Here was further cause of conflict within the group of founders who were de facto the determiners of both IWN's policy and its practices. Over time those of us who had attended the AJC Dialogue had gradually co-opted other women who were considered suitable not only because of their prior feminist activities but also because of their professional or semi-professional theoretical knowledge or experience in the fields in which we operated. Ours was a very informal (and very feminist) mode of decision making and of governance, that had already proved itself highly successful in achieving certain goals. We sought consensus rather than confrontation, comradeship rather than competition.

The dilemma and the acrimony which emerged during our deliberations following the IDF discussion and Yael Rom's response to it led Naomi Chazan at the next "general meeting," which was again open to anyone interested, to propose that we become a membership organisation, with fees and formal procedures. Her proposal was accepted, not only by those present, but also – more reluctantly – by the "board."

Soon IWN found itself with a bloated board of twenty-four (!) members and an executive of six. We had committees and sub-committees, each headed by a member of the board. We gradually took on paid employees to replace the original "staff" of volunteers. Within a few years, the professional staff were significantly more expert in their respective fields than the board members.

IWN's activities in the field of parliamentary politics intensified after the 1988 Knesset elections, which resulted in a low number of women entering the legislature. In response, we began more actively and aggressively pursuing a policy of leadership training and consciousness raising designed to bring out the women's vote and ensure due representation of women in party lists of candidates. Prior to the Knesset elections of 1992, we campaigned intensively to encourage women to become members of political parties, where hitherto their main contribution had been to serve as backstage assistants, meekly fulfilling duties, stuffing envelopes, stamp-licking, making phone calls to remind lapsed members to renew their registration.

We ran training courses, not only to educate women on the political complexities of Israel's electoral procedures, but also to train them in making persuasive presentations, refining their arguments, lobbying, creating alliances, and the use of other political tools. Party membership would enable women not only to elect, but to be selected as candidates for their parties' lists. These activities encouraged women with political ambitions to join IWN , even to lobby for election to the board — a tendency further promoted as a result of the 1992 election.

Of the mere twelve women elected to the new Knesset, eight were "graduates" of the Network who had either served on its board or participated in its political training courses. IWN thus came to be perceived as a valuable springboard for leaping into the political arena. Membership grew, but many of the newcomers were motivated by personal ambition rather than by feminist ideology. For the first time, partisanship became evident, replacing our initial feminist mode of collaboration and consensus, which, however, gratifyingly continued to be reflected among the women MKs. These included Naomi Chazan, one of our founding members, and Yael Dayan who had succeeded Naomi as co-chair of our Political Committee. Naomi Blumenthal, Anat Maor and Limor Livnat, all three of whom had participated in our political training courses, were also elected. Shulamit Aloni, a staunch supporter of civil rights, and Ora Namir were both re-elected. Within a short time, this politically diverse group succeeded in overcoming partisan differences to form an ad-hoc committee on the status of women. Inured with the concept of collaboration on women-related issues, and no matter how much they differed on other matters, these MKs joined forces to establish a parliamentary committee designed to further legislation that would advance the status of women. Left and right-wing members alternated as chairwomen as partisanship gave way to consensus: IWN's model was replicated.

Throughout its parliamentary dealings, the committee was ably supported by IWN's lobbyist and our admirably efficient media expert. Members and staff appeared before it to present reliable data. The legislative achievements were widely reported and enthusiastically applauded, not only by women, but also by the courts and liberal sectors of society. Suddenly, women-related issues, previously so marginalized or totally overlooked, took centre-stage.

The role played by IWN, which received considerable media coverage, and the clear connection between it and the success of the MKs to whom it had given parliamentary birth, were not lost on women who had political ambitions. There was a surge in membership, which reached unprecedented heights in the mid-1990s.

Many of the new members, recruited by women who perceived IWN as capable of providing appropriate platform for their own entry into national politics, knew little about the realities of women's status and even less about feminist ideology. In this respect, they differed significantly from earlier members, whom they now outnumbered. Gradually, politicization infected the very spirit of the organisation. Partisan in-fighting abounded, replacing the tradition of decision-making by consensus.

The Network's very success led to its decline. Some candidates brought in their party colleagues as members to ensure they were elected. They even engaged in what in Israel are known as "deals," whereby candidates promise quid pro quo that they will ensure that their own voters also support a rival candidate, provided the latter reciprocates.

A particularly egregious example of political manipulation occurred at the annual general meeting in 1997, when a new board was to be elected. Shortly before the meeting was due to begin, a staff member who had been assigned to collect membership dues approached me with a dilemma. A board member who was standing for re-election had arrived with a busload of women who had never previously been members. She had proposed that, in order to save time, she herself would cover the membership dues of the entire group, each of whom would repay her. Taken aback by this unprecedented request, I reluctantly consented. The new members duly trooped into the hall and sat silent throughout the proceedings, asking no questions, raising no points for discussion.

Needless to say, the unscrupulous candidate's energetic recruitment paid off. She was elected to the board and, later, to the Knesset. Other new, inexperienced, uninformed women were, to my surprise and dismay, also elected. It became clear to me that there would have to be some kind of "in-house" activity, not only to educate the new members both on feminist issues in general and on the IWN agenda in particular, but also to create a cohesive body of women sharing the same goals.

I had retired as chairwoman in 1996 to take up a fellowship at Wellesley College's Center for Research on Women. Rivka Meller Olshitzky, a lawyer who had succeeded Frances Raday as head of the legal committee, was elected to replace me. At the first General Meeting held after my return to Israel, she abruptly announced her retirement. She had been in office for just over a year. Aghast and bewildered, the members turned to me, vociferously demanding that I resume responsibility until a new chairwoman could be identified.. Reluctantly, but in duty bound, I resumed the role of chairwoman. To my distress, I immediately became aware that the board I now headed was a very different one from before:, too diverse in background and outlook to meld at once into the unity essential to furthering a common feminist cause. I turned to Shatil, the subsidiary of the NIF that specialized in advising NGOs. They sent one of their most competent organizational advisors. I hoped, prayed, that he would succeed in creating a collaborative body with a clear common mission. However, the new board proved dismally incapable of determining IWN's agenda. Furthermore, its members were driven by unprecedented partisanship. Above all, there was envy of the extremely competent staff that had played so significant a role in IWN's achievements. In rapid succession, two excellent directors were driven to resign, Other staff members followed suit. A number of the veteran board members also resigned, frustrated by their failure to maintain earlier traditions of collaboration.

Finally, I myself came under attack. When the second director left and we had difficulty finding a replacement, I had taken upon myself many of the duties of administrative management, and continued to travel abroad to raise funds. But the double burden soon exhausted me physically. I sensed increasing hostility on the part of board members who resented my preference for the professionalism of our staff. Matters came to a head at a board meeting at which two members (one of them the unscrupulous MK who had earlier ensured election to the board) accused me of having personally profited from my travels. None of the board members had ever contributed a penny to the organization, though it is customary in most NGOs for each board member to donate even a small, symbolic sum towards covering costs. The baseless accusations took me aback. I left the room in tears, aware that I must withdraw from an organisation that had so perverted our initial ideals.

Over the years, due to partisan in-fighting and personal ambition, the IWN became an increasingly irrelevant body, remote from the glory days of its first decade and a half. In that comparatively short period, employing the classic feminist tools of consciousness raising, litigation and legislative advocacy, we had achieved a sea change in the status of women in Israel, their awareness of discrimination and their readiness to be actively engaged in improving their lot.

Our first newsletter had announced our plans for the future.. We proudly and confidently promised that we intended to bring about a revolution in the status of Israeli women. From 1984, over the fifteen years that followed until 1999, I continued to chair our organisation, IWN amply fulfilled that promise. We rapidly gained recognition as the country's main advocacy group on a wide spectrum of women-related issues and were respected for the professional expertise of its board members and, later, also of its staff. The remarkable breadth of its scope, coupled with meticulous investigation and eloquent expert advocacy, brought about a radical change in Israeli society.

SHOCK!

Palestinians

Mid-June 1967. Still in the elated state of euphoria elicited by Israel's miraculous victory, I was walking eastward along Jaffa Road, the city's main shopping centre, when I encountered an astounding phenomenon: Arabs, young and old, men and women, were streaming into the western side of the city. Excited, gazing in awe and wonder at the tall modern buildings, the well-stocked shop windows, the traffic, they greeted us with smiles and outstretched hands. Perhaps perplexed by the complexity of pedestrian crossings, the youngsters among them marched boldly along the middle of the road. Their enthusiasm and unanticipated friendliness aroused a similar response from us. We took their hands, extended our own and replied with "*Shalom*" to their "*Salaam*". The great stone wall that had for almost 20 years blocked even so much as a glimpse of the Old City had been torn down. We and they were now free to mingle as Jews and Arabs had done before the fighting broke out at the end of 1947.

As the weeks passed we became increasingly familiar with those from the "other side". They became our street cleaners, household helps, gardeners and builders. In the Mahane Yehuda market, the women crouched, selling fragrant herbs from their gardens – mint, basil, parsley. Little boys peeled juicy sabras picked from the prickly cacti that surround the city. Gradually, they learnt the basic Hebrew terms they needed in order to interact with us. We did not learn Arabic.

Not until 1986 did I meet an Arab woman similar to myself in class and educational background. Our meeting came about at the instigation of Father Emmanuel, custodian of the Dormition Abbey on Mount Zion, who had become a good friend of my assistant-principal at Pelech, Aryeh Geiger. When I arrived at the abbey, he introduced me to my counterpart, ushered us into his study, brought us cups of tea and left us alone together. In what language does one address the "enemy?" I knew no Arabic, she no Hebrew. Her English was hesitant. She had studied in Germany, obtaining a doctorate in botany, which she

286

taught at Bir Zeit University. My German was rudimentary. I knew as little about botany as she did about English literature. Nevertheless, we found a common language.

What did we talk about? Ourselves, our backgrounds, our family. Have you children? How many? How old? What kind of life do you lead? We didn't talk politics. An hour and a half later, when the Father put his head around the door to inquire whether we would like more tea, we were able to tell him not only that we wanted to meet again but that we had decided to bring a few of our friends to the next meeting. And so we did. But on the second occasion, the talk inevitably turned to politics and the conversation was fraught with an underlying tone of malaise. Each side had its agenda and view of the Arab-Israeli conflict, the war and its outcome. The Israelis did not want to be confrontational. We were in the delicate situation of being victors, wanting to make it clear that there was no feeling of triumph on our part: we desired dialogue and peaceful coexistence, and as feminists sought an end to armed conflict. At the same time, we were aware that in the eyes of our Arab interlocutors we were occupiers. It was more difficult for them to accept us than for us to seek collaboration with them.

On both sides, our "delegations" included women who were not only politically conscious but in one way or another involved in activities designed to further peace and coexistence. To my surprise, the Palestinians did not accept my new-found colleague as their representative, possibly because she belonged to the Christian minority. They did not invite her to further meetings, despite the fact that Father Emmanuel and even she herself had spoken of her as being a leader.

When the intifada broke out at the end of 1987, our meetings came to a halt, yet women's efforts to achieve peace did not. Rather, the violence compelled us to accelerate our activities. Israelis and Palestinians congregated at Paris Square, near the Prime Minister's residence, and at Zion Gate, where east and west Jerusalem meet. We wore black shirts and bore banners. We called ourselves Women in Black. Closer personal ties developed. Elsewhere in Israel, every Friday groups of Women in Black began demonstrating. A new movement was born. Women from abroad joined us.

Among them was Simone Susskind. A woman of considerable wealth, she and her husband were both ardent Zionists and equally ardent advocates of a peace process. In May 1989 they sponsored a women's dialogue, to be held in Brussels. I was invited to join the Israeli delegation. The Israelis' initial encounter with our Palestinian counterparts was one of welcome held at the Belgian consulate in Jerusalem. We were all markedly reserved, even frigid. In contrast to the camaraderie of the demonstrations, there was little mingling between the two groups.

What was the aim of this meeting? What outcome did our hosts hope for? The Israeli contingent included two members of Knesset: Shula Aloni and Nava Arad of the Labor Party. The remainder of us were a motley group. Many of us were personally unacquainted. The only ones I knew well were Naomi Chazan and Debbie Weissman, a fellow modern-Orthodox. In Brussels, further participants arrived from our respective diasporas: exiles from Palestine who still recalled the *Nakba*, the disaster Palestinians experienced during the War of Independence; my friend Bella Abzug, the fiery leader of American feminism, came with others from the US. She, Debbie and I were staying at the same hotel.

We arrived on Friday. Determined to mark Shabbat even away from home, Debbie and I had brought Shabbat candles, two small *chalot*, a miniature bottle of sweet wine and a jar of gefilte fish. We invited Bella to join us at this rudimentary Shabbat meal – a very different one from those she had shared with my family during her visits to Israel. Debbie and I walked to City Hall, where the official opening of our encounter could be attended by the general public. Shula, speaking for the Israeli delegation, delivered an unusually mild conciliatory speech. Then, to our consternation, Hanan Ashrawi, who was already perceived as a spokeswoman for the Palestinians, launched a relentless, scathing tirade condemning the occupation, Israeli oppression, injustice, denial and desecration of human rights. Nor was that the end. A senior employee at the Chinese Embassy added her own fierce condemnation of Israel. Debbie and I turned to each other in dismay.

"If it weren't Shabbat," I said, "I'd turn around and go back home right away." But it was Shabbat and we had little alternative other than to stay and try as best we could to outlive the approaching storm.

The next day, the first meeting behind closed doors at the European Union headquarters began just as badly, with one belligerent speech after another. Mutual recriminations: "You did such and such to me." "No, you were the aggressors." Woman after woman spoke, alternating between Jews and Arabs, both equally accusatory. Each speaker was allotted 10 minutes. What positive outcome could there possibly be to this confrontation? I sat in a daze, miserable. Why had I come? What had I expected? How far we were from mutual understanding! Then came an unexpected reversal. Lilly Scherr, a French citizen who had fought in the resistance to Nazi occupation, invoked Jewish suffering during the Holocaust as justification for the creation of a Jewish State.

Immediately after her, Mary Khass, who headed early childhood services in Gaza, responded angrily.

"Don't come to us with your Holocaust," she said scornfully. "We have our own horror." Dramatically, she related how, a week or so earlier, Israeli soldiers had chased a boy who'd been throwing stones at them, pursued him as he sought refuge in a kindergarten and beaten him viciously as her little charges watched, horrified, crying, clinging to her for protection. It seemed as if we were trying to outdo each other in terms of respective experiences of persecution and suffering. I don't recall which Israeli spoke after Mary but I shall never forget the next Palestinian. Tall, stately, beautiful, Suad Amiry is a professor of architecture at Bir Zeit, a resident of Ramallah. Turning to Mary, she reprimanded her.

"We cannot, must not, dismiss the Holocaust," she said. "We have to be aware of Jewish suffering. Because it is through their own suffering that Jews should come to appreciate and understand ours."

It was as if she had waved a magic wand or uttered some miraculous incantation. As her message of mutual understanding and sympathy sank in, Jews and Arabs were transformed, by a desire for rapprochement and conciliation instead of resentment and anger. Constructive proposals for resolving our differences were presented. Amity replaced the hatred and resentment. From time to time throughout the afternoon Naomi Chazan and Hanan Ashrawi left the room together, each time returning after some 10 minutes. The rest of us were puzzled by the recurrent exits and entrances. Our bewilderment was dispelled as closing time approached, when the couple returned with a document in their hands. It posited the partition of Palestine based on the principle of territorial separation, called for an end to the occupation, acknowledged the Palestinian right to self-determination and sovereignty, and the right of all peoples in the region to live in freedom, dignity and security. Each party would have the right to appoint its own representatives at negotiations organised under neutral auspices. The aim of the negotiations was defined as being "to achieve a just and permanent settlement of the conflict". Without hesitation, we voted unanimously to adopt the proposal and to publicise it in the hope and expectation that it would lay the foundations for a cessation of hostilities, for peaceful coexistence between two sovereign states – Israel and Palestine.

The Susskinds held a press conference the following morning. Excited, we gathered at the Jewish Community Centre, eager to publish the extraordinary conclusion of our deliberations. But we were overly optimistic. The agreement was to be signed by all the delegates. However, Nava Arad held out. She must first receive approval from her party leader, Prime Minister Yitzhak Rabin.

Alternately beseeching and berating, we sought to persuade her. In vain did Shula argue that all of us were there as private citizens, in no official capacity.

"It's alright for you," Nava snorted. "You're not in the government." And off she went once again, to telephone Jerusalem and request her leader's approval. Whether she failed to find Rabin or any other person qualified to grant the necessary permission or whether the response was negative, I never learnt. All I know is that, after waiting in growing impatience, all the journalists disappeared one after another. We had nothing to tell them. I burst into tears – of anger and frustration. We had come so close to a historic moment, been so elated by our unexpected arrival at mutual understanding, support and encouragement – so close to peaceful resolution of a struggle that had gone on for too long and cost too many lives. And now to be thwarted by red tape, by the need for approval from a male-dominated government that had so abysmally failed where we had succeeded. Simone, equally disappointed, sought to console us. While many of the delegates had to leave that same afternoon, she invited those who remained to dinner in her spacious home.

A warm May evening, a flower-filled garden, a long table set on the terrace. I found myself sitting next to Hanan Ashrawi, still feeling uncomfortable at the proximity, despite her collaboration with Naomi. The aftertaste of Friday's vicious attack lingered. In considerable trepidation I ventured to open the conversation not with any reference to the previous day or the sorrow of that morning but with a polite question about her professional background. It rapidly emerged that not only were we both professors of English literature but taught Chaucer and shared a love of his works. I learnt that she had studied at Cornell and told her that I had been at Cambridge.

"Oh, so you're English," she concluded.

"No, not quite," I replied. "I was born in Germany. My family came to England in 1934 as refugees."

"Refugees?" she asked, puzzled.

"Yes," I confirmed. "We had to flee the Nazis."

"Refugees?" she repeated, as if she found that appellation incredible when applied to Israelis.

"Yes," I reiterated. "Refugees."

She remained silent, as if digesting this unanticipated information. Suddenly, I perceived that this highly educated, politically deeply engaged activist had never conceived of Israelis as refugees. For her, blinded by the suffering of her own people, it was inconceivable that even Jews might once have been those compelled to leave their native land.

The meal at an end, we drifted into the living-room, reluctant to disperse. Seating herself at the piano, Rita Giacaman, a vivacious Palestinian responsible for public-health services in the Occupied Teritories, began to play. Startled, I recognised the melody: it was the popular Hebrew song "Hevenu Shalom Aleikhem", "We have brought you peace". The Israelis burst into delighted laughter, adding their voices to her playing. Soon the Palestinians too had learnt the simple text – a process made all the easier because the Arabic for "Peace unto you" is virtually identical to the Hebrew. And then, spontaneously, we joined hands and danced. Round and round we went, until we were breathless and elated. Yet it seemed impossible to separate. Rita changed the tune. "We shall overcome!" In unison, we sang and swayed from side to side, arms linked in sisterhood. It was a vision of what might be if women had the power to bring about change.

"Was it like this last year?" I asked Simone, referring to an earlier attempt to attain accord that had been attended by Israeli worthies such as Abba Eban and their Palestinian counterparts.

"Don't be silly," she replied. "They were men!"

Back in Israel, I intensified my participation in dialogue and in demonstrations against the occupation. In consultation with Rana Nashashibi, I established a connection between the Israel Women's Network and the Palestinian Counselling Centre, which she headed, making our well-stocked Resource Centre available to its members and launching a joint research project. Additional comparable alliances sprang from the Brussels meeting.

Every Friday I took my place at Paris Square, wearing my black T-shirt and bearing a banner reading "End the Occupation Now". On occasion, passersby joined us. Frequently, drivers paused to denounce us as traitors and whores. Women continued to come from overseas to take part in our protests. On one occasion hundreds of demonstrators filled the square, surrounding it from all sides, stopping traffic. Groups of sympathisers sprang up not only all over Israel but also abroad, eventually broadening their mandate to include denunciation of militancy wherever it existed. In 1999, while at a conference on violence against women in Valencia, I joined such a group. In 2001, after 9/11, New York women began to congregate in Union Square to voice their opposition to terror and their demand for an end to hostilities.

In 1995, while I was a Fellow at the Centre for Research on Women at Wellesley College, the Jewish Federation of Pittsburgh contacted me with an urgent request. Abba Eban and Saib Erakat were to speak at a conference being held at the university. The organisers were looking for an Israeli woman participant to counter a Palestinian. I agreed. I was amused to see the stilted way in which the two men gazed steadily in front of them while speaking, never facing each other, as if each wanted to dissociate himself from the "other". Then came my turn. To my surprise, I saw that my Palestinian counterpart was none other than Zahira Kamal, a Palestinian activist who was, like me, currently in the US. Plump and jovial, Zahira seemed as delighted as I was at the unexpected encounter. We embraced and spoke about the possibility of peace between our people. Unfortunately, having had their say, the two high-ranking men had not stayed to see for themselves that good relations between "enemies" were possible.

I met Hanan again during one of the frequent curfews imposed on Palestinians, when the Israeli authorities refused her permission to attend a conference abroad. Together with Shula Aloni, Naomi and a number of other peace activists, I travelled to her home in Ramallah to express sympathy and solidarity. She seemed to appreciate our gesture of sisterhood but when we next met, at the Silver Jubilee conference of the National Organisation of Women (NOW) in DC in autumn 1991, that spirit of collaboration appeared to have evaporated. A number of the Jewish members of NOW who had established a "caucus" of their own invited me to join them. I soon realised that the status of women within Judaism was not their major issue. Not one of them was an observant Jew. All were ignorant of halakhic restrictions (the formal corpus of religious ruling known as *Halakha* is oral law). Women's *iggun* (anchorage of women denied divorce) concerned them only in so far as it was clearly an infringement of equal rights. What did concern them was the anti-Semitism they perceived as underlying the intense feminist opposition to the Occupation, an opposition seemingly more profound than that to all other military action. Their concern was not ill-founded. They recalled their shock when, at the UN World Conference on Women held in Copenhagen in 1980, the plenum had adopted the "Zionism is Racism" resolution passed at the UN 5 years earlier.

Anxiety reached a peak when we learnt that Hanan, who had arrived in Washington as a member of a high-ranking delegation of Palestinian leaders, had been invited to address the plenary. As spokeswoman for the PLO, she was already famed for the fierceness of her attacks on Israel. She was sure to win unmitigated applause and admiration. Hanan's eloquence would surely elicit sympathy for the

Palestinian cause and engender renewed vilification of Israel. Considering themselves too uninformed to speak out on behalf of Israel, my colleagues approached me to rebut publicly any recriminations Hanan might utter. Although I felt inadequate and unprepared to make a coherent response, I was compelled to agree, secretly hoping that Hanan would temper her customary vehemence.

The only other Israeli present was MK Tamar Gozansky, the sole Jewish MK in the Communist Party, who had been invited as an official speaker, despite the fact that she had played no active role in Israel's feminist movement. For her, equality of the sexes was simply an integral part of social equality in general. Her English was not fluent and her delivery lacked fire. She was dull. Some 10 minutes into her speech, the boredom that had set in was suddenly dispelled by an audible buzz. Behind Tamar's back and unperceived by her, Hanan had swept on to the stage, accompanied by what appeared to be a guard of honour – two sturdy men, who stood on either side of her while she seated herself behind the podium. Tamar droned on, oblivious to Hanan's presence, but after a few minutes she became aware of the audience's restlessness and brought her speech to an end. Only as she was leaving the stage did she see Hanan but no sign of greeting was exchanged.

In sharp contrast to Tamar, Hanan's speech was impressively eloquent, her English impeccable, as she described the impact of the Occupation on the lives of the Palestinian population. The pathos rose to a height when she reached her account of the long curfew undergone by residents of Ramallah in 43 days of confinement to their homes, just at a time of year when they should have been celebrating Christmas. "So our children were deprived of the happiness of the holiday. No Santa Claus roamed the streets of Ramallah." I was appalled by what I perceived as wanton manipulation of the audience. How many Christians were there in Ramallah? And did Santa Claus freely roam the city's streets every year? I was too ignorant and lacked the ability to rebut her accusations. Yet I had– albeit reluctantly – agreed to respond should Hanan attack Israel. I was shaking with fright as Hanan, triumphantly completing her speech with a dramatically rhetorical apogee, swept off the stage as majestically as she had entered. The audience's applause was more moderate than I (and perhaps she, too) had expected. The newly elected president of NOW, Pat Ireland, announced that the Jewish members had requested permission for me to speak. I could not evade the responsibility of representing my country and my people. Nevertheless, I had one request to make.

"I want to address my remarks to Hanan." I said. "I have to speak to her and I want her to hear what I have to say."

"No problem," Pat replied and at once sent off an emissary to bring Hanan back on stage. As she approached, I walked towards her in welcome and embraced her, kissing her on both cheeks. I assume she recognised me, though she gave no visible sign of recognition. On the contrary, she appeared temporarily discomposed, presumably wondering why she'd been recalled. I then proceeded to address not the audience but her. I reminded her of my visit, our sympathy and our meeting in Brussels. I stressed that we, as feminists, must oppose male militarism, and join together in effecting peaceful coexistence and mutual recognition of each other's rights.

"We must stretch out our hands in peace," I concluded, extending my own hand as I spoke.

A moment of hesitation. Then she took my hand and I embraced her again. With no word of response, Hanan departed. Behind the scenes, reporters were waiting, to interview her. I was not deemed newsworthy. Only later, when I listened to the recording of the session, did I hear the roar of applause my remarks elicited. True feminists do not take kindly to their activities being exploited for narrow nationalist purposes. Their mandate is to create a world of equality and mutual respect: sisterhood.

When I returned, emotionally drained, to my Jewish colleagues, I realised the extent to which I had dispelled their fears and vastly increased their appreciation of, and support for, Israel. One of them, Gene Boyer, a founder of NOW, had been instantly converted to Zionism. She later became an ardent supporter of the IWN and a member of the board of Friends of the IWN.

As for Hanan, my only other encounter with her was at a women's peace meeting in Jerusalem at which I had at the last minute been asked to replace Shula as Hanan's partner at the opening session. By that time, Hanan was a member of the PLO's "parliament". She refused to appear with anyone of inferior status and abruptly left the hotel at which we were meeting. Evidently, my appeal to sisterhood had made no permanent impact.

The Schechter Institute of Jewish Studies

In 1990, as I was settling down to what I hoped would be a quiet life of retirement, I received a call from Rabbi Daniel Goldfarb of the Schechter Institute of Jewish Studies. He who identified himself as the chairman of its executive committee and requested a meeting. When we met at my home, it emerged that he wished to consult me as to who might be an appropriate successor to Ze'ev Falk, who had recently resigned from the post of Rector. I made a number of suggestions and with that presumed I had done my duty. Some weeks later came a second call. None of the candidates I had suggested had agreed to take the job. A second visit: had I any further suggestions? A few more names occurred to me – several of them retired professors of the Hebrew University. However, these too proved averse to returning to active academic life. Finally, on his third visit came the totally unexpected question:

"Would you be prepared to take the post?" I burst into laughter. Hearing me laugh, Moshe peered around the door.

"They want me to be Rector," I said; to which his wholly unanticipated response was, "Well, why not?" And so I became the academic head of an institution of which my only prior knowledge stemmed from having participated years earlier in an advisory capacity: to serve on a team charged with devising an MA programme of Women's Studies – a field in which Schechter was a pioneer.

The Schechter Institute comprised an unwieldy number of individual units, between which there was considerable overlap, although each one had its own board of management. The largest of these in terms of numbers of electives, courses and students was the MA programme of Jewish Studies. Several of the departments collaborated closely with another unit, the TALI Education

Programme, which devises teaching materials, teacher-training and ongoing supervision for an entire countrywide school system that aims to enrich Jewish Studies in the state school system. TALI (Hebrew for "enriched Jewish studies") has a subsidiary programme that functions in Ukraine, where it has established both schools and communities affiliated with the Conservative movement.

The Rabbinical School, the first of the Schechter units to have been established, prepared students for ordination as Conservative rabbis. They simultaneously took a number of mandatory MA courses, thus enabling them to acquire both an advanced degree and the title of rabbi. In short, Schechter strongly reminded me of the multinational Austro-Hungarian Empire. I was its emperor – a formidable role, particularly since each of the "nationalist" forces sought greater independence, chafing at the bit of having others determine their fate and their budget.

In the summer vacation that preceded the beginning of my first year at Schechter, I met key members of the academic and administrative staff individually. I wanted to become acquainted not only with the roles they played, their specific responsibilities, but also with their personalities. I sought both information and advice. While many of them expressed approval at my arrival from outside Schechter, one of them informed me in the most forthright manner of his disapproval, not only because he thought I was ignorant of the institution's *modus vivendi*, but because he felt that the Dean of the Rabbinical School should have succeeded Ze'ev Falk. I think he found it particularly galling that I, so lacking in Jewish learning, should by virtue of office be the Dean's superior. Nevertheless, he continued diligently to fulfil his role as general overseer of the physical plant and with time became a devoted collaborator.

The only person who seemed to remain permanently resentful of my infiltration was precisely the outstanding scholar of *halakha* whom I had unwittingly deprived of the title of Rector, a position in which he had temporarily replaced Ze'ev Falk. On my first day at the Institute, he marched into my room and demonstratively planted on my desk a daunting pile of files which, he made clear, were now my responsibility. His resentment at having been passed over was understandable. My qualifications for this particular post were negligible. As Dean of the Rabbinical School, he was not only familiar with the complexities of Schechter but had already – as the files testified – imposed some order on its awkward maze of components.

Everything at Schechter was a far cry from the formality of Israel's institutions of higher education. In the overcrowded building, initially constructed as a dormitory there was human warmth, collegiality between faculty members, an administrative staff both professionally competent and kind and welcoming towards colleagues and students alike, a rare openness and mutual respect. The students were mature not only in age but in the seriousness with which they took their studies. The majority, who already had experience in teaching, came to enrich their knowledge of Judaism and improve their teaching skills. They clearly enjoyed their days at Schechter.

In this congenial environment I found myself once again in a position to experiment and initiate new projects, introduce more effective means of collaboration and evaluation, exploit the collegiality so as to further greater efficiency. The incumbent President, encouraged and supported my innovations. I had as Dean of Education Professor Walter Ackerman, with whom I had become acquainted in Beersheba, where he had established the School of Education. A staunch Zionist, he had a very clear vision of what should characterise higher education in a Jewish state. While, his idealism had elicited little response from the cynical "old timers" in the Negev, at Schechter he was given a free hand to implement his vision.

At both Pelech and the IWN, I had learned the importance of public relations as a vital tool in fundraising. Schechter lacked exposure. Too few people, especially potential donors, were aware of its uniqueness. I insisted on the publication of a well-illustrated, informative *Annual Report* and Linda Price, head of the Public Relations Department, took up the challenge. Though it proved useful when I travelled to North America to raise funds, I was far less successful with individual donors than I had previously been. Nevertheless, I found the contacts I had formed in my earlier positions helpful. My feminist friends helped to fund *Nashim*, a journal of Jewish feminist studies. The Ford Foundation generously funded the creation of a Centre for Women in Jewish Law. Initially, its major mission was to conceive solutions for the problem of *iggun* and it published a number of pamphlets outlining various solutions. It was a time of unprecedented intellectual ferment, innovation and excitement for me personally and for the institute. Throughout, I benefitted from the wisdom of Robert Rifkind, a courteous and witty New York attorney, who served as chairman of the International Board of Governors.

One Yom Kippur, bored by the repetitiveness of the long day of prayers, I had read the section of the Mishna that describes the way in which this most solemn day in the Jewish calendar was celebrated in the days of the Temple. It included details of actions performed by the High Priest and his acolytes, changes of dress, exits and entrances, the people's involvement in dispatching the sin-bearing scapegoat to death in the desert and the point of highest tension, when the High Priest entered the Holy of Holies. Would he emerge, purified and purifying of the people's sins?

Clearly, this was more than ritual. It was theatre. The religious "performance" had not generated an entire literary genre, as it had in Greece, but where else in Jewish practice could one find a similar blending of ceremonial worship and artistic creativity? Where was there room for fruitful innovation, variations on a theme? Rashly, I decided to offer a semester's course on the topic. It proved amazingly enlightening. The students, who varied widely in ethnic origin, spoke about rituals practised by their parents and grandparents, not only on fasts and festivals common to all Jews but on occasions specific to their own ethnic community, such as the Maimouna among Moroccans, the Saharane among Kurds and - a very recent addition in Israel – the Sigd of the Ethiopians. The course generated a new "elective", for which I was able to elicit the collaboration of practitioners such as composer André Hajdu, dramatist Michal Govrin, artist Jo Milgrom, who transforms *objets trouvés* into Midrash, and film-maker Naphtali Gliksberg.

I first met Naphtali at a meeting to which I invited a very diverse group of professionals in various media to help me devise not only the Schechter curriculum but also a Centre for Judaism and the Arts. Naphtali enlisted a group of well-known artists – painters, sculptors, photographers, video artists, poets, novelists and composers. A year of weekly study of Jewish texts resulted in an impressive exhibition at the Mishkenot Sha'ananim. Some of the works proved too avant-garde for the general public but connoisseurs were enthusiastic. When I presented the concept of the Centre for Judaism and the Arts, I was in fact no longer at the head of Schechter, replaced by my disgruntled rival for the Rectorship. Instead, I was now chairperson of the Israeli executive committee. My successor invited me to present my proposal at a strangely hybrid forum composed not only of faculty members but also some of the senior (and even not-so-senior) administrative staff.

Naphtali, whom I had invited to head the centre, joined me in making the presentation. Too novel a concept, it was not perceived to be a natural component of an institution of Jewish study. We persisted in our arguments, stressing the prestige that would derive from it. Our audience seemed unpersuaded. But last-minute rescue was at hand. Liat Citron, the head of the Accounts Department, pointed out that since Naphtali had volunteered his service and the artists would not be remunerated, no additional expenses would be incurred.

"So why not?" she asked. Her argument carried the day. This major obstacle overcome, Naphtali and I left the room, exhausted but relieved. We were joined by Walter Ackerman, who shook his head in disbelief.

"Appalling!" he said, providing a much-needed dose of sympathy.

Intent on my function as the academic head of Schechter, I failed to untangle the complexities of its administrative structure. I sat through biannual meetings of the International Board of Governors, the majority of whose members came from the US, in a haze of non-comprehension. The same was true of the more frequent meetings of the Israel Executive Committee, which not only oversaw the implementation of the governors' decisions but also enjoyed a certain degree of autonomy. Among the members of this committee, a large number held positions in the Conservative movement, the World Zionist Organisation and other bodies that had some kind of connection with New York's Jewish Theological Seminary – whose rabbinical students come for a year's study in Jerusalem. To my mind, our president appeared to be performing his administrative duties in a most admirable manner.

Unfortunately, this proved not to be the opinion of the Board of Governors and, in particular, of its incumbent chairman, a wealthy American businessman and major donor whose opinion carried much weight. At the board meeting held at the end of my second year as Rector, he launched a biting attack on our president, citing his lack of efficiency and, in particular, his failure in the crucial role of fundraiser. To my astonishment, he asked me to take over, at least on a temporary basis, until another suitable candidate was identified. I was not interested in the position, for which I felt totally unqualified. He was adamant. He would do his utmost to help. After all, he argued, I had experience in heading an organisation. I succumbed to the pressure. It was one of the greatest mistakes of my life. The double burden was too heavy for one person to bear and, as I soon learned, I was totally ignorant as to the complexities of the Conservative movement in the US, with which I was expected to interact and collaborate, not only in order to enhance fundraising but also to create firm bonds of friendship and collaboration.

At the end of a year that was even more exhausting than the final phase of heading the IWN, I resigned from both positions at Schechter. I remained closely connected to it in my role as Chairwoman of the Executive Committee but was increasingly frustrated by my failure (and that of like-minded committee members) to effect structural change. Again I resigned. I was given a memorable farewell party. Steve Hornstein created a composition for solo harp in my honour. I was presented with a work by Joshua Neustein, one of my favourite contemporary Israeli artists. Bob Rifkind made a witty speech. Even my family appeared gratified. I have nothing but happy memories of my days in that spatially inadequate building, so geographically close to the elegant Givat Ram Campus of the Hebrew University, but so different in spirit from the latter's professional rivalries and its stress on academic research.

My Brother, Of Blessed Memory

MY BROTHER DIED on 4 January 2013, aged 91½. He died suddenly of a cause still unknown to me and destined to remain so. I believe that only his widow knows – perhaps not even she – but she refuses to speak about it.

His death was sudden and unexpected. Despite – or perhaps due to – a tendency to hypochondria that had led him to consult his doctor with exceptional frequency and undergo what seemed to me excessive blood and other tests, he had been in good health. A sudden death – presumed to be preferable for the deceased – leaves survivors without a sense of closure. Too much has been left unsaid, too much left unclarified and ambiguous. For many weeks I felt suspended and dissatisfied. I desperately wanted answers to unresolved questions but I knew that now I would never get them. My frustration intensified my grief at his loss.

My brother was five and a half years my senior. We never played together. He liked football and played the violin well enough to be in the school orchestra. A diligent student with an outstandingly good memory and profound intellectual capacity, he was highly esteemed by his teachers.

During the months when we were living in Mannheim awaiting our entry permits to England, neither of us attended school. He exasperated my mother by spending all his afternoons and many evenings out of the house playing football, participating in Zionist youth movement activities but also, amazingly for a twelve-year old, attending lectures by visiting Zionist notables. He also accompanied our mother to provide moral support when she went to the British Consulate in Frankfurt to try to expedite the long-awaited entry visas. In his neat handwriting and with full date at the head of the page, each time he added his own balanced report to her passionate, emotional accounts of the meeting. That capacity for cool, rational response remained typical of all his actions throughout his life. I do not recall his ever reacting with an outburst to any event. Except twice.

The first time was when he returned from the hospital after our mother's death, early in the morning, just as I was preparing to join him there. Typically, he had taken the bus rather than a taxi, as if to give himself time to overcome the immediate grief. Only when he arrived at our door did he burst into tears. The other also related to our mother. In 2008, sorting out the papers he'd brought from London when he came on *aliyah* some 15 years earlier, he came upon a thick file on which my father had written "Letters from my dear Perl". Inside, was what she had sent him in the course of the ten months of their separation, when he was already in London and we still in Germany. Letters of despair, anger, unfettered emotion; letters of pleading and rebuke, sudden hope fated to be dashed. Most were written on flimsy notepaper. Some were already fraying. We hired a German-speaking typist to transcribe them to a computer. For at least one morning every week over a period of several months we spent hours together in this way, for the first time learning about her personal tragedy. She wrote spontaneously, from the heart. The lines were crowded because she didn't want to waste paper; sometimes she apologised for not having written, because she had no money for postage.

One morning, when there had been a series of particularly painful letters and our amanuensis had just left, we happened to be standing opposite each other as I too prepared to bid him farewell. Spontaneously, we reached out and hugged each other, both of us weeping.

"She had such a lousy life," he said through his tears. It was only a minute before he regained his composure. In fact anything related to our mother aroused strong emotional response, including guilt. After our father's death, when she withdrew into perpetual widowhood, he had continued to travel abroad, often for comparatively long periods, leaving her alone in a house too large even for two. He recalled her sad face at the front window as she watched him drive off. We can never make amends.

My brother was a hoarder. When I was five years old, a kind visitor brought each of us an identical present: a hollow chocolate ball wrapped in silver paper, nestled in a string bag which one could either hang around one's neck or simply carry by hand. I chose the former mode, bouncing the ball as I walked around the house. Needless to say the ball broke into pieces but that made it no less delicious to consume, bit by broken bit. And then it was gone. My brother's ball, carefully set aside upon receipt, survived for years. Indeed I don't know whether its ultimate fate was to be eaten and if so, under what circumstances.

He collected obsessively: cigarette cards, coins, stamps, theatre programmes, news clippings. For many years he kept an orderly catalogue of visits to the cinema: the date, location, names of the film and the stars. Not long before his death, as we were reminiscing about a film we'd seen together over 70 years earlier, he brought out the catalogue to prove that he was more correct than me in recalling the circumstances in which we saw it. He collected intelligently and lovingly, focusing on the work of Jewish artists of the late 19th and early 20th centuries. At the *shiva*, a curator from the Israel Museum told me he'd been far more knowledgeable and expert than her on the Jewish painter Isidore Kaufman, several of whose works he owned. Everything he did, he did in depth. At a student dance in 1947 I was surprised to see him execute a tango to perfection, startling his flustered partner with the graceful expertise with which he performed the intricate twists of body and legs. He had, of course, taken lessons.

The range of his interests was wide: history, general and Jewish, opera, the arts, political science, economics (which he studied at the LSE, where he was named the most outstanding student in a decade). He read and spoke English, Hebrew, German, French, Yiddish (albeit haltingly), a little Russian and Italian. He understood Spanish. He was an inveterate, restless, traveller. He went everywhere, even to the Arctic, though not to the Arab countries hostile to Israel. What he had to say about the places he visited always indicated insight into local customs and culture. Wherever he travelled, he sought out Jews or relics of Jewish life and culture now lost. He found the *shtetl*s where our grandparents lived before they left Galicia or where they had died, like my maternal grandfather. He went to great lengths to find a guide or a survivor who could give him information on what no longer existed.

Nostalgically enamoured of a past he never knew, a culture that the Second World War wiped out, he immersed himself in Yiddish, supported the Yiddishspiel Theatre that developed in Israel, donated a Yiddish library in memory of our parents to Tel Aviv University (graciously adding my name to his as the donors), established a scholarship fund for students of Yiddish at the Hebrew University and endowed a chair in Yiddish at University College, London. At the *shiva*, the eminent professor of Yiddish, Hava Turniansky, told me he had become remarkably knowledgeable about Glückel of Hamelin, of whose unique diary Hava had published a scholarly edition.

I longed for my brother's attention and love. I tried to endear myself to him, in the hope of eliciting some degree of reciprocity. One summer, when I was probably five or six years old, he went to spend a considerable part of the holidays with my father's family in Mannheim. He was a great favourite of my grandmother's, petted and spoiled by my aunts. I awaited his return in eager anticipation. On the day he was due back, my mother baked a cake, we laid the table, I picked a vase full of flowers and drew a "Welcome" sign. I accompanied my father to the station to meet him and when my father kissed him tried to follow suit. But he pushed me away impatiently. I must have shown my sorrow at this rejection. Perhaps I even cried. He remained unmoved and unresponsive. My father, exasperated, slapped him, saying, "Give her a kiss!" That must certainly have endeared me to him! I can't recall whether he eventually relented so far as to brush his lips against my cheek. In any case, the joy of the occasion had dissipated. The cake, I assume, was eaten but my drawing and the vase of flowers were ignored.

This incident can be seen as a prototype of our relationship through the years. I constantly sought his approval and his praise of my accomplishments. Once, after a lecture I gave in London, he did indeed come up to me as I stood on the dais surrounded by members of the audience anxious to hear more, pat my arm and say, "That was very nice". In general, he was chary of compliments – so chary that I remember the few that he paid me very clearly. *London, December 1944.* The first vacation from my studies in Cambridge. He and I were staying in our London home, temporarily occupied by relatives, refugees from Nazi-occupied Europe. We were there to attend the annual conference of the Inter-University Jewish Federation, of which he was an officer. I was wearing a new dark-blue silk dress. One of the residents in the house, currently studying hairdressing, had brushed my gleaming chestnut brown hair into a fashionable pageboy style. My brother was helping me pin a jewel-studded butterfly brooch my father had given me. As he completed the task, he stepped back and said, in open admiration, "*Eine ganze Dame!*" ("A real lady!"). And only a short while before his death, when I sent him a memoir I'd written of our mother, he responded by thanking me, adding, "It brought tears to my eyes". Nevertheless, as I learned while going through his papers, he kept copies not only of all the off-prints I sent him but newspaper clippings that referred to me, even a very minute item from the local paper, which included my name among those pupils of Aylesbury Grammar School who had successfully attained the school-leaving certificate.

Primarily, I learned of his appreciation from others. "He was so proud of you," they would say. I suspect that what usually happened was that it was they who put the words in his mouth. "You must be very proud of her," they would assert – and he would acquiesce. But perhaps I'm mistaken. Perhaps he did think well of my achievements. I cannot tell, because he never spoke to me about them, save to criticise the fact I had dedicated myself too wholeheartedly to the school I'd headed for 15 years on a voluntary basis. He was justified in criticising me for my unsalaried work, since for many years he most generously supported me and my family, supplementing our incomes to enable us to live comfortably, far beyond our means. When clothing was still scarce in Israel, he continued my mother's tradition of shopping for us at Marks and Spencer. Was there a new fad or fashion? Walkman? Nike shoes? The Beatles? "Uncle Willy" provided a steady supply. He unquestioningly responded to every request for new books and records. It is to him that I owe the extensive library that I built up over the years after I left England. We took this generosity for granted and were shocked when, after his late marriage, it decreased and came to an end. During the war our relationship changed. The indifference he'd previously displayed gave way to friendship. The house my father had bought had only three bedrooms plus one very small dressing- room. Since one bedroom was filled with a stock of jewellery and watches brought for safekeeping from the London premises of Elco Clocks and Watches, my brother and I shared a bedroom. We both enjoyed "corny" jokes. Before going to sleep it became customary for us to exchange a Laurel and Hardy dialogue learned years earlier from the weekly *Film Fun*. "Nighty-nighty," one of us would say. "Pyjama-pyjama," the other would respond.

We went for walks together on Sundays, enjoying the park at Waddesdon Manor or the open roads around the village. And he taught me maths, expounding so clearly on the symbols of algebra that I came to love it, gaining high grades in a subject in which I'd previously failed. He should have been a teacher. He should have been the one to become a professor. Instead, he was forced to go into the family business. His desires and intentions constantly unperceived or opposed, he dutifully fulfilled expectations. He wanted to be an engineer. Instead, he was sent to study economics and commerce. He wanted to enlist in the army. My uncle insisted on his being granted exemption. He wanted to go on *aliyah*, like the cousins we both admired. In this too he was frustrated. His Zionism and loyalty to Israel were intense. From an early age, even while he was a member of the Blau-Weiss youth movement in Germany, he composed impassioned calls upon his contemporaries to join him in the effort to achieve statehood. Articles he wrote in the same spirit were published in Anglo-Jewish journals. These too I found in the boxes he left me. He had never shown them to me, nor had he sent me copies of his numerous, highly perceptive book reviews that appeared in the same publications.

I don't know whether he ever confided in anyone, revealed his innermost feelings. Nevertheless he did on very rare occasions disclose some hitherto unknown, unsuspected fact. Once, when I was visiting from Israel, conversation turned to *aliyah* and he revealed how much he had wanted to live in Eretz Israel.

"Why didn't you go?" I asked, in all innocence.

"Because you did," came the reply. "We couldn't both leave our parents." Was this *post factum* justification? Would he really have gone had the situation at home been different, my father still healthy? Or was it a need to justify his inaction, his inability to take the final step?

Among the papers that I found in the 25 deep folio box files that he left me and that his widow only grudgingly released to my care, I came across several letters he'd received from our cousin Yaakov, who had gone on *aliyah* in 1933. The first of these, dated only six months after we arrived in England, urged him not to come to Eretz Israel until he had completed his schooling, acquired a craft and learned Hebrew. To this advice, Yaakov added an admonition: "Join *Ha-Shomer Ha-Zair* (the most left-wing of all Zionist movements)!" Identical counsel came in another letter, two years later, when my brother, at the age of 16, finished high-school. He had yet to acquire a skill that would enable him to contribute to the building of the Land.

In 1946, having completed his university studies with honours in two degrees, Willy wrote to a Professor Pick at the Hebrew University. He kept a copy of the typewritten letter. In it, he enquired whether there was a Department of Economics at the Hebrew University. If so, he would like to apply for a position in it. If not, he would welcome the opportunity to establish one. The reply was brief and dismissive. A pity. Both he and the university would have benefited had the response been more affirmative and encouraging. Still wishing to fulfil his desire for *aliyah* but with a more appropriate profession, my brother turned to a vocational-guidance service to investigate whether he should study engineering – the career he had in fact wanted to pursue but had been compelled to abandon. He had the necessary qualities, the advisor told him, but surely it was inadvisable to begin a five-year course of study at his age. He seized every possible opportunity to compensate for not being an Israeli citizen. When the Yom Kippur War broke out, he immediately came in order to contribute to the war effort. Since public transport was severely affected by the conscription of buses and drivers, he travelled to and fro, picking up soldiers who needed to get from one place to another. He spent entire days and even some nights performing this task, staying until the end of hostilities.

It was not only with algebra that he helped me, while I was still at school. As my final year at school approached, he sent me the application forms for Newnham and Girton, the two women's colleges at Cambridge, neither of which were even dreamt of by the teaching staff at Aylesbury Grammar School. The LSE, where he himself studied had been evacuated to Cambridge. The LSE was an ideal place for him to study. More modern than Cambridge, it was a hothouse of Fabianism and British Socialism, an ideal combination in which he flourished and became an acknowledged leader. You're Willy's sister?" people would say in awe when I first arrived there, over a year after he had already graduated.

He made friends, mainly people who shared his intellectual interests and cultural tastes, and he kept them. He maintained correspondence with several of them over many years, filing each letter. In 1995 he presented me with the files containing all the letters I'd sent, first to my parents and then to him alone, from the time that I arrived in Israel 46 years earlier. He offered a similar collection to the widow of a friend who to my surprise, preferred not to keep them. He had one friend, a novelist, with whom he regularly each week partook of tea at a hotel across the road from the BBC. Occasionally in Europe at the same time as a professor friend, now resident in the United States, he would travel for several hours to spend some time with him. He seemed surprised when I asked why the friend, who was several years younger, never came to see him. He was dutiful where family was concerned. Every time he came to Israel he made sure to visit each one of our relations. After his *aliyah* in 1993, he regularly invited one or another of our two widowed cousins to accompany him to the opera. He went to great lengths to seek out and maintain contact with relations in the Soviet Union whom we had initially assumed to be no longer alive. Strangely, given his seeming strength of character, he was often indecisive, vacillating, though a professional graphologist would have discerned that his neat, precise, clear handwriting never varied, unlike mine, which, changing according to my state of mind and mood, often deteriorates into illegibility. Moshe would joke about my brother's practice of driving on the white line that separates the lanes of a road or motorway, as if to leave the choice open for as long as possible. When he was due to travel, he would reserve seats on several flights, each on a different airline, leaving that choice, too, as late as possible. Once, he appeared to be on the verge of proposing marriage to an eminently suitable young woman but failed to do so, leaving her, me and many of our friends bewildered and puzzled at his motives.

Finally, at the age of 75, he did marry. Born in Eretz Israel, his wife was well-versed in Hebrew language and literature, knew many passages of the Bible by heart and, although not religiously observant, was very traditional in her respect for religious practice. They came to live in Jerusalem, where he spent the last 15 years of his life in great contentment, still at first travelling far afield, going to Tel Aviv for opera and theatre, exercising diligently, seldom indulging in what he considered unnecessary luxuries (such as dining out), sitting on a comfortable sofa, the *Merck Manual of Medical Information* always at hand and frequently consulted. And reading, reading, reading. He read several books at one and the same time, going as deep as possible into a specific topic. Thus, a book on *fin-de-siècle* Vienna by Peter Gay led him to a biography of Alma Mahler, thence to Walter Gropius, next to Lou Salome and finally to Nietzsche. He absorbed, analysed and synthesised. Not long before his death, my oldest son, the one who was closest to him, noticed on the table that held current reading a book on the House of Rothschild, a dauntingly thick volume of over 1,000 pages.

"That'll take a long time," my son said.

"Yes," my brother ruefully admitted. "I manage only 120 pages a day."

Much of his reading was in German, essentially his mother tongue and the one in which he counted. I think the forced departure from Germany and German culture was something from which, subconsciously, he never recovered. In fact, arrival in England had been almost immediately succeeded by the language-related, humiliating experience of his bar-mitzvah.

Together with not being able to complete his brilliant progress at the *Gymnasium*, this must have been one of the many frustrations in his life. The greatest of these was undoubtedly the inability, due to the Anglo-Jewish mores of the time, openly to consummate his long relationship with a married woman who reciprocated his profound love. The need for secrecy led to ongoing subterfuge and deception. Only after her sudden death while he was abroad did he tentatively hint at the truth, which, with a woman's insight and sensitivity to minor, insignificant gestures, I had already intuited.

When I began my studies at the LSE, my first tutorial assignment was on a topic related to the Industrial Revolution. Lost in a field totally new to me, I turned to him for help. He gave me an essay he'd written on an allied subject. At once enlightened, I plagiarised sinfully. My tutor was overwhelmed by my brilliance. She must have been bewildered when subsequent submissions fell far short of that initial stunning one.

Relating to me as a "younger" rather than a "little" sister, Willy began in the summer before I went to Cambridge to suggest that I join him on weekends out of London, usually with contemporaries of his, and even, once the end of the war made this possible, on vacations abroad. We spent a rainy two weeks in the village of Lenk in the Bernese Oberland. Willy, who suffered from some respiratory disorder, went to the spa every day to take the waters. When the weather was fine we walked for miles, though I, inexperienced, had not brought sensible walking shoes. When it rained, we sat in the hotel's conservatory, each day collaboratively solving the difficult crossword in *The Times* – and reading. In the evenings we ordered hot punch and listened to the three-man "orchestra," which obligingly responded to our requests for the Viennese operettas of which we, like our parents, were especially fond. It was during that vacation that my brother taught me how to eat asparagus – a rarely-consumed, expensive luxury at home – without dripping butter on my chin and chest.

It was on that same holiday that his sophisticated knowledge proved for once inadequate. He loved whipped cream, which was unavailable during the austerity that reigned in England for many years after the war. Now, in this bovine-rich land, every one of the many farms sported a sign advertising its creameries. Irresistible. We picked one at random. We perused the albeit limited menu. Apart from milk of various degrees of fatness, there was whipped cream in bowls of differing sizes and there was an item called "meringue". For us, this denoted a delicate, lightly baked creation of oyster-shaped egg whites and sugar, in which a dollop of whipped cream nestled in place of a pearl. My brother ordered one in addition to a large bowl of whipped cream. The waitress was puzzled. No wonder. The Swiss interpretation of meringue proved to be yet another bowl of whipped cream. He heroically ate it all but on the way back to our hotel he vomited most of it up. A very rare example of fallibility.

In spring 1949 we went to Italy with two of his Cambridge contemporaries, now a married couple, Asher and Renée Winegarten. Tourism had not yet resumed to any noticeable extent. The country was poor and still war-ravaged. Few people, even those who worked in hotels, knew any English. Renée and I spoke some Italian but neither of us knew it well enough to comprehend the swift replies to our requests for directions in Milan, our first overnight stop. My brother had prepared for our journey with the aid of a pre-war, inevitably outdated

German *Baedeker*. Engrossed in this, he would read out descriptions of the noteworthy sites on either side of our car.

"On our left is a fifth-century basilica," he intoned.

"No, Willy," I responded. "There's a large hole in the ground. Must have been a bomb."

Undeterred, he continued to impart to us what would have been visible had the indiscriminate bombings not destroyed it.

Having spent too much time in Rouen, we were racing through France to Calais to catch the boat to Dover when one of the wheels sprang a puncture. Asher, who was driving, had no idea what to do. Willy calmly opened the glove compartment and took out the instruction manual. Step by step, he steadily went through a procedure in which he'd had no prior experience, while we stood by in wonder, our participation limited to occasionally passing at his request a screw that was just out of his reach. I do not recall ever seeing him flustered. He knew the right thing to do and volunteered his help unobtrusively, to avoid embarrassment.

My brother was an enigma. Just as he drove on the white line, so he seemed ambivalent in his attitude to me. I never knew, when I visited him, whether he would welcome me or merely tolerate my presence, showing an impatience to resume a more serious, satisfying occupation. I never knew whether my intense love for him was to any degree reciprocated. Did he resent the fact that my life was one of fulfilment, while his was not? Why, in the final month of his life, was he estranged from me, resisting or rejecting my suggestions that we visit him? Why were Moshe and I not invited to the annual Hannukah party that was the sole occasion in the year on which I met all his friends and acquaintances? Needing to determine the date of our own family party, I asked him for the date of his.

"We're not hosting one this year," he responded. Puzzled, I nevertheless accepted this decision. Soon afterwards, when mutual friends enquired why we had been absent, I asked him for an explanation. What had we done to warrant the exclusion? "It wasn't a party," he replied, "just a few friends." Already aware that this was a falsehood, I was deeply hurt.

The estrangement continued. Eventually, I surmised that he had been angry at the part I played in the mounting of the opera based in large part on our mother's letters to our father. Magret Wolf, our friendly typist, had composed *Refidim Junction*, which was commissioned by the municipal theatre of Wurzburg, where it premiered on 10 November 2012. Willy, like me, had gladly given his permission, even indicating that he would join me at the event. To my surprise, he soon reproached me for causing our mother's personal experience to be revealed to the public – and in Germany at that. My counter-argument was that precisely in this way would her suffering prompt sympathy and greater understanding of the fate of others. I failed to persuade him to accompany me. Only when I returned home, elated by the triumph of the performance, bringing a copy of the lavish souvenir programme with its copious text (including the essay on my mother that had greatly moved him), did he openly reveal his anger and resentment.

"Put it over there," he said drily, pointing to the chair in the hallway. "I'll look at it later."

That was the last time I saw him. My conjecture regarding the reason for the estrangement has never been corroborated or denied. I do not know whether it is correct. There is much that I shall never know. He died, suddenly, on Friday 4 January 2013. I miss him profoundly.

My Husband

"YOU HAVEN'T WRITTEN about Moshe!" my friend Omi reproached me. "You've written about your parents, your brother, your children. But you haven't written about Moshe!"

She had just finished reading the first draft of these memoirs. In writing about myself I must surely also have written about the one person most involved in everything I'd done since first meeting him in 1950? His words, actions, unfailing encouragement, the intensity of his identification with my ideals and initiatives, the comfort he offered when I was despondent – all were knitted into the fabric of my life. *Surely* that must be evident in what I'd already written.

"But Moshe appears in every chapter," I remonstrated.

"Perhaps so," she replied. "But don't you think he deserves a chapter of his own?" Of course he does – but how can I do justice to his "infinite variety"? I asked my children to come to my aid.

"Just send me a list of adjectives. You don't have to cite specifics." Within minutes, their replies arrived, adding to the list I'd already made myself. Here's what they wrote:

Joel: "Thorough; an enquiring mind; stubborn; organisational; the ability to activate people in a loving manner; excellent driver; sense of humour; skilled improviser; loved to cook but only from recipes".

Micha: "*Mensch*; a precious, modest man; magnanimous and sensitive".

Hephzibah: "Perfectionist; loving; humour, smile; consistent; diligent; energetic; modest; thorough".

Pnina (who knew him best both because she lived at home longer and because he taught her the skills of her profession): "Handsome, modest, didn't seek fame or honour; a leader – knew how to lead others but always gently; fostered his employees; authentic and pleasant towards others but never in a mocking manner; creative – thought creatively, found creative solutions; a hard worker; optimistic, trusting; honest and fair; reserved; did whatever he did with passion; thorough; a humanist who believed in the principle of human dignity; excellent sense of humour; a craftsman with a highly developed sense of aesthetics; faithful to *Imma*; protective of *Imma*; adored *Imma*; loved his work and his profession; was proud of his work but not boastful; sensitive to the sensitivity of others; never lazy; went into details; somewhat of a worrier but not obsessively so; invented wonderful stories when we were young!!; helped us devise Purim costumes and did our make-up; wrapped our school books, prepared excellent sandwiches to take to school; cooked well; was the best back scratcher and scratched my back for years (...till I married...); a wonderful grandfather to Batsheva and helped me enormously when I was a beginning mother. On the personal level, I felt very close to him. He showed me much warmth and love. I knew I could depend on him, his word was his deed. I felt he cared for me. I felt he counted on me to stay close to him and to *Imma*. He also unquestioningly helped me financially and professionally. On the whole, he trusted me.

"My sole criticism is about the way he related to his children. He loved those with whom he got along temperamentally but he distanced himself from the others. He didn't believe in venting emotion or speaking openly about matters. At the same time, he refrained from conflicts and rudeness. He wasn't sufficiently close to his grandchildren. *Imma* was the centre of his world and, out of a desire to defend her, he even perceived some of his children as opposition to *Imma* and himself."

The perception and precision of their comments were gratifying. They confirmed much, though not all, of what I had included in my own list. I recalled innumerable episodes that illustrate the traits to which they referred.

Moshe was dutiful. In November 1951, he decided to volunteer for the army. It was not an opportune moment for so drastic a move. I was six months pregnant with our first child. We had no familial support system. The managers at the Jerusalem headquarters of Barclays Bank (Dominion, Colonial and Overseas), recognising his gifts, had suggested he spend half a year in London to become more closely acquainted with the operations of the bank prior to promotion to a higher managerial rank.

Friends expressed surprise, even bewilderment.

"Since I've decided to spend my life in Israel," he explained, "I have to do my army service. Might as well get it over and done with. The sooner, the better."

At the recruitment centre the officer in charge expressed similar incredulity, even questioning Moshe's sanity. When medical tests confirmed his mental and physical fitness, he was inducted into the Military Police, where he was chosen as outstanding recruit at the end of his basic-training. Indeed, his intelligence and resourcefulness soon led to his being assigned to the Police Investigative Unit. In other words, he became a detective.

In 1976, his father had a stroke. Harry's third wife abruptly returned to the United States. Moshe went in search of a facility where Harry would be well cared for. Not one proved suitable.

"If I put him in any one of those, he'll die within half a year."

It was clear that Harry would have to live with us. The one bedroom was refurbished with a reclining armchair and a TV. Every morning, Moshe dressed his father and wheeled him to the synagogue next door to our house, where he had long been a faithful participant in morning and evening services. Finding his filial duties incompatible with continuing his intensive work schedule, Moshe applied for leave. He had a full two years of sick leave of which he had never availed himself. He became a devoted caretaker, arranged for Harry to be accepted into one of the workshops at Life Line for the Old, never revealing that we were ourselves covering the cost of meals and transportation. Harry was proud of the purses and spectacle cases he produced, which were sold in the organisation's gift shop. Because he so loved his work, Moshe, with customary ingenuity, set up a work table at which he could continue weaving in the afternoons.

It was utterly appropriate that Harry died on a Friday afternoon, as Moshe was lifting him out of the bathtub where he had just given him his pre-Shabbat shower. When I responded to his call for help, I found an inverted Pietà, the son bearing the body of his father, a towel draped over the dead body reclining in the arms of his son. It was the only occasion on which I saw Moshe in tears. All our children happened to be there that evening to share the Shabbat meal with us.

"You taught us what filial duty is," Joel said. Their own behaviour when Moshe became ill fully bore out that verdict.

Moshe did not relish his duties in the Military Police, which consisted primarily of hunting down defectors and draft-evaders. Accompanied by a colleague, he

314

would roam the streets of Jerusalem or scour the passengers in the overcrowded buses, demanding identification cards and evidence to indicate that the man had duly reported for service, as he himself had done. If no such evidence was forthcoming, the delinquent would be hauled off to the recruitment centre, often even without the option of returning home unattended in order to bid farewell to his family. In most cases, the victims of this arbitrary mode of recruitment were new immigrants. Many of them still spoke little or no Hebrew. Some had been unaware of the need to report for military service at the age of 18. Others, more adult, had assumed they were exempted. In every case, they were struggling to make a living not only for themselves but for an entire family of parents and siblings.

Moshe's inherent sympathy for the underdog led to his requesting a transfer to another branch of the IDF. It came at a propitious moment. The chaplain in charge of the Jerusalem headquarters of the Military Chaplaincy needed an assistant to help him communicate with the UN Mixed Armistice Commission that shared his quarters. Religiously observant native-speakers of English were in short supply in the IDF. Moshe was the obvious choice. Rabbi Eliezri was a modest, gentle man. He and Moshe took an instant liking to each other, their friendship further fostered by the fact that the rabbi's daughter was currently among my students.

For over a year, Moshe enjoyed the privilege of coming home after office hours and spending Shabbat with me. Then he was selected for officer training. Once again, he was cited for his outstanding performance. While such an achievement was gratifying, it unfortunately precluded his return to the easy-going practices of Jerusalem. Instead, he was transferred to the retinue of the Chief Chaplain, Rabbi Shlomo Goren, who had also specifically requested a native-speaker of English. Moshe fitted the bill. However, in his case the demand stemmed not from utilitarian considerations but from the rabbi's desire for what was essentially a press officer. Moshe greatly admired the liberal rabbinic rulings that Rabbi Goren issued in all matters related to the IDF. However, he felt distaste at the rabbi's desire for public recognition of his greatness and his inordinate pursuit of fame. On one occasion that pursuit aroused Moshes's disgust and anger.

In reserve duty, Moshe was in charge of a unit responsible for as far as possible identifying and burying those who fell in battle. These emotionally draining tasks frequently involved direct encounter with parents and spouses searching for their loved ones, wanting to bid a last farewell, to kiss the cold body of sons and lovers.

At times, they came in hope of discovering that the one they sought was not among the casualties.

In June 1967, Moshe was stationed at the Military Cemetery on Mount Herzl. Unlike the vast majority of Israelis, he felt no joy at the speedy victory and didn't share in the jubilant celebration of the liberation of the Old City. For him, the price that had been paid was too high, the general euphoria unjustified. Hence he was appalled when Rabbi Goren, having ensured that all the print and broadcast media adequately covered his triumphant blowing of the ram's horn at the Western Wall minutes after its liberation, summoned Moshe to serve as Officer-in-Charge at that site on the day it was first made accessible to the general public – *Shavuot*, which fell a few days after the cessation of hostilities.

Initially, Moshe remonstrated, maintaining that what he was doing must take precedence? Rabbi Goren was adamant. Moshe was duty-bound to obey. And so he donned the armband that bore the pompous title "Officer of the Wall", gritted his teeth and spent the day overseeing soldiers whose task it was to direct the throngs of people who made the pilgrimage from all over Israel, ensuring that they spend only a short while at this historic site before making room for the next group. He never forgave Rabbi Goren for that instance of false priorities. In Moshe's eyes, the arrogance far outweighed rabbinic scholarship.

"You haven't got a scraper!" "You need a one-cup espresso pot." "Your knives are totally blunt. They need sharpening."

These are but a few examples of Moshe's response to the inadequacies of the kitchens of friends with whom we stayed during our visits to the US. But he didn't content himself with criticism. He went out to purchase the missing items or mend the faulty ones. A stickler for appropriate tools and the correct methods of using them, he was recalled with love and humour when my friends celebrated my 90th birthday in New York. One of them even drew his gift of a scraper from her pocket, a souvenir of a long-ago weekend at her country home.

Unlike me, Moshe was scrupulously systematic. The difference between us can best be illustrated with reference to an excellent recipe for minestrone in Marcella Hazan's *Classic Italian Cookery*, which lists an overwhelming number of ingredients. Practical and considerate of the exigencies of cooking, Hazan describes the successive stages of adding each of the ingredients one by one. While one of them is already in the pot, the next can be prepared – peeled, diced and chopped – to be added two or three minutes later. I followed instructions. Moshe operated differently. He began by lining up all the ingredients, already sliced and

316

chopped. Each vegetable had its own bowl, the liquid measured in the appropriate jug – all before the cooking itself began. The draining-board was certainly more colourful and tidy than when I was in charge but the preparations took longer. He disapproved of my (or anybody's) slapdash style. "A half-ass job" was his stern expression of reproof.

Women loved Moshe and he loved them. He found them more reliable, readier to take risks, take up new jobs, and try out the new methods and ingenious systems he devised. That was as true in the later part of his professional life as it had been when he first started in book production.

At the Israel Programme for Scientific Translations it had been the complex sequence of translation, editing, typing and illustration of scientific texts. For the *Encyclopedia Judaica* it involved training an entire team in the art of illustration research, building up an impressive picture archive that included much hitherto unknown material. In the course of creating his *magnum opus*, the *Comprehensive and Historical Encyclopedia of Jewish Women*, he exchanged letters with innumerable contributors whom he never met in person. Some of them became personal friends, confiding in him details of their private lives. What shines through his letters is his generosity of spirit, his sympathy with women who were trying hard to successfully combine research, teaching and publication with the duties of home-making and mothering. He had learned, at first hand, from accompanying me throughout my tribulations, how much strength of body and mind is needed to achieve such success.

Moshe was modest. Only at the *shiva*, attended by hundreds, did I learn of the numerous people he mentored, encouraging them to take up professions that they would never otherwise have conceived as appropriate. I learned of the detailed routine he had developed for ensuring adequate emergency service if an earthquake were to strike Jerusalem (as he was certain it would, given past experience) and of how hard he had lobbied to ensure the provision of adequate equipment and personnel for such an emergency. As a result, ours is the only city in Israel fully prepared for catastrophe.

Moshe's instinctive sense of aesthetics, so evident in the books that he produced, extended to his clothes. His style was unique and unforced: colourful shirts, psychedelic ties, Fisherman's smocks, braces, hats of various shapes, materials and colours, fine suits for "best", to be worn on festive occasions. He was the first man in Jerusalem to wear tieless, round-collared shirts at formal events. I longed to add one of my pendants. It would have completed the outfit.

317

But we decided that such an ornament would be too extreme an innovation for the conservative middle-aged, middle-class concert- goers who, like ourselves, subscribed to the Israel Philharmonic Orchestra.

Moshe had flair. He had panache. He had integrity. There was no end to his virtues, his uniqueness. No words can adequately describe him. Omi, my dear, you're mistaken. Moshe merits not merely a chapter of his own, but an entire volume. Who, I wonder, will write it?

The sense of identity, of being part of a people, was (and still is) the primary element in my Jewishness. Once I came to Israel, I felt I had reached the acme of being a Jew: living in precisely such a "Jewish state", one with a Jewish majority, where Shabbat was a day of rest, the Jewish holidays were public holidays, the language spoken was the language of the Bible and of our prayers. A prophecy had been fulfilled. I no longer needed communal worship in order to express my identity. Breathing the air of the Promised Land and being part of the rebirth sufficed to give me a sense of wonder, awe and spiritual fulfilment.

For many years I did not pray with a congregation. But in 2008, in an unprecedented state of physical exhaustion and depression caused primarily by an inability to continue my writing, I turned for help to Dina Wyshogrod, a psychotherapist who teaches Mindfulness Based Stress Reduction. Under her guidance I began to practise meditation.

Early every morning I sought (and still seek) refuge from the exigencies of commonplace everyday duties and commitments: a quiet space where I can sink into myself, obliterate all distractions and – and what? How to describe the invasion of indistinct sensations that fill my mind, heart and innermost being? A wordless communication with an all-pervading, all-embracing spirit, the ineffable, the indescribable wellspring of life. I become part of a greater whole, of the entire universe. In this state of *hitbodedut*, exaltation, I experience the divine.

Yet I still yearned for community and ultimately, belatedly, I found it.

A poet, a visionary, a woman of infinite insight and compassion, Tamar Elad-Appelbaum had been my pupil at Pelech and studied at the Schechter Rabbinical School while I was its Rector. Repeatedly, she assured me that she would one day establish just such a community. The need grew stronger as Moshe sank ever deeper into a wordless depression. At last, on Independence Day in May 2013, a small group gathered to pray and rejoice together. From that moment, beginning in Tamar's living room, Zion grew.

Moshe was able to attend several of the Friday services at which we welcomed Shabbat. I held his hand in mine. "*Lecha Dodi*" – "To You, My Beloved...". One Shabbat morning we were called to the Torah together, he in his wheelchair, a single *tallit* draped over both our shoulders.

Two months later, as he lay dying in Sharei Zedek Hospital, our children around his bed, Tamar led us in singing the Sabbath eve prayers. Each in turn, we bade him goodbye.

"You made our Shabbat," said two women whose father, in the next bed, had just passed away. A moment of grace.

At 2.15 the following afternoon, Moshe returned his soul to his Maker. One second earlier, he had opened his eyes and looked into mine, with the same intense expression that accompanied his frequent reassurances to me: "I love you very much."

There were no eulogies at his funeral, only Tamar leading us at the graveside in singing the 23rd Psalm: "Yea, though I walk through the Valley of the Shadow of Death, I shall fear no evil, for Thou art with me".

Towards An Ending

ODDS AND ENDS of fabric lie jumbled in the needlework basket of my memory: finely textured alongside coarse, checkered and solid colours, slippery satin, sparkling sequins, plain flannel. But I lack the skill of sewing required to piece the scraps together into a patchwork quilt.

An old-fashioned, outmoded icebox, its shelves packed with scraps of unfinished meals, leftovers. Enough to scramble together a late-night snack for myself, unfit to set before guests.

Drawers crammed with decades of cracking celluloid negatives. But where are the darkroom and equipment I need to develop them, the albums in which to display the black-and-white photographs?

A wardrobe full of classic, timeless garments, some fashioned by the most skilful designers of *haute couture*. All are now too long or too wide for my shrunken, shrinking body.

Music plays enticingly. My feet tap in time, itch to dance. Why can I not will my knee to unbend?

Steadily, unrelentingly, the candle of creativity dwindles down.

It's a stale metaphor but I have none more vivid. From time to time the flame seems to flare up momentarily. That is a delusion. Energy is unsustainable, unrenewable.

Snatches of beloved poetry spring to mind, unsummoned. Wordsworth, Keats, Yeats and always Shakespeare. "When thou dost ask me blessing I'll kneel down/ And ask of thee forgiveness."

Popular melodies: "Somewhere over the rainbow", "September Song". All wistful, nostalgic. "And the days dwindle down to a golden few...".

Twenty years ago, I began in optimistic mood to write my memoirs. I had retired from work both salaried and voluntary. I was in Bellagio, a Land of Cockaigne designed specifically to stimulate, enable and encourage intellectual and artistic creativity. It was a balmy, rainless late summer, with Lake Como below and mountains all around. I went back to Jerusalem with 30,000 words completed. Years passed before I returned to the manuscript and continued writing.

Now almost all is changed. I have no husband. I share my home. I am at a loss for words, my erstwhile eloquence and rich vocabulary dissipated.

It is not now as it hath been of yore;–
Turn wheresoe'er I may,
By night or day,
The things which I have seen I now can see no more.

Moments of Being. Bicycling in Waddesdon Park, I round a bend and light, startled, upon a bank of golden daffodils. Surprised by joy!

Heard for the first time, the urgent "Libera Me" of Verdi's *Requiem* soars to the rafters of King's College Chapel. My scalp tingles.

Late-summer afternoons. The near-silence of my garden, with only a soft twitter of birds calling to each other. "Come home! Come home!"

Alone, seated in the vast expanse of the Sinai desert, waiting for my companions to return from hiking through a *wadi*. An intense stillness. The presence of … God? On the steps of the Dwellings of Tranquillity: opposite me, on the other side of the Valley of Hinnom, the late afternoon sun gilds the great stone walls of the Old City. Chimes herald Evensong. A muezzin's wail summons the faithful to prayer. The end of the day in the Holy City.

Softness, and peace, and joy, and love, and bliss,
Exalted manna, gladness of the best,
Heaven in ordinary, man well drest,

The milky way, the bird of Paradise,
Church-bells beyond the stars heard, the soul's blood,
The land of spices; something understood.

And now? The words no longer suffice. The traditional prayer book neither

321

embodies my belief nor expresses my innermost feelings. I can no longer pray to the Father, the King. The Divine Spirit that inspires me knows no gender. Unlimited in time and space, vast and all-embracing, it is a source of universal love, sustenance, joy. Schiller knew it. Beethoven expressed it in music that lifts the soul.

Seit umschlungen, Millionen,
Diesen Kuss der ganzen Welt.
Droben, übern Sternenzelt
Muss ein lieber Vater wohnen

Be embraced, o ye millions.
By this kiss of the whole world!
There, above the tent of stars
Must a loving [Father] dwell.

To that force, that source of life itself, I now address my songs of praise and gratitude. It inspires me to love all aspects of creation. It leads me to seek out the best, the noblest in myself, in others. It bids me love my fellow creatures. It leads us upwards, to the firmament, to perceive the wonders of nature, the depth of human feeling, the height of human achievement. It is everywhere around us, challenging us to awaken to its presence; beckoning us, summoning us to create a better world, a world of fellowship and human kindness. All that is required of us is to open our hearts to welcome and embrace it. No words are needed. No words suffice. Just as two lovers sit side by side in silence, ach absorbing the other's presence, so I sit absorbing and at the same time surrendering myself to the Divine Spirit.

Epiphanies

Sanctity

Exaltation